THE LIFE OF MADAME ROLAND

LONGMANS, GREEN AND CO.
55 FIFTH AVENUE, NEW YORK
221 EAST 20TH STREET, CHICAGO
TREMONT TEMPLE, BOSTON
128 UNIVERSITY AVENUE, TORONTO

LONGMANS, GREEN AND CO. LTD.
39 PATERNOSTER ROW, E C 4, LONDON
53 NICOL ROAD, BOMBAY
6 OLD COURT HOUSE STREET, CALCUTTA
167 MOUNT ROAD, MADRAS

JEANNE-MARIE PHLIPON
About 1764
From a contemporary portrait in the Musée Carnavalet

THE LIFE OF
MADAME ROLAND

BY

MADELEINE CLEMENCEAU-JACQUEMAIRE

TRANSLATED BY
LAURENCE VAIL

LONGMANS, GREEN AND CO.
LONDON · NEW YORK · TORONTO
1930

CLEMENCEAU-JACQUEMAIRE
MADAME ROLAND

TO

THE MEMORY OF

MADAME BRYNDZA

NÉE SOPHIE CLEMENCEAU

IN REMEMBRANCE OF HER FERVENT AND PENSIVE EXPRESSION
WHEN SHE PRONOUNCED THIS NAME

MADAME ROLAND

FOREWORD

It is not my intention, in this new work, to confine myself to a faithful enlargement of the small portrait already attempted, as photographers create a large figure with vague outlines from a clearly-defined snap-shot.

Mme Roland's life was short, but the story of it is full and varied. What it lacks in length it makes up in breadth.

Without detracting from the importance of her political career, one may note certain circumstances of her high-principled sentimental life which seem to merit attention and scrutiny. Thus I shall attempt to explain, for instance, the romance of her marriage with Roland, the tale of her dislike for Danton, the heroic poem of her love for Buzot.

Friendship as well had an important place in this ever-expansive heart, and the part it played was multiple, eager, liberal in an existence which even for a man would have been exceptionally laborious and which none the less evaded not one domestic duty.

M. Perroud, Rector of the University of Toulouse, was entrusted by the state with the publication of Mme Roland's correspondence for the collection of Documents Historiques. *This he accomplished with a method, a clarity, and a care that approach perfection. I take him as my guide, for his work is a masterpiece of a kind that serves the highest purpose and reflects the least glory on the author.*

My plan has a chronological form. This is not a fanciful portrait. Thanks to the Memoirs, *to the correspondence, to* papers found at Roland's house, to records of the time, to family traditions, to the testimony of contemporaries, reality will suffice and the colours will be perhaps bolder or more varied than if they were inspired by a romantic imagination.

I take for granted that Mme Roland is not unknown and that the reader is versed in the history of the French Revolution. I have not stressed with equal importance every feature of her life. At times I discuss and criticize those points I have isolated, in the belief that to reveal the originality of an individual is more important than to catalogue all the small acts which make up the span of life. Therefore I sometimes pass rapidly over long periods and linger upon the hurried times that were characteristically rife with sentiment or emotion.

All this with a candour and an independence which, alas, are scarcely in accordance with the scholarly methods taught at school, and if by some chance I succeed in giving a spark of life to this portrait, I can then compare myself to that little grocer who, on the Amsterdam quays, dreamed of the Mycenæan tombs rather than of the fine archæologists who revived Delphi, Olympia, and Delos.

May his good-fortune bless me.

M. C.-J.

CONTENTS

ix

LIST OF ILLUSTRATIONS

NOTE: The illustrations in this volume are reproduced by kind permission of M. Jules Tallandier, 75 Rue Dareau, Paris, the publisher of the French edition.

THE LIFE OF MADAME ROLAND

THE LIFE *of*
MADAME ROLAND

PART ONE

THALES AND THE NYMPH OF THE ILE NOTRE-DAME

> [The story of my life] would greatly aid
> an understanding of the human heart
> and teach great lessons to sensitive people.
> —*Madame Roland*.

THE POLITICAL career and death of Mme Roland were the consequences of her marriage. At first glance it might seem too fine a
match for the daughter of the engraver Phlipon, a girl "born in
humble conditions but of honest parents." But she was firmly set
upon it, while Roland resisted it to the very end.

Her intelligence and her sweet disposition first attracted and then
held captive the stern and elderly "philosopher." In spite of his
somewhat dotardly appearance, Mlle Phlipon had been flattered and
impressed by his attentions, for she believed she had found in him
a superior man.

They were a middle-class couple. That their relationship was
more intellectual than sentimental gives freshness and originality
to the tale. Contrary to what one finds in novels and published
letters of a more or less emotional nature, contrary to appearances
even, the main issue of this combat was not love. In the packet of
letters which remains there is nothing romantic, nothing picturesque. It is a record of life, nothing more.

The greater part of the time the principal players were leagues
apart. On one hand was this nervous man, this egoist so hampered

by doctrines that he might have been one of the early Romantics. He was forty-five—twenty years her elder—and seemed even older. His circumspection scarcely concealed his very masculine distrust of those warm sentiments which threatened to involve him in an unworthy marriage with a handsome and intellectual young woman who possessed neither family nor fortune.

In him was this resistance to an unwelcome passion, while in her we see the frantic attempt of a frustrated being to achieve fulfillment. The strange part of it is that they seemed to exchange personalities and each one spoke the language of the other. They acted and they wrote in complete contradiction of sentiments that were so obviously theirs. In reality she was all submission, tenderness, sweetness, while he was morose, touchy to the point of absurdity, and as unpleasant as it is humanly possible to be. He made every effort to conceal his feeling for her by harshness and sarcasm. As for her, she was not in the least taken in, and while managing him with masterly intuition, she gave free rein to a torrential power, which in this instance all her critics have mistaken for an irresistable passion. It is true that the intensity of her emotions was increased by opposition, but she still retained sufficient lucidity to recognize that her marriage would be a "strict bondage." This did not restrain her from writing with fine pride: "I am the only woman who can make you happy."

At twenty-four Mlle Phlipon's one decided taste was for study, but at the same time she was willing to consider marriage. Because of her disposition and her intelligence she was far superior to the mediocre people of her own class, but she had nevertheless made two or three attempts to find among her innumerable suitors one worthy to be her husband. At one time she had almost made up her mind to favour a sixty-year-old widower whose intellect was not displeasing to her, for *above all* she would have an "interesting" man, with whom she could exchange ideas and of whom she could be morally proud.

Because he failed in these respects to compare favourably with Roland, she dismissed him, and likewise a young man with whom she had been infatuated a short time before. There was nothing pleasing in Roland's person, but such shortcomings were entirely overshadowed by the intellectual and moral superiority she discerned in him and in which she believed to the very end. Guided by an obstinacy that the Ancients would have regarded as the inevitable power of destiny, she took him back again and again, after having lost him ten times, until the day she succeeded in acquiring the name of Mme Roland, a name so hard to win and one that led her to the guillotine of Robespierre.

It was in the reign of Louis XV. The master-engraver, Gatien Phlipon, engraver to Monsieur le Comte d'Artois, had had his workshop, since the year 1775, between the Place Dauphine and the Quai de l'Horloge in the second floor apartment of a house built in the time of Louis XIII. The Seine flowed below the windows. The Pont Neuf was at the corner and, according to Mercier, the Pont Neuf was to Paris

what the heart is to the human body, the centre of movement and circulation; the flow and ebb of Parisians and travellers . . . so washes this thoroughfare that to come upon any person one is seeking, one need but walk there an hour a day.

The apartment consisted of five rooms. Its proportions were handsome and it was furnished with a great deal of taste. We know that Mme Roland grew up in surroundings which today would be considered elegant and even luxurious.

The *salon* — "a pleasant room, neatly furnished, ornamented with pictures and mirrors," to quote the *Memoirs* — was hung with "Aubusson tapestry." Numerous mirrors framed in carved and gilded wood reflected the grey and blue light of day that came through the high windows. Several chests of drawers, a marble-topped desk in "veneered wood," a card table, a red-lacquered corner buffet ornamented with porcelains; these, with a few chairs, comprised the principal furniture of the room. Hanging on the walls were pastel portraits, dating from about 1760, of the engraver and his wife; a wall-dial painted green signed Gilles le Cadet and ornamented in gilded bronze; seven fine engravings by the best artists of the time; and last but not least a portrait of the child of the house, a pencil drawing executed "by a master."

Besides the tools of his craft, Phlipon's vast studio contained a number of pieces of statuary. The days were still quite recent when skilled craftsmen worked there together after the meals which, following the custom of the time, they shared with the engraver's family. The workroom produced patch-boxes, boxes for bonbons, little cases decorated with a riddle or a motto, snuff-boxes set off with saucy pictures, watch-cases engraved with emblems and attributes, frames for miniatures in which were interworked yellow, red, and green gold; and those large buttons, fashionable at the time, painted with landscapes, pastoral scenes, and even with *genre* pictures. At that period Phlipon employed every sort of craftsman whose work in any way related to his own: enamel painters, jewel-setters, chisellers, engravers of precious metals; and he increased his own income by trading in jewels. Merchants came there for business, artists remained to converse with the masters of the house. Desmarteau, the engraver, came there; Jollain, the Academy painter; Pigalle's pupil, Lépine; the younger Falconet; Greuze himself, and Latour who perhaps painted the Phlipon family in its heyday.

Mme Phlipon, née Marie-Marguerite Bimont, had succeeded in raising but one of the seven children who were born to her. On this daughter [1] she lavished every care.

She was at this time a woman of almost forty, rather stout, rather blowsy, quiet, and almost cold in appearance. She dressed after the fashion of the *petite bourgoisie* of her period. Her crinoline skirt was gathered in pleats at the hem. Her corsage was in the form of a long scallop-edged coat. Her hair was wound simply about the crown of her head and was at times concealed by a flounced linen bonnet.

She was prudent, reasonable, modest, and (although the contrary has been carelessly said of her) she was not over-pious. With one eye on the cook and the other on the apprentices, Mme Phlipon maintained an immaculate house and kept her "inconsequential" husband on the straight and narrow path from which he wandered as soon as she was dead.

The engraver remained alone with his daughter Jeanne-Marie,[2]

MONSIEUR PHLIPON   MADAME PHLIPON

From pastels of the French School of the eighteenth Century. Musée de Lyon

who, at one and twenty, had lost "a mother with a heavenly soul." She suffered such agonies of violent despair that her father confessor, Abbé Legrand said of her: "It is a fine thing to have some soul, but it is certainly uncomfortable to have so much." And indeed this girl was no ordinary person.

While her beauty was exuberant her bearing was reserved. The little shopkeepers of the quarter found nothing amiss with her except her dangerous inclination to study. Although she was an expert housekeeper, she gave no more than just the necessary time to household matters. The remainder of the day she passed closed away reading and writing in "her little study."

Through her we learn of that "hollow place in one side of the parlour mantelpiece which was transformed into a little alcove, lit by one small window. . . There a bed was placed, in so narrow a space that to get into it I must needs climb over the footboard. A chair, a little table, and a few shelves: this was my sanctuary."

If it be true that a day comes, a day that may seem exactly like any other, but on which the dice of Fate are cast, for Mlle Phlipon it was the day that M. Roland de la Platière, an unknown visitor from Amiens, crossed her threshhold.

Among the people in that city who comprised the set of Mesdemoiselles Cannet [3] and their mother, was this formal and virtuous gentleman, this serious worker who was usually regarded with more esteem than affection. His name was M. Roland de la Platière, and since the year 1767 he had filled the post of Inspector of the Manufactures of Picardy. Mesdemoiselles Cannet had frequently spoken to him in glowing terms of their great friend in Paris, Mlle Phlipon, whose portrait hung in the place of honour in the guests' *salon;* and as the duties of his post necessitated many trips to foreign lands and frequent visits to the capital, they spoke of bringing together these two people who would have so much in common.

Though they had talked of it, it had slipped their minds the day Roland came to take leave of them before departing for Paris. Half-seriously, but not without reproach, he had said to them:

"Am I never to meet that marvellous young lady of the Ile Notre-Dame ?"

"Ah, that reminds me," said Sophie, the younger sister, and jumping up she went off to write a letter which she gave to the departing guest.

This was in the middle of December 1775. The day was dark and cold. Mme Phlipon had been dead six months and the young girl's grief had scarcely abated. In a thoughtful mood she had retired to her sanctuary with the *Nouvelle Héloise* when Mignonne,[4] the maid, opened the door and placed a letter on the foot of the bed:

This letter will be handed you [wrote Sophie Cannet] by the philosopher I have sometimes spoken of, M. Roland. He is an enlightened man with excellent morals, and the only fault to be found with him is his great admiration for the Ancients at the expense of the Moderns, and a weakness for talking about himself.

Mlle Phlipon read with "avidity" this letter from her closest friend and then hurried to the hall. A visitor from Amiens, a friend of Sophie's, what an unexpected God-send on this dull day !

In the cold blue light that the shifting waters of the Seine cast upon the windows, a vision appeared before M. Roland de la Platière. He was standing in the middle of the room into which he had been ushered when he became aware of the presence of a beautiful young woman with her hair tucked up under a little cap, her ripening charms scarcely concealed by the white muslin negligé she wore with such grace, and her whole person sparkling with youth.

She for her part saw before her a man well into the forties, dressed in black, somewhat clerical in appearance, with a high forehead, long, unpowdered hair, a weighty manner, and a liverish complexion.

But she was not one of these heedless young women who are taken in by exterior graces. She immediately observed that "although lacking in worldly polish" the visitor's manners combined "the good-breeding of the well-born man with the gravity of the philosopher, and that an extremely subtle smile and an animated expression so transfigured him when absorbed in talk that it put quite a new face on him." This did not, however, prevent the young woman from noticing that his "features . . . were more respectable than winning," and that "if his conversation . . . teemed with interest . . . held the attention, his voice was harsh and inharmonious."

Their common tastes made their conversation engrossing from the outset, and they discussed Jean-Jacques Rousseau, an idol they worshipped with equal fervour; then Abbé Raynal, Voltaire, travel, and the government. Phlipon happened in at that moment, and, after having greeted the stranger, seated himself and listened in tactful silence to the fine discourse that was taking place under his roof. Roland left very late, promising both father and daughter to call again whenever he felt so inclined. He for his part had also enjoyed this first meeting, but it was never his custom to express his pleasure in flattering words.

While Mlle Phlipon felt a lively esteem for her new acquaintance, she expended little thought on him, her mind being then very much occupied by a young fop with literary pretentions called Pahin de la Blancherie.

This was a rather solitary period for her, for she found neither guidance nor comfort in a father whom she made every effort to keep close to her, but who was constantly absent from home. Although she hated cards she played piquet with him. Public affairs were not of the slightest interest to her, and her father's unceasing criticism of the government annoyed her, but to please him she made it a duty carefully to read the gazettes. "Too tender to be gay," to use her own expression — and a delightful one — she was left very much to herself. The more or less scattered family that surrounded her consisted of dull petty people.[5]

The engraver's mother, "Grandma Phlipon," however, stood out from this group as a worthy, jovial soul, not wholly ignorant, and very much preoccupied wth good manners. She doted on her granddaughter, and in former times had had her frequently in her home. She lived in retirement with her asthmatic bigot of a sister, Angélique, on the Ile Saint-Louis. What little money she possessed was inherited from a rich Mme de Boismorel in whose home at the Marais she had passed her life of widowhood as housekeeper.

The third Rotisset sister was married to a certain Besnard, steward at Soucy Castle at Fontenay-en-Brie, on the estate of the farmer-general Haudry, where she herself became housekeeper. A married couple so situated usually have the opportunity of setting aside a little money. The Besnards were no exception, and as they had no children of their own, the little Phlipon girl was to be their heir. Then there was Cousin Trude, a stern, devout maker of looking-glasses in the rue Montmartre, whose shrewd pretty little wife was to prove herself Jeanne-Marie's kindest cousin; and finally Mlle Desportes, still another cousin, who kept a jeweller's shop in the rue Bertin-Poirée, opposite the rue des Bourdonnais: a woman of sense who went in for the officious manner, took the tone of "a preacher" and in her own home entertained the tradespeople of the neighbourhood. The day was to come when she would be all eagerness to be of service to Mlle Phlipon.

By far the most interesting member of the family was a little priest, Curé Bimont.

A younger brother of Mme Phlipon, he had first been Vicar at St Barthélemy and later Canon at Saint-Cloud. He had just been nominated Canon of the Ste Chapelle at Vincennes. And indeed this young prebendary, this "little uncle" of the *Memoirs,* was a charming figure. He possessed the grace and ease of the eighteenth century and he dearly loved this grown-up niece whom he had instructed for a brief time when she was a child. It is highly probable that she had too speedily plumbed the depths of his Latin, for, to her intense disappointment, the course of lessons was of short duration. But although he abandoned his efforts to impart his scanty knowledge, he gave her a much rarer thing: a frank open heart. Until her marriage, or in other words, until she was twenty-five, she would go to Vincennes and there spend several days in the "canonical retreat," in that "abode of laughter" to which she might come in tears but which she would always leave in peace, imbued with new life, and even comforted. There she forgot the worries and vexations which were never lacking in Paris. There she indulged her taste for the arts, playing music, reciting verse, as on that day that Mlle d'Hannaches, the Canon's high-born housekeeper "who usually sat spinning in silence, suddenly started shouting at the hens" at the very moment that uncle and niece were declaiming in unison some of the finest lines of a Voltaire tragedy.

Curé Bimont had far too much admiration for such a well-instructed young woman ever to dream of disagreeing with her. Rather he was intimidated, and it later became evident that, instead of being a guide to her, he was obliging to the point of exaggeration. She wrote of him at a later date "that she could without the least effort make him think what she wished," and the other relatives were too inferior to have any authority over a character of such marked precocity.

At the time of Roland's first visit in December 1775, it was young Pahin de la Blancherie who was uppermost in her thoughts. A future magistrate, he was then twenty-two, and very well pleased with himself although he had neither position nor fortune. She had met him one of those Thursdays when she and her mother attended the amateur concerts of Mme L'Épine, the Roman singer and wife of the sculptor. Thanks to Sophie Cannet, who served as intermediary, Mlle Phlipon started a romantic correspondence with this insignificant La Blancherie. Phlipon, however, would not for a minute hear of such a badly-off young man for a son-in-law, and the young girl wrote her suitor that even though she bowed to the will of her father, she loved no one but him and would never marry another. In fact she had worked herself up to the pitch of believing herself madly in love with the flighty young fellow who was soon to cure her of her imaginary passion not only by paying court to a rich Mlle Bordenave, but also by promenading in the Luxembourg with a feather in his hat! Thus brought back to reality, she confessed her disillusionment to the sympathetic Sophie:

Ah, you would never believe how much that cursed feather annoyed me! I turned the matter over in my mind a thousand times, endeavouring to reconcile that silly ornament with the philosophical intelligence . . . which had made La Blancherie so dear to me!

And like a true Corneille heroine, she exclaimed:

I would prefer to see him in the arms of another with all his intelligence and discrimination, rather than tenderly and passionately at my feet after having renounced his principles.

Never would Roland occasion such a scandal! His tastes, God be praised, were in entire agreement with his principles, as far as "silly ornaments" were concerned.

La Blancherie was not, it is certain, Mlle Phlipon's first suitor. Before the completion of her fifteenth year, her professors, and then all the young men of the neighbourhood, had fallen in love with her. Twenty-five years later she thus described herself as she was at that age:

At fourteen I was, just as I am today, about five feet in height, having at that time acquired my full stature. I had a well-shaped leg, a nicely turned foot, extremely high hips; a full and superbly rounded bust, sloping shoulders; a firm and graceful carriage, a light, rapid gait; this is what first met the eye. There was nothing remarkable about my face except its extreme freshness, and a great deal of sweetness and expression; if one examined each feature separately one might well ask: wherein indeed does the beauty lie? Not one feature is regular, all are pleasing. The mouth is a bit large; there are a thousand prettier ones: there is not one that has a smile as tender or as winning. The eye is not large, its iris a warm grey; the eyeball full and protruding, the glance frank, open, lively, gentle, over it curves a well-made eyebrow, brown like my hair. It varies in expression like the affectionate heart whose emotions it reflects; it can astonish you at times by its earnestness and pride, but more often it caresses, and can always arouse. The nose rather worried me, for I thought the end of it too large; however, considering the rest of the face, or seen in profile, it did not mar the general effect. The wide, bare forehead, seldom covered at that age, was supported by the high arch of the eye. The centre of this brow that was so far from being the insignificant space found on most faces, was marked at times by Y-shaped veins which dilated at the slightest emotion. As for my chin, it turned up slightly and had those characteristics which physiognomists say indicate voluptuousness. When I compare these indications with all I know of myself, I feel that no-one was ever more intended for voluptuousness and at the same time tasted it less. A complexion vivid rather than very white, the brilliance of it frequently heightened by sudden flushes of turbulent blood stirred by the most sensitive nerves; a soft skin, a round arm, a pleasing hand, though not a small one owing to the long slender fingers that suggest nimbleness and preserve a sense of grace; white,

even teeth; the plumpness of perfect health, these were the treasures
nature had bestowed upon me. [*Memoirs.*]

The engraver was proud of his daughter and had hopes of her
marrying some worthy tradesman in an established business. All
the tradesmen of the Cité, even to the butcher, had offered themselves as would-be husbands. But the young girl did not take
them seriously, and in the glow of the lamp-light in the evening
she would write them tactful, ceremonious letters in which, "making believe to be a father" and laughing aloud, she would refuse
the offers made to Phlipon.

He loved and esteemed commerce because he considered it the source
of all wealth [she wrote]. I hated it because I saw it as the source of
avarice and dishonesty. . . Had I lived with Plutarch and all the other
philosophers only to unite myself to a tradesman who would judge or
feel nothing as I do?

But these fine words meant nothing to her father who went on
to cite the Mme Dargens, and the Mme Lempereurs who aided
their husbands as jewellers; he spoke of Mm. Delorme, Dubreuil,
and l'Obligeois, who were all very successful in their affairs:

"You have brought me up to use my mind and have allowed me
to form studious habits. . . I have seen very well, Papa, that the way
to succeed in business is to buy cheap, sell high, and overwork and
exploit your poor workman. I could never lend myself to anything
of the sort, nor could I respect anyone who made this his business from
morning till night. . . And how could I be faithful to a man I thought
nothing of ?"
"You have become very hard to please," sighed the disconcerted
Phlipon . . . "and what if you don't find your ideal ?"
"I'll die unmarried."
"There you are, up in the clouds. It's one thing to get up there,
but it's quite another to stay."

A worthy jeweller asked for her hand.
"He holds you in great esteem," said Mme Phlipon who felt her
approaching end and wished to see her daughter well established.
"He will be proud to follow your advice and he says already that
he has no objection to his wife nursing her children; you could
lead him. . ."

"But, Mama, I want nothing to do with a man I can lead about !"

A number of insignificant doctors of medicine and obscure barristers passed before the critical eyes of this girl who was becoming a greater and greater puzzle to her parents. Once she was on the point of accepting a young doctor named Gardanne. But, in her own words, "a doctor's garb is not alluring to a young girl; I was never at any time of my life able to imagine love with a wig !" Well, after all, she was more a woman than she thought or would have liked us to believe. But she found it easy to contemplate friendship with certain of these suitors. Her reasons were conscientious ones: "My own sentiments seem extraordinary to me; I find nothing so odd as to hate a man simply because he loves me and because I have wished to love him." Young girls are usually apt to accept, as if he were Eros himself, the very first man who speaks to them of love.

A RELIGIOUS crisis, the natural development of so ardent an imagination, came to its height at the time of her first communion.

As soon as the matter was discussed, the little girl, who but a short time before had thought God cruel because he changed the devil into a serpent, was precipitated into a strange state of devotion. It was the *Vie des Saints* that inspired her with the passion for sacrifice. One night after supper she collapsed in tears at the feet of her astonished and anxious parents. She who could never part from her mother without "shedding torrents of tears" and who could be teased into terror by the mere mention of the word "boarding-school," had made up her mind that she owed it to her conscience to enter a convent. The thought of separation made her desperate. But she did not weaken. She yearned to follow in the footsteps of the blessed, for only in so doing could one encounter the Almighty.

Her father exclaimed aloud at her ardour. Her mother, too wise a woman ever to commend excesses, was at a loss for words. However, after having taken the neophyte to call upon parents and grandparents and finding that they all approved of such laudable convictions, she resigned herself to fate and set about collecting information with the most scrupulous care. It occurred to her that M. Oajou, one of the child's first tutors, was a teacher in a certain devout establishment where young ladies were taken care of and instructed. The college of the Dames de la Congrégation was situated in the rue Neuve-Saint-Etienne in the faubourg Saint-Marcel.

In his *Tableaux de Paris* Mercier has written that the faubourg Saint-Marcel was then

a quarter inhabited by the poorest, the most turbulent, and the most undisciplined rabble of Paris. There is more money in a single house of the faubourg Saint-Honoré than in the whole of the faubourg Saint-Marcel. . . It was in this quarter that people danced upon the coffin of the Deacon Pâris and ate the earth of his grave, going even so far as to close the cemetery with the following inscription:

> The king hereby prohibits God
> To perform miracles on this sod.

Riots and mutinies have had their hidden source in this centre of blackest misery.

The truth of this was made evident during the Revolution, when Mme Roland, behind the iron bars of Sainte-Pélagie, knew how near she was to the spot where she had passed a happy year of her girlhood.

On the seventh day of May 1765 the little Phlipon girl made to God the greatest sacrifice in her power, and, in a storm of tears and a transport of despair, she entered the gates of the convent.

Nuns and boarders alike, won by the child's charm and intelligence, vied for her friendship, and one of them, Angélique Boufflers (called Sister Sainte-Agathe in the Order), a simple lay sister because she possessed no dowry, became her friend, a friend who was faithful to her to *the very last day*.

On Sundays the Phlipons never failed to appear at the appointed hour in the reception room to fetch their daughter. They would take her for a walk in the Jardin du Roi,[6] and in the evening she would return to where the convent stood embalmed in silence. She would fall to her knees, seeking to imagine the heavenly bliss of the elect in life eternal, and kneeling under those majestic arches before the mystical lights of the altar, with the innocent voices of the choir soaring about her, she breathed a strangely intoxicating air.

There was no break in the succession of days that passed each one just like the other. But one was to leave a lasting impression upon the child's mind. Let her describe it in her own words:

Several months had elapsed since my arrival at the convent. . . The appearance of new boarders came to arouse our little settlement. Some young ladies from Amiens had been announced. . . It was towards the evening of a summer's day, and we were walking under the linden trees. . . Suddenly the cry was heard: There they are ! There they are ! The head mistress put the two new-comers into the hands of the Sister who was then on duty. The crowd gathered about them, withdrew, returned, and finally quieted down sufficiently to stroll in groups down one pathway in order to scrutinize Mesdemoiselles Cannet. They were two sisters; the eldest about eighteen, with a fine figure, a lively appearance, and a swinging step; there was something sensitive, proud, and discontented in her that made her attract attention. The younger was no more than fourteen; a white gauze veil covered her sweet face and ill-concealed her streaming tears. . .

She was, it was said, the favourite of her mother whom she in turn tenderly loved and from whom she had parted in such grief that her sister had been sent to help her endure the separation. That night both of them were seated at my table: Sophie ate very little; her grief was a silent one that was in no way repulsive and would have melted a heart of stone. Her sister seemed much less interested in consoling her than in showing her own discontent at having to share her lot. And could one blame her ? An eighteen-year-old girl whisked out of a world in which she had taken her place, to accompany her young sister to the convent, might well consider herself an object of sacrifice. But in reality her mother's one idea had been to subdue an impetuous nature which she knew not how to manage. One had no need to listen long to the lively Henriette in order to gather all this: frank to the point of brusqueness, impatient to the point of temper, merry to the point of madness, she had all the high spirits of her age with none of its common sense; unequal in temper, forceful, at times charming, more often unbearable, her sudden outbursts were succeeded by the most touching remorse; she combined the most sensitive of natures with the most extravagant imagination: one had to love and scold her in the same breath and yet it was difficult to live with her and still cherish her. . .

The calm of a premature understanding characterized Sophie; too cool headed to feel very keenly, she had a taste for reflection and thought; quiet, never going out of her way to be obliging, she charmed no-one but she was ready to do anyone a service if the occasion arose, and if she lacked initiative, still she never refused a thing that was asked of her. She was fond of work and reading. Her grief had touched me, and I liked the manner in which she conducted herself; I felt I had found a companion and we became inseparable. I attached myself to her with that abandon which arises from a need to love. . . We worked, read, walked together. . . I shared everything with my Sophie. . . We wished each one of us to sustain the other and thus progress together on the road to perfection. . . Sophie had a certain advantage over me that I did not envy her; she was a good talker; I knew only how to respond: it is true that people liked questioning me, but it was not such an easy matter for everyone. The only real intercourse I had was with my good friend; the others but half suspected what I was. . . Henriette joined us at times, but very rarely.

Once out of the convent the little girl remained extremely pious and formed a secret resolution to consecrate herself to God. "Saint François de Sales . . . one of the most gracious saints in Paradise . . . had won me over," she said.

At that time she was living with her grandmother on the beautiful Ile Saint-Louis.

The island [says Mercier in his *Tableaux de Paris*] is a quarter that is closed off by the river and separated from the Cité. The corruption of the town seems to have overlooked it, for it has not yet penetrated there. No woman of easy virtue is allowed to live there: the moment one is discovered she is made to move elsewhere. The bourgeois watch over it; the morals of every individual are common knowledge; every girl who makes a misstep becomes a subject of censure and will never find a husband in the quarter. There is no better example of a third-rate provincial town than the island. It has been said, and well said: he who comes from the Marais is a stranger to the Island.

Mme Phlipon, very proud of her granddaughter, knew no rest until she had shown her to the Mme de Boismorel in whose home she had lived and whom she held in the highest esteem.

The fancy took my grandmama to call on Mme de Boismorel, either for the pleasure of seeing her, or for the purpose of showing off her granddaughter. Hence great preparations; my best clothes on rising, and off we went with Aunt Angélique, due to reach the rue Saint-Louis in the Marais about noon. Upon our arrival at the house, all the servants, beginning with the porter, fondly greeted Mme Phlipon with every show of esteem: all vied as to who should say the most civil things to her; she answered them all graciously and with dignity;

so far so good. But then they set eye upon the granddaughter, Mme Phlipon not having indulged herself to the extent of calling their attention to her, and the servants took it upon themselves to compliment her. I became aware of a certain uneasiness, difficult to explain to myself, but out of which I could make this much: that the servants could look at me if they wished but it was not their business to pay me compliments. We then went further into the house; a great lackey announced us, and we entered the *salon* where Mme de Boismorel, seated with her dog on what was then called not an ottoman, but a canapé, was gravely embroidering a bit of tapestry.

Mme de Boismorel was of the same age, figure, and corpulence as my grandmama, but her dress had less relation to good taste than to the pretension of announcing her wealth and quality, and her face, far from expressing any desire to please, bore evidence of a wish to be highly considered as well as the assurance that she merited such consideration. A rich bit of lace, crumpled into a sort of small butterfly bonnet pointed like the ears of a hare, was perched on the top of her head, permitting one to see some locks, maybe borrowed, done up with that feigned discretion which one assumes after sixty, while a double coating of rouge gave her very small eyes much more hardness than was necessary to make me lower mine.

"Eh, good-day, Mlle Rotisset," cried Mme de Boismorel in a high cold voice, rising as we drew near. (Mademoiselle? What! Grandmama is a mademoiselle in this house?) "But indeed I am glad to see you! And this beautiful child; is she your granddaughter? She's going to be very good-looking! Come here, my heart, and sit next to me. She's shy. How old is your granddaughter, Mlle Rotisset? She's a little dark, but the quality of the skin is excellent; it will get fairer before long; she is already very well developed. You must have a lucky hand, my good friend; have you ever tried it at the lottery?" — "Never, Madame, for I do not care for games of chance." — "I believe it; at your age one always thinks the game is won. What a voice she has, so sweet and full; but how serious-minded! Aren't you a little pious?" — "I see my duties and I strive to perform them." — "Excellent! You want to be a nun, don't you?" — "Still ignorant of my destination, I make no attempt to gauge it." — "How sententious!" cried the arrogant Mme de Boismorel, and with good reason. "Does your granddaughter read, Mlle Rotisset?" — "Reading is the thing she enjoys most; she spends a great portion of the day with her books." — "Oh, I can see that, but take care she doesn't become an intellectual woman: it would be a great pity." . . Mme de Boismorel took a few stitches in her canvas, stroked her dog, and looked fixedly at me from time to time. I carefully avoided her glances and turned my gaze to an examination of the room, for its decorations attracted me much more than did the lady who lived with them. My blood coursed faster than usual, I felt my cheeks flushing and my heart palpitating and oppressed. I had not yet begun to wonder why grandmama was not

JEANNE-MARIE PHLIPON
Age 15. Painted by her father

Original owned by Mme Alfred Chauvac

seated on the canapé and Mme de Boismorel in the place of Mlle Rotisset, but I was in the mood which leads to such reflections and the relief I felt when the visit was ended was like the sudden assuagement of physical distress.

The visits to the convent "were a poor substitute for the daily intercourse and intimacies of friendship. . . I supplanted these visits by writing letters, particularly to Sophie, and this was the origin of my taste for writing." The child's greatest joy was soon to be derived from letters which circulated between Paris and Amiens, between the Quai de l'Horloge and the rue des Jeunes-Mâtins.

"As for pens, they are tools that I am never without," she said.

Thus at a convent "at the age of eleven," the young letter writer found "these two treasures, a pious disposition and a true friend." "Truth and earnestness" were her ideals, but at eleven "meditation," the habit of self-analysis, had already destroyed her peace of mind. This child was not like other children who look with envy upon grown-up people, marvelling at their happiness. At the age of eleven she knew that she was happy and that her happiness consisted in "a tranquillity in which I delight." At eleven she knew that she had failed "through that inconsistency resulting from contradictory speculations."

This correspondence,[7] pitched on a lyrical key and pursued with enthusiasm, was for years her fondest diversion. She was seeking a noble style and the imperfect subjunctive held no terrors for her. Her reflections upon what she read, the narrating of her daily existence, discussions of moral and sentimental questions, fill these pages that so nobly hold their own among the letters of the eighteenth century.

In these letters to the Cannet sisters there is little mention of public events. "However, the interest she took in them," wrote M. Breuil, "her joy upon the reinstating of the Parliaments exiled by Maupeou, her grief at Turgot's disgrace, her ardent sympathies with the American cause, all these presaged the enthusiasm with which she greeted the ideas of 1789."

In a letter of May 17, 1775 which describes a riot (caused by an increase in the price of bread), in which "two unfortunates were hanged to serve as examples," the breath of the Revolution is already felt. Ill rumours were beginning to circulate about what was then taking place simultaneously at Péronne, Amiens, and Nantes. It was said that Abbé Terray was at Vincennes. In more than one passage the reader can perceive that taste for utopias which was the germ of what later became Girondist idealism.

In Mme de Staël there was this same sort of precocity, less surprising in her case, to quote M. Breuil:

Under the guidance of a learned mother, Mlle Necker pursued a serious and methodical course of study. Mlle Phlipon's only instructor was herself; thanks to a perfect organization of all the powers with which she was endowed, she gleaned a rich and well-regulated fund of knowledge from her scattered reading. At eleven Mlle Necker left her own room to mingle in her father's *salon* with men of letters of the day: Thomas Raynal, Marmontel, the Marquis de Pesay, Baron Grimm; they flocked about her, talking with her of her studies, stimulating her mind to form its own judgments. On the other hand we have the little girl of an engraver, enclosed in the narrow circle of her own family and friends, encountering only mediocre and uncultured people, and we can imagine all the resourcefulness and zeal it required to triumph over these adverse circumstances.

If social usage demanded it, Mlle Phlipon was willing "to make a few calls," but on condition that this be "for the love of the Good Lord": "Let us take pleasure in sacrificing our desires," she said, "for after all one must conquer and mortify one's own self if one wishes to be a Christian." If she was to tolerate amusements, they must be presented in a certain light: "One may agree to a game or even to dancing, if people insist, and if they are indulged in but seldom, and with great moderation." The world was filled with pit-falls and temptations. She was greatly influenced by her father confessor, and men said of her: "She is a bigot."

One day in company she was heard to remark that "it is easier to restrain one's passions than to gratify them." An Abbé objected as strongly as if she had "quoted Calvin or Mahomet."

Breuil later wrote of her:

When she renounced her faith she devoted herself even more to her duties, lest one imagine that she sought independent thought as a pretext for independent action.

Bossuet seemed to be the first who made her reason out her beliefs. How astonished he would have been had he known it!

This was the first step [she said]. I was still far from the skepticism that I was to know several years later, after having been successively a Jansenist, a Cartesian, a Stoic, and a Deist!

I no longer consider the atheist an unsound intellect; I could live with him as well as and better than with the devout man, for he makes more use of his mind; but he lacks a certain sense, and my soul does not entirely fuse with his: the most ravishing sight leaves him cold, and he seeks a syllogism whereas I give thanks.

Mature men of distinguished intellect began to frequent the house of the engraver, drawn by that sound, glowing mind which they fondly believed it lay in their power to direct.

The first recorded was M. de Boismorel, the charming Roberge whom grandmama Phlipon had brought up and who had always been to her as friendly and simple as Mme de Favières, his sister, had been arrogant and rude. He was very attentive to the learned maid of the Ile Notre-Dame and occasioned her the greatest joy by throwing open his library to her. When she was grown-up he paid her even more special attentions.

There she met M. de Boismorel's mother, that old lady who had once wounded her by her condescending manner, and with her an extremely pious daughter-in-law. But thanks to her dear Roberge, this time she was received with all the consideration she could have desired. They even thought her very well dressed:

"You don't care for feathers, Mademoiselle?"
"I never wear them, Madame, because as an artist's daughter who goes out on foot they seem to me to boast a situation and a fortune I do not possess."
"If your position were different would you wear them?"
"I cannot say. I attach very little importance to such details . . . and I am careful to judge no one from a cursory glance at their dress."

Although she said she spoke these "severe words so sweetly that their point was blunted," it is difficult to feel she was, to put it mildly, either kind or just. She was ill at ease and nervous in such surroundings and carried defiance to the pitch of exasperation. This was not her usual character, but even at the age of twelve she resented being examined from head to foot, an obsession which the following significant anecdote makes even more apparent.

It took place before the death of Mme Phlipon. The girl's great-uncle Besnard was, as we know, steward at Soucy Castle (the property of the farmer-general Haudry), and lived near the old feudal castle of Fontenay, and there Mme Phlipon and her daughter visited him in the summer season:

Old Haudry, who had built up his own fortune [say the *Memoirs*], was dead. He had left his great wealth to his son who, born in luxury, was later to squander it all. . . No sooner had we arrived at Mme Besnard's than she wanted us to pay a visit to Soucy, where Haudry's mother-in-law and sister-in-law lived with his son and did the honours of the house. This visit took place very modestly before dinner: it was without the least pleasure that I entered the *salon* where Mme Pénault and her daughter received us with the greatest politeness but with some superiority. My mother's manner and my own character, such as it was under the air of timidity I wore because of a realization of my own worth and the doubt that it was in this instance appreciated, hindered me from being myself; I was paid compliments which flattered me very little, and which I was able to cope with quite smartly until these ladies were reinforced by certain parasites of the Cross of St Louis who are always hovering around wealth like ghosts on the shores of the Acheron.

A few days later the ladies returned our call; they were followed by the company who had been with them at the castle; the visit to Fontenay gave them an excuse for a walk; I was much more pleasant and I knew exactly what dose of modest and dignified politeness was required of me to even things up. Once Mme Pénault asked us to dine; I was never more astonished than to find that it was not at her table, but in the pantry. I well understood that as M. Besnard had in other days performed his offices there, out of consideration for him I could not show displeasure at finding myself in the same place; but I felt that Mme Pénault might have arranged things so that we would have been spared the incivility of this gesture. . . On Sunday there was out-of-door dancing at Soucy. . . There, with the barriers of distinction levelled by enjoyment, and the question being only what each one was in himself, I no longer feared being put in any place other than the one due me. [*Memoirs*.]

Mme Roland was never to forget these insults to the little Phlipon girl and this rancour has done much to damage her in the eyes of posterity. Many years later, in the prisons of the Revolution and at the very foot of the guillotine, she recorded them with the same bitter resentment that she had experienced at the time. This show of malice on her part was so exceptional that, though it may well annoy us, we risk falling into grave error should we draw a general conclusion from it. However, this is what certain readers of the *Memoirs* have done — readers already prejudiced by their political views. After having labelled the author with "Vanity, Pretentiousness, Conceit" they have closed the book in the complacent belief that they had tapped the source.

M. DE BOISMOREL, a man of great distinction of mind, knew how to pick out for his young friend the points of interest in the ctiy.

The Paris of that day, while it drew the scum of the kingdom, was as well the centre of enlightenment and taste; preachers and actors, professors and charlatans, whoever happened to have talent for the moment was admired and followed in turn: but even the finest talent in the universe would not have long held the attention of a public that continually demanded something new, and which was attracted as much by display as by merit.[8]

On Saint-Louis' Day M. de Boismorel conducted Mlle Phlipon to the Academy where, after Mass had been sung by the Opera chorus, Abbé de Desplas spoke a eulogy on the Holy King. The Abbé was Almoner to Monsieur and hence not afraid to jeer boldly at the monarchy. His discourse was filled with philosophical jibes judged so inopportune that he was obliged to omit them from the text on publication. Mlle Phlipon, all ears, examined the Immortals at great length. Of Alembert she said: "His small face and his feeble voice made me think that it is better to know the works of a philosopher than his person." Neither did Abbé Delille please her overmuch, but La Harpe caused her to shed tears as he pronounced a panegyric on Catinat.

The following day M. de Boismorel took the young girl on a pilgrimage to Saint-Gratien, "where this great man (Catinat) ended his days in seclusion, far from the Court and its honours." After "a frugal supper" they went to visit the little home of Jean-Jacques in the valley of Montmorency, and there, seated upon the ferns, the sensitive Roberge enhanced the charm of this philosophical promenade by reading aloud an extract on virtue from Montesquieu.

Upon their return, she to the Quai de l'Horloge and he to the
Petit-Bercy where he had just bought some land, they wrote to
each other in verse and were rejoicing in their delightful relationship when suddenly "the sage of Bercy" as she called him, died of
a sun-stroke. His young friend grieved over his death, perhaps
even more than did his own son, and gave homage to this "venerable" friend (he was barely over forty), in a complaint that in
the solitude of her little room she sung to the playing of her
guitar.

She found companionship in Moré, the good Genevan clock-
maker, "the republican philosopher" who always had a book in his
tool-bag. He was a frequent visitor to the Phlipon house and was
greatly attached to the young girl whose cup of joy he later filled
to overflowing by sending her, on the first of the year 1778, the
complete works of Rousseau.

To have all of Jean-Jacques in one's possession, to have him there to
turn to unceasingly, there to console one, to enlighten one, there that
one may soar with him in every mood life offers, this is a delight, a
felicity that only one who adores him as I do can appreciate.

Among the intimate visitors at the house, the most unusual was
without question a certain M. de Sainte-Lette who had been sent
to the engraver's by M. Demontchery, an army officer who two
years previously had left for Pondichéry hinting that upon his
return he would be gratified to find the young girl still unmarried.

M. de Sainte-Lette had made a career for himself in French
Canada and in the Indies. A man of some sixty years, who,
according to the *Memoirs,* "possessed a proud carriage and an
eagle eye." "A self-avowed atheist," super-sensitized to things of
the mind, a "soul of fire and brimstone," a frend of Helvetius and
a disciple of Rousseau, Mlle Phlipon confessed that had he been
but ten years younger she would have "loved him perhaps more
than she might have wished." [9]

This romantic figure had a great influence on Mlle Phlipon and,
even more than Bossuet, was responsible for shattering her religious
beliefs.

M. de Sainte-Lette had a friend, a M. de Sévelinges d'Espagny,

collector for the tobacco farm at Soissons, who had just lost his
wife. M. de Sainte-Lette had gone to see him and brought him
back to Paris with him, and, in order that he find some distraction
from his trouble, introduced him to the household on the Quai de
l'Horloge. He was a nobleman of fifty-six with two sons, both
officers. A man of true distinction, a fair scholar, he had a pensive
air which interested Mlle Phlipon so greatly that one day she made
so bold as to submit him several literary essays composed a short
time before at the instigation of M. de Boismorel. Upon his return
to Soissons, M. de Sévelinges carried with him a copy-book of these
Loisirs. A literary correspondence, soon to become a sentimental
one, began between them, carried on through the intermediary of
Canon Bimont. His niece had explained to him that Phlipon complained of having too much to pay out for postage, and the uncle
was satisfied wth this excuse.

It was before Roland, however, that they were all soon to give
way. Because of him Mlle Phlipon lost no time in putting the
bragging la Blancheric in his proper place. His book, which she
had spoken of with enthusiasm but three months before, she no
longer risked showing to Roland, for she now believed it to be
"a work not of the first water."

But "when he [Roland] returned she was less disposed to please
him." "A terrible cold in the head spoiled her looks," and the
presence of the engraver made conversation difficult. She wrote
Sophie: "I know how to listen to him and understand him
[Roland], but I do not know how to communicate with him in
a way which might hold his interest." If the truth be told, she
was slightly piqued by Roland. In February this pique became
actual ill-humour, for the inspector failed to call again:

Apparently M. Roland has had enough of us; I rather thought so.
And quite right he is too.

She again turned to Sainte-Lette, who kept her mind occupied
by reading her his verses and in recounting to her tales of his
journeys. But in the spring M. de la Platière again put in his
appearance and the former intellectual intimacy was soon re-estab-
lished between her and the Cannet's friend.

Upon being introduced to the sanctuary of the little study-room, he was surprised and delighted to see with what books Mlle Phlipon nourished her mind. From the very earliest years books had played an important part in the existence of a precocious little person who enjoyed whatever she could lay her hands upon. At four she could read without having been taught: "From that moment," say the *Memoirs,* "my instruction was an accomplished thing, for from then on all I required was not to be left without books. . . No matter which were given me or what I could get hold of, they absorbed me so completely that nothing could divert my attention except bouquets. . ." She listed those books which were her principal reading-matter at the age of seven: a Bible in old French; a book on the Turkish Theatre; Appius' *Civil Wars,* and a *Treatise on Heraldry.* When other amusements failed, these volumes held her attention, and it required a *Treatise on Contracts* really to dishearten her:

I learned anything I was asked and I could have recited the Koran had anyone taught me to read it. I remember a painter named Guibal . . . a frequent visitor of my father's; an amusing sort of fellow who told me fairy-tales which I have never forgotten and which amused me exceedingly; he took an equal pleasure in starting me in science. I can see him now, with his slightly grotesque face, seated in an armchair. He would take me between his knees on which I rested my elbows while he made me repeat the Athanasian creed; then rewarded my obligingness by the story of Tanger whose nose was so long that he had to wind it around his arm when he walked.

At catechism she won such remarkable honours in the Gospel, the Epistles, and the Orison, that the instructing priest, Canon Bimont, was brought into the limelight and marked for advancement.

As for M. Garat, the priest at St Barthélemy (the Philpon's parish), "who had a passion to be in the pulpit and who could not utter two consecutive words once he got there," he was taken by surprise on the day that, inspecting his pupils, he believed he had thrown the little girl into confusion by asking her how many orders of Spirits existed in the celestial hierarchy:

I was convinced by the triumphant and malicious manner in which he asked me this question [say the *Memoirs*] that he believed me at a loss for an answer. I replied smilingly that although several were spoken of in the preface to the Mass, that I had seen elsewhere only nine could be counted, and I proceeded to name the Angels, the Archangels, Thrones, Dominations, etc. . . .

And further on:

In ferreting through the house I had unearthed a fund of reading-matter that I managed to spread out over a period of time. . . On the opposite side [of my study] was a large room in which my father had had his work-bench placed as well as many sculptured objects and samples of his own art, and that room was his studio. I often slipped in there of an evening or at odd moments during the day when there was no-one about. I had seen a hidden corner where one of the young men had put away some books. These I took one at a time and went off to devour in my little study, taking great care to return them at times when I would not be observed, and never mentioning them to anyone. In general they were good books. One day I noticed that my mother must have made the same discovery as I; a book she was reading I recognized as one I had already read; from then on I made no more bones about it and, without lying, but simply by not speaking of what had gone on in the past, I continued as if I were doing no more than following her example. . . The young man . . . was mannerly and possessed of a decent sense of tact, and was seeking instruction. He never made any remark concerning the momentary disappearance of his volumes. It was as if a tacit understanding existed among us three. In this way I read many books of travel, which I passionately loved . . . several plays by second-rate playwrights, and Dacier's *Plutarch*. This last work made more impression on me than anything I had yet read. . . Plutarch was the one pastureland that satisfied me. I shall never forget Lent of 1763 (I was then nine), when I took this volume to church in the guise of the *Semaine Sainte*. From that moment date the impressions and ideas which made me a republican before I even dreamed of becoming one. *Télémaque* and *Jerusalem Delivered* somewhat disturbed these majestic impressions. . . At times, at my mother's request, I read aloud the parts I did not like; this was a change from the meditations I so enjoyed and obliged me to go at a slower pace; but I would have preferred to bite off my tongue rather than read aloud the episode of Calypso's Isle, and numerous passages from Tasso. My breath came fast and I felt a sudden fire flaming in my face, while my altered voice betrayed my emotion. . . These works of which I speak gave place to others. . . One day when I was reading *Candide,* my mother left the table where she had been playing piquet, and the lady with whom she had been playing called me to her from the corner where I was and asked to see what book I was reading. Upon my mother's return to the room, the friend expressed her astonishment at my reading-matter; without answering her remark my mother told me purely and simply to return the book to the place from which I had taken it. I cast a sour look on that woman with her peevish face and her big stomach who was grimacing with such self-importance, and since then I have never smiled at Mme Charbonne. But, strange as it may seem, my good mother never altered her attitude but allowed me to read everything I found without question, although she knew quite well what I was reading. [*Memoirs.*]

Mme Phlipon had too much middle-class feeling not to fear that her daughter might, by her varied gifts, be made to overstep unwisely the limits of her sphere. Despite her happy meeting with a certain Abbé Jeauket, a German and a great musician who in Vienna had instructed Marie-Antoinette, she did not wish her daughter to evidence any taste for music and forbade her the clavichord and the harmonica as instruments of luxury reserved for young people who had been born ladies.

In compensation, this little girl

who read serious volumes, who had explained extremely well the circles of the celestial sphere, who could use both pencil and engraver's pen, and who at eight was considered the best dancer in a group of young people all older than herself who were taking part in a family gathering; this did not alter the fact that this child was frequently called to the kitchen to cook an omelette or clean vegetables, or scour a saucepan. [*Memoirs.*]

One can imagine her as she must have been at that time, in a wide skirt which touched the floor, a white kerchief, a short-sleeved jacket, and a pinafore.

But olden days are better evoked by pictures than by the written word. The childhood of this little girl was recorded by a fine painter, not an imaginative painter who depicted allegory as did Boucher, nor roguish scenes as did Beaudouin, nor the picture of manners intended to point a moral as did Greuze; but a painter who was the son of a carpenter, who took his models from among the humble folk about him; a painter satisfied to portray as best he could what he saw before his eyes; a painter who could make a radiant masterpiece of the common fish which the housewife had bought for the noon-day meal. In Chardin's works are

such subjects as a seated child playing wth her lunch; a little girl
fetching water from a pump; an apprentice playing cards; a little
girl washing clothes; a child with a shuttle-cock; a young tapestry-
weaver selecting wools from her basket; the son of M. Godefroy,
jeweller, watching a teetotum spin; the saying of Grace; the work-
ing-class mother; a young girl reciting the Creed; the morning
toilet; the little school-mistress; a young girl sealing a letter; the
preparation of various dishes on a kitchen table; the vigilant nurse,
or food for the convalescent; the portrait of Mme X holding an
engraved booklet entitled *l'Instant de la Méditation;* bunches of
flowers, implements of science, and instruments of art and music !

All of her childhood, her girlhood, her life as the young wife
are there. All of her life save the prison and the scaffold which
this good man, looking at life from under the green eye-shade
carpenters wear, would have been incapable of depicting. The life
he painted was not a life of the open air. The little Phlipon girl
was a city child, offspring of the *petite bourgeoisie* which later produced the *Tiers-Etat,* and which Chardin painted. "There is not
a woman of that class," said a pamphlet of the time written upon
the works of Chardin, "who does not believe his work to be a
conception of herself, who does not see therein her staff of servants,
her homely habits, her face, her daily occupations, her manners,
the moods of her children, her furniture, her wardrobe."

Mme Phlipon put all her wisdom into educating her daughter to
discreet and tempered tastes, not allowing her to pursue the study
of painting lest it draw her into dangerous company. But this
prudent mother put no ban upon books, she herself liking them
well enough as we have already seen. In guiding this hot-headed
girl she took but one precaution: that the works of Rousseau did
not fall into her daughter's hands. Mlle Phlipon discovered him
late, but early enough to be entirely swept away by him. "This
was a good thing," she said, "for he would have made me go
mad. I would have read no-one but him." Mme Phlipon had
"rightly judged it unwise so to influence a sensitive nature that was
more than ready to burst into flames." It "burst into flames nevertheless . . . for those who fought against inequality."

I was Agis and Cleomenes at Sparta; at Rome I was the Gracchi. . .
I withdrew with the people to the Aventine hill. . . Witnessing the
celebrations which took place in the capital upon the entrance of the
Queen and the princes, the thanksgiving after a safe delivery, etc. . .
I grieved at comparing this overbearing pomp with the misery and
abjection of the downtrodden people who pressed forwards as the idols
of their own creation passed by, and stupidly applauded the brilliant
equipage they themselves paid for at the price of their own necessities.

She was a great admirer of the English Constitution, as was
Roland. It was one of the favorite topics of those conversations
which were becoming more and more frequent and of such length
that the new friend asked the young girl to keep secret his visits
to her when writing to Amiens.

The result of this was that the brother of Mesdemoiselles Cannet,
Sélincourt, who was then living in Paris, was encouraged to regard
Roland as a possible husband for Henriette, and Roland received
several significant invitations which he made no effort to avoid. In
public life he never needed an example of courage. In private he
was irresolute to the point of cowardice. He had no idea what he
was after in going to the Quai de l'Horloge. Above all he was
afraid of himself. Should he ask for the hand of the eldest Mlle
Cannet ? Should he allow his family to make a good match for
him ? Should he remain in single blessedness ? Or should he
abandon himself to his infatuation, disturbingly sweet as it was,
for the scholarly and delectable Calypso of the Ile Notre-Dame ?
All his puritanical instincts rebelled against the various delights
such a union offered.

If the young girl seemed almost indifferent to the homage of a
man she considered so remarkable, it was because her thoughts
were elsewhere, as we know. To be thus casually received was
apparently just the way best to encourage the wary visitor, to
heighten his sentiments and to prevent him from perceiving their
increasing ardour.

He was that sort of person who is in reality his own worst
enemy, seeing evil in all tempting things, and fearing out of all
reason everything that attracted him. If at that moment he had
felt he was being sought after, it is certain that he would have

disappeared for good. But as Mlle Phlipon was otherwise absorbed at the time, he was taken off his guard. He instinctively hit upon an idea which flattered her more than any other. On the eve of departure for a long journey through Italy, he left her his manuscripts, giving her complete control over them in case "a misfortune befell him," and begged her to write him during his absence.

She felt she had been deeply honoured. Here was compensation for the shame of abandoning the "complete confidence" that had always existed between her and her friend! This time, very well satisfied with events, she wrote Sophie:

I am still further indebted to your friendship which has bestowed yet another blessing by introducing to me M. Roland, a sensitive, honest, and open soul.

The intimacy between them increased during that summer of 1776 when he spent much time in Paris preparing for the journey he was about to undertake at the instigation of his chief and protector, M. Trudaine, Superintendent of Finances. Roland, however, was far from giving his entire thought to the preparations for his commercial investigation. She who spoke the language of the Muses and the Graces was becoming more desirable to him every day.

We do not know why M. de la Platière made his unpleasant request as far as Sophie was concerned. We only know that from the month of June 1776 Mlle Phlipon followed a systematically deceptive course which grieves the reader of the correspondence that had hitherto been so open and sincere.

Annoying as it was for her in regard to her friends, she kept the secret of her relationship with Roland for almost four years, in other words, until the time of her marriage. Love is the destroyer of friendships. The two sisters had given her no cause for reproach and were entirely deserving of her confidence and affection. But Roland did not like them. They had been instrumental in his failure to live up to the austerity of his famous principles, and he was not disposed to pardon them for it. He inveighed against them with such embittered tenacity that Mlle Phlipon car-

ried obedience to the point of ingratitude and neglected those who
had completely absorbed her affections long before the appearance
of this stranger.

The bonds of friendship, however, were strengthened during
those trips Sophie and Henriette made to Paris to see the world.
They visited at the home of the two old cousins in the rue St
Dominique. Mesdemoiselles de Lamotte had a passion for rank, and
between knitting and backgammon they appeased their intellectual
appetites by reading the Psalms and looking after their own interests. They had taken into their home, say the *Memoirs,* a young
person named Mlle d'Hangard, "a stout dark girl, fresh complex-
ioned, and of almost terrifying good health," whom they intended to
present with a dowry should she marry a nobleman. "The most
curious thing about the house" was the lawyer, Perdu, "fat and
dressed to kill" who had been, so to speak, imprisoned by his sister
Mme Cannet in the home of these old relatives in order that he
end his days in more decency than he had begun them. He was
quite tittilated by the presence of the young d'Hangard, and looked
askance at his nephew, Sélincourt, the brother of Sophie and Henriette, who on his own behalf was more than disposed to pass
himself off as her suitor.

Through this household Mlle Phlipon made her first acquaintance
with a pretentious and ceremonious society which "behind her back
lamented that such a well-spoken young person had not been born
a lady."

THE time approached for M. de la Platière to leave for Italy.

On the sixth of August 1776, a day or two before his departure,
the traveller was invited to a farewell dinner at the Quai de
l'Horloge. M. de Sainte-Lette was present. Aided by Mignonne,
the young mistress of the house, who was no novice in the kitchen,
fairly outdid herself in her efforts to do honour to her guests.

Upon leaving, he [Roland] asked leave to embrace me [say the
Memoirs], and I don't know why it is but, even with the imagination at rest, a young person cannot manage this act of politeness without a blush.

"You are happy to be going," Sainte-Lette said to him in his sober, solemn voice, "but make haste to return and ask the same favour of her."

After his departure Mlle Phlipon had nothing more pressing to do than read all the papers Roland had left with her. Upon finishing them, she reread them, and meditated thus:

They concerned his trips, his reflections, his plans for work, anecdotes personal to himself; all revealing, to anyone who cared to seek them out, a strong soul, an austere integrity, rigorous principles, knowledge and taste.

As far as taste goes there may be some question. Roland prided himself on being a judge of the fine arts and was a frequent visitor in artists' studios. The Rouen library possesses letters of his written to the artist Descamps. He knew Pigalle and Couston, son and nephew of the two great sculptors and himself a sculptor. It is worth our while to listen to Roland criticizing their work.

But it was not in search of beauty that Roland went to Italy. In reality he could see no excuse for works of art that required an endless amount of work and served no useful purpose. At Strasbourg he wrote of the Cathedral: "It is very old. Its chancel in particular is extremely ugly." And again: "I was astonished to see the continuous effort that is wasted on preserving this tower, unable to reconcile the anxious concern of priests with the conservation of a monument which is of no comfort to the poor, etc. . ."

To the best of his ability Sainte-Lette filled the place left vacant at the young girl's side. Three or four times a week he appeared at the Quai de l'Horloge, and "when he dines at the house," she said, "he remains with me from noon until nine o'clock."

"Mademoiselle, deny it as you may, sooner or later you are going to write," he says.
"It will be under the name of another then," she answers him, "for I would rather eat my fingers than become an author."

Mlle Phlipon was of the opinion that "a woman who writes is always ridiculed." All her life she loved needlework and was a vigilant housewife. But this in no way affected the truth of her statement that: "I need study as I need food."

She played the guitar, the violin, set poems to music; her studies consisted principally of physics and mathematics.

Nollet, Réamur, Bonnet, who dream while others describe, amused me in turn, as well as Maupertuis who mourns even in describing the pleasures of snails.

Having to make a *précis* of Clairault's *Elements of Geometry,* she undertook the copying of the entire volume from cover to cover, including the graphs.

I know not what I might have become had I been placed in able hands; it is highly probable that had I concentrated upon one objective I would have gone far in that kind of knowledge or even acquired great proficiency.

Everyone lent her books. She read a bit of everything, and particularly what she could find in the library of a priest, a friend of the canon. It was there she came upon the *Fathers of the Church,* men of letters, and historians:

Cotron and Rouillé, who called Horatius Coclès a generous fool; Maimbourg, of as questionable good taste; Berruyer who wrote the *Histoire du Peuple de Dieu;* the chevalier Folard, quite another figure and one whose military points seemed to me to be more rational than the cogitations of the Jesuits; Abbé Banier, who amused me infinitely more than did Abbé Fleury; Condillac and Père André whose metaphysical system, applied to beauty in all its forms, was peculiarly pleasing to me; a few of Voltaire's poems and Nicole's *Essais de Morale;* the lives of the *Pères du Desert* and André Baillet's *Life of Descartes,* Bossuet's *Histoire Universelle;* Saint Jérome's letters and the romance of Don Quixote; and a thousand other things as well assorted. Gladly would I have said as did M. de Montesquieu: could I but forget that I am a Christian, I would consider the loss of the Stoics as a calamity to mankind.

Followed Pascal, Diderot, D'Alembert, Locke, Abbé Raynal, and the great playwrights:

I had no other ambition . . . except to know and to learn; I must needs use my mind, cultivate my earnest tastes.

Her style was improving, and beginning to rid itself of the commonplace and the bombastic. She was highly attuned to beauty, and had a profound understanding of painting. Her greatest enthusiasm was for Watteau. Diderot himself did not get beyond Greuze.

But Roland had not written.

One day, however, his brother Dom Pierre, the congenial Prieur de Longpont, called at the Quai de l'Horloge to give her news of the "ultramontane."

The traveller was roving through Italy and Sicily. He had been as far as Malta and upon his return journey planned to spend some time at Naples and Rome. By means of his good brother he sent a letter to Mlle Phlipon who answered him at Rome. Then he again relapsed into silence. Later we learn that this "charming little letter" had seemed all too interesting to Roland. It was for this reason that he had not answered it; but this way of reasoning never occurred to the young girl and her keen disappointment led her to ask her friends the Cannets "under the pretext of politics and customs," if they had had any news from Italy.

The truth was that at this time the husband and wife-to-be were each one looking about on his own behalf. Mlle Phlipon had finally seen through La Blancherie's mediocrity — either with or without a feather in his hat — and she was able to write of him:

When one has loved as I have it is terrible to see one's lover no longer as the finest example of his kind.

Hardening her heart she told herself that: "This fellow must be sunk in oblivion," and having thus lightly disposed of him, she turned her attention to Sévelinges with whom she was in constant correspondence.

As for Roland, his family was then urging him to conclude arrangements for an advantageous marriage. With that bourgeois indecency which bargains over everything, he haggled over the dowry, over the station of the prospective bride, and insisted upon the fulfillment, without any further talk about it, of certain promises made him by his mother and his four brothers — all church people — in the event that he should marry. If satisfaction were not accorded him "the thing will be decided negatively and irrevocably." And he added: "My heart would have to be very much involved to alter such a decision."

Neglected from February to September, Mlle Phlipon had turned
to the indefinable Sévelinges. After some correspondence concerning the prize subjects offered by provincial academies, the two of
them decided to enter the lists, for Sévelinges as well, let it be
understood, was a "philosopher." But it now developed that the
widower had had enough of solitude and was beginning to entertain "many thoughts upon the charms of an intellectual companionship." It occurred to him to go to Paris and call unexpectedly at
the Quai de l'Horloge on the pretext of buying an engraver's seal.
A cruel disappointment was in store for him, for Mlle Phlipon,
thinking him a passing client, received him absent-mindedly and
never recognized him:

This curious act made an unfortunate impression on me. . . [say
the Memoirs]. Our correspondence abated; presently it ceased entirely, as I shall relate.

What she failed to relate was that Sévelinges, upon receiving
several rather unguarded letters, permitted himself to suggest that
she come and live at Soissons "in the little house, at the end of
the garden . . . to talk philosophy." Did or did not the young
girl understand? It is amazing how she herself continued the
subject by proposing herself to him in a marriage that "instead of
following the usual rules" would remain "a celibate affair." Caught
in his own ambiguous snare, never did prospective fiancé evidence
less frankness. This woman of sense, plucky-spirited, clear-minded,
was to associate all her life with men who were incapable of considering the varied aspects of a case and coming to a definite decision. We have already had experience with Canon Bimont and
La Blancherie. We now see Sévelinges. We will later see Phlipon
and the family circle. We will see Roland. We will see the
Girondists. Among these people she stands out like one of Corneille's fine Roman figures, embodying in her woman's heart all
their will and conscience. This was the secret of her power over
them all, and of the charm she still has for "impartial posterity."

One fine day Mlle Phlipon was surprised to receive a letter for
which she had perhaps ceased hoping. It was dated September 17,
1777. Roland had reached Villefranche-en-Beaujolais the day

before, and there in the bosom of his family after a year's absence, he had suddenly remembered the nymph abandoned on the banks of the Seine.

He had written to her the day following his return. Nothing could have been more significant. Upon seeing again his own country he must needs seek out as well the woman who for him personified those qualities that made up the sum total of his own land. There is no doubt that the memory of his young friend thrust itself upon him in the very midst of his austere family. Doubtless, too, he sensed that to her it would appear no more than natural that he should turn to her again on his own hearth, surrounded by his mother and his brothers, in the moving hour of his return. Strange that so brilliant a young girl should be the means of bringing light and warmth to the old house that must have seemed so lugubrious to him after a whole year of sunny Italy.

Ancestors of the Rolands can be traced as far back as 1575, a family of the Lyons bourgeoisie which was often closely connected with nobility. Two members had been Lyons aldermen, one in 1690 and the other in 1723, and the Rolands could boast a Grand Penitentiary, a merchant's provost at Lyons, and a Member of Parliament in Paris. While the family had formerly been very prolific, it had through evincing a taste for the spiritual side of life produced such a number of priests, canons, and cloistered nuns, that Jean-Marie Roland de la Platière, head of the eldest branch of the family and father of the Roland who at present concerns us, was left as the sole heir to the family name. In 1720 he had made a brilliant match by marrying Thérèze Bessye de Montozan, a young lady of a family both noble and of great social prominence in the countryside, having placed itself in the front rank of important personages in the province by acquiring the title of Counsellor to the King in the bailiwick of Beaujolais. The De Montozans were established in the large patrimonial homestead at Villefranche.

Villefranche is one of those small towns of which so many exist [said Roland in his *Voyage en France* (1769)], fundamentally worthy but where petty vanities succeed in destroying even the best dispositions.

Its people are lazy and they live without reflection; gossips, small
people, petty affairs, these are the lot of all small towns. . .

The Roland's house still stands at 181 of the Grande Rue, at
the corner of the rue Sainte-Claire, a house so deep that it reaches
back to another small street which at the present day bears the
name of the family Roland. It was built in the sixteenth century
and decorated after the fashion of the time with beautiful iron-
work and finely carved wood. In the square courtyard upon which
handsome wrought-iron balconies open from each storey, an old
well still stands, and on the original wall near the entrance-way a
hand can be seen holding a basket of flowers with the following
inscription:

ANE CROPET
1594

The austere aspect of this dwelling-place is heightened by the
thought that it was once inhabited by severe men of the church
and their terrifying old mother. And we think with pity of that
young woman, brilliant both in appearance and mind, who was to
enter this relentless cage of stone.

At Thizy, not far from Villefranche, the Rolands owned the
beautiful property of La Platière, where the generation which concerns us was born. The father died in 1747, leaving his affairs
in a bad way, possibly the consequences of his wife's extravagant
tastes. Straightened circumstances caused the eldest son to sell La
Platière in the year 1750. There still remained a small property
called *Le Clos,* located in the parish of Theizé in the Lyonnais, to
which the name of La Platière was transferred in memory of the
family homestead. The people thereabouts have come to combine
the two names and call it Le Clos de la Platière.[10] At the present
day it is practically abandoned, standing there with its windows
obscured by the branches and vines that have overgrown it. Even
the memories which linger there fail to lend it any charm. However Mme Roland was happy enough in that spot, and Roland
wrote:

Our country house . . . is built on Lyonnais ground, and its principal outlook is upon one of the most magnificent hillsides of Beaujolais.

The greater portion of these slopes is covered by a dense forest from which we are separated only by a very narrow but profound valley. Further, we are surrounded by vineyards and behind us a very high mountain completely covered with vines obscures our view. This location might seem to some a dismal one. But what of that, it suits me very well. . .

Of the ten children that had been born to them, four of the five who survived took holy orders. The eldest, Canon Dominique, cantor in the Cathedral of Notre-Dame-des-Marais, ruled his brothers with an iron hand. It was he who managed the family affairs. His brother Laurent was a priest as well, but so delicate and weak-willed as to be of little real aid to him. With a mother of a strange and fantastical turn of mind, the sons lived in the house at Villefranche. The other two brothers, Jacques and Pierre, were Benedictines in the Cluny Monastery and had renounced their share in the family heritage.

Jean-Marie, the youngest son, who had "begun his schooling very badly," was sent off alone and without a mentor to the Jesuits at Roanne-en-Forez. There he fell ill.

I must confess [he said], that had it not been for this illness . . . I would have fallen the prey of this order, so sly and insinuating when it is after a thing, and so proud and insolent when it fears nothing.

His family next put him into business at Lyons. But from there he made his surreptitious escape in 1754, "upon having completed his twentieth year." On reaching Nantes he found work with a shipowner, with the idea of going off to the Indies. "The spitting of blood came as a warning that he could not attempt a sea-voyage without risking his life." He then journeyed on to Rouen, where a member of the family was Inspector in the service of the Godinot Manufactures. This gentleman found a place for him in the business, and there Roland remained ten years, and was, moreover, to devote nearly forty years of concentrated work as a member of the body of Inspectors of Manufactures.

In August 1754, the year in which his future wife was born, he was given the position of supernumerary student. Fulfilling the requirements of his service he went to Dieppe, and there he met the Cousin-Despréaux [11] family with whom he founded the little literary society called "The Greeks" in which he was known as Thales. Shortly after he returned to Rouen, and to his friends the Malortie sisters. He was in love with the younger, Marie-Magdeleine, but she was doomed to a premature death, and Roland, mourning her, wrote poems in which he called her his beloved Cleobuline.

Always eager to be on the move he had travelled all over France, and he knew Germany well as far as Berlin. He had been to Vienna, to Switzerland,[12] and to England, where he later returned with his wife. For eighteen years he had not seen his family, save for two "rapid appearances," but the touching welcome he had been accorded upon his last visit had reawakened his deep love for his own flesh and blood.

He was profoundly grieved at parting from his kin, and bidding them farewell was almost more than he could bear. Hence he made his departures in secret, and from the first halt in his journey he would write to his mother, who certainly cared little one way or the other, saying that he had left in this fashion to spare her the agony of his adieux. He deemed his brothers capable of sufficient masculine courage to withstand the ordeal, and they roused themselves at night to help him in his flight.

I make no attempt to describe my last farewells [he wrote in his *Voyage en France,* as though it were a feat actually beyond his powers]. I know of nothing more terrible than these moments of parting: the human structure is shaken to its very roots, and suffering benumbs and stupefies one's senses.

It is obvious that Roland suffered acutely from nerves, and a letter from one of his cousins, Mme Miot, bears this out.

You complain of being sad, apathetic. I see from the manner of your writing this that you are even more so than you say. I confess this makes me most unhappy. You are the victim of an unfortunate disposition or disorder of the soul. It may lead you to an even more desperate state. Do not give way to it, dear cousin, but rally all your forces, all your energies that in the past have served you so well.

We have already heard of Dom Pierre, the good Prior of Longpont.

This brother of mine, who is but one year my elder [said Roland], has a sensitive but an undemonstrative nature, more intellect than any of us, a great amount of penetration, philosophy enough to enable him to take things easily, and even more than that, but all without making a great show of it; one couldn't be more correct, more polite, more honest, and this is apparent in his face and his manner. I have always had more tenderness for him than for the others, and he is the only one from whom I have concealed nothing, absolutely nothing.

It was he who wrote in his beautiful scholarly hand to Mlle Phlipon and gave her news of the "ultramontane." He served as intermediary between the young girl and the traveller, and presently he was to act as the deciding agent of Fate.

Mlle Phlipon was overjoyed to receive Roland's letter of the seventeenth of September, in which several passages caused her to believe herself loved. She was ready to forget his seven months' silence and bear him no grudge although no reasonable excuse had been offered. Her response to him clearly shows that she wished to reveal rather than conceal her delight:

I am touched, enraptured, I am in despair; I pity you, scold you, I . . .

And further:

Happy man that you are to be so pitied! If I esteemed you less I would fear you more, but I will not tell you so. Your letter made me cry, and yet I am happier since receiving it.

She made these advances in the belief that she had been given cause to encourage Roland. Bitter indeed was her disappointment when a whole month passed without a response. But this time Roland had adequate reason. He had fallen ill at *Le Clos* and was recovering but slowly. Once more it was the Prior who sent news of him to Mlle Phlipon. His brother "who could still digest nothing but fowl, and even that with the greatest difficulty, counts so little upon the return of his strength that once out of bed he expects to walk with the aid of a cane."

During his convalescence Roland sent his travel notes to his young friend. But a coolness arose between them from his characteristic blunder in including a passage in which he described his meeting with a beautiful and interesting woman at Leghorn. Her own interest in Sévelinges was now at its height. But once in Paris Roland found little difficulty in superseding his rival.

But even with the Cannets she continued to preserve that strict secrecy on which Roland had insisted. Sophie came to spend four months in Paris, remaining from June to October with Mesdemoiselles de Lamotte, a happening which made the situation even more embarrassing. In the course of a stroll in the Luxembourg, Roland encountered the two girls, and Sophie later confided to Mlle Phlipon that her brother, Sélincourt, had the idea of marrying off Henriette to M. de la Platière. Mlle Phlipon did not flicker an eyelid. She was even now as far as her future husband was concerned, in a state of submission in which, despite the disconcerting attitude of her fiancé, she persisted through all the ups and downs of their strange engagement.

Thus she wrote of him to Henriette:

Our traveller interests me exceedingly. I see him very little. He seems to be always extremely preoccupied with his work.

Up to this time the Phlipons had lived on the Quai de l'Horloge. At the beginning of the month of December 1778, they moved because their house was to be torn down, and not, as M. Perroud believed, to effect an economy in rent. They moved into a house at the corner of the rue de Harlay. Their new quarters were smaller than their previous ones, and situated on the first floor. A partition was arranged for Mlle Phlipon so that she might have "a sanctuary" modelled upon her former one. She wrote to her friends in Amiens:

My little study seems to me quite delightful. I have taken the greatest satisfaction in arranging it. Here my books and my papers are at their best.

After a pressing courtship — and how badly this describes the attentions he paid her ! — Roland returned to his own home. Not a single definite word had he uttered, and for three months he neither wrote nor gave news of himself in any way. Alone and no longer under the sway of her charm, he was able to take himself in hand. But at the end of three months he was due to return to Paris.

In his state of perpetual indecision he had never made things clear to the Cannets. From certain signs he gathered that Henriette still had thoughts of making a match with him, but as far as any understanding with her went there was "nothing — nothing — nothing." This he stated in a letter written in Italian [13] and doubtless intended for the enlightenment of Mlle Phlipon. She was never the person to tolerate long periods of uncertainty and petty ethical cowardices, and she wished no misunderstanding to exist. But such a misunderstanding needed nothing short of a marriage ceremony to clear it up.

In the meantime Mlle Phlipon sent him little gifts. He for his part sent her one of those duck pasties for which Amiens is famed. On one occasion she wrote him at three o'clock in the morning, for she had dreamed he was coming to see her, accompanied by the Prior whose visit she was expecting.

She had many worries, however, for instead of remarrying her father [14] had taken himself a mistress. He spent money extravagantly, he worked spasmodically, and he gambled.

At the time of Mme Phlipon's death the family had not asked for an inventory of what remained in the way of a fortune, believing that no-one knew better than a father how to supervise the welfare of his only child. It was with delicacy, with dignity, and real grief that she allowed her friends the Cannets to divine the cause of her unhappiness, for she realized that Phlipon's present dissipation threatened to wipe out the remainder of what little was left to them. She was of age. All her relatives insisted that she ask her father for an accounting. But this idea was abhorrent to her and she went to Vincennes to seek the advice and the support of Canon Bimont:

It is a hard thing to bring justice to bear upon the author of one's days. I want my father to have my time, my attention, and my money, but I must have what is mine if only to preserve it for him.

It was in Roland that she would have liked to find a defender. At that time he was writing to his friend Cousin-Despréaux of a young lady who aided him in his literary work, "a young lady who has knowledge, talent, and above all a great mind."

Upon his arrival in Paris, Roland went like an old *habitué* to the rue Harlay. He got on famously with Mlle Phlipon, which only meant that he preached to her to his heart's content:

His conversation never bored me, and he liked to see that he was listened to with interest, a thing I do very well even with people not so well educated as he. This has perhaps won me more friends than my own ability to speak with a certain ease.

At first Phlipon had cast a suspicious and even an unfriendly eye upon Roland's frequent visits. Then he appeared to lose interest. People, however, were beginning to talk. The worthy Mignonne had gossiped to Sélincourt. Some vague rumours had thus got to Amiens. Mlle Phlipon felt she was obliged to offer some explanation to her friends.

Each time Mignonne sees me take up my pen she imagines that it is to write to that tall gentleman who called the other day with a lot of papers tucked under his arm.

There was one person, however, whom she could not deceive. This was a young man of twenty-three who for eight years had worked at the Phlipon home as "resident apprentice." Young L. F.—— only his initials are known to us—had long been in love with the daughter of the house, and, timid up till now, he suddenly gave vent to the most inconvenient fits of jealousy.

It is cetrain that in these long uninterrupted conversations Roland, irremediably smitten from this time on, must have lost a little of his austerity, and from the following quotation we gather that she offered some resistance.

Questo primo dolcissimo baccio impetuously snatched hurt me atrociously.

She was neither a child nor a prude. She was naturally proud, and as much for the sake of propriety as for the sake of tactics, it is probable that she had vowed never to permit the least liberty to any man except (as she put it) to "the man to whom she would be united by the most sacred ties." After this attack she followed her usual custom and retreated to her good uncle at Vincennes. Hardly had she arrived there when she wrote to Roland.

He had succeeded in convincing her that "injuries" such as he had committed were invariably provoked by the woman. She was quite willing to admit it. "I accept this as an axiom," she wrote. "I will take the responsibility for past errors as well as for any reproaches I might wish to make, but as to future wrongs, I shall forestall them with all the vigilance I can command."

This was cleverer than Roland suspected, and further on he was flattered to read: "Your animation intimidates and frightens me." But the young girl was determined upon maintaining in their "intercourse" that "happy security, that freedom, and that noble and touching intimacy that are the fruits of virtue." "It seems to me that caresses deprive friendship of its warmth," she wrote, "without them it is a sweet and natural thing; I no longer recognized our comradeship and my heart trembled. . . Leave me in that sweet peace so that I may always, always love you !"

But her flight to Vincennes had been a false move for Roland was annoyed and left for Amiens without seeing her again. "Am I then no better than a vile seducer ?" he asked himself in dismay. He did not hesitate to write her the following words, making no secret of his state of mind:

I innocently believed that we shared in common those emotions for which you upbraid and blame me.

The inference was that after all it would not be the death of him should he never see her again. And he concluded with: "I shall attempt to forestall the fatal moment in which you propose to forestall me."

Instead of this retreat, she had so confidently expected a proposal of marriage that she had already written Sophie, to whom she had entrusted her letters to return her the correspondence with Sévelinges as well as the letter she had written La Blancherie three years before. There is no doubt she wished to have these letters in order to send them to Roland.

Upon her return to the Cité she found nothing but troubles and

worries awaiting her. Mignonne, the maid, had fallen ill with
pneumonia and her young mistress put her into her own bed and
nursed her with the tenderest care. During these days she was
going through a "violent crisis" with Phlipon, as well as with relatives who had *plans for her,* this last a venemous dig at Roland
and one intended to have practical effect.

Indeed she herself was so disillusioned as she was uneasy about
Roland's attitude. The time for innocent poses was past, and she
knew they would no longer move him. She decided to write again,
and seven days after her first letter from Vincennes, she wrote him
in an ardent tone which was probably scarcely more natural than
her former one, and in which policy obviously played an important
part:

> Know me as I am or let me die. . . Blind ungrateful man ! Could
> I be happy if you were not ? You dare say this to me. . . You wrench
> my heart. . .

This time Roland replied as she hoped he would — to the *sog-
giogatrice de Melindo,* that is to the one who had subjugated
Melindo.[15] He was Melindo, just as at Rouen and at Dieppe he
was Thales to "The Greeks." Here we have him in one of his
rare expansive moods. He had been "moved to tears." He called
her "cruel one." He wrote: "I have but one heart. . . It loves
you. . ."

Occupied as she was with her patient, she answered him by an
enormous letter, but from then on the correspondence took on an
evasive tone. Roland would not be precise concerning his intentions. He disguised his handwriting so that all his letters would
be attributed to Henriette and Sophie and thus deceive the father
as well as the apprentice. Mlle Phlipon, however, seemed placated,
and one of her letters ends with this charming phrase: "My
friend, you have no longer the right to be unhappy, for you are
no longer unhappy alone." She wrote him at Mignonne's sick-bed,
and the little servant departed this life giving thanks to heaven
that her young mistress was near her while she died. Roland was
deeply touched by so much benevolence and wrote:

Prize your tears, my friend, for each one of them is a sign of virtue; your friend weeps with you. There is not one of your actions
that does not touch his heart. . . They call forth all my admiration
and fill me with that high esteem that makes the sentiment of friendship precious beyond all price.

And then he asked that she give him a definite yes or no. It was
well for him that when he finally did propose he chose a moment
when the young girl was dejected and almost ill with grief. Little
Mme Trude had insisted that she come with her to her own home.
Meanwhile Roland was counting the hours that must elapse before
he could hope for her answer. Without a moment's delay she
replied yes.

She was then twenty-five and she had taken some time to decide
what her future would be. It now seemed to her that Roland would
give her life a true significance. Besides his love, he offered her a
position she considered of importance. The day she would hear herself called Mme de la Platière, would be her hour of revenge on
Mme de Boismorel, on the Haudrys, and on the Pénaults. What
she felt for Roland was a complex enough emotion; one not inspired by instinct and still less by passion. She would have thought
herself frivolous had she sought such qualities as youth and grace
in her life companion.

She was not an intellectual climber. She did not crave homage,
honours, nor publicity. There is nothing whatsoever to justify one
charge frequently made, that she wished to play the part of an
important person. Neither was she a sort of female Julien Sorel,
requiring great subtleties of the mind. Her case was simpler and
more human.

But did Roland's family approve ? Obviously his parents and
relatives would look upon it as an odd misalliance, this marriage
of the forty-five-year-old son of an old bourgeois family with a
young person who was the daughter of a modest and poor engraver.
on the other hand did the Roland family of Villefranche ever oppose
the wishes of this last born son who was their one link with the
outside world ? Proudly Mlle Phlipon wrote him:

I would refuse to enter a family incapable of appreciating me suffi-

ciently to know that by so doing I was conferring an honour upon them,
and I could not bear to be indebted for such an alliance to a man who
felt he was doing me a favour.

She immediately followed her short letter of acceptance of the
sixth of May, which she wished to send him on "the wings of
the wind," by a longer, more explanatory one in which, by bringing
up the subject of Sévelinges, she evidenced more loyalty than discretion.

Nevertheless it was a very dangerous thing to write a fiancé all
the details of an intrigue with another,[16] and she even asked that
he read the letters she had entrusted to Sophie Cannet. Imprudent
though she was, she was careful to omit no point which would
place her in a favourable light, and she even attempted to even
things up by reminding him that he had courted a beautiful Italian
during his journey in Italy without troubling to send her news
of himself for months at a time. She did not deem it out of place
to mention that she was an excellent cook; M. de la Platière was
certainly not insensible to the advantages of such a talent. She finally
began to suspect that her radiant youth must give this severe betrothed much food for thought and that he probably feared nothing more than feminine frivolity. Whereupon she said: "I fully
realize that bitter trials have given me an indefinable seriousness
and austerity which may in some measure cloak my sensitiveness
with an appearance of harshness."

A letter usually took but one day to get from Paris to Amiens,
but this time there was some delay, and, in his state of uncertainty,
Roland experienced moments of actual anguish. He answered her
on the ninth of May. He was preparing the bridal home. She
replied:

Make ready our home. It will be the abode of faithfulness. . .
Make the plans we are to follow; I much prefer that they be yours,
for my pleasure in conforming with them will be increased . . . you
will enlighten me. I shall think with your ideas.

All this suited him perfectly, and with more decision than was
usual for him, he presently made reply:

May 19 . . .

I return to those things I touched upon in one of my preceding letters, not then having the time to enter into explanations. You will come to a house which is neither orderly nor disorderly; you understand me, or in case you do not . . . I mean there is nothing there. I made certain arrangements in Paris recently, shortly before I formed the plan of making more serious and permanent ones with you, and they will greatly straiten me until the end of the year. I want you to consider that this account I am making is a sign of the utmost confidence and is not meant as a discussion, but as a means of coming to an agreement in accordance with our mutual tastes, our common conveniences, and the state of my affairs which are to be yours. I consult you, or rather I give you the means of deliberation; I do not wish the decision referred to me. I have table linen, house linen, and linen for my own person for another two years; that is all I have. I have knives and forks for eight persons and two stew ladles, nothing more. I shall have to buy everything for the principal room and furniture for the entire house; as for those general indispensable supplies, I have nothing. I have just rented a house at 500 livres a year. All I have from now until next January unless I borrow (and I would not like to touch my capital right at the beginning), is 80 louis. Of these I need at least 40 for pressing and indispensable things for the house before you can put foot in it. We shall have to live there the rest of the year, probably buy extra things for the house, travel, return to Paris at the end of December or beginning of January. I shall undoubtedly have business to attend to at that time, etc. Another thing: you are quite willing to give up all your jewellery; had I thought you incapable of such a sacrifice I might not have been so capable of loving you; but you will need linen; a little to begin with; we will supply the deficit later on. You must have frocks; I cannot expect any remission as far as that is concerned; but you need nothing magnificent, nothing out of the way, but you must be dressed like everyone else, and first of all, like everyone else, you must have bonnets, headdresses, and so forth. Consider these points carefully, decide what is fit, because these things must be done — that's all I know. Tell me frankly, without embarrassment or constraint, what you think of all this. If you need linen immediately we can get it on credit from Rouen; this does not apply to the other things. Once more, tell me how much you need to do things properly from the start. Next March you can count on 50 additional louis for yourself and the house, deducting what I may have had to borrow before that date; as to current expenses, starting January next, for you, for me, in short for everything (for I don't want to be bothered about anything, not even about what concerns me personally), you can count on 300 livres a month, not including the rent of the house which I take entire charge of. I speak openly to you, my friend; I tell you all I know and all I can do.

To this she answered:

May 23 . . .

I now come to those things that we must deal with and in regard to which you have written me with the clarity, the directness, and the kindness which are so much a part of you. I need not repeat how much I appreciate all you are doing: our hearts were made to understand one another. . . I have estimated, dreamed upon, and examined in detail the expenditures we have to make in accordance with the rules you have set down, and I find them higher than they should be for our convenience. I can dispense with buying linen for the next two years, except for a few little things which I can pick up quite easily: but I need three dresses, one for summer, another for autumn and spring, the third, a very simple one, for every season. For this must be counted, including the making, the mending, shoes, and odds and ends, at least 25 louis. As for bonnets, cuffs, kerchiefs, which it is customary to have in lace, that will be 12 to 15 louis more, all keeping strictly to passable, decent things, without striving to be elegant, and without affecting to be simple. True I have certain of my mother's laces that I would like to make use of, but as none of them are whole and the pattern old-fashioned, it would be difficult to match them and even more difficult to prevent them from looking haphazard and pieced together. I have also attempted to dispose of my earrings for which I have no use whatsoever, and am delighted to see that my taste in this is at one with yours. At the present moment I am offered but half of 750 francs for them, the price at which my father counted them to me; I hope to lose a little less by waiting for a better offer.

With this she passed on to other things, adding no further word of gratitude, and we are convinced that in this was a wealth of delicate feeling. Roland wished the marriage to take place between the fifteenth of August and the fifteenth of September, and that she was marrying without dowry, without furniture, without a trousseau, and that her future husband was obliged to dress her even and see to her smallest necessities, was a state of affairs too far beyond the pale of convention not to be extremely painful to a young Frenchwoman. Her pride was put to the test. To say the least, she would have liked the subject to be disposed of in a speedy manner as though it were a mere incident among the other material preoccupations of the moment.

To complete the sum which her father owed her, Mlle Phlipon was obliged to accept "some gems" which she "no longer wanted."

I will get rid of them without delay [she added]. I have never placed any value upon jewels of this kind; I despise and detest them ever since I began to entertain the hope of one day having ornaments similar to those Cornelia called her jewels.

Mlle Phlipon's own generosity soon made the self-interested side of Roland's character apparent to her, and she doubtless felt she was taking much upon herself in writing him:

I wish, I ask, I insist . . . upon settling [on my father] an allowance out of my fortune. . .

Roland was certainly very much put out by this news which she broke to him without her usual *finesse*. He explained the change of mood which he experienced upon reading this "I insist," and felt he was greatly injured.

What then have I said that makes you think me a self-seeking man ?

With what charm and tender humility she asked that he forgive that "I insist" which "fell inadvertently from her pen." At that time, however, he was at his best and for the first and last time gave evidence of some forethought and consideration by "exacting" that his fiancée, who was reduced to doing the housework and cooking for her father whose affairs were going very badly, find a maid to replace the unfortunate Mignonne. Roland seemed at that time to possess all the ear-marks of a good husband. But the day of their union was still far in the offing.

He was reasonable enough, however, to accept with a good grace her confessions about La Blancherie and Sévelinges. "How well I know him !" she thought. And after all she had not been as indiscreet as we imagined, for he wrote her:

. . . Your ingenuousness, your precious candour spares us both the dangers of discovery through another channel, and I love you a hundred times more because of it.

He remained perfectly calm. It would have been impossible to be more rational. After a first reading of Sévelinges' letters, he was scarcely "disconcerted." A lover could hardly say less. She sent him the plan of a letter breaking off relations which she intended to write to Sévelinges. He made not the slightest objection. And then suddenly his exaggerated good nature forsook him. He became furiously embittered. Sévelinges was "infamous," the correspondence "much too light . . . out of place and ridiculous . . . and of the utmost indiscretion." The letter to Sévelinges had been sent with Roland's entire approval. He now judged it "neither delicate nor frank . . . out of place from every point of view," and the answer she received — (and sent him immediately) — "full of good lessons and insulting offers." She replied:

If I find it sweet to learn the truth, is it not principally because it is you who show it to me. . . I would have to agree with you in spite of myself even if I wished to disagree.

What gentleness after Roland's unsparing terms! However, she called his attention to the fact that he had approved her letter to Sévelinges and asked him how "with so thin an opinion of her letter, could he have made no effort to prevent her sending it."

But his contradictions profited her nothing. She asked herself which she should follow — her heart or her mind? The truth was that "she had never erred except through reasoning too much."

You will be in turn my teacher and my confidant and the candour of a thousand little confessions will serve as fresh witness to the fruit of your lessons.

At twenty-five she had already given evidence of her sound reason. Neither was she lacking in self-confidence, at least as far as such matters were concerned. Was it then through tactics, and to flatter Roland's vanity that she adopted this humble attitude in flagrant contradiction of her true nature? Was Roland taken in? Without any doubt he was, but it was equally true that it was not the glow of love that warmed her letters; they were above all kind and submissive. From then on, though Roland was often churlish and ungracious, one feels he was more spontaneous. He was disturbed, this careful man. What was happening to him? Was a young girl to distract this Inspector of Manufactures from his serious work? It was not surprising that he made her suffer for her indiscretion by a few brusque rebuffs. Was it not possible that his resistance was a tentative and unconscious gesture of revolt against the mysterious force that was involving him ? The woman who wanted him for her own would lead him to the Girondist Party, to the flight of the 31st of May 1793, and finally to suicide at night on a public highway. In the course of the following months — from May 1779, when the secret engagement was contracted, until January 1780, when the marriage was celebrated — it would seem, considering all the strange incidents which arose between them, that Roland was floundering in the dark like a blind man, fighting a desperate battle against some fatal force. This reluctant fiancé with his uncouth ways and his peevish disposition was, in thirteen years of married life, to become a husband who lived in perfect accord with a wife he loved and admired to the extent of being unable to spare her for a moment from his sight, who had complete authority over him, and whose loss he could compensate for only in voluntary death.

The Phlipon family were bent on marrying off the young girl. At their wits' ends, the good people were willing to consent to a marriage even with the apprentice.

My opposition [she said] put them in mind of all those characteristics they like to call my eccentricities; they counted them off on their fingers, and I was lauded and blamed with an inconsistency and stupidity almost impossible to imagine.

It was then that Roland's strange pretension made its appearance, and he refused to make it known that he was Mlle Phlipon's fiancé and to ask her father for her hand. His intention was to keep one exit open and the way clear for an escape. Indeed there can be no other explanation of his obstinacy in insisting that she maintain absolute silence as far as her family was concerned. This was the origin and the cause of all the tribulations the fiancés were to endure, as well as of the break that was to follow. The young girl's situation was intolerable. Between the continuous anger of her father, and the vacillating attitude of her relatives, she had to keep at a distance, within the confines of a small apartment, the "sensitive and impetuous" apprentice who was smitten to the point of despair and made dramatic scenes all day long.

"Oh, my friend," she wrote plaintively to Roland, "how one does love at twenty !" Thereby implying: "Not like at forty-five !"

She wrote him in great sorrow of her anixety for her father:

Fits of grief and anger often lead him to form resolutions whose results I can prevent only by exercizing the utmost skill and diplomacy. He is losing his health. Before long he must be either ill, or dead, or insane. . . I am broken-hearted. I despair of ever again seeing my father as I would wish him to be. . . He is getting thinner and thinner and seems consumed with worry. . . He is lost . . . lost to me, and to happiness.

She wistfully remembered the happy days when her mother was still alive, and how on Saturday evenings the engraver would affectionately tease the little girl of whom he was so proud.

"It will be fine tomorrow," he would say. "The fountains will be playing at Saint-Cloud. There will be a lot of people . . ."

"Ah, if you would like, papa, it would be much nicer to go to Meudon. There won't be anybody there. We could walk in the woods looking among the trees for the nooks where the deer hide, and at evening we could rest in the hut of that worthy old man who brought us a bowl of milk and black bread under a honeysuckle spray."

In those happy days, Phlipon, always impressed by show and finery, "rather liked to appear in public" with "a well-dressed young woman whose fresh colouring would sometimes cause flattering remarks to buzz in his ears." She saw herself in new clothes, entering an exhibition of pictures on the arm of the proud engraver who, bridling with importance, would confidentially inform the friends he encountered:

"This is my daughter !"

In such surroundings Phlipon was at his best. When it came to the fine arts, there was much he could teach the young scholar. Their tastes were congenial. One day they happened to meet Greuze, that great man who depicted heart-rending scenes and moral lessons worthy of Jean-Jacques himself. The painter bowed to the beautiful young woman and she exclaimed with fervour:

"Ah, Monsieur, did I not already love virtue, you would give me a taste for it."

But now Phlipon was incensed with his daughter, and "flees her from room to room." Moreover he was constantly out and hardly ever came home except to go to bed. Perhaps he was thinking of remarrying, but his "creature" (as Roland called her), lost interest in the marriage the moment she learned he had to hand over to the notary what little money he possessed. The young girl had always said, however, that she wished to give her father "half her income and spend the remainder with him."

My aged relatives [she wrote] are highly gratified by my pacific intentions; they wish me a world of good and would accomplish marvels if I could prompt them during the conference. I cannot depend on their memory; they will remember my arguments, but will forget how to use them to the best advantage, and embarrassment will seal their lips. My Vincennes uncle, though possessing greater discretion, would be no cleverer and considerably lazier. . .

Had they not, one and all, strongly urged her to demand a settlement of those affairs that had estranged her from her father? Greatly vexed, he had appealed to the Besnards.

"Would you believe it," she said to Roland, "that these good people who have advised me, who approve of me and sing my praises, have no idea what they should say to my father to pacify him and bring him back to his senses? They listen to him without a word, censure him after he has gone, complain, and then tell me everything."

At last the agreement was signed, and the next day she wrote Roland:

We went yesterday to the notary, as I wrote you we would; my father's reluctance and discontent, which he has evidenced all along, broke out with fresh energy at the last moment. Here is the way I continued to act, however, both through duty and inclination. To begin with I had already made up my mind not to ask for an exact accounting of my revenue since my mother's death, but to leave that amount to pay for my expenses in food and upkeep. I have told you that the actual value of the property was insufficient to settle my share, that I had received some furniture on account and that my father was still my debtor in the amount of about one hundred écus. It would have been vile to allow him in his very distressing circumstances to borrow from strangers in order to pay a sum of money to his own daughter; I also thought it hard to brand him with the stigma of debtor; I therefore recognized, in the act, that I had received the sum as though it had been actually given me. While this act was being read and examined in our presence, the notary perceived an error to my loss, which referred to a sum of 500 livres that had been forgotten; a clause was added assigning me this amount, as the law ordained. I let the operation go through; how my father was to meet this expense was the question that then arose. I had not forgotten the embarrassment which the payment of the first amount would cause him; moreover I thought the law which granted me this sum severe, further I was delighted to have an opportunity of showing my father how I liked to do business with him. "I make no pretences," said I immediately, "of reckoning with such exactness. The law is inflexible, still as far as I am concerned I acquit and exonerate my father of this sum as of the preceding one." [17] After having signed I begged the notary to keep the contracts: the excuse I gave was that I wished him to make me models of discharges for future use, but in reality I wished to avoid the displeasure and ill-grace of taking them still warm from my father's hands. My heart was sore; it was in this month, in fact just about these days, that I lost my mother four years ago. I could not hold back my tears at hearing her named so often in these lugubrious documents wherein the dead are perpetually mentioned. I thought of her candid sweetness, her goodness, and the inexpressible tenderness which filled her eyes whenever she looked at me. I contrasted my father, sober, silent, frigid, repulsive as he is today, with that father of other days who all but idolized his daughter. . .

We came home; I approached my father with emotion. "The law," I said, "has just put me in possession of documents which you have hitherto retained, but I will take the income they grant me only if to share it with you. All that I wish . . ." "Don't talk to me of these things," he cried indignantly. . . "I do not know what I shall decide." With these words he left me, and I saw him again only at bedtime. I went to call on my grandparents. My poor grandmama moves and grieves me; she takes no joy in living because, as she says: "I do not see you as happy as I would have you be." I persuaded her with such success that all this is but a passing storm and that she must keep herself alive to witness better times, that she is quite consoled. I owe my notary about 220 livres, for my share in the expenses of the division. I do not have to pay him immediately; I am counting on 130 livres due me at the beginning of August to settle this debt, making up the deficit with what I hope to obtain before that date from those wretched jewels that I intend to sell. The result of these arrangements is that I have actually an annuity of 530 livres; this, net and unencumbered, is all my wealth. Well, this dismal transaction is at an end; our misfortunes made it imperative, besides it was the only rational thing to do. It grieved my heart sorely; moreover it leaves behind it a train of troubles because my father has turned against me, perhaps forever.

May he return to me sufficiently to accept without pain what assistance you will permit me to offer him. Beyond this my desires do not go.

And here she was practically without resources, with no-one to advise her, compelled to do the cooking and the housework, and to cap the climax she had to nurse the apprentice who had fallen ill. She had to meet all the expenses. Phlipon took no interest whatsoever in his house and she sold some of the jewels which the settlement allotted her for an amount greater than their actual worth.

What was preventing Roland from putting an end to all these worries ? She was of age. She could very well act without the consent of a father who, she considered, had forfeited the prerogatives of authority. There was nothing to keep her from marrying quite unceremoniously. We know that the Prieur de Longpont was already on Roland's side, and that he was received at the Quai de l'Horloge where he was making friends with the daughter of the house.

I would like to conceal my tears; no, I lack the will even for that. . . Adieu, sweet friend. Let not my grief torment you. I allowed my emotions to run away with me at a time when I was deeply moved. If I thought it made you suffer too much, I would no longer know the solace of telling you all. You are everything to me. I love you and everything is forgotten.

He did not suffer too much. In fact he did not suffer at all. But he was annoyed and he replied in an indifferent tone which must have cruelly pained the unfortunate girl.

What ! You give up ! Who then will console me when I am sad? . . . What has become of that strong mind which I thought so capable of bearing its own sorrows as well as mine ?

As to the end of the letter, it was penned by an extremely cool and sagacious fiancé.

Write me whether you want me to write you or not.

After this he remained eleven days without giving any sign of life.

The ensuing letters [18] ranged from the most easy and justifiable expansiveness to the brusquest sort of miscomprehension. No doubt he was dimly conscious that his inaction was a mark of his weak character. No doubt he was not very proud of himself. But he was dominated by his egoism. He feared he knew not what, and he was stubbornly determined to stand by his first resolution. And how stubbornly too must the young girl have been set upon marrying him that she persisted in writing him with the same tender and submissive grace. Why did she not rather dread the thought of a master so wholly devoid of charm ? What sort of a life would she have with this fussy, cranky, bilious man, and, even worse, with a man so sure of his own opinions and convinced of his own perfection ? Events were to prove her right. But let us not plead a love which M. Perroud, usually so clearsighted, interpreted as an overwhelming passion. True, Roland was not displeasing to her, and she who all her life had had a taste for friendship was certainly more attracted to this learned man than to M. de Sévelinges or M. de Sainte-Lette.

Fully to understand this correspondence, one must bear in mind that the young girl wrote about her "predestination." Nor should we forget, as we witness her persistence, that during her married life (if we omit the last months), she was entirely faithful to the promises she made during her engagement. It is a mistake to ascribe to her a headstrong character that imposed its own opinions, or to make of her an authoritative woman who spoke and decided for everyone. Her untiring sweetness to her husband and friends may seem incompatible with the intensity of her convictions, but this gentleness was to affect to no small degree her engaging and animated disposition.

Her letters still bore some traces of the phraseology of the time, but they were becoming rarer and rarer. Her clear intelligence is strikingly apparent in them all. Her style was already rich, eloquent, and clear, although it lacked that strength we are later to find in Mme Roland's works.

As for Roland, he wrote very badly. It is doubtful even whether his thoughts were clear to himself. At any rate he generally expressed them in the most confused and obscure terms. He disliked stating things precisely. His sentences are so involved that one does not know of what or of whom he was speaking. His style was generally awkward, cumbersome, frequently bombastic, and entirely devoid of any kind of charm. Pedantic and ponderous, his conversation must have been unspeakably boring.

But Mlle Phlipon had only too many reasons to worry over the silence which Roland insisted upon concerning their engagement. Finally he gave the young girl permission — and how grudgingly ! — to tell her relatives that she had a marriage in view, but on condition that "for nothing in the world she mention his name, nor let them suspect with whom."

He, however, found it quite allowable that he speak of it to his friend Cousin-Despréaux, although he did so with extreme precaution and in an amazingly calm tone:

> I have a plan of which I can say nothing to you except by word of mouth, one that will be thought strange, which already bothers me somewhat in itself and even more because of certain arrangements I made before I looked forward to it.

But Mlle Phlipon had determined to get out of a ridiculous situation. There was but one person close to her who could be of aid to her and at the same time keep a secret, and that was her cousin Mlle Desportes. She began by making half-confidences to her, and Mlle Desportes soon guessed that her niece was referring to Roland. The "preacher," as she was called, summoned Phlipon to her home and began by asking him if he intended to remarry.

Everything passed off marvellously well between father and daughter. At Mlle Desportes' they became fully reconciled. The young betrothed told him everything. The father gave his full forgiveness and sang the praises of Roland, repeating that his daughter's fortune, if non-existent at the present moment, would be a handsome one because of all that the future would settle upon her. And finally he himself promised not to remarry. On the 27th of June she wrote Roland a letter that fairly vibrates with joy:

> Kiss my letter, leap with joy: my father is pleased, he esteems you, he loves me, we shall all be happy. Peace, good-will, harmony, every-

where joy on earth. If you could have seen how we embraced each other. . . Ah, how I wept! This good papa, he loves me so much that he can't help himself. . . I dined *tête à tête* with my father for the first time since . . . since I don't know when. I hadn't eaten since the day before yesterday, I had the face of a Jansenist, my knees were giving way under me. . . Mlle Desportes sent for my father today. . . My father preceded me so that they sent for me suddenly; I ran; I remained in an adjoining room; I was on tenter-hooks; I hung between hope and despair, or rather I was in such suspense that I didn't even dare draw a breath.

At last they called her in. She dissolved in tears at the feet of a "confused" father who addressed his "sobbing" daughter in the following terms:

"Your behaviour still seems extraordinary; I cannot forgive you for making that request which the law fully authorized you to make, but which wounded and insulted me. . . If your wish is to remain with me, then it is a contradiction to proceed as if you were planning to leave me; all your motives are displeasing to me. If you had better ones I might judge differently. But in that case why should you have hidden them?" — "And what," I cried heatedly, "if I had some reason which in honour bound I must keep secret, would you then say I had committed a crime by having kept my word?" — "What secret could you be justified in withholding from a father?" — "One confided to me on condition that I keep it because various circumstances made it imperative that it be not communicated." — "Such ambiguous statements do not impress me; I want to see things as they are; give me a good reason, if you have one, or else leave me in peace."

With feigned discretion, Mlle Desportes wished to withdraw, for she already knew everything. But her young cousin detained her by saying:

"No, stay, I beg of you. . . But I ask that you preserve that same silence which I have maintained up to the present at the greatest sacrifice, for it was one which made me appear guilty." At this moment I took my father's hand; he was extremely affected, I was moved, but never was I more self-possessed. . . They both promised me, my father giving me his word with an expression of impatience and sincerity that I found singularly touching.

. . . I think I can flatter myself that my father will keep silent; I have seen signs too convincing to be in doubt. My father is ours, he has been won over, he loves us. Ah, if your honest, sensitive, lofty mind delights in making others happy, how overjoyed you should now be ! You have given me all that is dear to me. You have restored to me a father's good-will. . .

"You have shown me, my father, that the legal arrangement between us would have seemed quite natural had there been any question of my marrying; it is precisely such a question: there is my secret, you will soon know my reasons. A certain person whose choice honours me and will flatter you, I am sure, proved his esteem for me by acquainting me with his intentions. His sole idea was then to determine mine and to know if he could rely upon them. Extreme consideration for his family, and other matters of no less importance forbade his opening his heart to anyone, or even declaring his intentions to you, . . . From then on I felt the need to settle our affairs fittingly. I thought it would be better to arrange them between you and me; I was determined to bring you into it. On the other hand, I made no secret of the modesty of my fortune. . . I said that a happiness which caused you any privation would be far from a perfect one for me. The delicacy and the disinterestedness which had been the motives of this person's every action caused him to respond that he was no less concerned than I with your welfare and your satisfaction and that he would leave you a revenue sufficient to your needs. . . Convinced of his uprightness and his generosity as much as of his other excellent qualities, I made him an avowal which I fully expected you would one day approve with a joy equalling my own. You have a suspicion of whom I am speaking. There is no use telling you his name; at least, my cousin willing, I shall not speak it before her; this is a final consideration I give up for you alone." (I wished to stress the air of secrecy so as to impress my father even more.)

Never, no, never, can I depict for you the change which came over my father and the effect it produced; all his furious anger faded away like a cloud blown far by the winds. Compassion took possession of his soul, sweetness and joy were reflected on his features. The speaker flung herself upon the parental bosom and there shed the most delicious tears that had ever dimmed her eyes. I had found again my father of other days, the father who was proud of his daughter, who was overjoyed by his love for her. . . He whispered your name in my ear, gratified to show Mlle Desportes that in my choice he found but further proof of all that I had ever been to him; he sang your praises, and a little my own, with such an overflowing heart that I needs must interrupt him with kisses on his cheeks and hands. . . He added that if my fortune were nothing at present, it would one day consist of at least all he could collect, that he planned to enter into no alliance whatsoever, and that he gave me his word on it. But, my friend, all this so graciously that my head is still in a whirl; it was spoken with that tenderness which cannot be put on, in that natural and truthful tone that cannot be feigned. You are supposed to know nothing of his errors, neither of our quarrels; my father relishes the idea that you look upon him with consideration; he holds you in the highest es-

teem, he showers me with tenderness, he considers both of us as the
reason and root of all his happiness. Our union flatters him as much
as it affects us, he will bless it with his whole soul. (June 27, 1779.)

This was a masterpiece of negotiation and skill. In her father's
mouth she placed all that she herself had been burning to say, and
with good reason, for the past two months.

At first Roland accepted this *coup d'état* with a good enough
grace. He was certainly far from sharing his fiancée's enthusiasm,
but at any rate the first letter he wrote (the same day) was not
unfriendly. True, he was soon to adopt that frankly disagreeable
tone which people less proud would have found unbearable.

Don't use up pages in justifying or excusing something already done.
I won't feel it any the less.

It is quite evident that he was reproaching his fiancée for having acted without his consent. He was obliged to accept the accomplished fact, but he had no patience with the abundant explanations she insisted on giving him. She had put him with his back
to the wall, and there he found himself extremely ill at ease, and
further he considered it a bit too much that he was expected to
be grateful to her for having brought him to such a pass.

AT THIS period of her life the future Mme Roland was in a highly
nervous state. The agitation which was so often revealed in her
letters assuredly had a physical cause. It is true that in the years
that followed, Mme Roland gave constant evidence of her sound
sense. The austerity of her character equalled the weight of her
judgment, and her husband was not to be the only one who accepted her point of view. On all occasions her opinion was to be
consulted, and in the Roland family of four able-bodied, learned
men, she was to be the one they would seek out to act for them
in delicate negotiations. Nor were her friends to undertake anything without first consulting her. This hectic correspondence gives
no indication of the perfect balance and moral well-being that was
to characterize the remainder of her life.

But this disorder never manifested itself by the least irritation

with Roland. She wanted to please him at whatever cost and retain
her position as the beloved woman.

Her replies to his most peevish letters were filled with an un-
flinching sweetness and submission. As if it were a musical theme
played on every key, she seemed to pursue the touching and profound sentiment of that line from Zaire:

'Tis I who owe you everything, for I it is who love.

It was he who corrected a very humble and grateful pupil. She
put in her time copying one of Roland's essays on the *Trojan Wars,*
and dreamed of the time when she could finally "take care of so
dear an object." But he was not to come and see her, for that
would be too unreasonable ! As for him, nothing was further from
his thoughts. It had not taken him long to adopt a domineering
and ungracious way with her, even when he intended to say the
kindest of things:

If you do not wish to be taken to task, do not reduce the size of
the paper on which you write me, and remember that I do not like
you to send me blank pages.

In a letter highly characteristic of her facile manner, Mlle Phlipon
had responded immediately and without complaint to his hostile
missive of June 29th:

Go then, be obeyed, be loved, be happy, not in my way but in your
own. . .

In another instance — their letters being frequently interspersed
with Italian — she called him *baroncello* (little rogue), and again
in plain language, "indiscreet rogue."

She went a bit far in saying:

I have sometimes thought with bitterness, when reflecting upon the
character and inclinations of the two sexes, that the clever ruses of the
one have often more charm for the other than simple candour and
naked truth. This makes me none the less resolved to cling to the
latter. My choice is made for good.

"Truth," said Pilate, "what is truth?" Having said this he went
out. . .

How difficult it is to distinguish between truth and falsehood! The one frequently overlaps the other, but all through her life Mme Roland's character was as transparent as glass. If we seek among illustrious women for an example of honesty, we naturally turn to her. Artful she was not. She did not distort facts but she presented them in the light and setting she considered the most favourable. She had fallen too much into the habit, almost the mania of self-analysis, to be aware that she was far from clinging to "simple candour" and "naked truth." What was it her definite intention to procure? Her own happiness, and that of Roland. What did she succeed in procuring? Roland's happiness at the expense of her own, until that day so near her death when, in an outburst (premeditated) of that famous honesty, just a hundred years after the virtuous precautions of the Princess of Clèves and a hundred years before the inhuman follies of Ibsen's heroines, she confessed to him that she loved François Buzot.

L. F., the apprentice, growing more and more heated, had guessed that the rival was Roland and conceived of going to Amiens to kill him — no more, no less. Heavens, "how one loves at twenty!"

Mlle Phlipon reproved him in these terms:

Debased, degraded by shameful excesses, by the blackness of your projects which place you in the rank of the lowest of humans, you bring blushes to my cheeks. . .

Roland appeared very much troubled by this bloodthirsty plan:

Can you believe that should my affairs call me to Paris at this time that I would be afraid to expose my person to this assassin, or that I would not sooner demand the protection of the police?

Everything quieted down, however, and the young girl advised Roland of it in these words:

No, virtuousness is not an idle dream. It is to its power that I owe this last triumph and it is because of you, who are so loyal to virtue, that its seal is set upon our mutual happiness.

That the apprentice had guessed his identity was an even greater worry to Roland than to learn of his homicidal intentions. Roland had the mania of mystery, a common enough failing. In conse-

quence his fiancée suddenly received a letter from the baths of
Saint-Armand, Flanders, without ever having suspected that Roland
intended going there:

"You will be surprised to see from where I am writing," he said
without any further explanation. But he had hardly arrived there
when something occurred which annoyed him very much. In taking the waters whom should he meet but a lady from Amiens!
All was lost. Little good it did him to ask her to mention to no
one that she had seen him. She was not one of these ladies able
to keep a secret, and the bad temper of the exposed tripper vented
itself on the entire sex.

Mlle Phlipon was concerned that he had gone off thus to a
watering-place:

Why these mud-baths? Have you then a chronic complaint? Why
these waters? Why . . . my friend, I wish you an immediate re-
covery to sufficient health to allay your suffering, to appear as you
should in the eyes of the world, and to put me in a position to take
care of you myself with an attention that I would trust no-one else
to give you, least of all yourself. Write me, keep nothing from me. . .

Ever since the sensational revelation that had been made at Mlle
Desportes', Phlipon had waited patiently for a letter from Roland
declaring himself and asking for the hand of his daughter. How
little he knew this suitor, who had no idea of doing anything of
the sort, but who intended to marry a young woman who lived
under her father's roof without troubling to form any kind of
connection with the father himself. The fiancée who had written
him the joyous letter of the twenty-seventh of June had indeed
been brought down to earth. Despite her every effort, her doubts
and her unhappiness were apparent in her letters, and Roland wrote
her:

How you change from one state to another, both physically and
morally! This is not one of the things that astonishes me the least.
I confess that I myself would not be able to go to extremes with such
facility; moreover . . . as you accompany all this with full dissertations on cause and effect, means and results, appearances and truth,
right and wrong, good and evil, pretty and ugly, the strong and the
weak, the hot and the cold, the large and the small, etc., etc., etc.

What a singular love-letter! It seems possible to discern, in all this bitterness, a little envy for her easy and agreeable epistolary style which the husband was later to put to such good use.

But by the beginning of August, Phlipon had quite enough and he wrote Roland that if the marriage took place it would be without the parental consent. Phlipon put "questions" to him (according to Roland), and gave expression to "unreasonable demands" of which we cannot judge as the letter has been lost. But we have the document in which Roland commented upon it, and gave full evidence of his unpleasant disposition:

> I cannot believe that he pretends to have a right to discuss or even to consider a thing which is no concern of his. The sentiment which moves me and the point of view I take oblige me to consider as an insult any objection, or indeed any reflection made upon the matter. In uniting myself with you, our interests become common ones. But I wish no-one else to put his nose into our affairs, not even your father. . .

Without being in a position to judge, as half the text is missing, it would seem no more than a father's formal duty to question the conditions of his daughter's future, and in those letters which are preserved to us, Phlipon shows himself neither absurd, indiscreet, nor discourteous.

Roland blamed Mlle Phlipon.

> It is true that his impatience and your lack of firmness could do a great deal of harm to our affairs. Your father would have been more restrained towards you, and less urgent and precipitate with me. . .

Clearly he suspected the young girl had made her father write in order to hasten matters along.

She answered him with her usual patience, with humility, but ardently and tenderly, slipping into her letter, nevertheless, a little sentence which revealed her discernment and her anxiety:

> Believe me, my friend, I did not neglect to bring up *every argument which might justify you.*

On the twenty-eighth of August there was a particularly surly reply, and interminable reproaches. He had once written Cousin-

Despréaux that it had always been difficult for him to make women love him. It is not difficult to believe that this was true!

He asked all sorts of meddling questions about the financial status of his wife:

. . . if she has any debts whatsoever, or any decent or respectable obligation, if anyone has any resource against her; for, finally, such things can be somehow arranged, and between positive and negative there is a mean, and in any case, one must be well advised as to how matters stand.

We gather that this time the young girl gave some evidence of wearying, and even of losing patience. (Her letter is missing.) But he answered:

After all that, I can only say that the tone of your letter destroyed with a vengeance the good humour in which I returned from my trip. . . It is to be hoped that I will not often receive letters of this nature. It is likely that I shall never forget this one as long as I live.

Mlle Phlipon immediately sent him a very grieved reply:

It is evident that you did not understand the half of my last letter and that you misinterpreted the other half. . . Let us write otherwise to each other, or let us write no more.

The following day, the first of September, she not only wrote a second, but even a third reply to his wounding letter of the twenty-eighth of August. Evidently she was at the end of her courage, but in this letter she apparently made every effort to exercise restraint:

At times I thought I observed a little austerity in you, and I allowed myself to be injured by certain phrases which seemed harsh; as to this I kept quiet, believing that I had been too sensitive, believing, moreover, that I could interpret them otherwise than in the way they had been used. . . On the other hand *I lived in perfect assurance that I was the one who could best contribute to your happiness.* You are the most estimable being I have ever known, the only one with whom I would wish to share my life . . . our plans, our hopes have cultivated a fondness in my heart which must in any case decide my fate, and I say even more, *I am convinced that you cannot be happy without me.* Ah, well, in this mood, which surely makes plain to you what might become of me, I feel, I confess, a certain pride which would forbid my being yours if I thought you in the least doubted the happiness our union would bring. . . Think these things over seriously in your mind and come to some firm decision. I must shortly be yours in peace, love, and confidence, or be nothing more to you than a memory that you will have to efface.

This is a dignified and clear statement. Mlle Phlipon was true to herself. She had a great depth of sweetness and fidelity, but enough courage as well not to jeopardize her pride. She knew what was her due and, even at the risk of forfeiting her most coveted plans, she demanded respect for her character.

Roland then answered Phlipon, and the fiancée in turn replied:

Your letter has arrived. My father considered it icy in tone, and of a singular and astonishing brevity; astonishing because of the silence it imposes on certain questions, and the little concern it shows for me. I explained it, approved it, and upheld it as was seeming; I told him that a scrupulous and sensible man had no need to give an accounting, nor to be given advice; we discussed it at length, with warmth and with sorrow.

At the end of this letter a wish escaped her, doubtless one she had cherished a long time, and while reasonable enough, one with which Roland did not comply: "I hate all these written words. They no longer have any meaning. They are deceptive! Come, and let us have an explanation and understand each other." But this was exactly what he did not wish to do.

Meanwhile, deeply mortified at having been put aside in the question of his daughter's marriage, Phlipon evidenced in stormy scenes his odd and variable character. He said he had been treated as if he were an unimportant relative whom one no longer bothered about, and indeed he spoke truly. She appealed to Roland:

Sustain me, my friend, without you I would give up my life, so unpleasant has the world become. . . I really believe that your presence would subdue my father and that he will be eternally at me as long as I am the only one to answer him. . . I await news of you with great impatience.

Although she said: "I am not going to write much more," she took up her pen again on the following day. Mlle Phlipon was constantly in need of expressing her feeling; her fertile mind and her acute sensitiveness impelled her to write, to write even in the most crucial moments. Hosts of new arguments and convincing reasons occurred to her. At whatever cost they must be written out. For one of her temper, writing had a magic charm. And who has not found solace in writing a letter that is never to be posted ? Mlle Phlipon must surely have torn up a great many but, one after another, she sent four answers to the disquieting words which had again put the whole affair in the balance. She was not aware of what Pascal called the persecution of silence.

Roland's response had little in common with her vibrating pages. He wrote at great length upon the "outrageous affront" which had been offered him by a man who "giving nothing to his daughter," "had pretended to set himself up as the arbitrator of his (Roland's) fortune." He obstinately refused to come to Paris. He would not "treat with a man who had no foresight, no discretion, and no honour." As for seeing her, he said not a word. He reproached her with having suggested a break. He was "in the most horrid state of depression. Physically and morally I am violently over-wrought," he said.

Roland was one of the first romantics, and in a letter written at this time is a phrase remarkable because of the date on which it was written: "I believe myself destined and delivered over to misfortune." With typically masculine sentiment and without making any definite statement, he, however, let everything be understood by ending his letter with these words: "Be happier. This will be my dying wish. Write to me, however, I entreat you." All he wished to say was contained in these final words which meant in effect: our plans are broken off, but this is no reason why I should forego your letters. Despite our resolution to separate, which is an accomplished thing *write to me, I entreat you.* At the same time he sent his friend and confidant, Cousin-Despréaux, a note so worded:

. . . A curious adventure I have to relate to you may mean perhaps that I shall not need the 1200 *livres* in question.

In this thought he must have found a certain compensation for his loss.

But Mlle Phlipon did not, or pretended not to understand:

The state you are in puts me beside myself. . . The die is cast: we must be happy together or never know happiness at all. Adieu, hasten to write me and calm me with the assurance of a more consoling mood. I embrace you and am entirely yours, in life and in death.

The conferences between father and daughter began again and made the situation a bitter one. The engraver wrote the following letter (Roland copied it and joined it to his):

Mr [Monsieur], the discussion of interests can surely do no harm to the affair in question: very recently my daughter, making use of her majority which she attained three months ago, saw to it that I give her an exact accounting before a notary of the fortune of her deceased mother. This matter is irrevocably closed. . . You did me the honour, Mr, of writing me: I am entitled to that of answering. But having previously asked my daughter to inform me of certain things [19] which she very curtly and even, if I dare use the word, harshly refused me, I have with regret decided to tell you that she can enjoy to the full the privileges of her majority to hasten a definition of this affair.

Roland, already exasperated by the "Mr's," cried out that this letter "revealed a mind so foreign to his own that it made him shudder." He was bound by the highest esteem to the daughter of such a man, but he exclaimed: "Your father, my friend, your father !" which was ridiculous, for Phlipon did not count, and had never counted, and they had agreed upon that from the very first. In one letter, which is missing, she spoke of suicide. After having remonstrated with her, Roland attempted to console her by overwhelming her father — whom she loved in spite of everything — with a thousand insults; speaking of his "monstrous and undefinable" character, "of his idle life, his indecorous conduct, his low instincts." He took him to be "insensitive, unjust, false, depraved . . . unworthy to be considered a man." The answer to this, this time neither pained nor plaintive, showed in the final words an unimpaired resolution: "Until the last breath I am your friend."

The next day, having received no news, she wrote again: this letter is ardent in tone, very distracted, very fine.

The good distance you keep from all discord and talk, the numberless annoyances of the details of my affairs, the gloomy forebodings of your family, these form a mass of obstacles most arduous to over-

come. Enthusiasm alone could vanquish them, and this has been
deadened in you by fear or prejudice. . . You seem no longer to ad-
here to our plans save through deference to me, and because you are
bound by your word and by the tenderness of your memories rather
than by any allurement of hope. I need here remember only the name
of friend to assist you to make that resolution which will best serve
your happiness. . . But can I love you enough, or little enough, to
give you disinterested advice upon this subject ?

Having come to this point in his sentimental adventure, Roland
had an idea which serves to show once more how badly he
reasoned and how liable he was to act inopportunely. He had
doubtless waited until he had firmly made up his own mind before
saying anything to his family of his plans for marriage. But now
that these plans were on the point of being abandoned, he wished
to take them into his confidence. In his anger he must have felt
the need of being told how justified he was, and to enforce his
furious statements, he sent Phlipon's letter on to Villefranche. It
was a singular idea. Evidently he hoped that his family would
object to such a union and that he could make use of their opposition, notwithstanding his own sentiments, to bring about a definite break. This weakness of character marked him as the leader
of the Girondist Party.

In the meantime, Mlle Phlipon had regained her equilibrium.
In the following letter she very accurately summed up the situation:

What has now happened again to upset our plans? Is my father
any different today than he was and than I depicted him to you a
short time ago ? How you exaggerate ! Ah, it's quite enough that
his faults and his whims torment me. . . But, really, he is not a marked,
dishonoured, contemptible man. He has done nothing to be so and
he is generally looked upon as an honest artist. . .

She suspected that Roland was afraid of her:

"Live, breathe, *be brave,*" she wrote him; then, again resorting
to artifice, she tried to rouse him by speaking of a match suggested
by her Uncle Besnard, "one of these Court servants, so basely proud
of their servility, in the service of Mme Adélaïde." L. F., the
apprentice, was no longer her destiny, nor was Sévelinges, who was
three times her age, but "a brilliant match connected with the

Court," and likely to put her in the limelight. "I must go slowly in order to avoid this new interview without making too bad an impression on my great-uncle. I hope to succeed."

By gently and graciously asking that Roland write Phlipon his intentions, she forced him to define them, although she was quite convinced that he would avoid a frank expression.

And then once again she let her father give voice to all that she wished Roland to hear and yet feared to say directly to him:

My father is more convinced than you believe of our intentions to carry out our plans. We went to Mlle Desportes' to read the copy of the epistle he had composed for you: it was impossible to make him understand that it was rude and that it would make it necessary for me myself to withdraw: he insists that this request of mine proves that his concerning you was no more than an accommodation by which I dare not profit, that only your reply could clear up this point, that you could not do otherwise than applaud the thing he has asked of me,[20] and *that if you really loved me you would feel that these difficulties made by a father are not unsurmountable.*

But Roland held fast to his new position. The word friendship was used. "A project conceived in enthusiasm and kept alive by virtue" must be set aside.

Like a mournful echo she answered:

A time is allowed for hope. Let there be one for reason.

But she had lost her courage:

I was, I am uncertain, I change each day, I am harrowed by torments of perplexity and other torments that will henceforth always be with me.

She would enter a convent. Her only resource would be to have Roland as a friend as she could not have him as a husband.

You will be to me all that you can and will be; to you alone shall I describe in all its verity my situation and its needs, and I shall exemplify all the dignities the name of friend signifies or suggests. You will see my sentiments undergo the last proof to which they can be put. Write to me, advise me. . .

And Roland answered:

The transports of friendship are less violent, but all is not lost, my dear, if one still retain a steadfast and constant friend.

And further, after more invectives against Phlipon:

Love offers great pleasures, no doubt, and frightful griefs as well. Reason has no excesses, and in the end one lives to it regretting that one did not so begin.

This was the consolation he offered her!
It was thus to the future friend she wrote:

You love me, you will always love me; I know this, I believe it, I feel it, I am yours. I live only to strew a few flowers on the path you are to tread. . .

Let her take care lest he say again to her: "The transports of friendship are less violent."

The future, however, was to prove her right. It was Roland who was smitten, and not she. Her stratagem in speaking of love under the guise of friendship was to affect him strongly:

Write to me, I entreat you [she wrote], otherwise I could not long endure the anxiety which undermines me . . . if you delay in letting me know *the state of your heart and health. Make haste, sweet friend, to put them both at ease* if you wish me to survive.

Here was a pointed thrust:

You are no longer my future or promised spouse. . . Be then my confidant, my friend, *my father.*

How cleverly she aroused the masculine vanity of the man who had loved her and who, although twenty years her elder, had found favour in her eyes. He was, moreover, so conceited that this question does not seem to have been mooted at the time when Roland was eager and the young girl undecided.

From this moment, whether unconscious or contrived, her plan was extremely clear-cut, and it proceeded without a blunder. She understood thoroughly that Roland was at that point of sullen hostility which can cause an irresolute man to take a stand of permanent opposition against the one he loves. The more he loved her, to use the terms of men, the more he held her responsible for all the trouble she had brought upon him, and the more he guarded against a charm that would otherwise have captured him. But just because she defended his judgment through thick and thin and cleared him of any pretext of resisting, he was compelled to change his attitude. In agreeing to give love the name of friendship, she made him feel that he had never really given her up and that his deepest being was in revolt at the idea of losing her.

The jilted fiancée, however, asked him to inform the engraver that the marriage was broken off. This, she said, was necessary. "The silence into which he (Roland) has retired (begins) to make her an object for pity because of her constancy in openly cherishing a man supposed to be but slightly attached to her." She took a certain satisfaction in writing these last words; but Roland refused to comply and put the responsibility of the break upon Phlipon:

If your father were as you say he is, could he then be the sole person to look upon his own behaviour as kindly and not to see in his letter *a deliberated break inspired by coarse motives?* What can I write him after *the natural result of his letter,* a result which he desired and *forced into effect?* It would be false to ask you to believe that I will answer him.

It is evident that she hoped Roland's letter would draw out a reply from Phlipon in which he would ask pardon and declare that he had entertained none of the intentions ascribed to him.

On the nineteenth of September, probably from Dieppe where he had gone to seek some slight courage from his friend Cousin-Despréaux, Roland gave in and wrote to Phlipon in his worst style, indulging even in the childish trick of using the abbreviated "Mr" that had so scandalized him in Phlipon's letter:

I found in her [your daughter] qualities sufficient to compensate for other things, and I hoped that, flattered by my choice, you would be inclined to make these compensations permanent as far as I was concerned and triumphant in your daughter's eyes.

Far from that, after having depreciated your daughter, the tone of your letter and the sentiments you voice therein would make it an offence [the plan of marriage], considering that they have alienated all the minds that an undiluted honesty could have and would have reconciled.

You knew very well what effect this would have, Mr, or else you believed me a base person, and my family made to be toyed with, something neither one nor the other could ever be; you surely did not believe it. Rejoice in your triumph. Nothing will ever make me believe your daughter less worthy of esteem, even should you make stronger declarations against her. It would be useless to try to blacken her name in public, your insinuations would never be believed: the only successful way to combat virtue is by greater virtue. I might say that they would serve no purpose other than that of showing up hers, of making it even more respected by everyone and by me in particular who know the great motives which serve as its foundation.

On the twenty-first of September the poor girl replied:

Your letter came; I know you wrote it for me; I am grateful to you as I should be for it. . . I had wanted this declaration from you. In the eyes of my father and family the affair that is broken off between us could only have been terminated by you. They persist in considering your reply the effect of a passing ill humour which you would have judged too accurately to take seriously had you any interest in the carrying out of our plans.

In spite of her thanks and her gratitude, twice already had the young girl fully justified her father and presented matters in their true light. Phlipon next wrote Roland a letter again typically his own both as to style and spelling. Obliged to go back on his first gesture, and give his consent, he did it with a good grace and even with a dignity that should have put to shame his unreasonable correspondent who was brooding down in Amiens.

. . . I heartily approve, Monsieur, your conduct towards your relatives in a matter of this kind. It is proof of your prudence and your sound way of thinking; if there be still time I give you with complete satisfaction and great pleasure my approbation; I accept you whole-heartedly, I shall then be at ease concerning my child's fate if this matter can take place. She has not much in the way of a fortune for the moment, aside from good opinions [?], but she has a sure prospect of being not badly off in a day to come, seeing that she is the one and only heir to several close relatives who, by the law of nature, will pass on before her. Thus, Monsieur, all at present depends on you, as long as it is true that there is a remedy for everything excepting death. And if there be really some esteem and affection between you two, etc. . . .

Mlle Phlipon perhaps exaggerated a bit when she made out that she had tried in every way to convince her father of the futility of the above letter. But Roland, who was devoid of any shrewdness, suspected nothing at all. Heavens knows he would have mentioned it! But Phlipon's capitulation had no effect whatsoever on

Roland who continued to cling to his pretexts. The young girl understood what he wished to convey and sent him a draft for a letter breaking off relations.

Sternly and coldly he wrote to put a definite stop to all parleys, for "all things must have an end."

He had "some work, a task that will take him far . . . happiness is but a dream"; and as for her, she has only to adjust herself to matters as best she can. That she should care for her health was all he could find to say before writing his definite adieux.

Even after the three months of torment through which she had just passed, it is evident from her letters that Mlle Phlipon was not at all convinced that there must be a definite break. She pretended to believe it, just as she had appeared to resign herself to friendship. But her instinct — and it did not mislead her — gave her unshaken confidence in Roland's love. But how could she manage to see him again ? She knew that nothing would induce him to come to the house because of the stubborn stand he had taken against the engraver. For this reason she planned to leave her father and live at the convent. Her mind was entirely made up. She would go to the nuns of the Congrégation Notre-Dame where she had been a boarder from 1765-66.

On the tenth of November, having broken with Roland, she wrote a remorseful letter to Sophie:

Oh, my friend, my dear and faithful Sophie ! Do not be offended, do not complain of the manner of reserve I have maintained about the reasons of my distress. I have never betrayed the sweet confidence which is the base of friendship. . .

She must have a certain sum, however, before she could go away:

At the present moment I need 300 to 400 livres. It would be well if I could have them within about twelve days; this would mean that I would take a step that would *influence the rest of my life.*

Remark this phrase: *the rest of my life,* and notice as well that at the same time she continued writing to Roland who had written her an abrupt letter received five days before.

He, however, was worried:

Ah, my friend, although I do not complain I am none the less filled with black grief that is undermining and killing me. . .

But for the third time she firmly stated — and stated it well — that Phlipon was neither a dishonourable nor a debased man. This nail must be driven into Roland's opinionated head, and he in return need sacrifice but a slight part of the austerity of his inviolable principles:

That a man dissipate a part of his fortune through carelessness, or spend it on a not too squalid wench, or through neglecting his work, he is doubtless at fault, but if there be nothing indecent and dishonest about him I do not see what can be done to him, and how those unenlightened as to the circumstances of his private affairs have the right to reproach him.

Roland objected violently to this point of view. The pleasantest phrase in his letter was this confession:

Let me know if this philosophy you extol is more useful to you than to me. I believed it good for all things and learn more every day that it is good for nothing.

And then he remained two weeks without writing.

It was understood that he accepted friendship. He complied with the desire she evidenced to continue the correspondence, but finally confessed that he would like "a personal conversation."

At last he had written those words which must have made the young girl leap with joy!

So you are yearning for a personal conversation. *I no less.* But where, when, and how?

This question she had already answered by installing herself in the convent on the seventh of November 1779.

There she had found great consolation in her old friend Sister Sainte-Agathe, a humble lay sister of the Congrégation, who had already known and loved the little Phlipon girl when she had been a boarder at the convent.

A place at Court was proposed to her. Had she been the vulgarly ambitious woman that so many people have thought, she would have made no bones of abandoning the old, ill tempered Roland. But she had not a moment's hesitation:

It is a position dependent on a caprice of the Queen, and has no
other object than her entertainment. I am not inclined to risk moving
. . . for a situation . . . which, everything considered, would be an
excellent one for anyone who combined a common mind with a com-
pliant and artful disposition.

She remembered a sojourn to Versailles she had made in her
youth with her mother, the Canon, and his distinguished housekeeper, Mlle d'Hannaches, who wished to show her the Court.
They had had to reason wth her before she could be persuaded to
take the trip. Even before this when her parents had taken her to
view the King's Coronation robes, she had met their beatified
admiration with a superb: "And what do they mean to me, a
simple citizen, these frivolous decorations !"

We were lodged in the chateau; Mme Le Grand, Lady-in-waiting to
the Dauphine, acquainted with Abbé Bimont through his son . . . not
residing there, lent us her appartment. It was at the top of the house
in the same gallery as that of the Archbishop of Paris, and so near
this dignitary that he had to mind himself lest we overhear him. We
ourselves had to observe the same precaution. Two rooms, rather
poorly furnished, and at the top of one an arrangement where a valet
might sleep, the approach to them made detestable by the odour of
the privies, such was the habitation that a Duke and Peer of France
was proud to possess so as to be able to grovel more readily every
morning at the rising of Their Majesties. And yet it was the rigorist
Beaumont himself. We witnessed every repast of the entire family,
the services, the walks, the games, the presentations, during that week.
Acquaintances of Mme Le Grand procured us special favours; Mlle
d'Hannaches entered arrogantly into every place, ready to fling her
name into the face of whomsoever might offer her opposition, believing
that her six hundred years of high lineage should be apparent on her
grotesque countenance. . . I was not unmoved by the spectacle of a
great ceremony; but it made me indignant that its object was to exalt
a few individuals already too powerful and of very slight importance
in themselves; I preferred the statues in the gardens to the people of
the chateau and when my mother asked me if I was enjoying myself,
I answered: "Yes, on condition that it finish soon; a few more days
and I will so despise the people I see that I will be unable to control
myself." "How then have they harmed you ?" "They have made me
feel injustice and look upon absurdities." [*Memoirs.*]

Upon her return from Versailles, seated in her little study, she
wrote Sophie: "A benevolent king . . . yes, perhaps . . . but were

I given a choice of governments I would instinctively choose a republic."

From the moment Roland weakened, he was a vanquished man. Lest he take fright she wrote less from that day on. She took care not to appear triumphant. She wrote in that reasoning and tender tone which was peculiarly her own, calling Roland "my dear Thalès," relating to him her plans for her life at the convent. He said to her: "No-one could put more wit and skill into maltreating a fellow being."

From the Congrégation she had rented a little lodging for 20 écus. "There I shall be in my kitchen, and I hope to manage with my 530 livres." Before leaving she gave her father the little she had saved and which he needed greatly. She intended to apply herself to her guitar, her geography, and to look for pupils. With all the exaggeration of her years, and with her particular fondness for fine phrases, she wrote: "I have known every grief, I fear nothing but remorse."

At first Roland's letters continued to pass through Mlle Desportes' hands. Then he began to write directly. He was occupied with his candidacy for corresponding member of the Academy of Sciences, and in correcting his *Lettres d'Italie* which "the piety ! ! ! of the royal censor, pruning-hook in hand, had slightly mutilated."

Understanding that now that he was weak and uncertain he wanted more than ever to appear firm and brave, she spoke frequently of "the strong mind" she knew he possessed.

She said:

I, for my part, have enough emotion to give, as far as need be to our relationship, that extra amount of affection that is almost always supplied by one or the other of the two. . .

Roland wept upon reading the last pages of this letter. He wrote in reply:

Yes, I love you; I want to see you, to listen to you, although you have, by your frigidity, cast a mortal cold upon the means of bringing this about. Oh, my friend, how well I know what your position is ! How it grieves me ! It is continually in my mind, it pursues me everywhere. Without working you can manage to occupy your mind, you can at least find some diversion. As for me, I work like a dog; five or six days of the week I do not even go out; I pass entire sleepless nights; and with all this I accomplish nothing. . . I am dissatisfied with everything I do; I, for my part, have violent and terrible crises. . . I have almost never seen things in so black a mood, nor contemplated life with more disgust. . .

He was weakening. He was going to succumb. He was already aware that he was no longer the master of his fate. His love was tormenting him, and he no longer concealed it.

In her happiness she made one false step. That same day, in an ardent letter, she spoke of love again: and she was wrong. Her diplomacy succeeded where her spontaneity failed. It was not yet the moment for the laying down of arms. The adversary immediately recovered himself:

Everything disgusts and repulses me . . . if this goes on I shall throw the helve after the hatchet and betake myself far from these savage humans who caress only that they may bite, and who end by poisoning one.

At this time Roland was probably disappointed at not having been appointed to replace the Inspector of General Manufactures at Rouen. But it is without doubt to her that he is referring in this harangue. Under cover of caresses and poison he is rebuking her for the enthusiastic effusions with which she responded to his sufferings and regrets. He quickly resumed his quibbling and peevish tone. Never before perhaps had he shown himself so obdurate. Never before had she been so sweet. In the name of friendship she made him the most touching of appeals:

Come close to your friend, know her, rend the veil which absence, the inadequacy of written words, and so many contradictions and wrongs have put between us; I am dying to see you and I live in anticipation of that moment. . . I know of nothing that could be termed good, or wise, or desirable, if it failed to bring peace and joy to your heart.

And further:

What has become of your trip ? When can I see you ? Come, be forever, in the name of friend, all that you can be to the tenderest and most faithful of hearts.

On the third of December, Roland wrote again, and so rudely that one wonders in exasperation how she could have wished to pass her days with so unjust and crotchety a human being. Nevertheless, she persisted, and with the deepest admiration one reads this passage in which the future Mme Roland, as well as Jeanne-Marie Phlipon, fully reveals herself:

My fondness for you still leaves me rights on your affection and your happiness. I feel this. I believe it. It was this that dispelled the depression into which your letter first plunged me, it is this which sustains me, restores me, and gives me the confidence to encourage you. I say it to you with justifiable audacity, that there is but one sensitive, upright soul who is deeply enough aware of your true worth, and sufficiently devoted to your person, to be capable of lightening the burdens of your laborious career, and that being is I.

As the time drew near he now began to regret having said that he would go to Paris and see her. From the very beginning of his letter of the tenth of December, he mentioned plans well designed to discourage his friend:

My departure will not take place until the 20th, or more likely until the 24th, so that I will reach Paris the night of the 25th, and will leave early on the morning of the 26th for Longpont, where I expect to stay until the second or third of January and not appear in Paris again until towards Twelfth night.

She mastered herself sufficiently, however, to feign at least that calm which he reproached her with not possessing. But Roland had still other disappointments in store for her. On the nineteenth, the day before his intended departure, he announced that he had decided to postpone it until the twenty-seventh. Above all she must not get it into her head that he was anxious to see her. He was much more eager to see his brother the Prior. That she must fully understand.

At the end of December when Roland finally did come to Paris, he passed through the city without going to see his friend who by this time was convinced that all was lost. Roland was a man who persisted in the execution of his plans. He passed a week in Longpont with his brother the Prior. He did not return until after Twelfth night, exactly as he had said. But would he again be able to evade his fate ?

Yes, he would. Upon his arrival in Paris, he went to the Hotel de Lyon in the rue St Jacques. Having said he would be there the sixth, he did not arrive until the ninth, and could not make up his mind to call at the Convent of the Congrégation until the twelfth. But there, as he feared, he hopelessly succumbed upon "again seeing at the gate" the woman he had wanted to banish from his heart.

The next day he sent the young recluse a few agitated lines:

Glory in your retreat, my friend! What then is your power that you can put me into such a state!

Owing to some misunderstanding he had no news from her and he was desperate. He returned to the hotel to see if her letter had come. But there was nothing. Only upon returning for the third time did he find it awaiting him. And the impatient lover wrote:

You love me. . . Well, why does this not mean everything? Are you then an enigma? . . . if there were a mistake it was the one I made in seeing you. . . Had you hated me, I doubt if you could have hurt me more.

He wrote this the day after his visit to her, that visit at which he lingered until long after the closing hour. We know he was a man prone to make endless calls. And now he reproached himself with this and wondered what the nuns had said and thought of him. Good heavens, was he compromised?

He had seen her on the twelfth. In a letter dated the twentieth he finally pledged himself.

It was his brother, the Prior, this brother from whom he kept nothing and who understood how uselessly his younger brother distressed himself, who carried the following letter to the convent:

"It is so necessary to me that you be happy!" There is your text, and therein my consolation. Woe is you if you forget it, or if ever you contradict it! Content yourself with your own observations! And for your own sake, do not invent monsters merely for the pleasure of combatting them. Know at last, and know it well, that my family loves me, that they wish for my happiness. . . If you have sufficient confidence in me, and enough in yourself . . . my brother will see you: do not tell him that I wrote you once before to announce his visit. . .

My friend, my good friend! I shall see you Sunday; cause me no more pain; you have already endured too much. Farewell.

The pacifying influence of a brotherly counsel is here clearly seen, and sustained by the Prior, Roland finally made up his mind. But he was still timorous, for the twentieth was a Thursday and he thus allowed himself two full days in which to regain his poise.

Mlle de la Belouze, a person of prominence in the parliamentary world, and a cousin whom Roland — exceedingly snobbish — respected to the point of exaggeration, came to pay an official visit on the fiancée. Without the least doubt, Mlle Phlipon was dazzled by the worldly appearance and polished speech of this high and mighty lady. Her presence definitely proved that Roland did not intend to change his mind. Never would he have asked a person of this degree to disturb herself if his resolution were not an irrevocable one. It is evident that he was infinitely more bound by the steps taken by his brother and Mlle de la Belouze, than by his own words to the woman he loved.

As for Mlle Phlipon, prostrate with success, she was suffering "a collapse that disturbed her exceedingly."

Farewell, sweetest friend. You know I love you. There are many things I would say to you, but pens no longer have the skill to express how much I feel. I wish to write no more sweet words and other pretty things, for they seem to me fit to describe only moderate emotions. True and ardent love has no expression other than silence; and thus I hold my peace.

Who knows what she really felt when she had finally attained this end? We are at times inconsistent with our ownselves, and when we have reached the pinnacle of satisfaction that we had strived for with all our might, an inexplicable disillusionment pervades us and mocks our years of effort. Was the reality of an old and ill tempered Roland suddenly uppermost in the thoughts of this fresh and beautiful young girl? It is possible. It is probable. For it was the same young girl who one day said to Sophie: "I love you because you are attractive."

Before the ceremony, there was one task to be performed: the announcement of her marriage to the friends she had deceived.

She had not yet shown much concern about it. She was indifferent to everything that did not immediately concern Roland.

She had recently written Sophie a very gratuitous remark, and one which which leaves a disagreeable memory: "M. Roland came to see me yesterday. We discussed philosophy."

A few days later she must finally tell the truth and confess to a deception which would naturally cut to the quick her loyal friend. But far from being ill at ease, Mlle Phlipon seemed to rise above the situation:

> Dare I flatter myself that the veil which always masks the circumstances of an unexpected event will in no way lessen your esteem and trust ? It is you who can now complete my happiness; the measure of my wishes will be filled if Sophie does me justice and believes me always her best friend. . .
> In this great change, I do not forget, my good friend, that it is through you I came to know the one with whom I am about to unite my lot forever. I like to feel that you are the cause of my happiness and that I owe it to your friendship. Even for you *this will be an exquisite joy which cannot fail to touch your tender heart.*

Mlle Phlipon left the convent to return to her father's house in the rue de Harlay.

The contract was drawn up on the twenty-seventh of January by Durand, the notary, on the Place Dauphine; the bans were published on the thirtieth, and the marriage took place quietly on the fourth of February. It was solemnized by the Canon of Vincennes in the Church of Saint-Barthélemy,[21] in the Phlipons' parish, where the bride's mother and grandmother had been baptized, married, and interred.

Dom Pierre Roland was his brother's witness, and Sélincourt, then practising law in Paris, was gracious enough to act as witness to the bride.

Cousin-Despréaux, the confidant of Roland's tergiversations, had to be immediately advised. Scarcely was the marriage over, when the newly wed Mme de la Platière took it upon herself to tell him that she had had her revenge. It was she who, in fine and ceremonious phrases, announced the marriage to Roland's most intimate friend. Roland added several lines in a familiar tone, incongruous

enough with the body of the letter, and terminated with these
words: "I sought happiness. I now believe it exists." And then
she again took up her pen to call Cousin-Despréaux' attention to
the fact that her husband was "worried and troubled" by the delay
in the publication of the *Letters d'Italie* [22] *à Mlle X*. From the
very first she adopted the rôle of the modest collaborator of an
eminent man.

This letter was the first of innumerable writings in which Mme
Roland assisted her husband. His admiration for the facility and
pertinency of her pen scarcely dated from this moment. But he
was soon to recognize — although probably without admitting it —
that she was greatly his superior. *From the first to the very last
day,* they preserved this habit of working together. For a long
time she approached his work with profound humility, with timidity lest she see "a shadow" darken her husband's countenance.
The submissiveness she had promised him was her law.

PART TWO

M. ET MME DE LA PLATIÈRE

IN EXPLAINING her marriage, Mme Roland wrote the following in her memoirs:

. . . If marriage was, as I thought, a strict bondage, a partnership in which the woman took upon herself the responsibility of two people's happiness, was it not better that I put my talents and my courage to this honourable task rather than continue in the isolation in which I lived? I must here dilate upon the very sensible reasons which, I believe, decided me; I was not, moreover, moved by the train of thought which was the fruit of meditation, but only by what experience had permitted me to observe. I became the wife of an honest man whose love for me increased the more he knew me. My marriage was a rational one and there was nothing that tempted me away from it. In the devotion I gave to it, there was more spontaneity than calculation. By force of considering nothing but my partner's happiness, I soon perceived that there was something lacking in mine. I never for one instant ceased to think my husband one of the most estimable men alive, and one to whom I would always be proud to belong; but I often observed the lack of gaiety, and felt that a dominating character, added to the fact that he was twenty years my senior, made too great a disparity between us. When we lived in retirement, the hours were sometimes difficult to endure; were we in company, I found myself well liked by other people, some of whom might have come to mean too much to me; I submerged myself in work with my husband, another extreme measure which had its drawbacks; I accustomed him to never doing without me for anything in the world, or for one instant, and I wore myself out.

These critical lines were penned during the summer of 1793, thirteen and a half years after her marriage, when Mme Roland, a prisoner, had good reason to regard with a vindictive eye the fiasco of her sentimental life.

But the truth was that at the time of her marriage she did

not in the least believe that she had decided in favour of "an honourable task," nor that she had chosen "a strict bondage." She was not persuaded by "very sensible reasons" alone. If in 1793 she really believed what she said, it only proves how much one can forget and that posterity should take with a grain of salt even the most sincere confessions.

On the other hand it is impossible to think of her as a woman who blossomed in the sunlight of a happy love. Her case was one of those which falls between two categories. At twenty-five, and un-married, an intellectual love stimulated by resistance, deceived her as to her own feelings. As a young wife she was reduced to seeking happiness in the performance of her duty. Like nurses who find gratification in consecrating their lives to the ailing, so was her fondness for Roland a result of the good she did him.

Between 1780 and 1789, that is to say between the time of her marriage and the first months of the Revolution, there is a scarcity of original documents. The young wife lived the life of her husband, and the voluminous correspondence with the Cannet sisters slackened and then ceased. The *Mémoires particuliers* devote but a scant dozen pages to this period.

It was, indeed, the least interesting time of Mme Roland's life, or rather the life of Mme de la Platière. The young woman was immersed in domestic matters, and Roland kept her employed as his secretary. She lived a provincial life, either in dull company or in a remote part of the country where she supervised the harvests, the fruit crops, the vintages, and passed her evenings either in sew-ing, while her people shelled nuts, or in working for her husband until two in the morning.

WE HAVE already remarked that friendship occupied no small place in Mme Roland's life. Since her convent days, when she discovered Sophie Cannet, we have seen her surrounded by friends whom she dearly loved. It is worthy of note that from her earliest years her friendships were mostly with men. Once married, she found it easier to satisfy this predilection which suited the inclinations of her heart as well as her intellectual tastes.

But one of these friends, François Lanthenas, was already acquainted with Roland at the time of his marriage.

At first the young married people lived with Phlipon, but there they remained only a brief time. Whether because quarters in the rue de Harlay were too cramped or whether because living under the same roof as Phlipon was disagreeable to Roland, they soon moved to the Hotel de Lyon, facing the Chapel Saint-Yves. There, either through devotion or economy, the young wife did the cooking for a husband who, we believe, had liver trouble.

It was necessary that Roland remain in Paris. The Trade Managers required his services to reform the Manufacturers' statute, and to this work he devoted all that liberality of mind which he brought to public affairs. He spent his leisure hours on his *Descriptions de Quelques Arts,* and in correcting the endless *Lettres d'Italie.* In her memoirs Mme Roland was to write with a bitter irony rare enough from her pen, that:

He made me his copyist and his proofreader. I performed this task with a humility at which I cannot help smiling . . . but it came from the heart. I so frankly respected my husband that I readily believed he knew better than I, and I was so afraid that a shadow might darken his countenance, so strongly did he hold to his opinions, that it was only after quite a time that I gained sufficient confidence to contradict him.

In the middle of the summer, the medical student, François Lanthenas, took up his lodging above the Rolands in an attic room of the Hotel de Lyon. He was a young man of twenty-six, the youngest of twelve children, and hence divested by the law of primogeniture. His father, a merchant wax-maker at Le Puy, was a wealthy trader whose affairs extended far and wide. He had put this son in college and, although he had no marked talents, kept him there until the age of sixteen. Then he found him a small post.

The business house in which he was placed had sent him abroad, and it was in Italy, probably in Naples or Sicily, that he had met Roland. They got on well together and in the course of events met again at Lyons, where, having no taste for his work, the young man was leaning towards the arts and sciences. Roland, always tender hearted towards his friends, went so far as to accompany Lanthenas to Le Puy and there persuaded the young man's father to allow François to take up the study of medicine. On Roland's advice, he moved into the Hotel de Lyon, where M. and Mme de la Platière were also living.

A sweet intimacy developed between the newly married couple and this indifferent, irresolute, weak-willed boy. His new occupation disgusted him as much as had his former one. He seemed to have no inclination, except for friendship. Mme Roland called him "the brother"; he named her *"sorella,"* and Roland, among the ancients as usual, outdid them all by calling Lanthenas "faithful Achates."

It was then very fashionable to take up the natural sciences. The three friends attended the lectures of Jussieu and Daubenton, and there they shortly made the acquaintance of Louis Bosc d'Antic, a young twenty-year-old botanist.

His was a noble and exquisite figure, this "botanizing Girondist"; a true scholar, a fine and honourable man, simple-hearted and chivalrous, a faithful patriot, a tried and trusty friend.

His mother had died young and he had been brought up in the country near Laon, by his grandmother, Mme d'Haugert. His father and grandfather, Protestants of the Castres country, had studied medicine. The former had drifted into the business of glass-making, when he learned that his religion forbade his practising this art. Correspondent member of the Academy of Sciences, he was profoundly interested in literature, and proved it by subscribing to Letourneur's translation of Shakespeare.

Following a custom fashionable at the time, and a very old one to boot, he had embellished his name with a "d'Antic," taken from heaven knows where. He had ambitions for a military career for his son, preferably in the artillery. But young Louis, with tastes less destructive than debonair, preferred wild blossoms to explosives and dreamed of plant collections, not of cannonades. To tell the truth, he enjoyed nothing better than combing the woods and fields for specimens of plant life. He was now employed in the postal service and only asked sufficient leisure to continue hs research work.

Thus it was that, during the botanical course in the Jardin du Roi, M. d'Antic observed M. and Mme de la Platière, accompanied by their friend Lanthenas.

They made friends immediately. The young man with the sensitive face was from the first moment attracted to the virtuous husband and the intelligent young wife. From then on their lives were so closely intermingled that it would be well-nigh impossible to separate one from the other and relate each life apart. It can truly be said that this friendship survived by thirty-five years the drama of 1793 — for it was still inviolate in Bosc's heart when he died in 1828.

Between the month of August and the month of December 1781, Roland took his bride to Villefranche to present her to his mother and brothers.

The young bride was suddenly intimidated and dreaded this first meeting, which, however, passed off with the greatest ease. Without any hesitation and with her usual simplicity, she adjusted herself to the family's scale, which must at times have been no easy matter. She immediately became one of the household. She asked her husband, who was going to Lyons on business, to bring back "numbers for the game of loto . . . and some melons, if possible."

From Villefranche the newly married couple went to pay a visit to *Le Clos*. On the twenty-ninth of September 1780, she wrote Sophie:

I arrived in Villefranche on the ninth in the bosom of a respectable and highly-esteemed family who made me welcome in the most touching way. The mama, lively and in good health, over eighty, full of spirits, strict as to her own habits and lenient to others, received me with emotion, and in again setting eyes upon her dear son (whom all the family welcomed in the same fashion), she displayed the greatest satisfaction. After the visiting and the hubbub of the first moments, we escaped to the country. . .

I there met the brothers who inspired in me all those sentiments the word "brother" signifies, and I was delighted to play my part in that sweet intercourse, in that relationship that was hitherto unknown to me. . . The old estate is rather lonely, but agreeable; the country is mountainous and almost entirely cultivated with vineyards; some woods on the high places; the landscape varied; the sky is beautiful here, the air healthy, the evenings delicious. We spend much time in the fields. Everywhere, the vintage, etc. . . .

After "two months passed in the sweetest confidence and intimacy," she returned from Beaujolais. At the end of January, we find Roland installed at Amiens, but without his wife whom he had sent off alone to pay a wedding visit to Cousin-Despréaux in Dieppe, and to Mesdemoiselles Malortie in Rouen, where she was accorded the heartiest welcome.

During her trip, Roland was occupied arranging the house, with a care and solicitude that astonished even himself:

I am fixing up your room as best I can. I cannot tell you how much I want you to be passably comfortable in your quarters. The thought of seeing you well installed and happy is singularly on my mind.

He was very much affected by the "happy event" which was to take place. In February he had confided it to one of his brothers as well as to Lanthenas, and he wrote to his wife: "Take good care of yourself, and consider how much pleasure I shall take in seeing *him* running about. . ."

The house in the rue du Collège in which they lived was a large building that had been uninhabited for some time past. It had a carriage-gate, stables, a courtyard, a garden, and a vineyard "to grow grapes for sparrows." It adjoined the Cloister Saint-Denis, which still served as a cemetery and had the reputation of making the quarter unhealthy. "They die like flies here," said Mme Roland in a letter to her husband. "I never go into my dressing-room that I do not see them digging a pit or filling it."

There the couple lived three years. He performed the duties of his post conscientiously, at times revealing the independent viewpoint he owed to Trudaine's teachings, and which alienated his superiors. She was an excellent wife and a thrifty and orderly housekeeper. Completely devoted to her husband, she assisted him in his reports on the use of fertilizers, the manufacture of hats, the improvement of woollens, etc. She read over and corrected his manuscripts and at the same time kept a watchful eye on the servants.

My new cook arrived this morning; I no longer have any illusions about that breed. . . She is a fair cook and quite pleasant, still she is not of the old stamp. . . I have to watch and direct everything for economy. She seems willing and I am getting her accustomed to doing with little.

And again:

I think it injudicious for women to despise housework, for it is better to do common things well than to show up one's incapacity for higher matters. I do not know whether it is the conviction of my own weakness that makes me reason thus, but I have too much pride to wish to be other than myself, and there is nothing I would dread more than to have the appearance of an abortive man.

Roland had been fifteen years in Amiens when he brought his young wife to reside there. He had formed a little circle of friends whose hearts Mme Roland immediately won.

Of prime importance was the Cannet household.

It was Roland's desire during our marriage [say the *Memoirs*] that I see little of my good friends. I complied with his wish and frequented them again only when time had put at rest my husband's anxiety as to any rivalry in my affections. . . Still, if you deprive a sensitive woman of the sweets of friendship with persons of her own sex, you take away a necessary nourishment and expose her to other things.

Let us here take note that when he requested that she decrease her visits to her friends, obedience seemed as just and natural to her as when, at an earlier date, he had asked her to deceive them as to their matrimonial plans.[1]

There was, in that vigorous nature, a certain docility which is somewhat puzzling, but which we must respect if we wish to understand her. Any other character of this cast, instead of yielding to her husband, would have forced him to accept her friends.

Roland associated but little with his superiors, the most important of whom was M. d'Agay, the superintendent of the province. His closest acquaintances were Mme de Chuignes, a distant connection; M. de Bray de Flesselles, attorney to the King at the finance office;

M. d'Eu or Deu de Perthes, general director of the Farms "for customs, gabels and tobacco," and Mme d'Eu or Deu de Perthes and her devoted admirer M. Devin, general collector of the aforementioned Farms, and a great student of books and botany. Then there was Dr. d'Hervillez; Reynard, the natural philosopher; l'Apostole, the apothecary, as well as several "venerable" old ladies who were called "the mothers." And lastly, there were those manufacturers who were friendly with Roland because he supported them against the merchants who were all powerful at the Municipality. Mme Roland frequented this little world and was not impressed. At the end of a year she wrote to her husband:

. . . I swear to you that for all the inhabitants of Amiens, foreigners and the rest of them, I would not give one *iota*.

When she went out it was more to go walking than to pay calls; sometimes, taking herself very seriously, she went botanising on the ramparts. By this she not only added specimens to her plant collection, but brought herself closer in spirit to her friend Bosc. If she went to the *Comédie,* it was "to weep like a little girl at the theatre for the first time." It was her custom, however, to remain in her dreary house in the rue du Collège, copying out Roland's writings, studying English, and playing the harpsichord that had been lent her by the Concert Society of the town.

On the fourth of October 1781, she gave birth to a little girl whom she called Marie-Thérèse Eudora.[2] Roland's mother and eldest brother were godfather and godmother by proxy. The baptism took place in the parish church of Saint-Michel, behind the cathedral. A disciple of Jean-Jacques, it was natural that Mme Roland should wish to nurse her child. More than a month after her confinement, however, a serious ailment (the nature of which we ignore) made this impossible. Roland, compelled to go to Paris at this time, was extremely anxious. In one of his letters he sounds an entirely new note:

You conceal your condition from me, my dear. I gathered from yesterday's letter that you were better. But you wrote Agathe [Sister Sainte-Agathe] that you had been bled and that you had dreadful dysentery, all of which I have just learned at five o'clock. I have looked everywhere for a carriage to come to you post-haste; I have been unable to find one. I had already written two or three people apprising them of my departure. If my health permitted it, I would set out on foot, etc. . . I will never forgive myself for having been the last to learn of your condition. I kiss you with a distracted heart.

He came home in the greatest haste and displayed true solicitude for the young mother, placed a good nurse by her side and did not leave her until all was well. But the infant began to sicken and the doctor despaired of saving it. Mme Roland then gave a remarkable demonstration of her strength of character and her motherly intuition. In spite of the doctors, the nurses, the old wives, she insisted that she could make her milk come back, and she actually succeeded. Thus, at the cost of great suffering, she saved the life of her child.[3]

Mme Roland was an emotional and jealous mother. She had found a little nurse, Marie Marguerite Fleury, who took care of the child and was to remain eighty years in the family. The cook seemed to give more satisfaction. "After I was put to bed they went on with the laundry until three in the morning and we were able to profit by today's breeze and get a lot of things dried." But several days later the cook injured her heel. "Because of this accident she goes limping about, she won't get up early, and things don't move at that lively pace I wish to be the rule of the house, and there is nothing much I can say. I fear that buxom female has some of the slowness fairly common to those of her height and bulk."

The young mother was very well pleased with her nurse. Upon her departure, she wrote Roland:

I paid her very liberally yesterday evening, but though I am hard up at this moment, I felt I could not do less by her. She has been with me thirty-six days and I paid her at the rate of twenty sous a day; I also gave her an extra écu for some little things I will tell you about. I put all this money in a green net-work purse which pleased her exceedingly, as well as what I said to her. I had some difficulty making her accept everything.

But Roland belonged to quite another school. Referring to some small gifts made to a woman who came to help with the house, here he was in his usual quibbling mood:

It seems to me that in your generosity you show perhaps little consideration for our means. I think, my dear, it would be more prudent to avoid superfluous expenses and take no risks, so as to be able to meet the necessary ones.

The young woman, much abashed, answered that she "recognized the significance and importance of his remark." She feared further reprimands. "What do you think of what I did for my nurse ? You will tell me, I hope. . . Next time I shall be guided by your opinion." Further, to allay his fears, she made it clear that she had given no New Year's gift to the cook "who had only just arrived," nor to Saint-Pierre, Mme de Chuignes' lackey who came to her on New Year's day with "his mug all befloured."

A trip to Beaujolais in September, with little Eudora, who was then eleven months old, broke the monotony of the year 1782. The Villefranche Rolands had forgiven her not being born a boy and, through Canon Dominique who was in friendly correspondence with his sister-in-law, they urged that she be brought to see them. Moreover, the husband and wife considered it wise that they pay a visit and see if the promises to give them *Le Clos* were to be kept.

Following this, Mme de la Platière, who had been urging Sophie Cannet to marry a M. de Gomiécourt, paid a Whitsuntide visit to Sailly-le-Sec, M. de Gomiécourt's property. Roland was often in Paris at this time, occupied with the important work he had undertaken for the *Encyclopédie Méthodique* of Panckouke's library, the *Dictionnaire des Manufactures*. He was not always pleased with what he saw in the capital: "Since I have remarked on the street so many people who should be on the gallows," he said, "from the very depths of my soul I abhor a state and customs. . ."

She wrote him by every post. Through economy she addressed her letters to Bosc, from whom she kept nothing secret, and he would open the envelope and add a few lines to his friend.

Here is a sample of her letters as a young mother:

January 27, 1783

I began the day by a little tune on the spinet, after having caressed and played with my little girl who follows me everywhere, pulls at my clothes, calls me mama, and asks for kisses that I am always more than eager to give.

This was the beginning of her great friendship with Bosc. At first the correspondence [4] had consisted of questions and responses on useful bits of information concerning Roland's work, but before long it was friendship alone that sustained it. She treated him a little as though he were her son. She spoke to him in a playful, intimate, and extremely affectionate tone.

Here are a few typical lines, dated the twentieth of March 1783:

You are a good child who well deserves to be dearly loved; your last letter shows sensitiveness and reason. . . Discriminating tastes, wise plans, true emotions, here are the seeds of happiness: you have them in you. . . I am losing patience, and I am learning little, not even the music you selected for me and which, moreover, is on the whole easy enough.

And on the fourteenth of April 1783:

Isn't it enough then to leave these poor women alone instead of sending them to the devil besides ? Young man, you are far from tolerant; but as your little grudge is amusing, it is forgiven you. . . After which your friends can content themselves with asking you to chase over fields and bushes for them sometimes, but not other things. . . In spite of the trouble you have taken to describe all your work, I am not at all sorry for you. . .

Another letter to Bosc written July twenty-ninth gives us an interesting piece of information: Mme Roland was not a feminist.

Some women might not admit it, but I believe as much as any man that you are superior from every point of view. In the first place you have strength, and everything that goes with it or that results from it: courage, perseverance, wide horizons, and great talents. . . Be proud, be fierce, be clever and learned; it is not because of us that you are so, but because of all that, it is right that you should be our masters. But without us you would be neither virtuous, loving, kind, nor happy, so retain all your glory and authority; we have and seek no other supremacy than to govern your manners and to be pre-eminent in your hearts. I would never ask more than that. It often angers me to see women disputing you certain privileges that ill become them. . .

It is common knowledge that Mme Roland showed herself a skilful negotiator in the matter of the patents of nobility, which her husband's family had not hesitated to put into her hands. This was, indeed, a strange mission to confide to so young a woman.

LOUIS BOSC

From a contemporary crayon

Original owned by MM. Pilastre, his descendants

JEAN-MARIE ROLAND

Drawn from life by Gabriel. Cabinet des Estampes

Roland, who had already started certain proceedings, knew what the difficulties were, but this did not prevent him from setting his wife off on false tracks, or from drawing up for her a plan of action the errors of which she was quick to perceive. In bad odour with his chiefs, the Superintendents of Commerce, because of his austerity and vanity, he had attempted to dispense with their influence, a thing wholly out of the question. Everything, in reality, depended upon M. de Vergennes who must be instructed by M. de Calonne, Roland's official chief, who could in turn recommend him only upon the motion of the Directors. Mme Roland's prompt and practical mind was not long deceived, but she had still to persuade her husband to accept her point of view.

She left Amiens in March, accompanied by little Marguerite Fleury as lady's maid, and leaving her husband and daughter in the care of Louison, the cook. She alighted at the Hotel de Lyon where she had engaged two rooms. As in 1782, Lanthenas still lived at the top of the house, and was half-heartedly completing his study of medicine. From the moment of her arrival, Bosc abandoned both the Postal Service and botany for her sweet sake.

During the two months of her sojourn in Paris, she displayed an unparalleled activity. She filled the rôle of solicitress with all the devotion and intelligence she possessed. Her health suddenly revived and she spent her time in goings and comings, in endeavours, proceedings, and visits. With the intention of reaching M. de Calonne, she launched herself in the subordinate world at Court. She frequented the home of Mme de Candie, first lady-in-waiting to Mme Elizabeth, as well as the house of a secretary to M. de Vaudreuil, First Falconer of France. An old woman who was first lady-in-waiting to Mme Adélaïde sent her to a M. de la Roche, clerk in one of the departments of the General Controller's office, to ascertain if it would be possible to obtain the assistance of the Princess. But the trips to Versailles resulted in nothing. On the fourth of April 1784, she wrote to her husband: "Here I am then, a downright ... intriguer, a very stupid calling, but anyway I am doing it and not by halves, for otherwise it would not be worthwhile." Her letters were full of youthful spirits. She was very popular and, after the retired life and troubles of the past years, one feels she was thoroughly enjoying herself when she wrote to Amiens: "My thirty years don't scare people away."

However, when Mlle de la Belouze, who had given her many letters of introduction asked her to talk about Eudora, the young mother was "amazed to feel her eyes filling with tears . . . the memory of her little voice . . . came calling at my heart," she said, "and I am no more than a mother with all a mother's frailties. . ." She was also very much concerned over her husband's health:

I kiss you with all my heart. For goodness sake, do not neglect to put plasters on your backside, I implore you to do it, it is very important. If I thought you were overlooking this care, I would simply go off and leave matters up in the air here, for not one of them is more important than your health.

Moreover, in Paris she was working for Roland in more than one way. When the letters of nobility gave her a moment's respite, she went to Panckouke, and when the *Dictionnaire des Manufactures* was in the printer's hands she, in passing, won the heart of the publisher. One morning when she was feeling "extremely gay and somewhat saucy," she "made so bold as to correct the works of (her) husband . . . without his participation." On the other hand, she did not fail to keep Roland posted as to everything which might be of interest to him. She wrote him an account of "Lavater's work." Gluck was no longer a favourite. Pilatre's and Rozier's courses were deserted. On the twenty-seventh of April she wrote:

There is an equally great crush today at the Français for the *Marriage of Figaro*,[5] a sorry play in which there is a great deal of naughty talk, they say, and which was played at Court and has been several times forbidden. At any rate, it will appear in the capital's theatre.

And she continued to run to one place, hasten to another, beg for interviews, hurry such and such a one, return ten times to the same place where she had succeeded in getting no farther than the antechamber.

Her task was complicated by Roland, who had not only made enemies, through his disagreeable disposition, but who was besides in bad favour for having published in his works matter which might be considered manufacturing secrets.

After having manœuvred her position, the most difficult thing was to approach the terrible Superintendents of Commerce, and among them, the most ferocious of all, M. de Tholozan. At his home the young woman was accorded a very disconcerting welcome. He received her in the morning, in his night-cap, and in a temper which, as soon as she had begun to sing Roland's praises, broke out in these impatient words:

"Take care not to present him as a superior man. That is his pretension. But we are far from judging him so."
And then I had to listen to a tirade, but a tirade such as it would be impossible to imagine. Pedantic, unbearably proud, thirsting for glory, all kinds of pretensions, an ungovernable character, perpetually contradicting, a bad writer, tactless methods, aspiring to domineer, incapable of subordination, etc., etc., etc. . . .

The good wife was not in the least discouraged, but argued adroitly and even embarrassed her interlocutor who ended by telling her that "she could be of great service to her husband and that it was a pleasure to listen to her."
One after another, she charmed them all. Soon all of them were so well tamed that they worked together in one accord for her success. Her friends were amazed. Lanthenas wrote Roland that he had put "his affairs in exactly the right hands in confiding them to his better half." And as for M. d'Antic, although crushed by the death of his father, he, upon hearing Mme Roland speaking with regret of her harpsichord, made the charming gesture of sending to her room in the Hotel de Lyon, a *forte-piano* on which she "doted," and which was her greatest pleasure.
She had others, however. She would go to the Bois du Boulogne with the two friends who shadowed her footsteps, and there "sucked eggs robbed from under the hen"; or she would run to Vincennes to see good Canon Bimont; to Alfort, to the professors of the Veterinary School; to the Jardin du Roi to listen to M. Fourcroy who was starting his courses; to Chaillot to see the fire-engine, the rage of the moment. They heard La Saint-Huberty; they saw Guimard dance. . . They went to a concert where, in an adjoining box, she recognized Pahin de la Blancherie, who seemed not to

see her. And dear Bosc, who had lost his heart, wrote naïvely to Roland:

> . . . I wished to speak to you of your wife, of my excellent friend whom I should like to see by your side, and yet whom I should like to keep always in Paris; but the mere thought of her puts me in such a state that I haven't an idea in my head. I love you both, her even more than you, if I dare confess it. She has probably told you that it was I who put her up to her plots at Versailles. . . I can assure you that she manages with surprising dexterity; I have been astonished at her gift for interesting the coldest individuals and turning even their objections to her own advantage.

And did not this sly puss have the effrontery to allow those who were astonished that she took "so much trouble for a daughter . . ." understand "that she expected an heir within a few months. . . This makes the matter more touching, and they watch my progress while I laugh up my sleeve," she wrote merrily.

The letters to Roland became joint ones, and Lanthenas would write on the margins of the "dear sister's" letters, and Bosc would embrace "the little sister," if, having received nothing by one post, she grieved at having no news of the "good man," as Roland called himself.

> In reality, my dear, you are a very bad man [he wrote him]. How can you be so? You know how weary is your lawful wife of her tasks, and yet you allow two days to pass, two whole days, without providing her a moment's relaxation in the reading of one miserable letter. This is terrible! And didn't we swear about you yesterday on our return from the fire-engine; you should have heard the vengeful plans! They kept us busy for more than an hour; we almost wept (but they would only have been tears of rage). However, you mightn't believe what happened afterwards. . . Guess! We kissed each other very soundly, very soundly, and you were between the two of us.

If we read all these spontaneous letters consecutively, we feel there could have been nothing questionable in this companionship. Like all Roland's friends, Lanthenas and Bosc were in love with the brilliant young woman. But in the course of her lifetime, it is impossible to perceive one hint of artifice or coquetry. No mysteries. No innuendos. Honest and good-natured, she wrote in a warm and hearty tone: "What is a woman over thirty who is well-behaved and not pretty, or no longer so, if you prefer," in direct contradiction of the opinion of all her contemporaries. In her letters to her friends she spoke of her "fat face," or even: "I am thin as a cuckoo." And again: "Bless me! What a flatterer you are becoming. You call me a fine lady. I'm putting on airs, you should see me! I have almost three chins."

Roland finally ended by losing patience with the familiarities Bosc was taking with "his better half," and from the experience we have had with him the pen he wielded must have been no feather. Bosc himself was rather lacking in a sense of humour, and he replied:

What the devil are you trying to quarrel about? We were jesting with you. This does not mean we feel less sorry for you. We speak of you none the less with pleasure. We don't wish for you less, we don't love you less. And yesterday when your better half told me the approximate date of her departure, I thought more of your reunion than of her departure, which, in spite of my being exceptionally busy, will certainly make a very considerable void in my life.

Roland calmed down. He became the perfectly behaved child:

You are quite right [he said], and one must be fair; but where is one to find this woman you are debauching? Every day I hear of new pranks, and if it is not you who are the author of them, at least you take part in them. What have you to say for yourself? . . . Tell me seriously, are you determined to keep her very much longer? Do you know I am beginning to weary of so long an absence, and if it is not soon cut short I shall end by growing angry. . . I embrace you with all my affection.

Mme Roland had just written her husband upon the same subject:

Concerning friend D'Antic, I understand nothing that you have written, and I see moreover, by your letters, that you are none too sure how you ought to take the matter. I repeated to him what I had written you. . . When you lions try to sport among yourselves, your voices are too harsh and your claws too sharp; leave it to us little birds to do the chattering, we who know how to flit about your ears without injuring others. The truth of it is that this poor friend is in the saddest state of mind one could possibly imagine. Distaste for everything, complete apathy, really miserable; health suffering from it, as is inevitable.

Mme Roland referred to the state of depression in which the

death of his father had left young Bosc, but her real thought was
continually in Amens. She wrote Roland:

> . . . I would not care to purchase the greatest success at the price of
> an absence as long as the one I have just endured. I feel more strongly
> than ever that no good can equal tender affection and intimate devo-
> tion. . . I am eager to return and revel in it; I no longer live; my
> heart, all of me is unceasingly with you and our child. . .

And Roland, on his part, wrote his friends:

> Send her back to me, I don't say when you are tired of her, but as
> soon as possible. You will make me very happy. She has sweetly
> accustomed this good man to her; and now he finds it difficult to do
> without her.

In spite of all the conquests Mme Roland made among the "bears"
who "growled" at the Superintendence of Commerce, in spite of
their influence, one might even say, in spite of their zeal, it was
evident that the matter was not progressing. But she had at least
one triumph to her credit. Having learned that the General In-
spectorship at Lyons was vacant, she persuaded her new friends,
the Superintendents, to promise this position to the inspector they
could not tolerate.

On the twenty-first of May, Roland, whom she had questioned in
haste, answered:

> I only take the time to tell you that for everything and in all things,
> do as you judge suitable, and I shall subscribe to everything in advance.

What a change! Moreover she had forgotten nothing; she had
thought of the salary and of the gratuity, of the moving and the
installation, and M. de Tholozan himself declared that "the total
salary would equal that of the highest-paid province inspector."
But judging Roland "too quick-tempered, too stubborn," he relied
on his wife to "moderate him."

> In short, my dear friend, Le Clos, the greenness, Eudora, the delicious
> peace, the lovely affection, we shall have all that and I care nothing for
> the rest."

Roland was delighted with the result his wife had obtained, but
she scarcely dared believe he was satisfied and was very much worried. Reassured, she wrote him: "How greatly I needed . . . to

be convinced . . . that this change was in accord with your desires !"

Roland, almost good-humoured, came to Paris to fetch her. They both wished to make a pilgrimage to Ermenonville before returning to Amiens. She remembered the day she had gone on a venture to pay a visit to J.-J. Rousseau. She had written to announce her coming, but he could not believe that such a letter had been written by a young woman, and when, with timid glances and flaming cheeks, she appeared at the rue Plâtrière, she had found Thérèse, Levasseur on the threshhold barring the door. "She was," she said, "a woman of at least fifty, wearing a round bonnet, a clean and simple house-dress, and a big apron. . . A woman who looked severe and even hard," but to this young *bourgeois* girl, so particular on the score of good manners and cleanliness, she did not appear the sordid creature that we visualize in thinking of the one who signed herself: *La fâme de gangaque*.[6] This round bonnet, this clean house-dress, this severe manner, at once endowed her with an unexpected dignity.

In the house in the rue du Collège, little Eudora did not recognize the tender mother who had nursed her and who, in the face of such a welcome, burst into tears. Even "when the child had taken up again her accustomed ways," Mme Roland "could not think of the disappointment of her return without a terrible swelling of the heart," as she described it to Bosc.

The leave-taking in Paris had been an emotional one. Lanthenas, who had been greatly worried by a slight ailment, had sent for the doctor for "the dear sister" and showed his genuine devotion. As for M. d'Antic, it was quite another matter. He had taken offence when Mme Roland had declined his company for the outing to Ermenonville, which she wished to make with her husband. But this slight tiff was soon forgotten. Hardly had she gone off with the happy Roland when Bosc wrote her an awkward and touching letter, all filled with tenderness and melancholy:

It is ten o'clock; if you are not already in the thickets of Ermenonville, you are not far distant. I rejoice in those pleasures you are revelling in together. I can feel tears welling in my eyes when I think of those you will shed, seated on the shady lawn before the *Ile des Peupliers,* in thinking of your happy lot, of Eudora, and of what she may become. . . The quality of being a mother should develop in you the liveliness of emotion this state produces more than the one of bachelorhood which I profess. Albeit I would have preferred to have been there with you, more to enjoy your happiness and that of your husband, and the bonds that unite the two of you, than to have been happy myself.

Had circumstances favoured my wish to join you, fatigue would not have permitted my doing so. I have not the hope of even passing my days in solitude, as I had planned. My present existence is no longer my own; it is extremely painful to me.

Everything worries and disturbs me. Will you believe me that simply because I have noticed the word "friend" more frequently repeated in your last than at other times, my peace of mind is troubled.

Farewell, be happy always. Perhaps I will not reach that point of corruption where the happiness of others becomes a torture, but I feel I am on the way. I need something to turn my course.

A week later, Lanthenas, who had taken four years to obtain his M.A. degree and was working dispiritedly for his doctorate, arrived at the Rolands' just as they were on the point of leaving on a six weeks' trip to England, where they intended to investigate on the spot the effects of the Constitution. The three friends, accompanied by M. Deu, spent the month of July 1784 in this abode of liberty.

Upon their return, Lanthenas remained with them in Amiens. Mme de la Platière wrote Bosc:

I haven't talked to you about the trip which was an extremely satisfactory one. . . I will always remember with singular interest this country whose constitution I had already known and admired through Delolme;[7] and here I saw the happy effects of it. Let fools protest and slaves rejoice.

This time, upon their return, Eudora recognized her parents, but a fresh disappointment, which Mme de la Platière confided to Bosc, awaited her at Amiens. She had a falling out with Sophie Cannet. M. de Gomiécourt had "behaved badly" and she had taken him up sharply, "too sharply, perhaps, for gentle people, once irritated, are worse than others. . . We now will hear nothing more from each other. I am more affected by this than I can tell you."

August came, and the time to leave Amiens drew near. Roland, who had a sincere respect for friendship, did not want to leave the provinces of Picardy and Normandy, where he had made his career and where he had lived for almost thirty years, without paying a visit to Cousin-Despréaux at Dieppe, and to the Malortie ladies at Rouen. In passing through Paris, the family stopped several days at the Hotel de Lyon to see Bosc, who, half-gloomy, half-jealous, took offence on an absurd pretext: while travelling, Mme Roland, concerned over her husband's health, had consulted a professor of the Faculty of Medicine, Dr. Le Roy, instead of contenting herself with the advice *by correspondence that Bosc's father had sent them some time before his death!*

Nevertheless the four of them, the Rolands, Bosc, and the inseparable Lanthenas, betook themselves to Crespy-en-Valois to see Prior Jacques Roland, and to Longpont to Prior Dom Pierre.

Then a curious scene was enacted, the memory of which is preserved in one of Mme Roland's letters to Bosc.

You left me cut to the quick and crushed [she wrote him] at a moment when a hundred leagues were about to be put between us, at a moment when you were to leave us for perhaps a long time, at a moment when I, broken-hearted, clasped my husband's hand, my daughter's, and yours in mine, renewing in my overflowing soul that blessed vow of friendship, made all the more sacred because vowed in a silence that not one of us could break — at this moment you tore yourself away from me, you fled from us! . . . I remained motionless in my seat, my child in my arms, my eyes bathed in tears, fixed upon that door through which you had just passed. . .

This letter (of the twenty-third of September 1784), must have been left unanswered, for on the third of October Mme de la Platière, returned at last to *Le Clos,* wrote again:

Well, our good friend, what has become of you. . . I wrote to you from Longpont; our friend Lanthenas will bear witness to the utterances of our hearts; we flattered ourselves, I confess, that we would find news from you here, or receive some upon our arrival. . .

A letter dated November seventh, shows us that Bosc finally replied:

The intensity of your feelings more than makes amends for the suspense we suffered. . . I firmly believe this, for the consciousness of our rights upon your friendship is inherent in that sentiment which we have for you and carries with it the assurance of bringing you back to the truth ! I mention this to you for the last time. I shall continue our correspondence in that former tone which we have no reason to alter and you will know that, far from estranging ourselves from our friends who are not well, we revive the devotion which unites us to them forever.

In the following letter Mme Roland brought in Eudora in a touching way:

My dear Eudora has a bad cold for the first time in her life; her cough tears my heart, alarms and tortures me. The poor little thing remembers you well, but less your games than the condition which she saw you in before our departure. "Mama," she said to me this morning with her little intonation which already presages a deep feeling, "M. d'Antic is crying !" She brought tears to my eyes as well.

At other times, Roland writes in a simple, fraternal tone, in which his wife's influence can be seen. But it is only just to say that he also was kind-hearted. He was a tender, even an indulgent father; a true friend who could establish loyal relationships and whose letters were not entirely devoid of charm. It is to be suspected that the untiring patience of "his better half" — who was always ready to share his views so as to moderate them — had greatly improved the condition of his nerves.

To her husband's letters Mme de la Platière added long postscripts. But nothing availed; Bosc had made up his mind to be angry. In March, however, he again took up his pen. And Mme Roland, in great delight, wrote to her husband who was then away on a tour of inspection: "D'Antic had become nicer than ever. . . The most wearisome existence would still be sweet to me as long as there were good to be done and friends to cherish." And elsewhere: "I feel my heart at peace when I know my friends are happy."

The Rolands passed the first months of winter [8] at Villefranche, having taken but a small lodging at Lyons. The household got on well enough with the Canon, but Roland's mother had little by little discouraged first her daughter-in-law's sweetness and then her diplomacy. There was nothing left to resort to but patience.

As long as I retained some hope of finding a heart in the midst of the eccentricities of this bizarre character, I worried myself as to a means of winning her, and I was disconsolate at my lack of success. Now that I see her as she is, a selfish and capricious being, the essence of contrariness, who never experienced any pleasure except that of molesting others by her whims, who triumphs in the death of two children whom she overwhelmed with grief, and who would smile at all our deaths and scarcely make any pretence about it, I feel I have come to the point of indifference and almost of pity, and I have no longer any indignation or hate except in short rare moments.

Mme de la Platière's life was that of a provincial lady, a good wife, good mother, and good housekeeper. Whatever annoyances she may have felt, she made it a duty to pass the plate in church and offer the consecrated bread. She paid deadly visits, gave big dinners, as is the lavish custom in Beaujolais, arranged dinners whose menus we still have and from which we learn that an eel pasty accompanied a terrine of woodcock and half a hundred crayfish "as side-dishes," with "fresh black truffles."

As for Roland, he was continually on the move, either inspecting in Beaujolais or on the way to the little lodging in Lyons, and his wife was ill at ease when he went off on horseback, with a servant, because of the wolves in the woods.

The social life at Villefranche was even less interesting to the young woman than the life at Amiens, nor did she meet with any notably good dispositions among what she called, in moments when she must have been completely discouraged, "the Caladois [9] rabble."

At Lyons she had, through her husband, met more interesting people, and she was pleased to receive them when the occasions at the Academy brought them to Villefranche.

This growth all over France in the eighteenth century of small provincial colleges, was a significant detail of the intellectual movement. They were often very much curtailed, but always active, and it was considered a great honour to be accepted by them.

At one of the annual sessions of the Villefranche Academy, Roland read a "much applauded" paper. His wife, it was said, had some part in it and the young Mme de la Platière received public eulogies which cannot have contributed to her popularity.

Shortly after, the session took place of the Lyons Academy to which Roland had been recently elected, and he made a speech of grateful acknowledgment. It was there that, later, he was to make known his *Thoughts on Plutarch,* an essay on the old master inspired by the little Phlipon girl and corrected by Mme de la Platière.

The correspondence with Bosc [10] was then very regular and very genial. Calm was restored. The husband and wife swamped him with errands:

They are advertising everywhere [he wrote Roland] three big volumes of Necker. I have seen that man commit so many stupid actions that I would be greatly surprised if he did not say equally stupid things about them in so many volumes.

Very charmingly, Mme Roland asked Bosc to go to Vincennes for news of good Uncle Bimont.

Then Phlipon gave her a great deal of worry.

On the morning of the twenty-second of December 1786, she sent Bosc letters for the engraver, to whom she had suggested a retirement to Chatillon. In her memoirs she speaks of the "errors . . . which had just dispersed the little she had inherited from her grandmama." She also said: "We paid some debts he had contracted, and persuaded him to retire from business . . . assuring him a pension.[11] She had already once asked Lanthenas to settle up Phlipon's affairs. There was first the back rent to pay, but with the hard condition Roland imposed, that the receipt be made out in his name. In truth this father-in-law appears to have been extremely remiss.

Bosc collected the revenues at the City Hall. He inquired what sort of cement should be used to repair the terrace at *Le Clos* "which is cracking and which lets in water," and what varnish to stain and polish the window-panes as was done in Paris. Moreover, Mme de la Platière must be kept advised as to "scientific life," the museums, theatres, recent writings, and the Academy; she asked above all for books, demanded technical information for Roland's work, and sent flowers for him to identify. The poor fellow was, moreover, very inefficient. Frequently she gently reprimanded him: "You are an admitted braggart, a great promiser of nothings. . ."

AT FOUR years of age "that little rogue of a Eudora" yawned over every book. In spite of the lightness of her reproof, one feels that Mme Roland was scandalized. This baby wanted stories told her, but the mother, who highly disapproved of "tales of magic," tried to beguile her child with virtuous tracts and moral examples. Still infatuated with her Rousseau and concerned, as were all the intelligent women of her time, with evolving a scheme of maternal duties, she adopted "Julie's plan" and discovered to her dismay that she had gone far wide of her mark.

Eudora was not yet four when Bosc already reproached this terrifying task-mistress for demanding too much. She paid no attention to his reflections in which she saw nothing but weakness, and later she wrote him:

At five years and six weeks, Eudora reads well, is beginning to know no other plaything but the needle, enjoys making geometric figures . . . add to this . . . that she has no false ideas as far as I know on any subject.

When she was six the programme became quite terrifying!

Two things surprise us: as soon as she was up, at six in the morning, Mme Roland made her daughter read the catechism, which shows that she did not know how to dispense with that convention and direct her according to her own ideas. On the other hand, in spite of that new theory that hygiene must play a large part in education, she could not make up her mind to have her child "inoculated." At six and a half, Eudora was still not vaccinated and her mother asked Bosc "to find some good reasons which would decide her." Her taste for science was powerless before the most timorous of all emotions. If Eudora were the least indisposed, Mme Roland went to the same extremes of anxiety as any modern mother in whom maternal love has become, it is said, a neurosis.

With neither railways, automobiles, or steamboats at their disposal, these people of the eighteenth century moved about with the greatest facility.

In the summer of 1787, Roland took his wife and his daughter (then aged six), to Switzerland, where they spent a month and a half. The Prior of Longpont accompanied them. They visited all the principal cities. At Zurich they saw Pastor Lavater, about whom Mme Roland was enthusiastic. Upon her return to *Le Clos,* she wrote Bosc:

A letter from this good Lavater, kissed with an ecstacy which would seem laughable to many people, and I will keep it as other people keep the letter of some royal personage in their archives. . .

In the autumn of 1787 Canon Dominique finally decided to give up the property of *Le Clos* to the family.

Mme Roland's interest in the soil was now greatly increased. From that time on, something new was manifested in her. The country seemed to show her in her true light. The manor, the vineyard, all took on for her a hitherto unknown importance. She made plans to put them in order again and prolong her days of sojourn in the country.

She wrote Bosc:

I have been in town since Wednesday. I am leaving today or early tomorrow morning. I pine for peace and the open fields. I feel I am in my rightful place only on the back of the horse which takes me into the fields, or on the grass where I rest; it is there I have left my daughter, and it is there I shall see again my husband [Roland was then in Paris]; it is there I feel nature, that I love life, and that the study of one single flower seems finer to me than the lessons of all your masters.

Beasts and people, the lady of *Le Clos* set them all going with a spirit hitherto unknown to them, and she believed she had found her fate in the command of a working household. She put up dried pears which she knew would be delicious, and:

We are drying grapes and apples [she said], we wash, work on the linen, we have white wine at lunch and sleep on the grass to get sober; we follow the grape-pickers, rest in the woods or the fields, bring down the nuts; we have garnered all the winter fruit and it is spread out in the attics.

She depicted herself marvellously well in her letters. Sainte-Beuve observed:

M. ET MME DE LA PLATIERE WITH THEIR DAUGHTER EUDORA AT ZURICH IN THE SUMMER OF 1787

Silhouettes by G. Lavater. Original owned by Mme Marion, great-great-granddaughter of Eudora. Now in the Château de Rosière, near Bourgoin, Isère

. . . The country above all inspired her . . . her autumn letters breathe the vintage and smell of the fruit. . . We have a Sévigné of the *bourgeoisie,* and better still, a Sévigné-Georges Sand.

At the same time Mme Roland's philosophy became less bookish. In the place of Rousseau's abstractions, she substituted the realities of village life. Human sympathy brought her close to the poor she aided and the illnesses she cured. She discovered a profound truth, better known to the common people than to the *bourgeoisie,* in: "One can do good without being rich." Her generosity was an involuntary gesture. "It seems to me that my hands would always be open proffering aid if the power to administer it were always in them," she said with a simple charm that dispels any idea of affectation.

Nothing but poverty ! Sometimes one is amazed or touched by descriptions of the hard and savage life of so many remote peoples, without reflecting that our peasants, for the most part, are a hundred times more miserable than the Caribbeans, the Greenlanders, or the Hottentots. Thus death seems a release to the one who expires and to those who witness it. I have just seen it in a woman of sixty, who could have been saved had she been taken in time; but these people suffer for whole months without stopping their work; they go to bed without a word . . . never think of a doctor, or, fearing the expense of having one, call in the priest and in agony depart this life thanking God for having delivered them. Evidence, however, of an interest in their lot, surprises and touches them; they are ready to do anything suggested to them by a person they feel sure has naught else in mind but their good. It is a fine school . . . the death of the poor.

The Revolution was approaching and had already manifested itself in riots in Lyons. Mme Roland, however, interested herself not at all in public affairs. "I imagine you are as bored as I am by the gazettes," she wrote Bosc on February 10, 1787. "The difference between us is that I at times force myself to the point of speaking of them, without the least idea what I'm talking about." The truth is that she was concerned only with the change of ministers, and then only from the standpoint of whether or not the new-comers would be favourable to Roland's career. She scolded Lanthenas severely for having "taken a fancy for defending juniors" and for expounding in a pamphlet the iniquity of the rights of

primogeniture.[12] Roland, well placed to bear witness to the confusion of the administration, declaimed at times against those in
office, but did not see that something else might be preferable to
replacing them.

On the other hand the Inspection of Manufactures had been for
some time strongly attacked by free trade theoricians and by the
majority of the merchants. Roland's position was threatened with
being abolished by the very partisans of his own beliefs.

An Assembly of Notables, composed of a hundred and forty members of the clergy, the nobility, and the magistrature, had been summoned by Calonne the twenty-ninth of December 1786. Young
Mme de la Platière did not even listen to what Canon Dominique,
who was deeply engrossed in this new development, had to say of
it, but answered him "merely by haphazard yes's." On the eve of
the Revolution, it was the elder brother who, of the whole family,
showed the greatest interest in the march of public affairs.

Tell Lanthenas [Mme Roland wrote Bosc] that as long as he wants
to put himself on good terms with my brother-in-law, he should insert
political news into his letters.

In 1788 one sentence in a letter to Bosc is for us the first symptom
of Mme Roland's awakening to the impassioned movement which
was soon to claim and master her. Following a month's illness
she wrote:

It is two weeks now since I have left the corner of my hearth and
since I have renewed my acquaintance with emetics, drugs, and other
pleasant things from the chemist's. But how can one speak of one's
private miseries when there are so many public ones ?

In Paris, Parliament had dared to hold out against Loménie de
Brienne. Arrests had taken place. "Large bailiwicks" were spoken
of, the dispossession of Parliament, etc. Mme Roland was soon to
complain of the newspaper censorship, of the "falsified reports."
Here is something new. "And then," said she, "who is this M.
Carra who has just published two pamphlets, *M. de Calonne, the
Complete Man,* and *A Little Message to M. de Calonne* ?"
But only in relation to her family interests did the mind of the
Inspector of Manufactures' wife fix its attention upon the acts of

the Ministry, and even in the matter of the great "bailiwick of Lyons" she merely wrote Bosc:

It is only we plebeians into whose pocket anybody can put his hand, and no-one will say "Mind !" to him, who won't approve this business of registering and this formation of a plenary court sold to the King.

Suddenly the news came that Loménie de Brienne had declared the nation bankrupt, and that Necker had been recalled. Roland wrote to Bosc in a very urgent tone, asking him for news. Mme Roland was particularly disturbed because "the man [was] vindictive" and Roland had put audacious "notes" in his *Dictionnaire des Manufactures*. Not long before this, she was saying to Bosc: "Why then do you no longer write to us, you who have no vintages to keep you busy ? Is there really any other occupation than that ?" Now the general disturbances were beginning to affect her. "You say nothing to us, my dear, even though the Parliaments are acting and showing themselves up in a very astonishing manner. . ."

The letter is dated the eighth of October 1788. On the fourth they had held country festivities at *Le Clos* to celebrate at the same time the close of the vintage and the birthday of Eudora, who was entering her eighth year. "Our Colettes and Lucases [danced] their gay rigadoons [while] drinking our wine with a right good will," wrote the lady of *Le Clos*.

She wanted to know, however, at what point were the *Notables* who were working to give a form to the future Assembly of the States General, and, before going to spend a month in Lyons, if she still asked Bosc for information on all the varieties of turnip and radish, still she had subscribed to *La Comédie,* which had suddenly taken up the opposition.

From that time the *bourgeoisie* took its stand against the nobility. The nobility spoke arrogantly of the "Tiers-État," and the "Tiers-État" was quite ready to scoff at the nobility. Minds were in a state of ferment. The temperature of the nation was rising. Mme Roland's destiny was about to be fulfilled.

PART THREE

THE TRAGEDY OF THE MUSE

Plutarch had prepared me to become a
Republican . . .—*Memoirs*.

FOR SOME time past Lanthenas' letters had frequently made mention
of relations he had established with America through the intermediary of Brissot de Warville, a Republican doctrinaire whom he
valued highly.

Warville, like the Rolands, had been drawn to England by his
interest in the Constitution, and near the close of the year 1788, he
visited America to investigate the Land of the Free. He came
back a disciple of Franklin and an admirer of Washington. Taking up his pen, he set himself the task of seeking in the events
of the English and the American Revolutions, ideas likely to rouse
the feeling of his own countrymen in the cause of liberty. The
Academy of Chalons-sur-Marne, following the lead of the Academies at Lyons and Dijon, honoured his writings. But M. de
Miromesnil and M. de Vergennes cut short the activity of the small
provincial groups who, in the eyes of these gentlemen, kept the
public mind in a dangerous state of ferment.

A defender of the oppressed, Warville soon founded in Paris the
society of *Les Amis des Noirs*. In his memoirs he says that this
society and the society of the *Adeptes du Magnetisme,* founded
by Bergasse, were responsible for the great majority of writings
published in 1787 and 1788 against the Ministry. His ideas were
shared by Lavoisier, Sieyès, Grégoire, La Fayette, Condorcet, Bergasse, Pétion, Carra, Valady, etc., besides Pahin de la Blancherie
(one of the little Phlipon girl's first suitors), who had published
a paper entitled *Reflections on the Arts and Sciences.*

M. and Mme de la Platière read M. de Warville's works with
the greatest admiration. On the twentieth of March 1789, Roland
wrote him: "Sir, I have been your faithful follower on your American journey," and further on we note these predictions: "To my
mind there is a revolution under way, but what I see is the domination of intrigue, the tyranny of factions, and, presently, death
for everyone." Following her custom, Mme Roland added a personal *post scriptum*: "I join my good wishes, Sir, to my husband's,
and our feelings are so similar that, etc. . ."

Lanthenas,[1] like the rest of Paris, was then very much fascinated
by a book entitled *Letters of an American Farmer,* in which Saint-
John de Crèvecœur, inspired by the society Granville Sharpe and
Clarkson had established in England, described life in America as
similar to that of the shepherds of Arcady.

M. and Mme de la Platière naturally admired this book, but their
enthusiasm met with nothing but hostility in those around them.

For some time there had been discord in the paternal home.
Roland, "who had a passion for independence," could not agree
with his elder brother who was full of "the prejudices of domination." It must not be forgotten that Roland had long professed
advanced views, that he had weaned his wife from her religious
faith, and that, because of the liberal principles expounded in them,
his *Lettres d'Italie* had met with the disfavour of the Superintendents of Finance. Let us hearken to him in his *Voyage en
France*: "I, and others, have strongly inveighed against the monks
whose possessions spread over immense tracts of land, but are there
not others even worse ? They at any rate spend their wealth where
they live, while the fortunes of the others are consumed in the
capital." (Here already we have a foretaste of that hostility to
Paris which was to prove so fatal to the Girondists.) On the road
to Beauvais, he remarked: "Always great castles, great parks, a
large quantity of game, and hardly any human beings. This country, considered beautiful by Parisians, seems to me extremely
mournful, for I am as shocked by the opulence as I am by the
misery that invariably accompanies it."

"My brother-in-law is more bigoted, despotic, fanatical and stubborn than any priest you have ever listened to," wrote Mme Roland. "Moreover, I am convinced that his contempt for our principles will cause him to do us all the harm he can." In truth, the Canon was exceedingly hostile to those ideas which were irremediably cutting off his brother and sister-in-law from Beaujolais society. Things came to such a pass that M. and Mme de la Platière had to leave Villefranche and retire to their little apartment in Lyons, Quai Monsieur, Maison Chamburcy, where the lack of space necessitated boarding out little Eudora in the home of a Protestant pastor who had been recommended by Rabaut Saint-Etienne.[2]

Something even more important than the *Dictionnaire des Manufactures*[3] diverted Mme Roland from the education of her little girl. Only quite recently, however, for Mme Roland was slow to be moved by the impulse of the women of her time. Not immediately did she become one of those who, in Michelet's words, took "the fatherland for their bosom friend, and right eternal for their lover."

But now a common interest was in every heart. The convocation of the States General had aroused boundless hopes. In the provinces, the members of the Third Estate assembled, deliberated, prepared themselves with respect and gravity for their new mission. The *bourgeois* was about to come to the fore.

In the past, the *bourgeois* had been a timid soul, wanting both in instruction and in character. A humourist of the period said rather wittily that: "In the scale of human beings, the *bourgeois* should be placed between the man and the mule. He marks the middle place between these two species. He is the link between the two. Frequently he possesses the latter's upright bearing, sometimes he tries his hand at thinking like the latter, and this not always successfully."

The *bourgeoisie* was terrified by the revolution it had created. The Legislative Assembly and the Convention were, for the most part, composed of *bourgeois*.

Meanwhile, the press, though rigorously censored, was responsible for the infiltration of myriads of pamphlets inspired by a burning criticism of social conditions. The insolent acts of the Court —

they were later to be called mistakes — at the meeting of the States General, had a violent repercussion on the heated public mind. The costume that the Third Estate was compelled to wear in the presence of the gilded nobility, the contemptuous reception, the long wait in the rain before a barred gate, the threatening tone of the King when he commanded that "the deliberations of the Three Orders should take place in separate rooms," the thundering voice of Mirabeau, the haughty reply of President Bailly, all these things excited Mme Roland to the pitch of frenzy. From one end of the land to the other blazed a sacred fire, but these rages of altruism, this fury of proselytism, still contained as many tortured fancies as it did well-defined ideas. Awaiting she knew not what, Mme de la Platière worked harder than ever with her husband. He had sent to the Emulation Society of Bourg-en-Bresse a treatise entitled: *Summary of the Causes likely to make a Language Universal, and Some Observations on those Languages having the greatest tendencies towards Universality,*[4] the idea of which had doubtless been inspired by Rivarol's famous discourse on the *Universality of the French Language* (1784). His wife had aided him with this work.

At this time she was particularly interested in foreign languages. She frequently quoted Ariosto and Tasso, Milton and Thompson, whom she read in the original. She showed a marked preference for the English language. Of Shakespeare, so badly understood in France even today, she wrote: "Shakespeare . . . knew no other law . . . had no other teacher than nature and his genius." Elsewhere she said: "The English are the novelists of Europe." Although we have since had the Russians, her words still ring true.

ROLAND was dangerously ill that spring, and, nursing him, his indefatigable wife suffered the greatest agonies. Her letters to her friends were reduced to mere cries of despair:

He has inflammation of the lungs and a putrid bilious fever. I am in constant fear of losing what I hold dearest in the world, and with smiling lips and a heart sick with anguish I encourage him with hopeful words in which I no longer believe. Pity me, weep for me, for my grief will soon know no bounds.

"What I hold dearest in the world . . ." when a woman employs such terms concerning someone other than her child, it means that love has won the first place in her heart. But where is the woman who would neglect a charming little girl for the purpose of burdening herself with a person who had only a "severe bondage" to offer her? Though she did not suspect it, there was something in Mme Roland that was stronger than her maternal love, and this was not her wifely affection but her vocation. Roland was the instrument with which she was to fulfill her destiny. He must not die. All her passion was concentrated on the task of saving him. A nature such as hers would always find sufficient strength to weather a crisis. She said:

I did not sleep or take off my clothes for ten days. For six months I endured the anxieties and agitations of a precarious convalescence without suffering the least indisposition. Thus it is that the heart gives us strength and doubles our capacity for action.

Suddenly the most incredible news flew from Paris to the provinces. Almost at the same moment the Rolands learned of the dismissal of Necker, the taking of the Bastille, and the King's capitulation; La Fayette, the hero from America, had been placed in command of a national militia; Louis XVI took the red, white, and blue cockade from the hands of the Mayor of Paris, the Queen and the Court were plotting against the nation . . . and then silence. Letters failed to arrive, the post no longer functioned.

As soon as news came through again (in the last days of July 1789), Mme Roland vigorously criticized the behavior of her friends which she considered weak and childish. Her letter to Bosc amazes us by its violent tone and by the use of certain terms which were never again to appear in her vocabulary:

You are nothing but children. Your enthusiasm is but a short-lived blaze, and unless the National Assembly gives those two illustrious persons a regular trial or some generous Decius cuts off their heads, you are all. . .

M. Perroud, surely an impartial commentator, if there be such a one, has been struck by the incongruity of this one letter in an immense correspondence.

We must remember, however, that at this time the success of the Revolution was perpetually jeopardized by plots. Even in the Lyonnals, a municipality had asked Louis XVI to prosecute the betrayers of the divine right of kings. "Let them be tried by the Assembly . . . let a terrible punishment safeguard the people forever from the most heinous crime man can commit. . ." At the same time a sort of peasant warfare had broken out in the provinces. It was said that the crops were in flames, that murders were being committed. . . What was to become of *Le Clos* ? And, moreover, Mme Roland, worn by the fatigues and anxieties of her husband's illness, may have lost a measure of her habitual poise. Besides, who knows whether to "ask for heads" in '89 was as serious a matter as in '93 ? In any case, this letter is such a rare exception that the political enemies who seized upon it with such savage glee, have never found another of its kind to quote.

The following day Mme Roland wrote Bosc:

I am writing you no more about our personal affairs. Who today is the traitor who has any affairs except the nation's ?

And she ended another letter thus:

Farewell, let us be citizens. Let the people be happy and our private troubles will come to naught.

A rumour of panic, and Mme Roland made up her mind. She went to defend *Le Clos,* riding five hours on horseback, alone, through the countryside. To her disappointment there was no disturbance for her to face. This "great fear" which, in the beginning of the Revolution had swept the villages like a typhoon, was, for the most part, the hysteria of over-excited minds.

At this time, Roland was asking news of Bosc and Lanthenas who had spontaneously thrown in their lot with the revolutionary movement. He seemed to be modifying his dislike for Necker; "the abominable Necker," he had formerly said of him, "that smirking, bloated man, always threatening us with the horrors of bankruptcy." But were they not going to bring the Queen and the King's brothers to trial ?

The fourth of August gave the Rolands the opportunity of mak-

ing a notable sacrifice to the Revolution. Deputy Maury, a cob-
bler's son, had been the only one in the Assembly to protest against
the abolishing of titles and privileges. M. and Mme de la Platière
did not hesitate when the fatherland was at stake; henceforth they
were to be known as M. and Mme Roland. M. de Warville, as
well, became M. Brissot, and M. d'Antic, M. Bosc. The revolutionary opinions of the couple were in perfect accord. From then
on Mme Roland showed a resolution and vehemence which never
weakened.

> The French are easily won over by the fine appearances of their mas-
> ters [she said]. I am convinced half the Assembly has been stupid
> enough to be moved by the spectacle of Antoinette asking them to take
> care of her son. Zounds, as though a child were at the bottom of this
> question ! The salvation of twenty million men is at stake !

At this time two deaths in the family touched the Rolands very
closely. At the end of September, Canon Bimont, the "dear Vincennes uncle" passed away. There were no more rural dances at
Le Clos to celebrate the vintage: the Prieur de Longpont, tortured
by gallstone, had but two months to live.[5] At any other time,
Mme Roland's letters to her friends would have been full of grief.
But now she considered it high treason to dwell on her private
sorrows. She had said this, and she kept her word. One of her
noblest traits was that she conscientiously lived up to her principles.
She expressed herself always with the boldest independence and the
most complete altruism. She had once and for all made up her
mind to allow no personal consideration to distract her from the
way she had chosen to follow in the pursuit of justice.

ROLAND was very anxious to take part in the reorganization of his
department. He drew up memoranda after memoranda and asked
his Parisian friends to distribute them and recommend them, that
was "if they found them good." In March 1790, he was elected
member of the General Council of the Commune in the capacity
of "notable." One of his first reforms was the abolition of the
Lyons customs, and the aristocracy who wished to ruin him tried
to hold him responsible for the riots which broke out after the passing of this measure. Public rumour charged him with a thousand

atrocities, and at Villefranche his servant was stopped by passers-by and "asked whether they were not afraid of being seized." The old wives said that Mme Roland had visited all the hovels in Lyons and bribed the poor to revolt. Still they lived in such retirement and were so little known that a great many people took Roland for an abbé, "either because of his attire or his discreet appearance." Mme Roland prevented her husband from going to Lyons, for "if it be glorious to give one's life for one's country, there is no reason to risk being killed in a brawl." But she wanted to "see things at close quarters," and as "it was not yet the custom to tell idle tales to women," it was she who went after news.

The city was in a state of great ebullition. The theatre increased the agitation by expounding public events. In the *Courrier de Lyon* of the second of June 1790, we read that at the previous evening's performance "three ladies wearing baldrics in the colours of the nation" had been observed in the audience, "and that the public had shown by their cheers how much they appreciated this adornment." Wednesday, July 14, 1790, the first anniversary of the taking of the Bastille, was in Lyons as well as Paris the occasion for great patriotic celebrations. During the morning, on the Place Bellecour, four priests performed Mass at the same time on a four-faced altar in the presence of an immense crowd.

The counter-revolutionary manifestations were more rowdy than the others. One went to them as to a battle. After a free performance of William Tell, a very dull five-act play in verse which caused "the spirit of Liberty to flame in every heart," the *Courrier de Lyon,* filled with enthusiasm at the sight of an audience composed entirely of the people, declared that this had been "one of the most brilliant evenings since the theatre had been erected. . . There were no lavish frills, no farded elegance. This time the first boxes offered the smiling picture of natural simplicity."

Through Lanthenas, the Rolands had entered into correspondence with Camille Desmoulins and sent him an article on the occurrences at Lyons, which he subsequently published in his paper, *Le Courrier de Brabant*. But this was not their only connection with the Paris press.

In his book *De la France et des Etats-Unis,* etc., Brissot (ex--Warville) had more than once quoted and praised some of the passages from the *Dictionnaire des Manufactures* and the *Lettres d'Italie*: "Sound reasoning, a courageous patriotism, and a trained mind characterize these writings," he had said. "He [Roland] sees the causes of ill and, what is rarer, has the courage to make them public."

Bosc, having received from Mme Roland a letter of interest to those concerned with the public welfare, showed it one day to Lanthenas, and Lanthenas took it to Brissot who printed selections from it in *Le Patriote Français.*[6]

This soon became an accepted thing. Mme Roland, although she insisted that her name not appear, set herself the task of composing letters in the form of articles and addressed herself more to the public than to any one person. At the same time, she began a sustained correspondence with Brissot who, astounded by her serious tone, her well-digested views, and her admiration for heroism inspired by classical literature, introduced her letters to the readers of *Le Patriote Français* saying: "We have received from a true Roman," etc.

In the retirement of *Le Clos,* or in her little room in Lyons, Mme Roland earnestly meditated in unconscious preparation for the struggle that was to come. Like Joan, she heard voices. But over three centuries had passed and now it was no longer an archangel, no longer saints who spoke or took shape before her. Plutarch's heroes and the ideas of the philosophers had replaced these symbols and their splendour was no less dazzling. Mme Roland's ideas and emotions were inseparable. She was concerned with restoring to man the consciousness of his own dignity, enabling him to develop for his own good, and hence for the good of all humanity, the gifts which nature had bestowed on him and which an unjust social system had repressed. She was concerned with giving man a concrete meaning for the word "fraternity," for the word "equality," and for the finest of them all, that word that cannot be uttered without a heart-felt thrill, that sublime word, that sacred word — Liberty ! The idea of the fatherland was to follow.

Mme Roland believed she had done a daring thing in not fearing
to write Bosc: "Discard natural history and every other science
save that of becoming a man and propagating a public spirit." She
"thundered" against certain deputies, among them La Revallière-
Lépeaux, Creuzé-Latouche, and Leclerc "who still go to the *Jardin
des Plantes!* A fine time for that! The hour had struck, not for
botany, but for the nation.

In order that the great work be victorious, this zealous patriot
would have preferred the security of a well-considered method to
the perilous risk of improvisations and the spontaneous acts of individuals. Let us take a very remarkable passage from one of her
letters to Brissot (1790).

*"The Revolution, imperfect as it may be, has altered the face
of France. It has given her a character, and we had none before."*
And elsewhere: *"Since the French have acquired a fatherland . . .
it should, for all those worthy of such a blessing, create a powerful new bond that brings them closer together."* She was later to
make this admirable definition, and to the King himself.[7]

Fatherland is no longer a mere word to be embellished by the
imagination: it is a being to whom we have made sacrifices, to whom,
because of the very anxieties it causes, we grow more attached day by
day; a being we have created by dint of great effort, who rises clear
of a host of disturbances, and whom we love as much for the sacrifices
it costs us as for the hopes it inspires.

Since the time of Joan of Arc, a nation had existed only in terms
of power. During the religious wars, the concept of a nation had
been like a stream flowing in the heart of the earth. With the
exception of Henri IV (who had some idea of a fatherland in his:
"Paris is well-worth a Mass"), the kings had looked upon the country as though it were a fief granted by God. These unenlightened,
barely intelligent kings were, in a certain way, nothing more than
spoiled over-grown children who were taken as models of behaviour by followers who certainly had no reason to broaden or
uplift their minds. The Court was the fatherland of courtiers, and
privileges were their rights. Who had ever told them otherwise?
When the Court moved to Saint-Germain or to Fontainebleau,

they were quite as happy there as they were in Versailles. Why not transplant the Court across the Rhine? A greater distance to go, that was all, and the times were so troubled that there would be annoyances to put up with on the way. But once there the lords would gather around the prince again, and only the aspect of the scenery would be changed. There were even relatives to be found in that country. Through his German-Saxon mother the King belonged to it, and there the Queen would find the language of her youth. The Emigrants had the excuse of not being fully aware of the odiousness of their behaviour. The idea that they were traitors would never have occurred to them unless they had indulged their minds in thought, and such was not their custom. It would have required a Danton to explain to them that one's fatherland is not merely the soil beneath one's feet.

Mme Roland said:

I recall with emotion those moments of my youth when, in silence and retirement, I revelled in the study of ancient history and wept for vexation that I had not been born a Spartan or a Roman.

She had not altered, she had matured. With scrupulous care she imparted to her friends those acts and thoughts which might serve liberty's cause, and still retained her modest rôle of the respectful and submissive wife. She did not seek to put herself in her husband's place, but brought him invariably to the fore, serving his interests with the most excessive devotion, eulogizing him at every opportunity, praising at all times his "severity," his "austere virtue," and his "violence in combating abuses." But her natural strength of character made her greater than the rôle she had spontaneously accepted as her own. Penned as they were, in the remoteness of her province, with but mediocre means of keeping informed, her direct and penetrating views astound us when we take them from her letters and compare them to historical facts. She foresaw events and judged events with an astonishing shrewdness.

This is what she had to say of Mirabeau:

This Mirabeau is a genius whom I admire and fear. In two instances he supported such bad principles for such bad reasons that since that time he inspires me with mistrust: look at his opinion on the *veto* in particular.

Seven months later Mirabeau was negotiating with the Court.

She was also uncertain of Lafayette, whom she "would like to be able to esteem"; but his absolute *veto* occasioned her strong doubts and she could not reconcile "the General's opinion on the freedom of the press with the proclamation against it."

On this subject may be read her entire letter to Bosc, written on the sixth or seventh of October 1789.

All sorrow ceases, all pain is postponed, all private affairs fade into insignificance.

Despotism has been unmasked; the nation is under way. Let all good people rally and let their union strike terror to the hearts of sinners!

Courage and arms: these we already glimpse, but they are not enough. We must have a regulated administration, sure methods, prudent progress, and an enlightened vigilance.

The first thing to do is to seize all the Paris banks, form a public bank and name capable citizens for its administration, thus serving the double purpose of removing all money from the Court and providing for the needs of the people.

The second important act is to establish a committee for supplies.

The third, to establish connections with the provinces so as to be assured of provisions and aid of every kind.

In all probability the Court will remain seemingly quiet until it is reinforced by foreign troops; watch must therefore be kept to prevent their entering the kingdom.

Flanders would seem the first province through which they would try to bring them; therefore it is indispensable that attention, means, and confederation be brought to bear on this side, but without neglecting any other frontier.

All mail, all dispatches from the Court to its various subordinates in the capital, should be stopped and submitted to inspection by a committee formed for that purpose.

In the details of the measures to take for assuring provisions, it would be advantageous to permit comestibles to enter Paris tax-free and give the butchers the right to dispense with the Sceaux and Poissy markets and bring their livestock direct.

After a methodical confederation has been established with the provinces, it would be pressing to resolve that each province recall her own children, officers, and soldiers, under penalty of public disgrace and disinheritance, so that each would thus be in a position to form a body of troops for its own defence and so direct events in favour of the common good.

These solid foundations once laid, a plan would needs be drawn up to reach Versailles, on one side from Paris, and on the other with aid from the provinces, and remove the deputies and transfer them to Paris under the protection of the nation for the Constitution of which they would then labour without remission. I say "remove" them; for 'tis a part of judicious conduct, as of the Roman Senators of olden days, to remain in the place assigned them and where they are united; but it is the duty of the nation to watch over their safety, to shield them, and protect them.

This great undertaking demands extreme care: there will be royal troops to face and Paris to hold; therefore a provincial army is needed to march from one or several sides upon Versailles, while a portion of the Parisian troops goes out from their side and an adequate number keeps guard in the capital.

Above all, we must watch our supplies.

The Court's plan is surely to leave it to time to undermine forces and resources, to effect a state of exhaustion and then profit by it by wiping everything out. Once the public bank is established (and for that there is not a moment to be lost), it must be posted up that not only grains will enter free, to be paid for in cash by this bank, but that a premium of encouragement will be awarded.

Currency must be facilitated in every way, the bank well regulated and so conducted as to serve as an example and model to all the provinces.

Up till now, no outstanding leader has come to the fore: this may be a blessing, but we need an administration, councils, committees of the divers parties, and all this under the jurisdiction of the supreme Court of Electors. We need a rational plan, quick foresight, great activity, indissoluble union and tireless wisdom.

Let France awake and live ! Let man resume his rights and Justice begin her reign, and from one end of the kingdom to the other let the universal cry be heard: Long live the people and death to tyrants !

Those who can do naught but think should disperse their ideas far and wide: see that a copy of this letter goes to the Committee of Electors.

P. S. If the theatres in the capital continue to play, as they presumably will, vigilance of the citizens should be brought to bear on them; they should be allowed to present only plays fitted to nourish sentiments compatible with present conditions: some of the great Corneille, but not *Cinna;* Voltaire's *Brutus,* his *Catiline,* his *Death of Cæsar, etc.* Little things pave the way for great ones and nothing should be neglected in the regeneration of an entire people. These cares should also be extended to the small theatres and whatever supports or inspires softness, bad habits, and slavishness must be suppressed.

Mme Roland wished to place the deputies in Paris "under the protection of the nation." She wrote that on the very day the people were transporting the Assembly. A little later she conceived the idea of a camp outside Paris, a plan which the Minister of War, Servan, put into effect in June 1792. Her project of a provincial militia was already "Federalism." On the seventh of June 1790, at the very moment the Assembly was discussing the Civil Constitution of the Clergy (which was not voted until the twelfth), Mme Roland, in absolute ignorance of the Assembly's activities, wrote:

I am out of patience with the rubbish of this old hierarchy, archbishops, primates, bishops, etc. Nothing but hypercritics, meddlesome theologians, ambitious, sectarian, intolerant, blood-thirsty abettors of stupidities and corruption !

As early as 1789, she who was to work so much for the propagation of liberal ideas, was already insisting that patriotic printing presses be installed for the purpose of instructing the people and "diffusing light." Roland, for his part, wrote Bancal: "We preach patriotism, we elevate the mind." Which was to say that in their long walks he never ceased preaching new doctrines to the peasants. All along the way he talked of liberty to anyone he met.

Our legislators [wrote Michelet in a particularly fine page] looked upon education as a complement to the Laws and put off the question until the end of the Revolution; it was precisely the one by which they should have begun. The political symbol, the Declaration of Rights, once having been presented, the Laws now demanded living men as their base; men must be brought into being, a new spirit constituted by every available means: popular assemblies, newspapers, schools, plays, festivals, the Revolution augmented in their hearts, and all the people made the living subject to the Law, so that the Law would not come in advance of popular thought, not come as a stranger, unknown and uncomprehended, but would find the house in readiness, the fire burning on the hearth, and the eager hospitality of welcoming hearts.

Such was Mme Roland's belief as well. She considered the instruction [8] of the people of prime importance, on a par with the freedom of the press, and she never ceased working for the propagation of revolutionary ideas. As for the freedom of the press, she wanted it to be "unlimited." She had already said so and she

repeated it in a letter written the twenty-third of August 1790.
The law was not passed until the sixteenth or seventeenth of April
1796.

Hardly had Mme Roland spoken of counter-revolution, than it
broke out in numerous parts of the country. While so many
others were deluding themselves with optimism, she was writing:
"This country is lost." And she added: "My heart bleeds for all
that I foresee." On the fourth of August 1790, her agitation was
a true foreboding of the Terror: "I saw the terrifying red flag
hanging on the Town Hall (at Lyons). . . My heart shrank at the
sight. I grieved over the abused people."

THROUGH Bosc, through his neighbour, Creuzé-Latouche, and
through Lanthenas, the Rolands had entered into correspondence
with Henri Bancal des Issarts, of whom we have already made
mention once or twice. An Auvergnat, and a notary in Paris, he
was the son of a manufacturer of silk hosiery established in Lan-
guedoc.

After a short time of practising his profession, this notary discovered that his briefs no longer interested him. He rid himself
of his notary's office in exchange for a certain sum, and connected
himself with Brissot's advanced group, probably aiding with his
deniers to found the *Patriote Français,* and began himself to write
revolutionary articles.

Henri Bancal's passion for botany was equal to his distaste for
slavery and, although he was one of the first members of the
society of the *Amis des Noirs,* he missed not one of the philosophical outings which Bosc conducted on Sundays in search of
plant specimens in the Montmorency woods. It was in this way
that Bancal des Issarts chanced to become the proprietor of a modest
refuge that they had happened on in the most secluded part of the
woods.[9] It was the priory of Sainte-Radegonde, a small church
property, at that time almost completely abandoned and in the eyes
of Bosc (and his group of strollers), a sanctuary of such charm that
he persuaded Bancal to buy it.

But in this group of fervent disciples of J.-J. Rousseau, Bancal des Issarts' fortune had inspired a plan of a newer and even more original character. It was to buy in common, for the purposes of cultivation, one of the vast ecclesiastical estates that were to be sold for the benefit of the nation, and there to found a *Société agricole ou d'amis,* whose plan (*Plan of a Society for promoting the emigration*) had been drawn up by Brissot following the American principles of Saint-John de Crèvecœur,[19] and which had as its aim the regeneration of man through the benefits of a rural education.

The Rolands were eager to support this plan and Lanthenas, clearly recognizing a future Arcadian shepherd in the ungowned notary, persuaded Mme Roland to write to him. Bancal's fortune, said Lanthenas, could best be employed in purchasing the greater part of the coveted "national property."

Bancal had returned to Clermont-Ferrand to present himself at the elections and see the cause triumph in his candidacy. Mme Roland, all the more interested in the future delegate from Auvergne because he had been in Paris the editor of the *Patriote Français,* invited him to stop at *Le Clos* when, as was his intention, he passed through the provinces preaching to the inhabitants the truths of revolutionary gospel.

The moment he arrived, Mme Roland recognized him as one of those twin souls with whom the interchange of thought was made delightful, and from the very outset a fine and sensitive relationship was begun in the name of Republican principles. They played at battle-dore and shuttle-cock before the house. They took rambling walks across the country, and Roland was not jealous. In warming to the cause of public weal, they encroached upon forbidden ground, but the young woman never doubted her ability to control with ease the perils and surprises she encountered there. Bancal was from the first filled with enthusiasm for the vital and tender mind that burned with the fire of sentiment and yet was cooled by the strength of reason. From the moment he set eye upon her, Mme Roland had exercised a curious supremacy over him and as he took his seat in the saddle when the time for parting came, he wept like a child.

"Send me a copy of the Declaration of Rights," she said with tear-drenched eyes.

And a lively correspondence straightway began. They had much to say to each other, for their attachment was founded on the perfect concurrence of their political beliefs. A perfidious agitation, however, had penetrated to the very heart of this "rustic lady." That this new friend had succumbed to her from the first was nothing unusual. This was the case with them all. But no other had ever disturbed her tranquillity nor caused her to abandon her open ways.

Virtuous woman that she was [wrote Michelet], her strength was never sapped by inactivity, that idle musing in which women droop and fade. She was hard-working and active in the highest degree. To her, occupation was the guardian of virtue, a sacred idea. From the first breath to the last, duty hovered over that beautiful life. She herself bore witness to this: "No-one," she said, "less than I has known voluptuousness."

An initial letter to Bancal, prompted by an undeviating but trembling heart, bespoke, for all its air of honesty, a timorous emotion, unspeakably touching in this woman who was perhaps the most courageous who ever lived. It lies before us, penned in that perfectly lined and formed calm hand which Mme Roland preserved even in the darkest days, and to the very end. This letter moved Michelet to admirable commentaries, and he wrote that "one could only read it kneeling down." [11]

October 8, 1790, *Le Clos*
. . . My mind teems with a thousand thoughts which I would doubtless find easier to express were they accompanied by less tumultuous emotions. Why are my eyes thus dimmed with tears that fall unceasingly and yet are left full to overflowing?

My principles are unshaken, my heart is pure, and yet I am not at peace!

It will be the greatest delight of our lives and we will be of service to our fellowmen, this is what you have said of the affection that binds us, and this consoling thought has not yet brought me peace! . . . The thing is, I am not assured that you are happy and I shall never forgive myself for having caused you grief. And, too, that I thought I saw you attaching your happiness, or at least a portion of it, to means I consider false and to a hope I must forbid you to entertain. Ah, doubtless the affection which draws us together and unites two frank sensi-

tive minds that partake of the same tastes and are equally enthusiastic
for the public good, must cast a charm upon their life and set a new
value on it; doubtless the virtues such an affection nourishes must contribute to society as well as to the glory of those in whom they dwell;
these are the foundations of my faith and the rock on which I firmly
stand in even the wildest moments of the storm.

But who can foresee what effects violent or too often repeated emotions may produce ? And are they not to be dreaded when they produce no more than this languor which succeeds them and which mo-
mentarily alters the moral being and leaves it far inadequate to the
situation. But I am wrong; you have never had to face this unworthy
alternative. You may at times be sad, but you could never be weak,
and it is only weakness which brings one to despondency or to grievous
excesses. The impetuousness natural to your sex, the activities of a
keen imagination, produce slight blunders only, like those of a fleeting
dream, as long as the heart be nourished by a profound sentiment that
purifies vain illusion in its sacred fire. The thought of your strength
restores all mine; heavenly joys would be mine could I but imagine
that I had not disturbed your happiness and even in some way augmented it. . . How this sweet hope brightens my life ! It is this kind
ray of light which would make the earth smile and restore the sky's
serenity. Tell me, or rather, instruct me still as to your progress, your
plans, what you may know of the public weal, and what you propose
to do for it. . . Alas ! You will soon be far away. . . But you are
going to the centre, where the fatherland is now summoning those
who can serve her well, for she has need of mustering her forces; thus
if the distance between our dwelling-places is increased, at least com-
munication will be quite as rapid.

Why is it that this page I write cannot be sent to you without subter-
fuge ? Why should not every eye see what we would dare show God
himself ?

To be sure I can call heaven as witness to my wishes and my plans;
I find solace in the thought that heaven sees me, hears, and judges me;
what are they worth, these social contradictions, these human prejudices, through the midst of which it is so difficult to guide one's heart,
if courage of sacrifice and constancy of character be not united with
purity of intention and a scorn for empty formulæ so that the line of
duty be maintained ?

When shall we see each other again ? A question I ask myself often
and dare not answer. But why seek to penetrate the future when Nature's wish was that it remain hidden from us ? Let us leave it undisturbed behind the impressive veil that conceals it, since it has not been
given us to see beyond; we have but one way of influencing it, no doubt
a great one, and that is to store up for its happiness by wise employ-
ment of the present. . . Thus the dearest friends can endure separation
because of the pleasure they derive from consecrating the moments of it
to virtues each has inspired in the other. What duty would not this

sweet obligation render a delight! How can we complain, how bemoan our lot in life, as long as we have hearts to appreciate this compensation, and should I have alarms and fears for you who are so well aware of it? No, they would but do you harm; forgive me those that have already shaken me, forgive that tender anxiety that approaches too close to weakness in a sex whose courage even at times lacks the emphasis of strength.

. . . I say naught to you of affairs, that is a chapter I reserve for public correspondence; our two friends are in the big city and I am deep in the bustle of vintage-time. The fine days we passed here were not succeeded by others like them; the very evening of your departure the weather changed, and, by an eccentricity very rare at this season, twenty-four hours have not passed in the entire week without thunder being heard.

It has just rumbled again. I rather like the tinge it gives our fields; a noble and sombre one; but even were it terrifying it would not frighten me. The wonders of nature which make most people blench, and present an imposing aspect even to the eye of a philosopher, are to the sensitive being who is preoccupied with larger interests, only incidental scenes inferior to those enacted in the theatre of his heart.

Farewell, my friend; it is almost a cruelty to talk to you when you cannot answer. But if there be any severity in employing this questionable advantage, you will forgive me for it.

Roland, too, wrote often to the one he called "our dear friend," but the young wife noticed that her services were required less and less to pen a letter to Clermont-Ferrand. Were Roland's suspicions aroused? There is nothing to prove it — he was, moreover, too sure of himself not to be sure of the woman who had the great good fortune to belong to him. Their entire joint life, at least until the end of 1792, passed thus without Roland giving evidence of the least sign of sentimental worry.

After her emotional outburst in the letter of October 8, 1790, Mme Roland seemed to have rapidly regained her poise. Her letter of the twenty-sixth: "It is a treat to write to you, good friend," was lively, gay, full of the harvest and vintage-time. At the end of the month she wrote:

". . . I understood what you meant to answer me; I understood everything." If she were guilty of a sub rosa correspondence (and, if true, this was the one instance of duplicity in her entire life as a married woman) Bancal's letters at least were always joint ones to the husband and wife. "It is impossible, my friend, that we should ever misunderstand each other; imagination wanders, reason errs, and even philosophy is at times misled or misleading, but an upright heart always leads back to the truth, this is its inevitable tendency. . ."

For her, the danger was past. But such was not the case with Bancal. He was a restless dreamer, at the same time positive and complex. Racked by a torment that gave him no peace, he left for England and Mme Roland wrote to him shortly after:

At last you have attained your ambition: you are observing an interesting people; you are broadening your mind and you are not forgetting your friends. I predict you will become learned if this continues.

She asked that he keep her informed of current opinion and send her books, particularly Burke's *Reflections on the French Revolution* which was then doing us so much harm in the British Isles.

No other ambiguities are to be found in the correspondence which followed. But one feels it was the dearest and most important of all to this woman who was the perfect friend. Bancal was not more tender hearted than Bosc, but he was less of a dreamer, and he was more intelligent and a better worker than Lanthenas. Even in the gravest times, not only did Mme Roland not forget that her letters were impatiently awaited in London, but she herself felt the need of sharing with Bancal the news of the events that occurred and her own thoughts on them. With what heartfelt understanding did she console him upon the death of his beloved father! Lanthenas took up the pen and continued her letter for a bit: "Mme Roland having been called away," he said, and when she returned it was to urge Bancal to make up his mind to leave foreign shores and come and recuperate in her home at the hearth of friendship. "You are educating yourself for your country, you speak of returning in the spring. That will probably be a stormy period. . . It is not yet a question of dying for liberty: there is more than that to do." Finally Bosc, who was charged with sending the letter to Bancal, added vigorous words concerning the efforts of his political group.

This letter, written in three hands, but in which Mme Roland played the leading part, was very characteristic of her way with her friends. From first to last of a very beautiful and very voluminous correspondence, Bancal was a true inspiration to this great friend who spoke to him as one man to another and sent him many of her noblest thoughts.

It was to him that on August 18, 1790, she wrote these lines in which, if one be just, one cannot help but read the sum total of her endeavour and the explanation of her sacrifice:

By bringing us into life in the day of the dawn of liberty, fate has made us a wasted generation which must do battle for that liberty and bear her to triumph. It is for us to perform our tasks well and thus prepare the happiness of succeeding generations.

When Bancal was in Paris she had said to him:

You ask me so gravely to take care of myself for the sake of the country, that you make me wonder of what importance the achievements of an insignificant little individual who has but small ways of serving, could be to the fatherland.

These few words give us some hint of how Brissot's friends, and his paper, had come to respect this provincial muse. Although a hundred leagues away, from the middle of 1790 she exercised so great an influence on this group that she felt it necessary to remind Bancal: "If you see Brissot, be sure and tell him that I don't think my opinions are laws." This faith she inspired "reminded her how severe she must be with herself." And, reverting naturally to the woman she was before the Revolution, when she lived her rural life with no thought but for her husband, his daughter, and his friends, she added: "I have been in ignorance of everything that is happening for three days now. I have heard nothing but the sound of the thrashers beating the wheat, I have seen nothing but our animals and accomplished nothing but jam."

As early as December 1790, Mme Roland's style had attained the height of its vigour.

She wrote to Bosc:

Have the extent of the Ministers' responsibilities decreed. Restrain your executive power, organize a national guard. A hundred thousand Austrians are at your frontiers, the Belgians are defeated, our money is slipping through our fingers, we are paying princes and fugitives who spend our pennies on arms with which to subjugate us. Zounds, Parisian though you are, you see no further than your own nose. . .

On the twenty-second of January 1791, in a letter to Bosc, begun by Lanthenas, she took the pen from his hand and exclaimed:

What ! And you too, you would like to console yourself with amusements ! Is such the rôle of a patriot ? Rather, fire your own courage and that of all good citizens. Demand, thunder, terrify. . .

Still writing to Bosc, this *Cornélienne* heroine exclaimed:

The wise close their eyes to the sins and weaknesses of the private man, but when the public safety is at stake, the citizen should spare not even his own father. . . Come to life and let us hear of your efforts in the same breath that we hear of your success.

Roland, already a *notable,* was presently elected municipal officer at Lyons. There, before the General Council, he demanded the recall of the regiments sent to Lyons after the sanguinary uprisings of July twenty-fifth.

When the bad weather set in, the Rolands returned to town; but this time they left little Eudora, who was then nine, at Villefranche, in the Convent of the Visitation of Ste Marie. It was at that moment that Mme Roland, the elder, died at the age of ninety-two. Her daughter-in-law did not wish the brothers to remain on unfriendly terms. She persuaded Roland to copy out a conciliatory letter which she had composed to send Canon Dominique.

But she would be the first to reproach us for lingering upon family matters when those of the nation were in the balance. Even as she wrote to Paris: "You Parisians, you don't know how to make use of your Assembly and you are simply paving the way for slaughter at the frontiers. . ." (January 24, 1791), she was remarking with satisfaction that by his speeches, pamphlets, and his tireless activity, Roland, as well as his friend Champagneux, founder of the *Courrier de Lyon,*[12] had become one of the heads of the democratic municipality. On the first of February 1791, Roland was deputed by the city of Lyons, together with Procurator for the Community Bret, to inform the Assembly that a debt of thirty-nine millions, contracted before the Revolution principally by royal

order and for the benefit of the King, was now incumbent on the
State. It is easy to imagine Mme Roland's excitement upon receiving this news. Probably the idea of separation occurred neither
to the husband or wife. Eudora was in safe keeping in Villefranche. The date of departure was quickly settled, and Bosc
charged with finding lodgings.

The accommodating Bosc, destined as usual to run errands, fixed
his choice upon the Hotel Brittanique in the rue Guénégaud.

The travellers reached Paris on the twentieth of February 1791.

Their first concern, immediately they arrived, was to pay a visit
to Brissot — ex-M. de Warville — with whom they had corresponded since 1789, but whom they had never seen.

This honest man lived with his three children and his humble
wife in a state of poverty that was close to destitution. The son
of a cook in a tavern near Chartres and the thirteenth child (four
were to come after him), he had managed to acquire some learning. One of his first cares had been to embellish his name with
the one of Ouarville, a village of the Beauce where his father owned
a bit of property. Anglophile that he was, he himself admitted
that the idea had struck him to give his name an English air, and
he spelled it thenceforward with a "W," which left the pronunciation unchanged.

Brissot [said M. Lescure] [13] was better suited to the wings than to
the stage, more to the study than to the rostrum, to council rather than
to action. His only weapon was his pen and all he could do was write;
he was neither fashionable nor worldly, neither gallant nor eloquent.
The sole one, perhaps, among all the men of the Revolution who had
a determined, immutable end in view: the proclamation of the
Republic.

Brissot conducted the Rolands to Pétion.[14] Mme Roland, enthusiastic from this first meeting, wrote upon leaving: "Oh,
Liberty, it will not be in vain that unselfish citizens consecrate themselves to your defence !"

Lanthenas had undertaken to send news to Bancal, who was still
in England.[15]

Mme Roland was ill the first few days we were here. She went to
the National Assembly, however, and she is convinced that Liberty

and the Constitution should not and will not remain in the hands of the men who were most prominent at the moment of the Revolution.

The major importance these men attached to the moves and opinions of the woman who was from then on to hold such sway over their thought and conscience, can be felt in Lanthénas' words:

On arriving in Paris [said Sainte-Beuve] she straightway joined the vanguard. Hers was a masculine brain. Thus she dominated all the men of peaceful and gentle disposition who surrounded her.

Mme Roland returned to Paris eleven years after her marriage and seven years after the affair of the patents of Nobility. When, filled with emotion as we can readily believe, she went to the "rue and Ile Saint-Louis" to visit her old relations, the Besnards, and the dear Sainte-Agathe who was still in the Convent of the Congregation, they did not find her changed.

Of all the intimate little world that had constituted her youthful surroundings, they alone remained. The engraver, Phlipon, was dead; Canon Bimont was dead; Grandmama Phlipon was dead; and the innocent Angélique and the kindly "preacher," and as for the Trude family, they had for some time past lived in retirement near Meulan, at Vaux.

But neither affection nor duty could hope to turn her from her apostolate. She was to give herself with all her ardour and all her reason, as women of that temperament will, to the work of renaissance that had fallen to the lot of her generation.

She had succeeded in introducing an element of passion into her devotion to a severe old man and in spending the intensity of the suppressed desires of her blooming youth in attachments that were above reproach. Now adequate sustenance was offered her lively talents that had been so long famished. In an instant they recovered their full force, their boundless ardour, and were ready for a bold attack. At last Mme Roland entered into her true existence, a brief life of thirty-two months and eighteen days. Her principal thought was for patriotic duty for the sake of future generations. In this she gloried, found peace with herself, and fulfillment of her inner life, and at the same time a field of action for her freedom.

We have already spoken of her "argumentative gentleness" (the phrase is Michelet's). From then on it was inspiration, directed by an earnest conscience, that was to be her guide. She was to be a leader, but in the one way a woman of her kind can lead — a leader fired by idealism — and her officers, although they possessed a true individual generosity, were to prove on the whole filled with weaknesses and timidity.

From the first day she saw that "the patriots had no organization, no union to make for the success of the good cause."

Nothing was more severe [wrote Michelet] than Mme Roland's first glance at Paris. The Assembly horrified her, and she was filled with pity for her friends. Seated in the tribunes of the Assembly or the Jacobin Club, she saw behind the masks of the participants; her penetrating eye perceived the insincerities, the cowardly acts, the baseness, the whole farce of the Constitutionals, the evasions, the indecisions of the friends of Liberty. She spared not one of the men she saw in action. She had no patience with procrastinations or with compromises. Young, ardent, strong, severe, she called them all to account, would not hear of delays or obstacles; she demanded that they be men and act.

I have seen my country freed [she wrote Bancal on the seventh of March 1791]. I admired all that this Liberty meant and I no longer regretted not having been born under a government other than my own. After my personal duties, my first thought was for this National Assembly which had done so many things or which had at least invested with a lawful character all that had been actually accomplished by the force of circumstances and that of public opinion. Had I not already been a patriot, I would have become one at these meetings, so evident was the dishonesty of the Blacks (as the Right was then called). I contemptuously observed the Blacks affecting the superior speech and flowery manners that give the Assemblies such a theatrical air; but the strength of reason, the courage of honesty, the insight of philosophy, the knowledge of the study and the eloquence of the bar should assure the patriotic Left of triumph were they all untainted and remained united. . . I have heard the subtle and captious Maury, who is nothing more than a very talented Sophist; the terrible Cazalès who is frequently an orator but often, too, an actor and a barker; the ridiculous d'Eprémesnil, a true mountebank, whse insolence and pettiness lead eventually to ridicule; the dexterous Mirabeau, more enamoured with applause than anxious for the public good; the captivating Lameths, made to be idols of the people and unfortunately to lead them astray were not an eye kept on them; little Barnave. . . What more do I know ? The Assembly weak and corrupted. . . However I am hoping everything will be carried on by that strength and that belief which made everything begin.

She also said:

It is not likely that the National Assembly will have finished the constitutional work under four months' time, and surely not one of its members would allot that period to its achievement. Each and everyone of them works precariously, by fits and starts, with no predetermined method and often in contradiction of the Assembly's decisions; it is like a big machine which circumstances have started off and it is difficult to foresee what its effects may be. Unfortunately the most obvious thing today is that the mob will always alter and deteriorate in proportion to the freedom it is allowed. The people brought about the Revolution because they had had enough of slavery; the awakened nation forced its representatives to rise to the heights to which its own indignation had swept it; now that the foundations of the constitution are laid, the nation idly watches what the legislators she herself selected are going to do; *and they, left to their own devices, prove themselves as a rule nothing more than mediocre men, or men corrupted by the old regime.*

"It was settled," say the *Memoirs,* "that everyone come to my house four evenings in the week, because I was frequently at home, had comfortable lodgings, and because my quarters were not at a great distance for any one of the members of these small committees."

Mme Roland had an extremely good disposition. She was cordial, with that sort of generous cordiality that welcomes the guest by offering him the best of everything one has. Sainte-Beuve found her the perfection of grace and ease, and her tact is already well known to us. She must have been a delightful hostess; but at this time all her energies were devoted to thought and reflection, to work, and to a sense of duty. At these receptions "a pitcher of water, and a sugar-bowl were set out as refreshments." Never a word passed her lips, but she remembered all that was said. No-one addressed her until the meeting had broken up.

This arrangement suited me perfectly [she wrote]. It kept me informed of the things in which I took a lively interest; it encouraged my taste for following political argument and studying men. I knew what rôle suited my sex, and I never forsook it. The conferences took place before me without my taking any part in them; seated outside the circle and near a table, I did my needlework or wrote letters while they debated; but even if I wrote ten, which was sometimes the case, I lost not a word that was uttered and I sometimes had to bite my lips to keep from speaking out.

They had all been dumbfounded and captivated upon meeting the author of the articles in the *Patriote*. They had known this correspondent from the provinces only through a style so firm and a trend of thought so strong that they had scarcely expected to find her a young and alluring woman.

Soon they gave allegiance to no political idea unless it had been sanctioned by this new-comer who possessed the faculty of sharpening wits and hastening action. Surrounded by these men who, time and again, needed to consult her and gain strength from contact with her generous mind, she naturally became the centre of a group. She admitted it herself: because she could be found in the rue Guénégaud, in her *salon*, it was there that the "patriots" collected after the meetings of the Assembly or before those of the Jacobin Club, to consult upon the best way of directing or dealing with events. There were Brissot, Robespierre, Pétion, Louis de Noailles,[16] Creuzé-Latouche, Bosc, Lanthenas, etc., and later Buzot, and a talented woman Bosc had brought, Mme Sophie Grandchamp.

Mme Roland has, in her *Memoirs,* written her first impressions of each one. Let us take the passage that deals with Robespierre:

Robespierre appeared to me then to be an honest man. Because of his principles I could forgive him his bad diction and his tiresome delivery. I noticed, however, that he was always deep in thought at these meetings; he gave ear to all opinions, rarely voiced his own, not troubling to explain it, and I heard it said that the next day he was the first to take the floor, where he made the most of the arguments he had heard his friends using the night before. He was sometimes mildly reproached for his conduct; he got out of it by hedging about the matter and his cunning was accepted as a kind of over-weening conceit which was really a great worry to him. However, this did not make for confidence. . . Never did a trusting smile appear on Robespierre's lips; on the contrary, they were almost constantly contracted in a bitter sneer of envy which he would have liked to pass off as disdain. As an orator, he was worse than mediocre; his common voice, his awkward expressions and his vile pronunciation made his delivery highly tedious. But he defended his principles with heat and tenacity. . . I esteemed Robespierre for this, and I showed him I did,

MAXAMILIEN ROBESPIERRE

From a painting by Adelaïde Labille-Guiard

and although he did not attend the meetings very regularly, he would from time to time ask me to dinner. I was struck by the terror which seemed to pervade him the day of the King's flight to Varennes; I met him that afternoon at Pétion's, where he said anxiously . . . that he didn't expect to live another twenty-four hours. Pétion and Brissot said that on the contrary the King's flight meant that he was lost . . . and that the people must be prepared for the Republic. Robespierre, as usual sneering and biting his finger-nails, asked what a republic was.

A simple warm demonstrative friendliness characterized this still unstable group. Among its famous members, certain like Robespierre, outgrew it; certain, like Danton (even when accompanied by his Fabre d'Églantine), were never at their ease.

History sorely lacks a beautiful portrait of Mme Roland: a pastel by Latour, for instance, or a bust by Houdon. To recapture a vision of the woman who was soon to be the Gironde's queen, we must refer to the portrait sketched of her in the prison of Sainte-Pélagie by another prisoner whose identity is unknown, who was neither very skilful, nor very gifted, but who was sincere, and whose wavering line was hampered neither by convention nor by the wish to flatter his model. The portrait made by Bréa at the Revolutionary Court is more attractive than the others, and the one reproduced by Champagneux in the edition of the *Memoirs* he published in 1800, is also of interest to us. But the miniature of the Archives differs strangely from the others.

Without neglecting these land-marks, let us attempt to form a fair idea of the person of Mme Roland, taking into consideration certain characteristics found in her letters and the *Memoirs,* and above all, the opinion of those who knew her. First of all, here is what she herself said of her various portraits:

My portrait has been done several times, both painted and engraved: not one of these likenesses gives any idea of my person; it is difficult enough to catch because I have more soul than face, more expression than features. An ordinary artist could not render it; it is possible that he would not even perceive it. My countenance brightens in proprotion to the interest which is aroused in me, just as my wit responds to the sharpness of another's wit. I have found myself stupid with so many people that when I discovered my resources in a witty company, I, in my credulity, long believed it was to their skill and not to my

own that I was indebted. I am generally liked because I am afraid
of offending people; but not everybody thinks me pretty or appreciates
my real worth. There is an old fellow . . . who knew me for ten
years without suspecting that I could do anything but add a sum or
sew a shirt. Camille [Desmoulins] was right to be astounded that
at my age, with so few claims to beauty I had what he called adorers.
I never spoke to him, but I wager that with a person of his sort I
would be cold and silent, if not actually repulsive. He was not strictly
truthful when he spoke of my court; I detest courtiers as much as I
mistrust slaves, and I agree perfectly that flatterers should be shown
the door. Above all I require esteem and kindness; admiration may
come later if one is so inclined, but I need to be singled out and loved;
and this never fails to be the case if one sees me frequently and if one
has sound sense and a kind heart.

There is one point on which all her contemporaries agreed: that
Mme Roland looked as though she were Roland's daughter, for he
was the type of man that the seventeenth century described as
an old fogey.

Concerning this there are several testimonies worthy of note. The
one closest to the period we are now dealing with, is that of the
Englishman, Arthur Young, who, shortly before, when passing
through Lyons, had had himself introduced to Roland and caught
a glimpse of his wife.

This gentleman [he said], already elderly, has an extremely pretty
young wife.

We cannot forego the satisfaction of quoting the following from
Lemontey's well-known description of Mme Roland:

I had seen Mme Roland at times before 1789: her eyes, her figure,
and her hair were of remarkable beauty and her delicate complexion
had a freshness and tint, which, combined with her reserved and candid manner, gave her an extremely youthful air. I did not find she had
that easy Parisian elegance which she attributed to herself in her
Memoirs; I do not mean to say that she was awkward, for simplicity
and naturalness are never lacking in grace. I remember the first time
I saw her she seemed to me the realization of the dream I had of the
little girl of Vevey who had turned so many heads, the idea of
J.- J. Rousseau's Julie; and when I heard her speak the illusion was
even more complete. Mme Roland talked well, too well. Self-conceit
might have been thought to play its part in all she said, but such was
not the case. It was simply the expression of a too-perfect nature. Wit,
good sense, neatness of expression, sharp reasoning, naïve grace, all these

came in an unstudied flow from between her ivory teeth and her rosy lips; there was nothing to do but be convinced.

During the Revolution I saw Mme Roland once again; that was at the beginning of her husband's first ministry. She had lost none of her bloom, none of her youthfulness, nor her simplicity; her husband looked like a Quaker and she like his daughter.

Her child hovered about her, with beautiful hair hanging down to the waist; it was as if inhabitants of Pennsylvania had been transplanted into M. de Calonne's salon. Mme Roland's entire conversation treated of public matters and I saw that my moderated opinion moved her to pity. Her mind was overwrought, but her heart remained gentle and inoffensive. Although the great breaks in the monarchy had not yet come, she did not close her eyes to the fact that symptoms of anarchy were beginning to appear and she pledged herself to fight them until death. I remember the calm and resolute tone in which she told me that she would bow her head, when necessary, on the scaffold; and I confess that the thought of this charming woman delivered to the executioner's blade had an everlasting effect upon me, for party fury had not yet accustomed us to such terrifying thoughts. Thus, in what followed, the marvels of Mme Roland's strength and the heroism of her death did not astonish me. Everything was consistent and nothing was feigned in this celebrated woman; which makes her not only the strongest character, but as well the truest of our Revolution. History will not slight her and other nations will envy us who gave her birth.

We have reason to believe that she was tall, vigorous, with well-developed hips and a very full bosom. Her neck must have been rather thick and a little short. Her head was large and crowned with superb black hair which, according to a family tradition, was said to have been carelessly arranged. Her greatest claim to beauty was her limpid complexion and her appearance of youth and health. Her eyes must have been very beautiful, her face remarkably expressive and mobile; her smile caustic, in unexpected contrast with the touching sweetness of her gaze; her nose, rather thick at the end — (we recall it caused her some anxiety) — set the mark of kindliness on a face that shone with intelligence, like those faces of Leonardo da Vinci, in which the sad gentleness of the eyes contradicts the gaiety of the smile.

A gentle nature, a strong soul, a solid mind, a very affectionate disposition, and an exterior which bespoke all this, endeared me to those who knew me. The situation in which I was placed made enemies for me; I myself had none; those who say the worst of me have never seen me.

Her plain frocks with flat sleeves and, at the very most, a ruffle around the bottom of the skirt, were gathered simply in below the bosom, but the material was brightly printed with fresh-coloured stripes or with vivid bouquets. A kerchief of white muslin, sometimes edged with a scalloped ruffle or a border of lace, was worn about her fine shoulders, covering them with more modesty than the mode required.

Mme Roland continued to write for the newspapers, but she left her articles unsigned. In her this anonymity was a matter of principle and reason. She believed that, conditions being as they were, feminine intervention could serve no purpose. She was afraid of doing her party harm by revealing her identity, and thus continued to maintain her rôle as her husband's secretary.

Women should inspire good [she said], and feed and fire all those sentiments that might serve the fatherland, but they should not appear to take part in the public work.

She found Paris greatly changed. The little girl born in the reign of Louis XV, the young intellectual of the Ile de la Cité, no longer recognized her city. Popular clubs had sprung up everywhere. Sometimes meetings were held in the streets. There were constant uprisings. The cobbles, at times, were wet with blood. The city was "over-run with foreigners, who flock from heaven knows where." Sinister faces began to appear. Incidents threatened to become insurrections. The people revolted because the King wished to go to Saint-Cloud. For one hour and a half he was forced to remain in his coach surrounded by a hostile mob.

This stupidity has its advantages [said Mme Roland], and is the price paid for the idolatry in which so many people still indulge; many mortifying remarks were made to the Queen, opening her eyes to the general feeling about her. I see the best-balanced minds now persuaded that we cannot avoid civil war and that the time is approaching when it will break out.

And further:

"Paris is greatly disturbed. You knew about . . . the terrors of the Court, which were followed by Montmorin's famous letter." Mme Roland had seen clearly in judging this letter "affected and

MADAME ROLAND [?]

From a painting by Prud'hon. Collection of Mme a Vicomtesse de La Rochefoucauld

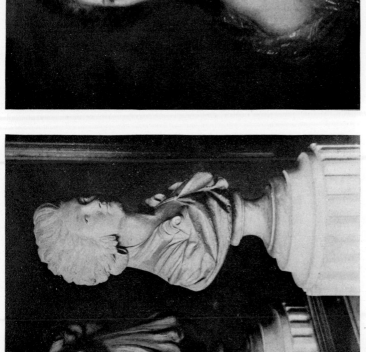

MADAME ROLAND [?]

Terra cotta bust by an unknown artist. Musée de Nevers

hypocritical." It was written to French ambassadors abroad in high
praise of the Constitution, declaring it was an "atrocious calumny"
to pretend that "the King was not free." It was later learned that
secret envoys left at the same time bearing contradictory messages.

As for Lafayette, every day he loses a little more of the confidence
we had in him [she said]. He is heading for oblivion or for death.

The people were despondent over Mirabeau's unforeseen end.
The curious page Mme Roland wrote Bancal on the fifth of April
1791, three days after the event, must be quoted:

. . . The papers will have apprised you of Mirabeau's premature
death: premature as to age, but doubtless not as to the use he made
of his life, and very timely as far as his reputation is concerned.

This hasty and almost sudden end of a very talented man who truly
served the public weal, leaves an inevitable impression of something
inexplicably solemn and sad. I am far from sharing in the enthusiasm
so many feel for that astounding being they mourn, and at the same
time I hate death for having so promptly seized upon this great prey,
while on reflection I cannot but applaud this act of fate.

It will perhaps be long before the people rightly estimate either the
man or the event. Truth penetrates with difficulty and there is much
here to unite in fostering illusion. Moreover it has made a tremendous
sensation; the people sincerely believe that they have lost their
best defender; Mirabeau's death approaches public calamity; his funeral
was more majestic than those of the proudest kings, and the most
enlightened citizens applaud this triumph eagerly, for to the public
mind these homages were in reality paid to Liberty, because of all that
Liberty owed the man who had just passed away. As far as I, personally, am concerned, I consider Mirabeau offered us the most monstrous jumble of a genius who recognized good, who could have put it
into effect, and who did at times, but with a corrupt heart that trifled
even with virtue. He usurped a reputation through works not his
own; he sold his ability and truth to avarice and ambition, for gold,
for which his dissoluteness had so great a need. Without discussing
again his conduct at the time of the *veto* and the decree on the right
of *peace* and *war,* he was a coward and a traitor to the last degree
in *the organization of the public treasury,* in the question of the
regency and in the matter of the *mines.* I was indignant over his
perfidious silence, over his contradictory speeches and his villainy.

Mirabeau hated despotism, from which he had greatly suffered;
Mirabeau flattered the people because he knew their rights, but Mirabeau would have sold the people's cause, for corrupt men who crave
authority are always considerate of the Court, and he in particular
wished to be of service because he was striving for the ministry. Had

he lived longer, he would have been found out, and his reputation ruined before his death; he died an honourable man, at least in the eyes of the populace, and it was a stroke of good fortune for him. The common men in the Assembly were astounded to see disappear the man whose influence had so often swayed them; the factious Lameths mourned him in the manner of Cæsar on the death of Pompey, all the while rejoicing at being delivered from a rival whom they feared and whom good citizens regret just because of the counterweight he was to the Lameth intrigues. The day of Mirabeau's death, the Assembly was occupied with the great question of the equality of distribution, or rather with the power of making a will; in announcing this event it was learned that Mirabeau had a work on the subject; he had given it the day before to the Bishop of Autun, who was requested to read it. It was an excellent speech in which the best principles of Justice and Equality were expanded with that vigour and those salient forces which characterized its author; this was a wreath he laid upon his own tomb. The patriots could not refrain from regretting a man so capable of serving truth; the *Blacks* trembled at the ascendancy he was exercizing for the last time upon them. However, with his customary facility for compromise, his conclusion was not the abolition of the power of making a will, although this would have been the logical consequence of the principles he laid down, but with reservation of a tenth part at the disposition of the testator.

I could not help thinking that had Mirabeau been alive and present at the end of the discussion, he would have finished by granting even more if he had seen the Assembly demanding it. This was his supreme art: first to expound good principles, then to fit them to circumstances so that he seemed to be the champion of truth, then to so restrain the two factions as to become the dictator of the Assembly, whereas he was naught but his own idol and sacrified the Republic to his reputation or to his personal interests. All the journalists seized upon his death as if it were a choice piece . . . and each one played it up according to his talents. Brissot is the only one I know who has the wisdom to escape idolatry with such prudence as not to offend public opinion. Doubtless he will one day tell the truth, but we are not ready for it; if one hastened to disclose it, it would only be reviled.

We purposely cut short this fine quotation to draw the reader's attention to the last sentence which seems to shed a ray of light upon Mme Roland's relation with the men of her group.

It is a certainty, and it is understandable, that at the time she left her provincial home, Brissot had a real influence upon her. He was the leader of the "Patriots," as his party was then called, and the director of the most advanced and influential paper. As much as his ability, she admired his activity and his zeal. It was at this period, of very short duration, that she said in a letter to Bancal (May 12, 1791):

Brissot, constantly devoted, as you know, and for whom I would wish two assistants whose pens equalled his own, to conduct the Assembly and the capital. . .

But it was more his disinterestedness than either a great nature or a superior mind that explained his influence over her. Mme Roland's puritanical principles, her republican virtues, found a patriotic pledge and a moral satisfaction in Brissot's poverty. Brissot's wife would wash in turn the three shirts that he possessed and dry them at the windows of their attic-quarters in the Palace of Saint-Cloud.[17]

Mme Roland believed that Brissot "escaped idolatry" through "wisdom." At any rate it was not through lack of genius. Pétion was idolized, and Marat as well. It would be perhaps fairer to say that Brissot did not put himself in the first ranks because he had his own measure, and above all because he was not an orator. He had a tendency to temporize, a characteristic he had in common with his present and future friends, with the exception of the Rolands. They were both opposed to every act of postponement; but, as it did not take Mme Roland long to understand, not one of these men could have put up with a more openly determined policy. She must have reflected that in her home in Beaujolais, she had progressed far beyond them all, but her convictions had but little to do with the world of actual affairs. She thought she owed it to the public weal to subdue her tendencies, and we well know her resources of patience and diplomacy.

Nevertheless, she must have been often out of patience with the deletions to which the director of *Patriote* subjected her articles, much to the indignation of Bosc and Lanthenas. These two, incapable of criticizing her in any way, had certainly, by their admiration, contributed much to her uncompromising attitude and her nascent taste for personal domination. Thus she forced herself to mind whither she was going and to consider her words. But what a trial for her to hesitate on the brink of action! "It is all that remains for honest people to do [to wait], unless a general insurrection comes to save us from death and slavery; but *there is still not sufficient force or public instruction to let us hope for that. Don't come to preach peace and the courage of mere patience to us. . .*" Here let us consider the state of Mme Roland's mind. This is necessary if we would follow and understand the changes in her public character, up to the day when, in prison, she was at last at liberty to judge men and the history which they made. The following passage, which dates from near the close of her life, is remarkably precise and instructive in this regard:

All the ability of subordinates cannot compensate for the lack of character in a minister; for those who govern, weakness is the worst fault of all, particularly in the midst of warring factions. Garat and Barère . . . one vested with executive power and the other a legislator, would ruin all the States in the world through their half-measures; their passion for would-be conciliatory methods puts them always on the devious path that leads to the precipice and to confusion. . . We need statesmen . . . rigorous in principle, firm and rapid in action. . .

But if she was willing to make momentary concessions in public affairs, her private letters preserve their natural tone. Moreover the atmosphere was becoming charged and no-one felt it more than she. She had already written Bancal: "German soldiers are stationed at Porrentruy. . . The National Guard is still not organized and there are no more arms to give them. . . I believe that civil war is inevitable." And she was on the point of writing Brissot on the twenty-eighth of April 1791: "Throw your pen in the fire, generous Brutus, and go plant lettuces." Soon she would say:

"It is the art of people of character to lend it to those who lack it."

Ah, no, she was not gentle with the Constituents! She saw them from too near. She wrote Brissot:

The Assembly is no longer anything but an instrument of corruption and tyranny. . . I saw today that Assembly that one cannot call national; . . . reason, truth and justice are there smothered, reviled, and spurned . . . there is nothing to do but hide one's head or stab one's enemies to the heart.

It is in this letter that we see for the first time from her pen the name of Buzot and, by a perfidious irony of fate, linked with that of Robespierre: "the vigorous Robespierre, the wise Buzot. . ."

She asked herself in real anguish if there were not thirty honest men in the Assembly (capable of understanding sound principles), to shock the others into action. "My heart is broken," she added. "I vowed this morning never to return to that abominable cave where justice and humanity are a mockery."

The discussion which had aroused her ire was one concerning the organization of the National Guard.

Certain deputies, Dubois-Crancé, d'André, Rabaut Saint-Étienne, got a resolution passed that it should comprise only *active citizens* to the exclusion of *beggars*.

How is it no-one has noticed [she exclaimed] that in all the big manufacturing cities there is a considerable number of workers who, as a result of the panics which imperil all industry, are for the moment unable to support any tax whatsoever and are even reduced to accepting temporary aid from the board of public relief ? Thus at Lyons in the winter 1789, more than twenty-five thousand souls were abandoned to misery. These workers are however of use and are good citizens, honest fathers of families, loyal to the Constitution and ardent in their support of it; and have they not the right to bear arms ! The arbitrary authority of town councils is to reject them ! For have we not had at Lyons the example of a town council which, under pretext that such and such ones were not on the list of taxes for '89, would not allow them to enter when they solicited permission to share the rights of active citizens ! [18]

She did not hesitate to give vent to her vehement indignation in her letters to Bancal. During this time, he was absorbed in the *Société des Amis des Noirs,* believing in all sincerity that he was serving the cause of the French Revolution by fraternizing with the "generous Quakers of England," whose influence, through Brissot as well as Mme Roland, was strongly felt by the Brissotins.

"I would never have the courage to write you all the ill I think of our Assembly," she said. ". . . I am absolutely convinced that it will produce nothing more than ill-advised decrees (May 5, 1791)." Doubtless she did not fear the success of the Counter Revolution, but she perceived "the obstructing force of the executive power, the worse organization of finances . . . a swarm of bad decrees and constitutional vices which hinder the exercise of liberty, halt the progress of instruction, establish an aristocracy of wealth, oppose the regeneration of the national character and morals . . . prepare, in short, new shackles which the people will not observe and which they will find themselves burdened with unawares." [This is a remarkable enough prediction of the 18 Brumaire.] "I see the Assembly so corrupted that it seems to me all its acts are necessarily defective, which is proven only too well every day . . . *on the Left there is not a single man of character . . . the best patriots seem to me more concerned with their own petty glory than with the wide interests of their country, and, in truth, they are all mediocre men, even as far as ability goes. It is not wit they lack, but soul. . ."* (May 12, 1791).

The severity of which Michelet spoke went far. Mme Roland was to say: *"France was as if drained of men. It is a surprising thing, this dearth of them in the Revolution. There have been naught but pigmies."* Each bit of news, and heaven knows that news was not lacking, made her take up her pen: [19] A few aristocrats are emigrating. . . The Pope was burned in effigy at the Palais-Royal. . . The removal of Voltaire's remains will be celebrated by a ceremony, the plan of which is truly superb." She approved the strong organization of the Criminal Court: Pétion, president; Robespierre, prosecuting attorney; Buzot, substitute. The members of the Assembly would not be re-eligible; she thought this "an excellent thing."

Mirabeau had said of Robespierre: "He will go far, for he believes everything he says." It was Robespierre, above all an ideologist, who proposed this foolish act, one prompted by false ideas but on which he counted to win him admiration: that the Constituents were not to be allowed to apply and amend the laws they had studied and voted. Malouet [20] saw this clearly. "There was but one more mistake to make," he said, "and now it has been made."

But Robespierre, with his eyes on the future, said that "in every part of the Empire there were fathers of families who would willingly embrace the profession of legislator so as to assure their children morals and a fatherland. . .Intriguers would keep away? So much the better. Modest virtue would replace them. . ."

Mme Roland's disinterestedness was destined to mislead her to the point of blind approbation. She too had not failed to fall into that final error.

It was then thought that the Revolution was an accomplished thing. However, the new city was still to be erected on the ruins of the old. With what just cause did Duport [21] accuse Robespierre of always talking "principles, high generalities, without getting down to ways and means, without taking any responsibility, for it was hardly a responsibility to preach uninterruptedly on natural right."

Some were already aghast at their own destructive acts, and sought to atone for them by every means. "It was pitiful," said Rivarol, "to see these men who, after having been the incendiaries, now offered to fight the flames."

Mme Roland herself was carried away by the illusions which then beset even the most practical minds. Talk of Utopia was on every tongue, and Mme Roland wrote: "We need new men and honest people, enemies of luxury, friends of liberty. They will vote for the unlimited freedom of the press, general instruction for every class of society . . . particularly that one heretofore considered as the people. . ." And then: "Common rights . . . universal fraternity . . . security of the happiness of nations. . ."

A rational heroism took the place of the argumentative gentleness of bygone days. Virility ? That is the falsest description of all, and in employing it the public merely proved that they accepted a conventional idea in the place of a real person. She was, on the contrary, a woman, and she had her moments of weakness, but it was a secret to be whispered only to a friend: "I long for my country place," she said in confidence. "I have had enough of Paris. It was fine to see it at the time of the Revolution. But now it grieves me. I would leave it without regret."

On the twenty-sixth of June 1791, her letter to Bancal was on the table, sealed since the previous day. At ten in the morning, she feverishly tore it open to add a few words:

I wrote you yesterday afternoon. I unseal my letter to tell you, with the cannon roaring and in the wildest commotion, that the King and Queen have fled; the shops are closed, everything is in an uproar. It is almost sure that Lafayette is implicated. This means war.

All France believed this too. Louis XVI and Marie-Antoinette had been looked upon as hostages securing the emancipated nation from the vengeance of neighbouring monarchies.

A levy of a hundred thousand volunteers was immediately decreed. If foreign invasion did not at once take place, it was because the King was allowed to keep the crown.

Of a sudden, here was Mme Roland a Republican — the first after Brissot who had already published his views in 1787. She had instinctively quailed when Mirabeau, for whom the republican form of government was "a desperate resource," had forgotten himself so far as to say: "If they are unreasonable, I'll ——— them into a republic!" She quickly converted her friends to the new idea, but "the Jacobins," she said, "go into convulsions at the mere thought of it.[22] The first time the word was uttered, the deputies vehemently protested: "We are not Republicans." Taking the floor, Vadier declared that he "detested the republican form." Marat was still a Royalist and a Catholic in the year 1791. Robespierre, as usual, held back, and was later to declare, in a burst of sincerity: "The Republic slipped in among the parties without anyone knowing how it happened." But an impudent remark of his can bear repeating: "Accuse us who will of republicanism. I declare that I hate any kind of government in which the factious reign."

MME ROLAND, who had from the first considered that the flight of Louis XVI "was far from being a misfortune, for the hatred of kings and the word Republic were yesterday voiced in every quarter," passed in one moment from "the highest hopes" to "anxiety and fear." This meeting of the Assembly, which should have been "the finest of all those ever held or that ever will be held," had left her thoroughly disillusioned. "With an energy in keeping with his character," Robespierre denounced all that in the eyes of good citizens appeared suspicious in the event. Lafayette and Bailly had confessed at the bar, that since Whitsuntide the Research Committee had discovered plans for escape, and that this was not the only

indication of treason, for the Assembly had retained the ministers
of the King, who were all obviously hostile to the Revolution. "In
vain does that vigorous D'Anton [23] exert his eloquence against
Lafayette and loudly accuse him." Without justifying himself,
Lafayette paraded his zeal, "and was applauded." Sieyès preached
against "mistrust," Barnave in favour of "union." Nothing else
resulted from the deliberations of an Assembly which should have
been "the source of the highest resolutions at a time when we are
beset by the gravest and most decisive circumstances of our history."
Mme Roland was filled with contempt for the incapacity of those
who fail to accomplish their tasks or who fall short of their aspira-
tions.

"For six months they had been doing nothing but lulling us to
sleep; I smiled at the awakening, now I am dismayed to see that
they are again trying to calm us in the same manner." She foresaw
that Louis XVI would call upon the enemies' armies, at the same
time obstructing the Assembly which he would continue to direct
. . . "I perceive," said she, "that we are surrounded by snares, de-
luders, assassins, and if we still hope to attain Liberty, we shall
have to wade through a sea of blood." She wished an address presented to the National Assembly requesting a change of ministers
and a different composition of all the committees. "*All primary
Assemblies should present this address at the same time*. Could
not one of the clauses of this address solemnly request the French
to answer by a yea or nay whether they wished to retain the
monarchic form of government ?"

The Revolutionists had a great proneness for historical sym-
bolism.[24] After some theatrical manifestations in the ancient manner, they were convinced that they had accomplished something
both concrete and permanent. That Mme Roland's good sense was
shocked by this, is shown in her ironical words:

Let them make fine proclamations, exhorting us to be on our guard.
Let them decree pompously that all citizens should be on the watch,
should unite, and should have confidence in an Assembly that makes
such touching protestations. Now, I ask you, does this give us any
cause for satisfaction or put our minds at rest ? The Jacobins held

a meeting; they were numerous, they had noble impulses, and the oath — for we have become relentless swearers — the oath of liberty or death was passionately repeated.

And, indeed, an eloquent gesture pleased them more than a good decree. On the twenty-second she returned to the Jacobin Club:

They were as numerous and the meeting opened with the same solemnity as on the preceding day. I don't know whether I told you with what inexpressible fervour they knelt down, unsheathed their swords, and again took the oath to live or die. This outburst was paltry compared to the frank and gay intrepidity of an entire people.

The day following the Jacobins' oath, Mme Roland wrote — still to Bancal: "Yesterday . . . June 23, 1791 . . . at five o'clock in the afternoon, while we were with Robespierre and several others, considering ourselves in imminent danger . . ." the news suddenly arrived "that the King and his wife had been arrested by a small municipality at Varennes, near Stenay. Fifteen to twenty thousand [?] national guards surrounded Chalons-sur-Marne whither our great rascals had been taken. What is to be done with them? It seems to me it will be necessary to imprison the royal dummy and bring his wife to trial."

The King's arrest was followed by a state of general perplexity; the various parties vacillated and deliberated in confusion. In her letter to Bancal, dated June twenty-fourth, Mme Roland gives us an interesting account of the proceedings: [25]

They are bringing back Louis XVI, his wife, children, and sister. . . Tomorrow he will be within our walls. . . Monsieur and his wife are at Mons; the Emperor has gone there; there is great activity along the frontiers. . . We are unprepared, we have little ammunition, we are lacking in discipline and we have no sure able leaders. On the Flemish side, the country is open and undefended; through the Ardennes the enemy could almost reach Paris. . . Lafayette is "under suspicion." . . He must be relieved of the command of the National Guard. . . A host of deputations, fragments of battalions, all the magistrates, etc., have come to the Assembly and have again sworn fealty to the nation, and the entire Faubourg Saint-Antoine filed by, the men armed with picks and sticks, the women festively . . . in good order . . to the music of the national band. . . And the band played Ça ira, the people taking up the refrain and sending the King and the aristocrats to the devil.

Meanwhile the Jacobins were on the point of playing into the hands of the Orléans faction, which was trying to turn the King's flight to its own profit. "This gives full scope to traitors and suspects," said Mme Roland.[26] Robespierre, however, was getting ready.

"As to my opinion, here is what we were thinking and saying to Buzot after midnight. It would be inept, absurd, abhorrent even, to put the King back on his throne... A regency? Whom could we name as regent? Monsieur? d'Artois? Condé? Orléans? ... who is vicious and contemptible... No doubt but that the best and fairest measure would be to bring Louis XVI to trial," but no-one had sufficient courage. Let him be suspended "as used to be done with prevaricating magistrates." Whereupon she indicated the measures which should be taken without delay: put the frontiers in a state of defence, and, before all else, order ammunition. Her imagination, nurtured on wide knowledge, was a spur to her initiative. With Camille Desmoulins, she said:

I find Brissot unsatisfactory at this important juncture. His paper should instruct us, instead of being filled with news gossip. The hours are fleeting; it is not possible at the same time to conceive, observe, talk to a great many people, and do the writing in time for the press. It is now we are feeling the lack of an association and all the advantages it would have brought us, an association such as we had imagined, composed of three or four very independent people devoted to the public safety, whose one task would be to ripen opinion, and who would have a printing-press expressly for this purpose. But they would need to be in perfect agreement, lay aside every personal consideration, and seek in this association merely those things which could safeguard it and make it flourish, with no thought as to rank and profit. This understanding, and the high degree of energy and altruism it requires, are the very qualities so hard to find in three or four men who, at the same time, esteem each other sufficiently to tolerate differences of character, intelligence, and talent. Why is it that a few intelligent men of your acquaintance, and mine, have not formed such a group, which, in these revolutionary times, would have been able to perform great things?

Thus Brissot was led to speak plainly in public upon the question of whether the King should be brought to trial. Mme Roland, who was present at the meeting, wrote of the cheers and the furore:

Three times was the entire Assembly swept to its feet; arms were stretched forth, hats hurled into the air in an enthusiasm impossible to describe. May he perish who, having felt or shared in this emotion, is again willing to become a slave !

We have quoted this curious passage in full because Mme Roland's opinions and activity seem to spring from every line. It was she who, thenceforth, in the person of her husband, became the most important member of the association of which she had dreamed, in the first rank of that élite who performed "great things." She had the "altruism," she had the "intelligence," she had also perhaps the "talent." Devoted to the public weal, she had more organizing ability, more ardour, more moral courage, more decisiveness and practical sense than all those timid argumentative men. The day Roland was called to the ministry, she believed her idea of an association was on the point of realization. But, alas, instead of being comprised of the three or four chosen in accordance with her patriotic hopes, her positive conscience, her ideals of justice and her puritanical scruples, this council was to prove the most incoherent and imperfect of them all. Like all present and future "union" ministries, it was an ill-conceived, poorly assorted gathering, a prey to weaknesses and private obligations, incapable of concerted action, and hence inadequate; a part of it was even ready to betray the Revolution.

At the end of July 1791 came a reaction. A number of warning symptoms justified the apprehensions of the Patriots. Mme Roland's letters to Bancal increased and at times she wrote him every day: "Many people are being arrested, the machinery of despotism was never more formidable. . ." The Jacobins had closed their doors. She was present at the final meeting in the women's gallery where a terrified man had come to seek refuge. Having witnessed with disgust this cowardly exhibition of fright, she wrote spiritedly:

Heaven forbid that such a fine Revolution be made but for a few factious spirits to the detriment of the good people who only required support to make it perfect !
Three carriages have just gone by. . . Marat, one of the best known members of the Cordelier Club . . . was imprisoned in one of these on

his way to gaol. . . If this continues, you will be hearing that Robispierre's courage in defending the rights of the people has been bought by foreign powers. . . To be sure I am not comparing the energy of this worthy man to the excesses for which Marat is reproached, but it seems to me there is a propensity to judge them in the same spirit and with the same injustice.

She had already written a short time before: "Brissot, who triumphed yesterday at the Jacobins, is atrociously slandered." The affair of the Champ de Mars, which had never been entirely cleared up, was to her a cause for despair. Was it just of Mme Roland to accuse Lafayette? Curiosity had led her to the Champ de la Fédération where she saw not more than two or three hundred people scattered before the altar of the fatherland, "who, bearing on pikes declamatory bills," incited the crowd against the fugitive King. After what had been "justly called the massacre of the Champ de Mars," she was to witness "Robespierre's fright." It was said, indeed, that the Feuillants wished to bring him to trial:

Roland and I were both very anxious on his account. We went to his house in a remote part of the Marais at eleven o'clock at night, with the intention of offering him a refuge, but he had already left his domicile. We went to Buzot's to tell him that, without deserting the Jacobins, it might be well if he went to the Feuillants to see what was happening there and be prepared to take the defence of those they intended to persecute.

But Buzot, more clear-sighted than Mme Roland, replied: "I will do all in my power to save that unfortunate young man . . . though I am far from sharing the opinion of certain people on his account . . . etc." [27]

Had there been a royalist plot at the Champ de Mars? Certain patriots had been advised not to sleep at home, and the Rolands had given shelter to the Roberts, whom they hardly knew but to whom they had consented to deliver a letter.

She recalled the times when "the Bastille had kept people quiet," and she remarked that "those who are not deluded are even more reserved at this time, for the risks are the same and their proximity more immediate. . ." "Malebranche," she said, "reproaches the French for accepting probabilities and thus swerving from the truth."

This brought her to the topic of confidence, and she considered that the French had not changed.

> They have confidence in everything, and through this they lose their freedom. True, this confidence is extremely convenient; it dispenses with the necessity of watching, thinking, and forming opinions. It even flatters their pride, for by considering it a virtue, they can indulge their laziness.

Such a passage is remarkable from more than one point of view, but this time it prompts us to criticize severely the perspicacity of Mme Roland's judgment. The woman who was so astute as to make the above remarks, had placed her confidence in that very Robespierre who was to employ his execrable and bloodthirsty politics to the end of slaughtering her and her party with methodical and even mechanical indifference. It worried her to see Marat led to prison — she would not have objected to an insane asylum where he would have been quite at home. She sheltered Robert who, on a question of personal interest,[28] was to become her bitter enemy. We know that she was clear sighted, and that she often divined things she did not know. It is necessary, however, to observe the errors she made.

MME ROLAND was longing for the peace of *Le Clos*. She already blamed Paris for the misdeeds of its inhabitants, and wished to flee its corruption: "I have now had quite enough of Paris, at least for the time," she said. "I need to see my trees, after having seen so many fools and scoundrels."

Roland, who had seemed effaced by his wife, was none the less much in evidence among Brissot's followers. He had accomplished the mission with which the city of Lyons had entrusted him, and had obtained an exemption of thirty-three millions out of thirty-nine. There was nothing more, then, to keep the Rolands in the burning dusty city in the month of August, and as for the affairs of the fatherland, Mme Roland found them increasingly disillusioning:

> The progress of the legislature is still . . . an actual overthrowing of the Constitution [she said], a mockery of the Declaration of Rights. Here we are with princes, non-eligible citizens, and an inviolable King

surrounded by military assassins subject to his orders; with paid electors, etc. . .

Even before the fresh air of the country, friendship had been the great pacifier of her overwrought nerves. To be sure, Mme Roland admired the great gifts in those political men who were her intimates, but not one of them was superior in uprightness of character and fortitude of heart to her old friend Bosc (he was then scarcely over thirty), and to not one of them, doubtless, did she show a tenderer affection.

At the period we have just reached, Bosc was probably rather closely associated with a "woman of merit" named Mme Sophie Grandchamp, of whom we have already spoken. He had promised to present her to this Mme Roland of whom he thought so highly. So highly, indeed, that Mme Grandchamp looked upon the newcomer with some displeasure, and when Bosc neglected to fulfill his promise, she did not think it at all necessary to remind him of it. Months had passed when, one morning in the middle of August, he arrived unexpectedly at her home to take her to the Jacobin Club. Mme Roland was on the point of leaving, and the young women had only the time to catch a glimpse of each other:

He [Bosc] introduced me [she said] and, turning to Mme Roland: "Here is an Athenian whom I present to a Spartan." [29]

Mme Grandchamp was very much disconcerted because this took place before a large group of people.

I would have difficulty in describing my feelings. I can still see that famous woman, seated by a little table, dressed as an amazon, her black hair cut like a jockey's, her bright colouring, her eyes penetrating and soft. She welcomed me charmingly, but as she was obliged to leave, we were unable to talk. Placed as I was beside her, I paid little heed to the meeting, I thought only of looking at and listening to her. She spoke with a purity, a choice of expression, and an energy which the silvery tone of her voice made all the more remarkable. We parted at about eleven, and I was left meditating and ill at ease. Her departure really pained me; I regretted ever having seen her, for now I wished to be always with her.

It was love at first sight, as we can see. Twice Mme Grandchamp called on Mme Roland without finding her at home; the

third time, Mme Roland was doubtless a little absent-minded for
Mme Grandchamp found her "embarrassed and constrained." Mme
Roland returned her visit. There the love was reciprocated. Here
they were, kissing each other, using endearing terms, no longer
able to live without each other, to such an extent that Mme Roland,
who was on the point of leaving for *Le Clos,* invited Mme Grandchamp to accompany her. But there was not another place inside
the coach, and moreover Mme Grandchamp was none too sure that
she wished to go, for "other bonds held her !" Was she referring
to Bosc ?

Mme Roland . . . provoked, disappointed, strode up and down my
room. . . All of a sudden she stopped and exclaimed: "Why did I not
think of it before ? My maid has a place in the back; I can easily
dispense with her for a few days. We shall leave tonight; at eight
you come to dinner, my friend, at ten I take you with me. Farewell,
I have not a minute to lose."

It must have been a trial for Bosc to see his great friend lavish-
ing her energies and affections on all the new interests she had
found in Paris. In other days he had shared her touching solicitude (with the exception of Roland), only with Lanthenas, and the
latter was so apathetic that it was not too painful a thing to bear.
But first came Bancal, and then the Revolution and with it the
newspapers, and then the tide of affairs and men that had swept
with Brissot into the salon of the rue Guénégaud. Intimate hours
became extremely rare, for did not Mme Roland belong wholly to
the public weal ? What was there left of her for her friends ? She,
so sensitive, no longer even saw the pain she caused. And now
here she was leaving Paris, leaving for *Le Clos,* this time without a
thought of asking him ! This in itself embittered him, but worse
was to follow. Was it possible ? Mme Roland was taking with
her Mme Grandchamp, the close friend he had introduced to her !
She too was forsaking him ! And neither of them had told him
a word about it ! Yes, they had plotted this together, plotted against
him, to oust him from their plans, to leave him alone in Paris
and go off happily, to enjoy in peace the charms of the country,
in the paradise he had lost !

The moment Mme Roland learned of his distress, she wrote him at eleven at night:

I do not reproach you for your error, in my eyes it is the result of a hasty emotion which gave you no time for reflection, and once recognized this fault becomes almost a merit. Let your bad resolution go at that; come, as you promised me. . . But in truth you will do more than anger me, you will profoundly grieve me if you do not come; it would mean you were worse than unjust.

The next day, the one previous to her departure, in the midst of worry and packing, even though weary and in poor health, she flew to the rue des Prouvaires, to the touchy friend who had gone out expressly to avoid a too speedy reconciliation.

Scarcely had she returned to the rue Guénégaud than she took up her pen: "I have just come from your office and from your lodgings, all in vain. I was tired . . . but I would have gone to any extreme to have avoided taking with me the pain of abandoning a friend in your frame of mind. . ." She redoubled her explanations, her protestations, her assurances. She coaxed him, she called him her friend and her son, ending by saying that he would be both to her forever. But he was determined to be angry, and in his absurdity he resisted for more than six months the joys of an untroubled friendship.

If she felt saddened by this unforeseen and somewhat ridiculous storm, the journey soon distracted her and calmed and refreshed her overwrought mind that had, for several months, known no relaxation. She was a woman, and still young. Little by little, contact with kindly nature restored all her being. She was like a flower put into water after a dark journey, and the two women laughed at the inconveniences of the road, not neglecting to leave behind them pamphlets of revolutionary propaganda.

Mme Roland was delighted with her companion whose wit and knowledge won all the other mail-coach travellers during the three-day trip.

Since Sophie Cannet, Mme Roland had had no woman friend. In the letter she wrote Roland upon her arrival, she said:

I am still more than glad for the arrangement which has procured me Mme Grandchamp's company, and I am indeed infinitely grateful to her for the trip. It was an undertaking for her health, for the interruption of her work and her usual connections; I wish very much that you would come to know her better; there is not another woman with such a mind.

This same letter likewise informs us of the Roland's relations with the Buzot family:

I had promised myself that I would write Mme Buzot by the same mail; she cannot imagine how I was touched by the display of interest she was good enough to show; I left her with some precipitance, because I had to tear myself away, but never will this moment leave my heart. Tell her, as well as her worthy husband, how dear they are to us; speak for both of us, for you love them as much as I.

Canon Dominique, attentive as usual, came to meet his sister-in-law on the banks of the Saône, as far as Riottier harbour. Eudora awaited her mother with the greatest impatience, an impatience which her mother perhaps did not entirely share, for at Villefranche she went directly to the house where she spent two hours supervising the cleaning while Eudora, in her convent, sent three consecutive times asking her to come. Mme Roland went to Sainte-Marie "with the intention of leaving the child there until the next day," so as to put her house in order, but the poor little girl flung herself with such heart-breaking sobs into her mother's arms that she no longer considered leaving her. Mme Roland was one of those parents who have to be proud of their children before they can passionately love them. Eudora was merely a charming little girl, very pleasant and very sweet, but fond of play and heedless as one is at that age. She did not do honour to her mother, who was apparently little affected by her beauty, for she never spoke of it. In no way did Eudora resemble that young Manon Phlipon who at seven gave lessons to her priest, astonished the painter Guibal by reciting the Athanasian Creed, and, by her promise of extraordinary wit, made herself the talk of the entire Ile of the Cité Notre-Dame. The fact that at ten years of age her daughter had only the mind which one has at ten, greatly discouraged Mme Roland. To listen to her, one would believe she had given birth to a feeble-minded creature. Sadly, seriously, she spoke of the "nullity" of this "only child":

There is no use disguising it [she said to her husband], your daughter is sensitive, she loves me, she will be sweet, but she hasn't an idea, not a grain of memory; she might just have come from a wet-nurse, and she gives promise of no wit. She has embroidered me a very pretty work bag and she does a little needlework; beyond this she has taste for nothing.

Did Mme Roland remember the time when she was disturbed by a certain coldness which she thought she observed in the prudent Mme Phlipon ? She then longed for a greater intimacy with a mother she adored. She did not see that, after having been too intellectual for her mother, she was still more so for her child.

That year the country was nothing but disappointments. As there had been no rain since Saint-John's, there would be neither fruit nor vegetables. The grapes would ripen too early and a thousand worries would result. Mme Roland urged her husband to come with the inseparable "brother," that is to say, with Lanthenas, to oversee the work of the fields. At heart she was already regretting Paris. Her thoughts had remained there, and she considered ways and means of returning: "I suspect," she said to Roland in the course of the same letter, "that the big interests are not in the best hands in the world, and I for my part would look with pleasure upon the assurance of a sojourn in Paris. . . All the nothingness of the provinces has seemed to tumble about my ears. I have felt myself buried in emptiness and obscurity."

Roland stood at the legislative elections at Lyons, and was defeated. Mme Roland was certainly more than disappointed. In writing to Bancal, candidate for Clermont-Ferrand,[30] she exerted all her energies to soften the expression of discontent to a mere melancholy which contrasts strangely with the vehement letters of the past months. Was she not endowing her husband with her own emotions when she wrote:

As for us personally, it is not without pain that I see our friend [Roland] flung back into silence and obscurity; he is accustomed to a public life, it is more necessary to him than he himself knows; his energy, his activity become disastrous to his health when they are not employed according to his tastes.

In Roland's letters to his wife, there was no indication that he

was anxious to remain in Paris. At any rate, he was just as much
concerned with his own private interests as with those of his country. On the twelfth of September 1791, he wrote:

> The disorder of the public treasury is incalculable, irremediable, in-
> decipherable . . . see too the risks we run through being restricted to
> Le Clos, with a surcharge of taxes such as, combined with the enormous
> deficit, the horrible waste, the war and other miseries, would naturally
> put the machine out of order ! . . .

A little further on he added in evident horror:

> An engraving representing a large dinner scene has just been put
> up for sale on the walls of the Mint. Gargantua is at table. On one
> side is the family, on the other his wife standing holding his head in
> one hand and accepting in the other a large glass of the blood of a
> man whose throat is being cut by the butcher of Nancy, in order to
> give it to drink to Gargantua whose mouth is already open. And she,
> with an atrocious leer, is saying these words: "If only this glass could
> serve as a bath for me !" It is the most terrible reproach, the most
> horrible caricature that has yet been made. It makes one shudder to
> think of it.

Upon Roland's return from Paris, the two women left for Lyons
for the purpose of outfitting Eudora. Bosc continued to mope,
and Roland, deserted, wrote him:

> Concerning my womenfolk, you are too hard on them; they talk of
> you all day long; you do not answer them, you will have nothing to
> do with them. Where is all this going to get you, any one of you ?
> Do you want to break off ? Will you find elsewhere tastes more in
> keeping, notions more alike, or more reciprocal sentiments. I defy
> you to. . .

Mme Roland was far from happy at Lyons. "How I am to be
pitied," my friend said to me. "The work I am doing disgusts
me and wears me out." [31] (The work on the *Dictionnaire de
Manufactures*.) She wanted to keep Mme Grandchamp with her,
but this wish made Mme Grandchamp aware of those other
"bonds," that were even dearer to her. On her return to Le Clos,
Mme Grandchamp, in an ill-temper, wrote: "The house looked
exactly what it was to me: ugly, inconvenient, etc."

Ever since her return to Beaujolais, Mme Roland had written her
husband that there was reason to believe that a sojourn in Paris

would be of great advantage to Eudora. "Everything shows us that the air of the provinces is asphyxiating for her." She did not admit, and perhaps not even to herself, that she was seeking pretexts to prove that Paris would be favourable, necessary even, to the good of her family. She seemed profoundly saddened and out of her element. When she complained to Bancal that she could not reconcile in her life her work for her husband and her daughter's education, there was something so absurd in it that we must seek elsewhere for the cause of her evident discomfort. The absorbing companionship of Mme Grandchamp had no effect on this gloomy and unreasonable mood in which we see Mme Roland for the first time. On the other hand, these two women were extremely capricious. One day they adored each other and wanted never to be separated, and the next they scarcely spoke. This time the vintage left Mme Roland indifferent. How they had changed her in Paris, our "rustic lady" of former years!

There is an extremely simple explanation, however, that might occur to the suspicious mind. Could it be the image of Buzot that was troubling her thoughts ? Was it to see him again that she sighed for Paris ? It is impossible to answer yes or no. After having known her through the medium of autograph papers, and not through the words of more or less prejudiced authors, it would seem that, if in the autumn of 1791 she was languishing in the wilds of Beaujolais, it was because her active mind, her hopes, and her thoughts were left behind with the Revolution. It is almost certain that nothing had yet distracted her from her vocation. A year was to pass before she would be disturbed by that emotion which she invariably confused with the cause of Liberty ! One might even be tempted to find a delicate proof of this in the over-agitated part of her letter to Roland: ". . . I had to tear myself away . . . never will this moment leave my heart." Had she at that time considered Buzot in any way except as a friend of noble character, and as a talented man able to serve the cause of the public good, she would have kept from her husband such evidently suspicious impressions, nor would she have been in such haste to write Mme Buzot — whom she broke with almost completely a year later, that

is to say when she saw clearly and resolutely into her own heart.
It was from public life that she, in saying farewell to the Buzots in
September 1791, had had to "tear herself away." From this sprang
her emotion, as well as the regrets that followed it.

But there was even more.

On the thirteenth of June 1793, when Buzot was impeached
before the Convention, Deputy Duray, who like Buzot, came from
the Eure, stood up to fling his stone:

> Buzot's marked want of patriotism dates from the thirtieth of Sep-
> tember 1792. At this time he received a letter from the Roland woman
> [laughter], he gave it to me to read: the Roland woman complained
> because the Paris counter-Revolution had issued a warrant against the
> virtuous Roland. . . She set forth the dangers her husband was run-
> ning, saying that the one way of saving him would be to name him
> deputy at the Convention. Since that time Buzot has been against
> Paris. [*Moniteur,* June 15, 1793.]

On that day in September '92 when Mme Roland wrote Buzot —
and she was at liberty to write him as she wished — it was not upon
politics, and this was indeed so much the case that he did not
hesitate to show her letter to a colleague. And here we must
recall a remark which we have already mentioned: *"In October
1792,"* she said elsewhere, *"I had no other ambition than to keep
my soul pure and my husband's glory intact."*

The rumour had spread in Lyons that the Rolands' long stay in
the capital was due to Roland having been imprisoned as a supposed counter-Revolutionary, and one day Mme Roland heard
shouted behind her: "Hang the aristocrats on the lamppost!"
Upon returning to *Le Clos,* she exclaimed: "This gives a despair-
ing idea of the people's stupidity." Mme Grandchamp was still
there. Alternately the husband's and then the wife's confidant, she
had promised to do what she could to persuade Roland to return
to Paris, while Roland was counting on her to overcome his wife's
aversion to the country.

Mme Grandchamp was on the best of terms with Roland, who
was very attentive to her, listened to her opinions and was extremely shocked to find that his wife had neglected to put all his

works into her visitor's hands as soon as she had reached *Le Clos*. He brought them to her without further delay, obliged her to read them, and then to give her opinions. At the end of her visit, Roland even asked Mme Grandchamp to read his work on *Pelts* for the Panckoucke Encyclopædia, to annotate it, and to suggest corrections. Then he left for Lyons. "We are lost," cried Mme Roland. The two women were in league against Roland and realized it was not the moment to offend him, but on the contrary, to secure as much influence over him as possible. Mme Grandchamp, still unacquainted with Roland's fastidious and quibbling vanity, believed she could make everything right by saying that she would so soften her observations that he would not take offence, but Mme Roland only repeated: "We are lost. I know the manuscript by heart. . . Your notes, however intended, however modified, will irritate Roland beyond all hope. . .," which was to say that Mme Grandchamp would thus lose all the influence she possessed, and would never be able to dissuade him from passing the winter in the country.

ON THE fourteenth of September 1791, the King signed the Constitution, in spite of the strong remonstrances of the Princes.

Mme Roland revolted against the vestiges of the old regime — particularly the right of *veto* — which were retained for the purpose of obtaining the King's signature. But the public had not so much penetration. A great wave of jubilation was sweeping the country. There was public dancing and embracing. Everyone thought the Revolution was accomplished, that there would be no war, and that the French people could at last enjoy their conquests. It was not yet known that, returning from the solemn meeting where he had pledged his word, Louis XVI had, that same evening, sent a secret message to Emperor Leopold calling the Austrians to the frontiers of the kingdom of France. With her highest hopes destroyed, it was a humiliated Mme Roland who bitterly contrasted this reality with her fondest dreams.

Idle, now that she took no more interest in the work of the fields which in other days had seemed to her so fine a task, she wrote

Robespierre a ceremonious and respectful letter. However, she spoke to him as equal to equal, and it is worthy of note that she no longer brought her husband to the fore. She said: "The little town where I have a home . . .," and: "In the depths of my retirement I learn with joy the result of your successes. . ."

This was the man in whom she believed, she saw as much sincerity as energy. Curious pages, these, and terrible to read, for they make one feel from what heights this woman, but a brief time later, was to fall. How can one read without a shudder such phrases as: "You have done much, Monsieur, to prove and propagate these principles [those of equality and liberty]; it is fine, it is consoling to be able to bear witness to this in an age when so many others still ignore the career intended for them; a great one is still in store for you if the remainder of your life resemble its beginning, and you are on a stage where your courage will have full play." She had no particular reason for writing him, but she "had faith," she said, "in the interest with which [he would receive] news of two beings . . . who liked to express [to him] an esteem which they accorded to few people. . ."

It was to return in some way to the Revolutionary movement that she had written this disquieting man, it was so that she would not be forgotten. She was not at ease with him. He had always shown a coldness to her in which she had felt, with inexplicable certainty, a remote, a furtive aversion which she could not explain and which she could, perhaps, not overcome. Mme Roland was one of those women so accustomed in all encounters to win every heart and mind, that she was entirely put out by a rebuff. Such women rely upon their charm as they do upon their sight and touch. If it fails them, their very need to regain power hampers their talents and destroys their tact. Who cannot help but feel that this letter was an error, almost a lack of dignity ? And this was not the only one, as we shall see. It is probable that Robespierre did not respond. If he did, it must have been drily and briefly and not without disdain.

On this same date, September 27, 1791, a decree passed in Paris abolished the Inspection of Manufactures.

Roland thereby lost his salary of five thousand *livres,* but as he had been in the service almost forty years, he considered that he could apply for a pension. Mme Roland welcomed the opportunity and lost no time in proving to Roland the necessity of going to Paris to validate his claims. It was probably a hard battle to win, for though all-powerful in her husband's mind, still she did not deem it superfluous to further her cause by arguments which Mme Grandchamp cleverly inserted in her letters to *Le Clos.*

More than ever now, did Roland's correspondence strengthen the impression that he then felt there was not the slightest necessity to return to Paris. On returning to his country home, he had found the house fallen into neglect, his grounds in bad condition, etc. At the end of September, he wrote Bosc: "I am going to devote myself to the repairing of the ills of a too-lengthy absence."

He was thinking of taking up again, for the Panckouke Encyclopædia, the work that had occupied him as inspector of Manufactures. Following a new family arrangement, he considered enlarging his estate and sent Lanthenas to Marly to M. de Nervo, Lord of Theizé, to acquaint him with the fact that he desired to buy ground. Add to this that Roland had been re-elected, first to the district administration, and, two months later, municipal officer at Lyons. He was obviously firmly rooted in the country, but for a long time he had no other will but that of the woman who manœuvred him with skill. By this time she had no illusions as to the unimportant place he filled in the world. When she had married him, she, as well as he, had believed that an Inspector of Manufactures was a personage in the kingdom. Now she knew of what it consisted: "It is one of those very secondary places in the administration, which gives no authority, pays very little, and for the duties of it, it suffices to possess honesty, merit, etc. . ."

To return to Paris, however, was a hazardous undertaking. The Rolands' income was slender. To make up for what was lacking, they must rely on problematical work furnished them by libraries of their acquaintance or by new friends. No matter. One after the other, Mme Roland overcame all obstacles. On the fifteenth of December 1791, the family arrived in Paris — this time Eudora accompanied her parents — and once more settled at the Hotel Brittanique, but on the third floor, in very restricted quarters.

MME GRANDCHAMP wrote that she had made every preparation for the Rolands' arrival, and that she was extremely disappointed to receive a note from her friend bidding her not to come to the hotel to meet them. But the next day she was unable to keep away. Roland was sitting by the fire, and so irritated was he by the corrections she had made of his thesis, that he scarcely stopped his reading to greet her, while Mme Roland had "red eyes and a tremulous voice." It was clear that Roland was in the worst of humours and had just made a scene.

It was natural for Mme Roland to put a great amount of energy into a search for the work the couple required. Roland, who was always active, set about securing his pension and again occupied himself with the *Dictionnaire des Manufactures,* which had been completed in October 1790, but which had not been printed before now (January 1792), because "there is no work more important than the duties of a citizen." He was also considering founding in Paris a periodical devoted to agriculture, commerce, and the industrial arts. Panckouke would be the editor. Roland was returning to his old pursuits.

Had it not been for his wife, it is probable that Roland, influenced by his brother the Canon, would have gradually withdrawn from politics. He was physically tired, and morally disgusted with all he had seen in the last seven months. The necessities of life must have worried him, and he was not the sort of man for adventure. But he was easily persuaded by fine-sounding phrases. His wife was eloquent, and once convinced herself, she had no trouble in convincing him. She had but one thought, to return to public life. True, upon her arrival in Paris, she had found to her disappointment, that the personalities who had gathered about her in her *salon* in the rue Guénégaud, were scattered far and wide. Pétion, suddenly popularly acclaimed, had been named Mayor of Paris, and both he and his wife were inflated by "a conceit that was hardly democratic." Roland went to see him on his arrival, but Pétion did not call at rue Guénégaud, and when Mme Roland visited Mme Pétion, she met with a "cold reception," nor did Mme Pétion escort her further than the door of the *salon* when she left, but allowed her "to traverse unaccompanied, a number of rooms." Mme Roland was "deeply wounded. . ."[32] Should Republicans judge people in this way?"

Moreover, Buzot had returned to Evreux at the close of the Constituent Assembly. For some time Robespierre had seemed to be tending towards a more personal form of politics. "We see much less of Brissot," say the *Memoirs*.

Roland was extremely irritated, and wished to return to the country. Mme Grandchamp (in league, of course with Mme Roland), settled the matter by renting for the couple a small apartment at 51, rue de la Harpe, on the second floor, overlooking the court.[33] The Rolands were to move in after Easter.

The Legislative Assembly [34] which, to quote Taine, "the Constituent had already deleted of its staff of honest men," met on the first of October 1791. The majority of the deputies — there were 745 members — consisted of four hundred provincial lawyers chosen "from the lowest ranks of the bar," the greater number of which had not attained their thirtieth year. The Revolutionary party was now split in two, the Gironde and the Montagne, in other words, the left and the extreme left. In the centre were those who were contemptuously referred to as the *Plaine,* the *Marais* or the *Ventre,* and they formed the most numerous group. Those who were undecided — and there were many — often voted with this latter group.

The left was called the Gironde, because of the young deputies from the Bordeaux country who predominated through their exceptionally brilliant oratorical abilities. Guadet, Vergniaud, Gensonné, Ducos, Boyer-Fonfrède, all lawyers, caused a great sensation. They were joined by other deputies who shared their opinions, and this custom, begun in the Legislative Assembly, persisted at the Convention, where among the Girondists were Normands such as Buzot, an old member of the Constituent; Abbé Fauchet, Constitutional Bishop from the Calvados; Isnard, deputied by the Var; Brissot, who came from Chartres; Pétion, also from Chartres; and the former followers of La Fayette, and some of the first Jacobins, such as Manuel and Condorcet.[35]

The word Gironde was little heard at the time. In designating the "Patriotes," Mme Roland's group, the term "Brissotins" was used, and this was more exact,[36] for little by little the party had centred around Brissot. Later we shall hear "Rolandistes," "Buzotins," "Bordelais," etc.

It is not difficult to imagine how the Rolands again came to the fore. In the absence of political personalities, Mme Roland had to content herself with Bosc, Lanthenas, and Bancal who had finally returned to Paris. These men Mme Roland swayed as she wished. She had but to express the desire of seeing her husband again in power in the Revolutionary party, and immediately they set about it.

Lanthenas and Bancal exerted their influence at the Jacobin Club, where the former was Vice-president, the latter Secretary. Bosc, who was working regularly on the Correspondence Committee, had Roland admitted there in the capacity of secretary, and naturally Mme Roland took some part in her husband's work.

Matters were at this pass when, in March, a crisis arose in the ministry.[37] In calling Dumouriez [38] to the Foreign Office, the King had apparently showed a certain consideration for the Assembly. Demouriez, entrusted with the task of forming a ministry, in the utmost seriousness requested the chiefs of the Girondist majority (ineligible according to the decrees of May 19, 1790, and April 7, 1791), to designate some capable administrators to replace the outgoing ministers at the Interior and the Public Tax Office.

Mme Dodun, a wealthy *bourgeoise* of that time, whose husband had made a fortune in the *Compagnie des Indes,* had been smitten with revolutionary ideas — or perhaps only by one of their exponents — and had offered to Vergniaud an apartment in her house at five Place Vendôme.

Often a number of politicians would meet there at lunch and discuss current affairs before betaking themselves to the Assembly meeting. This was called the Committee of the Place Vendôme.

Republicans without a mandate mingled with the deputies, and Roland had been invited. He, however, was never much inclined to go anywhere without his wife, and although his friends all went there, he appeared but seldom. In conversation with Brissot,[39] one of them there suggested Roland for the Ministry of the Interior.

Brissot, Paris deputy, who had become very powerful through *Le Patriote Français,* appeared to approve the idea.

Mme Grandchamp has said very plainly that it was Lanthenas who thought of Roland for the ministry, but she added: "I permitted myself to tell Lanthenas that I did not think our friends fitted to lead an administration in such stormy times. . . They had little knowledge of either men or the Court, and would fall into all sorts of traps." She was well-acquainted with Mme Roland's candour.

On the twenty-first of March, Roland who had passed the evening with Mme Grandchamp, left her house at nine o'clock. At eleven, the bell rang. It was a note from Mme Roland: Dumouriez had come to advise Roland that the King had appointed him Minister of the Interior. Roland had asked until ten o'clock the next morning to give his answer. "It is you who will decide, come as soon as possible," wrote Mme Roland. Next morning early, Mme Grandchamp in great perplexity hurried to the Rolands. She found them in bed, after a sleepless night. She "burst into tears," for she was about to lose their friendship because of "the honours that would be heaped upon them." But Roland cried: "I shall accept only if you promise to share our lot." He had already created a post for her. She should read the papers and make press-cuttings which would be given him on awakening. This entire scene is excellent *bourgeois* comedy. Finally Mme Grandchamp consented. She remarked that her friends were very uncomfortable in their small quarters; "they had no clothes, no money." And moveover, Mme Roland was ill. The landlady had lost her respect for them since their inglorious return. Now she altered completely. She offered her entire house from cellar to garret to Mme Grandchamp. Mme Grandchamp told her to put the first floor in readiness against the return of the Minister who had gone to take his oath of office.

Then she went out to borrow funds. She found every purse open, but a thousand errands kept her going and coming; she ran about all day and came home at seven, exhausted with fatigue.

I thought I was dreaming when I entered the *salon;* my friend who had seemed that morning on the point of death, had recovered her freshness and charm. She was surrounded by a number of people who were showering her with compliments; Roland took his share in these civilities and seemed satisfied. I threw myself into an armchair near the fireplace, and there observed the new personalities before my eyes: the room was crowded with ministers, chiefs of state, and the principal deputies. Two lackeys, standing outside the door, opened one or two panels of it, depending on the rank of the visitor; it was he himself who informed them of the proper amount. I asked myself if all this were really serious. Only the day before, living in one room and a study, situated on the poorest floor with a simple country servant, surrounded by the most utter poverty, a man was worrying about his livelihood, and a woman wished to end her days. This over-night upheaval was sufficient excuse for my doubts and surprises. Fortunately I was able to abandon myself to my own thoughts and to the observations this spectacle gave rise to. When I left I was deeply distressed, and I resolved not to keep the indiscreet promise that I had made, although it had been publicly announced.

The next day Dumouriez, who had just donned the scarlet cap, went to the Jacobins and embraced Robespierre, without, however, offering him a post in the government.

Mme Roland felt only dislike for this "court varlet" whose cynicism and brazenness were odious to her. That he had planned to attack the virtue of this Lucretia is quite possible. The tone he took with her was quite uncalled for and put her on her guard; she made him keep his distance and treat her with respect. He was prompt with the assurance that the King intended "in all sincerity to uphold the Constitution." Mme Roland suspected and mistrusted him, and thought no good could come of a Roland working in conjunction with a Dumouriez.

We know but little of the emotions Mme Roland experienced during this extraordinary period. True, we have the letters she wrote Bancal, Champagneux, and Albert Gosse, in which she gave them this astonishing piece of news. Evidently her calm was a forced one, but if she succeeded in deluding her friends, we are not so easily taken in. There had never been any hint that she had imagined she would attain such prominence. How her brain must have spun ! In the course of that night, between Dumouriez' visit and Roland's official acceptance, not a wink had she slept in that shabby room in the Hotel Brittanique. Her imagination, however, must not have been idle. She was aware of her power. Her husband and those about him were in constant need of her approbation, of her ability, of her intelligence; she was the power behind them all; it was she, in reality, who had been named Minister of the Interior. There was nothing vulgar in these thoughts of hers. Hers was no common vanity, but weighing her responsibilities, she considered herself equal to the task. No doubt she was close to believing that day, that she alone was to remake the Revolution, restore to it its pristine majesty as well as that spiritual beauty which it had possessed in the first days of 1789.

In a letter Roland wrote before his return to *Le Clos* on the twelfth of September 1791, he said to his wife:

Lanthenas and I are still waiting; we are uncertain and anxious. Brissot continues to vacillate and usually ends by backing people who are both mediocre and untrustworthy. . .

We are familiar with Roland's pretentiousness. He esteemed Brissot anew, however, when the latter showed sufficient judiciousness to single him out for the ministry. "I have already recounted," says Mme Roland in her *Memoirs,* "how Roland became a member of the government unawares. Impartial posterity cannot but find in his public career, the proof of his enlightenment, disinterestedness, and virtue."

The *Patriote Français* took under its protection the minister its director had created, and gave the public a certain amount of information regarding this unknown man.

M. Roland Laplatière must not be confused with a certain M. Laplatière, the author of *A Gallery of Eminent Men.* The former is a municipal officer at Lyons, a writer known for his interesting, ingenious and useful works. . .

And on another day:

. . . a learned man who has written on several sections of the administration, a man not without experience in this connection, who enjoys an honourable reputation, and whose age, habits, and marked personality, as well as the high principles expressed in his work . . .

But indeed Roland was entirely unknown. Outside the Brissot group he was so little known to the political world that the Feuillants, as well as Robespierre's friends, were disturbed by the choice.

An engraving of Roland, dating from the end of his ministry, shows him in three-quarter view in an oval frame. The face is lean and bony, the forehead bald, the hair, planted high on the head, brushed back and falling, in the Quaker fashion, into sparse curls. The neck is as gaunt as the face, the nose is thin and pointed, the eyes anxious, the lips tightly drawn.

At the top is the name:

JEAN-MARIE ROLAND

Below is this inscription:

RESOLUTION OF TUESDAY, JUNE 18TH
1792
M. ROLAND TAKES WITH HIM THE REGRETS OF THE NATION

Roland was fifty-eight, but appeared much older. Because of the devoted care he had received, he was now in better health than during the preceding years. Notwithstanding, his contemporaries considered him "a venerable old man." We know he was "a gifted man" and "virtuous"—he never missed the opportunity of telling us so—but in justice to him it must be noted that he usually copied what had already been written by his wife. Therefore, it was she who paid this homage to her husband. His part was to repeat what she had written, thoroughly convinced that what he took such pains to copy out was no more than a blatant truth.

THE Ministry of the Interior was in the rue Neuve-des-Petits-Champs, in the former house of the General Control which had been magnificently renovated by M. de Calonne. The Brissotin Ministry, to use the expression of the time, comprised, besides Roland for the Interior and Dumouriez for Foreign Affairs, the

MADAME ROLAND

From a drawing made in prison by a fellow prisoner. Original
belongs to Mme Marion. Now in the Château de Rosière.
A copy signed Mélanie Guérin belongs to Gen. Marillier

JEAN-MARIE ROLAND

From an engraving by Augustin de Saint-Aubin after a painting by Bonneville. Original owned by Mme Marion. Now
in the Château de Rosière

Marquis Grave for the War Department, Lacoste for the Navy, and for Finance the Genevan banker, Clavière.[40] A Minister of Justice [41] was lacking, and Mme Roland brought her friend Bancal's name to the fore. But Bancal, absent as usual, had just left for Auvergne.

The Council's first anxiety was caused by the Extremist Party which was then forming to the left of the Brissotins. Robespierre, resentful at having been put aside by Dumouriez, was the soul of this opposition. Closely associated with him and another bitter enemy of the government, was the old actor Collot d'Herbois. At one time there had been a question of presenting him in opposition to Roland for the Ministry of the Interior, and he was furious at having been rejected. Other men, no less embittered, lurked in the background and were soon to centre around Robespierre.

No-one at the Assembly of the States General ever forgot this "lean, rigid, and obscure little lawyer from Arras," to quote Michelet; the man who came into the limelight by interrupting a debate on famine and pillaging with an argument of unheard of audacity: "The ancient statutes," he had said, "authorize the selling even of the sacred vases to succour the poor."

He had green eyes and a pale face — the face of a cat, Buzot said. His hair was well dressed and powdered. Behind great spectacles, his eyelids were sensitive and reddish. There was something mechanical in his walk. He bit his finger-nails unceasingly, and his dress, more than painstaking, was foppish, even gaudy.

La Revellière-Lépeaux, Barbaroux, Causen, the pamphleteer, have all told the same story of their audiences with Robespierre in the rue Honoré, at the carpenter Duplay's home. There Robespierre lived like a God on his altar, surrounded by his own painted, engraved, and sculptured likenesses.

In a pretty little salon, he received the hommages that are rendered to divinities [said Étienne Dumont];[42] His hair well brushed and powdered; garbed in the most immaculate of dressing gowns, he was installed in a great armchair before a table loaded with the finest fruits, with pure milk, with fragrant coffee. The entire Duplay family, father, mother, children, sought to read in his eyes all his desires so as to fulfil them instantly. . . I spoke twice with Robespierre, he had a sinister appearance. He never looked directly at one; he had a continuous and painful blinking of the eyes. . . He told me he was as timid as a child, that he always trembled upon approaching the tribune and that once he began to speak he was no longer aware of himself.

To bring back this man, this ideologist, to fortify the government with the already relentless power of his teeming brain, this was a task which would have baffled a Mazarin, but which Mme Roland undertook with a light heart.

We know already that on more than one occasion she had not hesitated to make advances to him. Confident of her captivating powers of persuasion, and impelled by the majesty of her cause, having sharpened her wits, banished the irony from her smile, and enhanced the melting softness of her eyes, she received him one morning in private.

This meeting rivals the story of Patru's library or Mme de Maintenon's visit to Saint-Cyr. Physically even, how greatly they differed, these two. He, a young man of thirty-four, narrow-shouldered, sharp-featured, with an unsmiling mouth and a cold eye. She, a deep-bosomed, handsome woman, with a warm heart, an open mind, and an extended hand.

Here is a precious note to Bosc, dated April 1792:

I am at home with Robespierre who asked me for an interview; I shall be alone and I will do all I can to be so this evening at seven; don't come any later; I expect you, and sweet friendship will welcome you with tenderness and serenity. . .

If Bosc responded this time,[43] it is to be doubted whether he found Mme Roland as serene and gracious as she had promised to be. Robespierre, indeed, was preparing to inflict on her the humiliation of an irremediable defeat. He, who was to attempt to "seduce" one by one his political enemies, saw very well that he stood not the least chance of annexing this woman. As for her, all her faculties were to count as naught before this underestimated adversary. Believing that she could sway him in the same way that she had her enthusiasts, she was disconcerted by the alien coldness of a man she could not fathom. But Mme Roland embarrassed Robespierre — a thing he must never have forgiven her — by an ease and simplicity which her culture had left unspoiled. He was constrained and calculating as usual, both too nervous and too cowardly to speak out.

When he left her with a ceremonious and derisive bow, that gift of divination and quick thinking which we have cause to believe was hers, must have made her quail.

In her confidence she must have thought some such thing as: "I won Roland, I shall win Robespierre." But wait. A certain distance is required to take the measure of a man. Doubtless she profited by this harsh lesson, but that day must have deprived her of much of that boundless self-confidence which had been hers since the triumph of her marriage.

"The Court and the intriguers of which the Court makes use . . ." Thus had Robespierre, upon leaving Mme Roland, spoken before the Jacobins with a perfidy rife with obvious insinuations against the new ministers. Mme Roland was beginning her apprenticeship in calumny.

ALMOST all historians have spoken of Mme Roland as the leader of the Girondists, but moderns reject this opinion after an examination of the facts.

Bonneville de Marsangy seems to have come nearer the truth in writing:

For a long time she seemed only the soul of a faction, the queen of the Girondist party. On closer consideration we see in her the convinced personification of that mass of ideas, of emotions, and of hopes, which we call the great principles of '89.

The Gironde was a rather scattered party in which were often found people with little in common. It was comprised of the Committee of the Place Vendôme, with Vergniaud; the *salon* of Mme Sophie de Condorcet,[44] a centre of atheism and Encyclopædia spirit; the mayoral group over which Pétion presided with a self-sufficiency better explained by his popularity than by the importance of his position; Brissot, more or less isolated, who drifted from group to group; and finally, Mme Roland's *salon*. As in 1791, it was there that the first patriots met, already outdistanced by those like Robespierre and Danton, who had gradually strayed away. There were many reasons why this group was the most celebrated one. While it could not boast Vergniaud, still it was the most brilliant, the most courageous, the most disinterested, the most in evidence, and it was, moreover, centred about a handsome woman who was the personification of civic purity. Mme Roland clearly wished to make her *salon* of the Minister of the Interior in 1792 the rallying-point it had been in the Hotel Brittanique in 1791. She had always been sociable, she had always felt the need of communicating with others. Her receptions, although very simple, excited so much envy that the opposition went so far as to describe them as orgies.

The Council of ministers met four times a week. In the *Notes Historiques* which she wrote after the *Mémoires Particuliers,* Mme Roland said:

During Roland's second administration, as in the first, I was resolved to receive no woman, and I scrupulously lived up to my word. My circle was never a very extended one, and women never formed the greater part of it. After my closest relatives, I saw only those people whose tastes and works were of interest to my husband. I felt that, in the ministry, I might be surrounded by very inconvenient or even dangerous people; I considered that the mayor's wife, Mme. Pétion, had taken a very wise decision and I esteemed it was as praiseworthy to follow a good example as to give one. I had then neither a following nor visitors; in the first place, it was time saved, a thing on which too high a value cannot be set if one has ways in which to employ it. Twice a week only, I gave a dinner. One for my husband's colleagues among whom were several deputies; the other to various people, were they deputies, head clerks in the offices, or such others in affairs or concerned with the common weal. Taste and cleanliness reigned at my table, and the ornaments of luxury were never in evidence; there we were at ease, without sacrificing much time to it, because I had but one course and because I shared with no-one the responsibility of doing the honours. The usual number of guests was fifteen, on rare occasions there were eighteen, and once only, there were twenty. Such were the meals that popular orators described in the Jacobin tribune as sumptuous feasts, where I, a modern Circe, corrupted all those who had the misfortune to be seated there. After dinner there was some conversation in the *salon* and then everyone returned to his own affairs. We sat down at table about five, and at nine there was no-one left at my house. Such was the court of so-called conspirators of which gossip crowned me queen.

Other days we were often, my husband and I, quite alone, for the round of occupations advanced the dinner hour till quite late so that my daughter dined in her room with her governess. Those who saw me at that time will one day bear me witness. When the voice of truth can again be heard, I shall perhaps no longer be alive, but I shall depart this world in the confidence that the memory of slanders will be lost in maledictions, while mine will at times be recalled with tenderness.

Before the time had come when she was to write with rare moderation of the atrocious mortifications which made her accept death with less bitterness than life, she was to begin, with Roland's acceptance of the ministry, a progressive descent. The first step of it was Robespierre's definite separation from the Gironde.

The question of war arose.

The government's programme was to rid the administration, the diplomatic service and the army of the men and the spirit of the old regime, to restrict the clergy, and above all to retaliate by an offensive to the threatening manifestations of Prussia and Austria.

From one end to the other the country was living in mortal fear of foreign invasion and of the revenge of the Emigrants. As long as this general panic lasted it was impossible for affairs to resume their normal trend or to succeed in the foundation of a new order. There was but one remedy; to force the European powers to recognize the Constitution and disperse the Emigrants who had collected beyond the frontiers.

On the twentieth of April, it was decided on the motion of Merlin de Thionville: "Let us vote war to kings and peace to nations," while Condorcet asked that it be "understood by all the world that France seeks no conquests but wishes only to establish the liberty of peoples."

The Gironde and the Montagne now came into violent collision. Even in the face of a common peril, the parties did not forget their differences. The country had now to undergo a revolution within the Revolution.

In all justice to the Girondists it must be noted that in spite of their lack of cohesion, they were not divided and accepted without a tremour the terrible responsibility of war. Robespierre, through demagogic [45] ambition, pretended to believe that they were merely seeking an opportunity to win the favour of a monarchy whose one remaining hope was war.

In his *Memoirs,* Barbaroux has written:

Robespierre who, as Condorcet has said, hasn't an idea in his head or a sentiment in his heart, Robespierre still held the tribune (of the Jacobins), poisoned the people with his flattery and was already serving his apprenticeship in crime by his instigations against the Republicans. . . It would make a curious and atrocious story, the tale of Robespierre's contradictions and calumnies. While the question of war was being treated by the Jacobins with great solemnity, he never ceased saying to those who contradicted him: "So you want war?" To be sure, no-one wanted this scourge, but the Austrians were there, it was no longer a question of whether or not one wished to fight.

Precisely at this moment, the future was hanging in the balance.

On the twenty-fifth of April, five days after the declaration of war with Austria, Guadet, supported by Brissot, appeared at the Jacobin tribune to answer the attacks of Robespierre. A memorable meeting, where for the first time men who had hitherto fought side by side publicly opposed each other.

On this same day, Mme Roland broke off relations by this vehement and uncompromising letter to Robespierre:

April 25, 1792
Ten o'clock at night

I wished to see you, Monsieur, because I believed in your great love for Liberty, in your complete devotion to the public weal, and in talking to you I found the pleasure and utility which rejoices good citizens when they express their sentiments and clarify their opinions. The more you seemed to me to differ upon a question vital to those men whose intelligence and integrity I esteem, the more important did it seem to me to draw together those who, having but one end in mind, should come to an agreement upon the methods of attaining it. When the soul is proud, when the intentions are upright and when one's every thought is for the good of the people, with all personal consideration and secret ambition laid aside, it is one's duty to reach a decision upon the ways of serving the common weal.

It pained me to see you were convinced that no intelligent man could differ from you upon the question of war and yet remain a good citizen.

I did not do you the same injustice; I know excellent citizens whose opinons are contrary to yours and I found you no less estimable because you thought otherwise than they. Your prejudices grieved me, and in order to have none myself, I hoped that I would come to know your reasons.

You had promised to explain them to me, you were to come and see me . . . you shunned me, you told me nothing, and in that interval you stirred up public opinion against those who differed from you. I am too frank not to confess to you that this way of acting did not seem frank to me.

I do not know whom you consider your mortal enemies: I know them not, and to be sure I do not receive them in all confidence in my home, for this privilege is accorded citizens whose integrity is proven and who have no enemies save those who are foes to the safety of France.

Remember, Monsieur, what I said to you the last time I had the honour of seeing you: uphold the Constitution, see that it be executed by popular favour; that was what seemed to me the citizen's guide wherever he might be. It is the doctrine of the respectable men I know, it is the end for which they are working and I look about me in vain for those who might be called conspirators, which is the term you use.

Time will clarify everything; its justice is slow but sure; it constitutes the hope and consolation of good people. I shall await its confirmation or justification of those whom I esteem. It is you, Monsieur, who should consider that this justice of time will make your glory forever eternal, or will annihilate it for all time.

Pardon the austerity of my opinion; it is at one with the principles I profess and with the emotions that impel me, and I could never appear anything but what I am.

Death was already on the way.

BUT Mme Roland's positive mind never wasted time on useless recriminations, whether against herself or against others.

She had immediately felt the necessity of reorganizing the ministerial offices where the action of the republican minister was paralysed by the routine of the old regime. Through a certain Gibert whom she had known in the Quai de l'Horloge period, and who was an employee in the Postal Service and a lover of all the arts, she met one of his most valued friends, a man named Pache. She acquired a taste for him upon learning that he, the son of a servant of the Duke de Castries who had had him educated, had voluntarily (after certain rather profitable financial operations), renounced the pension which an "ex-minister" paid him.

This Pache was a widower of fifty, burdened with a family, and on first glance seemed an intelligent and modest man. He was in reality a true Tartufe, who knew marvellously well how to play the rôle of the virtuous Republican. "But," said Mme Roland in her *Memoirs,* excusing herself for having thought Pache an honest man, "when hypocrisy sinks to such horrid depths it is less shameful to be duped by it than to have the perversity to suspect it."

When Roland entered the ministry, it was agreed with his wife that he take Pache into his office, but Pache accepted only on condition that he be unpaid, wishing, he said, to serve the State without remuneration. It is not difficult to imagine the delight of the candid Rolands who were furthermore to see Pache work in the ministry from seven in the morning till three in the afternoon without eating anything at the dinner hour except the piece of dry bread which he had brought in his pocket.

Mme Roland, moreover, considered it of the greatest importance to "disaristocracize" the Postal Department and had Bosc entrusted with this important work. (May 11, 1792.)

At the same time she took note of the ability of a postal clerk named Antoine Lemaire, author of the first *Lettres du Père Duchesne,* and founder of the *Courrier de l'Égalité.* Bosc was his chief. Mme Roland asked Bosc to release him from his duties. "Do it quickly, for the fatherland," she wrote him in one of those immunerable little communications which replaced and which certainly must have been less difficult than our telephone calls.

Bosc obeyed at once, of course, and twenty-four hours later Mme Roland charged Antoine Lemaire with the mission of preaching to and enlightening the troops.

At the same time Lanthenas introduced her to young Louvet who had been made famous by his novel *Faublas.* She commissioned him to found — principally against Robespierre and in support of the administration — a newspaper of propaganda. The first number appeared on the sixteenth of May 1792, under the title of *La Sentinelle.* "Roland," she said, "paid for the printing from a small sum he had collected in the ministry for the formation of the public mind" — a beautiful expression compared to our dreadful word propaganda.

In one of Mme Roland's note-books, very much like our own, we find a detailed statement of these funds:

> . . . funds put at the disposal of the Minister of the Interior who will undertake to have made and published good writings to enlighten the people and spread the ideas and the sentiments which are requisite to the triumph of good Order and the Constitution.
> As a result M. Pétion gave M. Roland: on the thirteenth of May the sum of six thousand francs;
> On the fifteenth — given M. Louvet, five hundred francs.
> M. Louvet was chosen to draw up a newspaper under the title of *Sentinelle,* which would appear several times a week or every day, according to the press of circumstances. The five hundred francs were given him as indemnity for the time and the attention he would devote to this work for a period of two months.

When at a meeting Roland read out the following convocation:

> Gentlemen, a decree of last evening sent me this morning, prescribes that the members of the council . . . give an accounting of their work today at one o'clock . . .

it was more to his wife than to himself that the decree was addressed. We can imagine her working desperately all morning putting in order the data that made up the Minister's report. She examined the provisions and supplies, the hospitals and the foundling-homes; the roads, the bridges and causeways, the charitable workshops, agriculture, manufactures, arts, commerce, the public mind, and ended with eloquent patriotic exhortations. In reading these papers one cannot but be impressed by the care and respect for good order which was one of the characteristics of this scrupulous woman.

Mme Roland's activities gave her no rest. She hated half-way measures. She knew that weakness meant at the very least a loss of time, for if one has done a thing by halves it must be done again. But if time is a fleeting and precious thing to us, what must it have been to the people of the Revolution who crammed such an unbelievable amount of work into the space of four or five years. It is tragic to think of her whose great soul we are attempting to evoke, so distressed over the passing of time. She had only a few more months to live, and she acted as if she knew it. Her brain was seething, her blood was on fire. The task she had set herself was a stupendous one. In a note to Bosc written at this time, she said: "I am in a hurry, I stifle my own ideas, but I love you with all my heart."

Thus Mozart, stricken with a mortal disease, once wrote: "I go on (with my work), because composing tires me less than repose."

To comprehend such a life, we must keep in mind that Roland's first ministry lasted two months and twenty-three days, from the twenty-third of March to the tenth of June 1792; the second, five months and twelve days, from the tenth of August 1792, when the crown was overthrown, to the twenty-second of January 1793, the day following the King's death. The Rolands' public life comprised in all two years and three months, to which must be added for her, five months and eight days of imprisonment. If we consider the principal features of the lives of the "giants" of the Revolution, we can readily see that, as a general rule, only a very brief portion of their careers was of any interest. Not all of them could compare with the Girondist Muse. As proof of her superiority, moreover, one has but to read their memoirs and then hers.

One might say that J. -J. Rousseau was responsible for the failure of the Revolution and wonder how things might have fared had Voltaire been its patron saint. His logic would have better served the innovators who had not only to liberate a country from an old regime but had as well to invent for their governmental system laws which would give France her dignity and power.

Voltaire, it is true, did not possess the emotional enthusiasm which to that generation was as necessary as salt. It is curious to note that the Revolutionists knew him principally as a minor or a tragic poet.

Rousseau's readers reacted according to their worth and character. They had hungrily absorbed the paradoxes and the metaphysical declamations which opposed nature to civilization. Some drew conclusions which led to anarchy. Rousseau was all abstractions, conventionalities, utopias, vague sentimentalities, false humanitarian love. All this led his disciples to the "Terror." Mme Roland had

too much good sense to wish for the complete collapse of the old
world. There were many things she wanted to retain, and the
Revolution, in her eyes, should be directed only "against abuses,"
that is to say against the right of might, in the name of Justice
and Liberty.

Historians unsympathetic to Mme Roland do not criticize her
with detachment. They treat her as an adversary, and because she
was a woman, they ridicule her. This tendency to mock would
seem perhaps a bit misplaced, and even rather ungrateful if one
consider what this disinterested woman suffered for the "happiness
of future generations." But is there a man alive who can without
emotion read the words she spoke when she saw opening before
her infinite horizons of hope for those descendants whom she would
never know ?

She has been accused of accepting the King the moment he called
Roland and his friends into power. But for the first time she saw
her ideas about to be put into effect, and what more could she ask ?
She had too much *bourgeois* good sense not to content herself with
this until something better should develop, and we know that she
was so little inclined to make concessions that it was she herself
who caused the downfall of the ministry by her celebrated letter to
Louis XVI.

In the luxurious house where Mme Necker had held sway, Mme
Roland lived with the same simplicity as at *Le Clos*.

However the day she encountered in the ante-chamber of the
Roland ministry, that M. Haudry, the former farmer-general at
whose home she had dined in the pantry, she said indeed that this
offered her a theme for meditation on the reverses of fortune and
the instability of human things. It is impossible not to understand
the satisfaction she took in the good and just revenge which Destiny
had accorded her.

Of course she immediately became a target for beggars, but she,
a good Republican, refused on principle to favour "introductions,"
and this immediately won her a host of enemies.

She worked without respite, frequently in the minister's office, and at times remained there even during the audiences. In his memoirs Barras has written a rather curious page concerning this.

He had been sent to Nice on a mission, and from there he corresponded with Roland whose practical views and organizing schemes he greatly admired.

Upon my arrival in Paris [he said] the Minister received me with great consideration. I sat without speaking in his study, waiting for his wife to leave before bringing up serious matters. Roland, interpreting my silence, said to me: "My wife is not unacquainted with the affairs of the ministry."

Mme Roland was not without exterior charm. It has been said that she might have shown more reserve in her affections, for in her *Memoirs* she speaks of several deputies she admired, describing Deputy Barbaroux as handsome as Antinous and thus she called him. Such acts belong to private life. . . As for me, I cannot reproach myself with having on that occasion, any more than on any other, encouraged Mme Roland's ambition to insinuate herself into public affairs. She seemed to me arrogant in her greeting and persistent in remaining with obstinate assurance in the Minister's room. I had too little gallantry to countenance her presence, which I considered indiscreet, and without uttering another word I bowed and retired. The next day I received an invitation to dinner and refused it for the same reason.

Étienne Dumont — another who did not like Mme Roland and admitted it — has in his *Souvenirs* supplemented Barras' censure of her by the following:

I was introduced to Roland; he was a man of simple habits, grave in his conversation, a little pedantic as far as virtue was concerned. . . Mme Roland, with all her charms, combined all the merits of character and wit. Her friends spoke of her with respect. She was a Roman, a true Cornelia, and had she had sons, they would have been brought up like the Gracchi.

In her home I saw several committees of ministers and the principal Girondists. A woman there seemed a little out of place, but she did not mingle in the discussions; she was more frequently in her office writing letters, and usually seemed preoccupied with other things, although she did not miss a word. Her modest attire in no way impaired her charm, and while performing a man's work she retained all the graces of her sex. I reproach myself with not having known the whole extent of her qualities; I was slightly prejudiced against political women and I found in her too much of that defiant tendency which results from an ignorance of the world.

Clavière and Roland, after having seen the King in the council, abandoned their previous judgments and believed he was sincere; she never ceased warning them against the deceitfulness of the Court (well, it was she who was right). She could not believe in the good faith of a prince brought up to believe that he was born superior to all men; she did not stop repeating that they were dupes, nor did she see aught but traps in the finest protestations. Servan, who had a gloomy character and a hypochondriacal pride, appeared to her for this reason an energetic and incorruptible man; she interpreted his passions as nobility of soul, and his hatred of the Court as republican virtue. Louvet, who had the same prejudice, became her hero. Louvet had much wit, courage, and vivacity. I was astonished that a virtuous woman could consider the frivolous author of *Faublas,* that professor of vice, as a severe republican; but Mme Roland forgave everything to those who declaimed against courtiers and who believed that virtues existed only under a thatched roof. She exalted very mediocre people, such as Lanthenas and Pache, simply because they had the same point of view. This exaltation did not attract me and prevented me from seeking her out as often as I would have, had I been able to know her living as we came to know her dead.

Her personal *Memoirs* are admirable; they are an imitation of Rousseau's *Confessions,* and are often equal to the original. She opens her heart and depicts herself with a force and truth that one finds nowhere else in work of this kind. Her intellectual development lacked a wider acquaintance with the world and connections with men of stronger judgment than her own. There was little breadth to Roland's mind, and none of all those who were her associates ever rose above popular prejudice. She never believed in the possibility of combining liberty with monarchy and she viewed a King with the same horror as did Mrs. Macaulay, whom she considered a being far superior to her sex. Had she been able to communicate to her party the strength of her mind and her intrepidity, royalty would have been laid low, but the Jacobins would not have triumphed.

Mme Roland, whose style was energetic and flowing, was inordinately fond of writing and induced her husband to write too much as well. It was an administration of writers. The greatest reproach that can be made against Mme Roland is that she enjoined her husband to publish the confidential letter he had written to the King and which began: "Sire, this letter will never be known except to you and me." [46] Dismissed from the ministry, he could not resist the satisfaction of revenge.

This is not an impartial opinion, and perhaps not a sincere one. "The Letter to the King" had, among the partisans of the Revolution, an immense success. We have an assurance of this (and there is no question of its sincerity), in a letter from Mme Jullien to her son.

Read carefully in the *Moniteur,* Roland's letter to the King. It earned him his disgrace at Court and will win him the admiration and esteem of all France. This blindness of the King is the scourge of humanity. . . Roland is immortalized.

An even better judge to oppose to Étienne Dumont, is Barbaroux. He said:

Rebecquy [47] had perhaps cause to complain of this minister's [Roland] denunciations after he had been misinformed as to his conduct at Avignon when he was commissioner of the Bouches-du-Rhone. But, having read this letter, he pressed it to his heart and said to me: "I am this man's friend forever." That he thus forgot his resentment made him all the dearer to me; it is the origin of the close friendship which unites us, and of our relations with Roland.

Let us again listen to É. Dumont:

Upon entering the Council, Clavière decided that the King was well intentioned, and spoke of this openly. This occasioned many disputes. I remember one in particular. It was at the Rolands'. Clavière related an instance when the King had surprised him in ignorance of an article in the Constitution; he had drawn his book out of his pocket and said to him laughingly: "You see, Monsieur Clavière, I know it better than you." Clavière spoke in the same way. Brissot became angry. They first resorted to sarcasm and then to accusation. The conversation grew bitter. Clavière appealed to Roland who dared neither to agree nor to disagree; afraid of appearing either weak or deluded if he dared be just to the King whose minister he was. I drew near Mme Roland. She was at a desk where she was pretending to write. I found her pale and trembling; I asked her to intervene to quiet the storm. "Do you think so?" she said to me hesitantly, and at the same time she cleverly and gently changed the conversation and prolonged it sufficiently to give the two friends time to calm down.

Mme Roland's friends, supported by Brissot's paper, had as one man taken a violent stand against Robespierre. Bitter and resentful since the Girondists had come into power, he did his utmost to secure the "approbation of the people" in order to strengthen his place in the opposition. By perfidious means he created popular discontent, using against the government news of the army (which was bad news), and suspicions which the Marquis de Grave, Minister of War, justified only too well by his dealings with the Court. Collot d'Herbois seconded him. Dumouriez sought to negotiate with everyone. Danton did nothing at all.

The ministers were not at ease in their relations with the King who was pretending to be good-humoured and credulous, and, had it not been for Mme Roland's good sense, he might very easily have won them over.

During the council the King read the gazette, questioned each one concerning the matters relating to his province, and displayed, with considerable skill, that sort of interest which the mighty flatter themselves they possess. He talked genially of general affairs and protested, with seeming candour, that he really wished to assist the working of the Constitution. For two or three weeks Roland and Clavière were almost enchanted by the King's intentions. They trusted his word and rejoiced like honest people at the outcome of events. "Good heavens," I said to them, "every time I see you leaving for the Council in this gullible mood, I am convinced that you are going to do something stupid. I have never been able to believe that a king born under despotism, brought up and trained to practise it, could have any inclination for constitutional government. Louis XVI would have had to have been an exceptionally intelligent man to wish in all sincerity for a Constitution that curtailed his own power, and, had he been such a man, he would not have let matters come to a pass which necessitated a Constitution. When Roland went to the Court for the first time, his round hat and the ribbons on his shoes created a certain scandal. The master of ceremonies was very much distressed and, pointing to Roland, said to Dumouriez:
"But, Monsieur, no buckles on his shoes!"
"Ah, Monsieur, all is lost then," Dumouriez answered with all the coolness of his irony.

The ministers, however, had not waited for Robespierre's insinuations before suspecting the patriotism of the Marquis de Grave. Finding himself cornered, he decided, on the first reverses the army suffered, to hand in his resignation. (May 8.)

Colonel Servan[48] whom the Rolands had known through Brissot and whom they held in high esteem, was proposed, not to say demanded by the Minister of the Interior. He was Mme Roland's candidate. We have two admirable letters which she wrote Servan the day after, and the second day following the Marquis de Grave's resignation. Her character as a leader is here shown in all its force:

May 9th, Year IV,[49] from
Paris

Yes, Monsieur, I wished it, willed it, I hold to this opinion and you shall justify it. Enough of doubts and fears, they are no longer in season; where there's a will there's a way . . .

The men who have held office up to now have proved noxious to the commonwealth and to themselves because they knew not how to speak their minds; they said they wanted the Revolution and at the same time they showed guilty consideration for all its enemies. One must be firmer and franker, go openly to the goal, make the Constitution function, and show Europe a ministry which wants it in all sincerity.

Place good citizens about you, so as to be less hampered in your course; take your colleagues to task when their conferences degenerate into mere conversations; and never once assemble without coming to some useful conclusion.

My coachman cannot serve you because he has but two carriages and they are both engaged, one by M. Clavière. He has not been long established, he is a child of the new regime. I am having M. Pétion's coach-hirer sought out to save us all the trouble of the details, and I will send him to you as soon as I shall have seen him. Make use of me as you see fit.

When you can tear yourself away from business and partake of my soup, I shall receive you gratefully; I shall be even more grateful to you when you give me the opportunity of serving you. So do not spare me any of those details which may trouble you.

Our friends embrace you. Here we are comrades in arms and fortune: we must save the common weal or perish with it.

And on the morning of the tenth of May from Paris:

. . . Up to the present time the new ministry can be excused if it has not done everything we expected of it; it has been impeded by a noble.[50] Now that you are all plebeians, or almost all, and true revolutionaries, in two weeks from now you must show great character and imposing methods, or it will be evident that you are worth no more than the others and the wheel must spin again until a better man appear. Remember, my worthy friend, that justice is the moral virtue of men in office and that firmness is the most difficult quality to preserve there.

I will not ask you to excuse these expressions. I cannot see you often; my friendship must be made known to you in some way.

I enclose a note prepared some days ago, which the confusion of the moment prevented my sending you until now.

I respect and love you and I confidentially hope to have more reason to honour and applaud you.

From the political standpoint, there is not a document which better explains Mme Roland's character. This one, indeed, was taken directly from nature. It is as authentic as a death mask. Obstacles did not exist for her, to ignore them was to deprive them of their force: "Where there's a will there's a way." It would seem too that we glimpse in part the secret of those tears which the warden saw fall at Saint-Pélagie, when the prisoner thought she was unobserved. Doubtless she wept for all that she held dear, for the ties which bound her to this earth, and which were about to be destroyed by the hand of man. But the realization of her lost strength, her fruitless work, her useless efforts, these filled the cup of bitterness to overflowing! Small men, great ideas, she had finally despaired of ever seeing the one rise to the heights of the other. In her retired province she had despaired, and even in 1791 in her *salon* in the rue Guénégaud had she despaired, although she had been proud to know and influence the Brissotins. No intrigues. Why was there always this talk of plots, of manœuvres? Were there not enough good honest men? Above all, purity. Her friendship would distinguish the good fighters from the bad. By this sign should they be known. To any other the door would be closed. She was too resolute to admit the "fears" of every sort which were continually set up as obstacles; too deeply convinced to endure those who were not "firm" and those who were not "frank." Precautions exasperated her, excuses wearied her. "Idle talk" seemed criminal to her, and she had no time for delays. "Go openly to the goal" — this was the prime necessity.

She would have liked to deceive herself as to the reason which contented her friends when they were obliged to admit that the Gironde Ministry, after forty-seven days of existence, had not done all that was expected of it. "It was impeded by a noble." The idea of treason has always pursued the French in the hour of their greatest trials. But "if, in two weeks' time" she said, "a group of able men, dauntless and sure as they should be for the fatherland, have not wiped out the old mistakes, done great things in the interior, and on the frontiers halted the Austrians," it will be proved, she wrote Servan, "that you are worth no more than the others." Regular orders follow, given in a tone that is persuasive simply out of deference to good form, for after all, it was a young woman who spoke, and it was the Minister of War she was addressing.

The Revolutionary mysticism which found atrocious incarnation in such indecipherable personages as Robespierre and Saint-Just, attained its height in Mme Roland. But her elemental, naïve politics, were soon to prove hopelessly inadequate. The lack of character of her soldiers did the rest, and furthermore they had no great intelligence. It was not an heroic Muse which Revolutionary France needed at that time, but a statesman who would have staked his personal fortune on the success of the Constitution. It was a time neither for generosity nor for sacrifice. Alas, the "noble victims" did nothing for the infant Liberty who, like the newly-born, came into being drenched in blood. A Richelieu, desirous of keeping order, could have easily quelled the anarchy by securing the support of a police force adequate to prevent Robespierre from doing harm, as well as to subdue the Commune which proceeded from him.

The Marquis de Grave's departure settled nothing. It was one of those useless operations. The Ministry, greatly constrained, continued to feel a secret opposition and could undertake no serious affairs. This time the fault lay with a certain Duranthon (and yet he had been recommended by Vergniaud), who had formed a secret alliance with what was called the "Austrian Committee," otherwise known as the private council of the King (M. de Montmorin, Bertrand de Molleville, etc.).

Mme Roland had soon ferretted out, if not the truth, at least the systematic opposition which immediately impeded every frank move the administration made. We know that she always went directly to the point. Therefore we are not unprepared for Roland's somewhat sudden move. One morning he brought to his colleagues a letter already composed — we know by whom — in which the King was demanded by law to reign in accordance with the spirit of the constitutional majority.

Mignet has said of Louis XVI that his ancestors had bequeathed him a revolution, and Rivarol: "Monarch whose first work upon ascending the throne was accomplished with a master locksmith, whose first injunction had to do with rabbits." [51]

A devout believer, he could not bring himself to decide the question of ratifications which the religious troubles had necessitated.

Besides he was in sympathy with the manœuvres of France's enemies and he put all his hopes in them. This was the sum total of all the reproaches of Mme Roland's letter. Moreover, Roland, Republican Minister for Louis XVI, had specified that he would undertake his duties only if he were provided with a secretary who would keep a record of the Council's discussions. In spite of the law which prescribed the presence of this secretary in the Council, it was in reality enforced but once or twice. Roland had been tricked.

The existence of the "Austrian Committee" had been pointed out to the Assembly the day before, and such Girondists as Brissot and Guadet demanded a true bill. The Assembly, to show the King its ability to deal with him, decreed the disbanding of his Guard. In spite of Dumouriez, who went from one side to the other attempting to conciliate the irreconcilable, the administration was already tottering. Roland, Servan, Clavière were in agreement against Duranthon, a recent deserter, and Lacoste, who had long been suspected by the pure at heart. But Clavière had advised against the proposed letter of the nineteenth of May, and had prevented its being sent to the King. On the twenty-sixth he wrote Roland:

I have, my dear colleague, thought over the matter of the letter you proposed writing the King. The more I consider it, the fewer reasons do I find to justify this step. . . Why turn the King against us, since we accepted our positions only for the sake of the common weal ? And since we are morally certain that, until peace is reestablished, we can be replaced only at the risk of increasing the misfortune of this lacerated land.

Servan had just triumphed in the Assembly. Pursuing an already old and extremely injudicious idea of Mme Roland's, he obtained the establishment of a camp of 20,000 armed volunteers outside Paris, for the purpose of protecting the legislators from the royal guard as well as from foreign invasion and popular insurrections.

On the tenth of June, Roland sent the King the letter which his wife had written and which, when it was made public, was greeted with the wildest enthusiasm all over the country.

Here is the text:

Conscious as I am of the dangers attendant upon present circumstances, I believe it my duty to put before Your Majesty's eyes the statement which I drew up yesterday in order that it might be presented to you.

I feel all the distressing difficulties of expressing certain truths, but the very safety of Your Majesty, as well as that of the State, demands that a minister and an honest man seek to be useful rather than complimentary. May this utterance of an open heart receive some attention from Your Majesty, and may you bring it to bear upon the resolutions which your wisdom and generosity will recognize as necessary to your own happiness and to that of France.

Had not this statement been already drafted, I might, after what occurred yesterday in the Council, have put it in another form, but upon reflection I believed it fit to let Your Majesty perceive all those things that I considered constituted the state of affairs and the general trend of thought. I have openly spoken my mind, and if these ills I have observed should come to harm the Empire, I shall not suffer the remorse of having kept to myself what I believed it expedient to make known.

I am, with profound respect,
Sire,
your most humble and obedient servant,
ROLAND

Sire,

The present plight of France cannot long endure. A critical state exists, wherein violence attains its height. It must terminate in a crisis as interesting to Your Majesty as it is of import to the entire Empire.

Honoured by your confidence and placed in a position which compels me to speak the truth, I make so bold as to withhold nothing from you; it is an obligation you yourself have imposed upon me.

The French have given themselves a Constitution; it has made enemies and malcontents. The greater part of the nation wishes to uphold it, has sworn to defend it at the cost of its own blood, and joyfully accepted war as a means of making it secure. The minority, however, fed on certain hopes, has combined all its efforts to acquire the upper hand. Hence this intestine struggle against the law, this anarchy which grieves good citizens and of which the malevolent make use to slander the new regime; hence, this discord which is spread and incited far and wide, for no portion of the nation is indifferent. Some wish the Constitution to triumph, others that it be changed; it is a question of upholding or of altering it. I refrain from considering the Constitution in itself, and deal only with what circumstances necessitate, and, detaching myself as much as possible from the matter, I shall consider only what is to be expected and what should be encouraged.

Your Majesty enjoyed great prerogatives which you believed were the rights of Royalty. Brought up to the idea of preserving them, you naturally were not pleased to see them go. The desire to have them reestablished was as natural as the regret in seeing them suppressed. These sentiments are part of the nature of the human heart, and must certainly have entered into the calculations of the Revolution's foes; they must have counted on a secret approbation until circumstances would permit an open patronage. The nation could not remain in ignorance of these inclinations, and they are responsible for her mistrust.

Your Majesty has thus been faced with the alternative of yielding to your early habits and to your own predilections, or of making the sacrifices which wisdom prescribed and necessity demanded. In other words, you could encourage the rebels and alarm the nation, or pacify the nation while injuring yourself in her eyes. Everything has its conclusion, and the end of uncertainty has come at last. Can Your Majesty ally yourself openly today with those who aspire to reform the Constitution, or will you generously and unreservedly consecrate yourself to its success ? This is the real question, and the actual state of things makes the solution inevitable. As to that highly metaphysical one of whether or not the French people are ripe for Liberty, its discussion has no place here, for it is no longer a question of judging what we may become in a hundred years, but of what the present generation may be capable.

In the midst of the agitations in which we have lived for four years, what indeed has come to pass ? Privileges, onerous to the people, have been abolished. The principles of Justice and Equality have been universally spread. They have penetrated everywhere; general opinion on the rights of the people has justified the belief that they should be recognized; the recognition of them has become a sacred doctrine, the hatred of nobility, long since inspired by feudalism, has been exasperated by the manifest opposition of the greater part of the nobles to the Constitution which overthrew it. During the first year of the Revolution the people looked upon these nobles as odious men because of the tyrannical privileges they possessed, but whom they would no longer have hated once those privileges were destroyed, had not the conduct of the nobility since that time strengthened all the reasons for dreading and fighting it as an irreconcilable enemy. Adherence to the Constitution increased in equal proportion; not only did the people owe such great benefits to it, but considered that it must have even greater ones in store since those nobles who were accustomed to making the people bear every burden sought so mightily to change or modify it. The Declaration of Rights became a political gospel and the French Constitution a religion for which the people are prepared to die. Its zeal has at times gone so far as to supplement the Law, and when the Law was not severe enough to condemn agitators, the citizens took the liberty of punishing them themselves. Thus it was, inspired by retaliation, that the property of Emigrants was exposed to destruction.

This is why so many departments believed themselves obliged to proceed with vigour against the priests whom public opinion had outlawed and would have victimized. In the clash of interests all emotions acquired the intensity of passion. Fatherland is no longer a mere word to be embellished by the imagination: it is a being to whom we have made sacrifices, to whom, because of the very anxieties it causes, we grow more attached day by day; a being we have created by dint of great effort, who rises clear of a host of disturbances, and whom we love as much for the sacrifices it costs us as for the hopes it inspires.

Every abuse it suffers adds fuel to the fire of enthusiasm. To what heights will this enthusiasm blaze when the enemy troops abroad unite with the intriguing forces at home to strike their deadly blows ? In every part of the Empire, there is intense feeling. It will burst out propitiously unless a reasoned confidence in Your Majesty's intentions can pacify it. But this confidence cannot be born of protestations; it must be based on acts.

It is evident to the French nation that its Constitution can be effective, that the government can command all the force it needs, the moment Your Majesty is absolutely resolved upon the triumph of the Constitution and will uphold the legislative body in all its executive power, removing any cause for anxiety on the part of the people and depriving the discontented element of all hope.

For example, two important resolutions have been passed, both of them of essential interest to the public peace and the safety of the State. Any delay in ratifying them arouses mistrust; if it be prolonged it will give rise to dissatisfaction, and, I must say it, in the present ebullition of minds, dissatisfaction may lead to anything.

The time for withdrawal is past; it is too late even to temporize. The Revolution has already been achieved in the public mind; by bloodshed shall it be accomplished and cemented unless wisdom forestall those misfortunes which it is still possible to avoid. I know it may seem feasible to solve and condemn everything by extreme measures, but when force has been used to constrain the Assembly, when terror has spread throughout Paris, and discord and stupor all about, all France will rise in indignation and, rending herself in the horrors of a civil war, will disclose that black anarchy, the mother of virtue and crime, which always brings disaster upon those who have provoked it.

The safety of the State and the happiness of Your Majesty are closely linked; no power on earth can sever them; cruel agonies and certain misfortunes menace your throne if it does not, through you, rest upon the foundations of the Constitution and find strength in the ultimate peace which its preservation should assure us. Thus the state of minds, the course of affairs, political reasoning, and Your Majesty's interest all make it an indispensable obligation that you join the legislative body and respond in the nation's name; they render duty a necessity, but the natural sensitiveness of this affectionate people is ready to find grounds for gratitude therein. You were cruelly misled, Sire, when you were persuaded to alienate yourself from and to mistrust this responsive people. It was by continually alarming you that you were made to act in a manner in itself enough to terrify your people. Could it but see you determined to make this Constitution on which it has staked its happiness succeed, you would soon receive its gratitude and thanks.

The conduct of the priests in many quarters, and the pretexts which fanaticism offers to malcontents, led to the enactment of a wise law against disturbers; let Your Majesty give it your sanction. The public peace demands it and the safety of the priests makes it expedient; if this law is not put into effect, the departments will be obliged to resort to violent measures, as they are already doing on all sides, and the incensed people will add to it by outrages.

The manœuvres of our enemies; the disturbances manifested in the capital; the extreme uneasiness caused by the conduct of your Guard and augmented by the approbation Your Majesty accorded to it by a truly impolitic proclamation under the present circumstances; the situation of Paris, so close to the frontiers, have made the need felt for a camp in the immediate proximity. This measure, whose object and urgency are apparent to all sound minds, only awaits Your Majesty's sanction. Why let delays give it the appearance of regrets when celerity would earn it gratitude?

The attempts made by the staff of the Paris National Guard against this measure already give reason to suspect that they were instigated by a higher power; the speeches of certain extreme demagogues have already aroused suspicions as to what their relations might be with those interested in the downfall of the Constitution; public opinion is even now implicating Your Majesty's intentions. Any further delay and the aggrieved public must believe it recognizes in its King a friend and accomplice of the conspirators.

Just Heavens, have ye stricken with folly the lords of the earth, and will they heed no counsel other than that which brings them to their ruin !

I know that the stern language of truth is rarely welcomed by the throne; I know too that it is because truth is almost never heard there that revolutions become necessary; and above all I know that I owe it to Your Majesty, not only as a citizen subservient to the Laws, but as a minister honoured by your confidence, or invested with the offices which imply it, and there is nothing which can deter me from fulfilling a duty which weighs upon my conscience.

In the same spirit do I reiterate my remonstrances to Your Majesty concerning the necessity and advantages of executing the law which prescribes a Secretary at the Council. The mere existence of the law speaks for itself so clearly that it would seem that its execution would follow without delay, for it is imperative to employ every means of preserving the necessary gravity, wisdom, and maturity in the discussions, and responsible ministers must have a means of stating their opinion. Had this existed I should not be now addressing Your Majesty through the written word.

Life is as naught to the man who esteems duty above all else; but after the happiness of having performed it, the good to which he is still sensible is that of proving that he performed it faithfully, and this in itself is an obligation for the public man.

June 10, 1792
The fourth year of Liberty
ROLAND

The following evening at eight o'clock, Servan came to Mme Roland beaming with delight.

"Congratulate me," he said, "I have had the honour of being put out."
"Which means," said Mme Roland, "that my husband is soon to share your fate. I am annoyed that you have been the first."

That morning when Servan had gone to the Château on business connected with the War Department, the King had turned his back upon him, and the Minister of the Interior was about to receive an autograph note couched in the following terms:

Paris, June 13, 1792
Monsieur, you will kindly hand over the portfolio of the Department of the Interior which I had entrusted to you, to M. Mourgues, whom I have just commissioned with this office.
LOUIS

Clavière, who was likewise openly in sympathy with Roland, was discharged at the same time. It was then the thirteenth of June; on the sixteenth Dumouriez, in spite of his diplomacy, was obliged to hand in his resignation. As for the King, blinder each day to the reality of the situation, he continued until the tenth of August to call in one by one the most vapid of the Feuillants for the final scenes of the monarchy.

The Girondists [said Étienne Dumont] who were preeminent in the Council, were favourably disposed towards the King. . . In a speech constructed with such skill that it was received without a murmur of dissent, Gensonné made strong declarations in favour of royalty and vigorously denounced anarchy. Gensonné's cold and feeble manner was very different from Mirabeau's, but he was listened to and applauded. The King was extremely gratified. I believe this was the last monarchic speech to be made in the Assembly.

The Assembly applauded Roland's letter to the King and gave
orders that it be printed and sent to the Departments.

The Minister of the Interior, who had remained at the Council
from the twenty-third of March to the thirteenth of June, was highly
complimented by the Assembly who voted "the regrets of the
nation." He left office with flying colours and, like a Roman family, the Rolands retired to their small lodgings.

Though weary and disillusioned, neither husband nor wife had
any thought of rest. Mme Roland did not say, as in 1791: "I want
to see my trees again." The ardour that sustained her was far from
spent. Moreover, her trusty followers had not swerved from their
leader, and they still turned to her for inspiration. They had been
joined by Barbaroux, the handsome young deputy from Marseilles.
With what patriotic exaltation he described his reception by the
people of Marseilles who had fallen upon their knees in their homes
and in the streets as the verses of the National Hymn rang out.

Servan, accompanied by Barbaroux, came often to the rue de la
Harpe. Both praised "the excellent spirit of the south." Why
should it not be the seat of the Republic "if the Court triumphed
and subjugated Paris and the north?" Poring over a map of
France with Mme Roland, they sought to determine the line of
demarcation. Should not every attempt be made to establish a
free government? Thank God for Marseilles! Thanks to its
people, swore Barboroux, good principles would triumph in the end.

In his memoirs he tells us of a visit to the rue de la Harpe:

One day when Rebecquy and I were returning from the Champs-
Elysées where we had discussed our plans, we met Roland and Lanthenas — that Lanthenas who has since then so odiously abandoned his
friend and the cause of Liberty. We embraced them fervently and
Roland expressed his desire to confer with us concerning the misfortunes of the people; we agreed that I should go to his house on the
following day, alone, so as to escape the suspicion of the spies. . .
. . . It was in their small lodging in the rue de la Harpe — the
refuge of a philosopher. His wife was present during our conversation
and took part in it. I shall speak elsewhere of this amazing woman. . .

They made ingenuous plans:

Let us arm Paris and the northern departments; and, should they
succumb, let us take the statue of Liberty [52] to the south and found in

some place a colony of independent men. As he [Roland] said these words, his eyes were filled with tears. The same emotion caused both his wife and me to weep.

Barbaroux gave new courage to every heart by promising to obtain six hundred men and two cannon from Marseilles.

Thus everything was settled !

These fundamental principles established, I took leave of Roland, filled with respect both for him and his wife. I have seen him since, during his second ministry, and I found him quite as simple as in his humble retreat, still the one man in office who opposed his own virtue to the enterprises of the iniquitous and his person to their daggers; while others talked, he laid the foundations of public morality and national industry. Had he not been forced out of the ministry, he would have effaced the memory of Sully — doubtless, a great man, although he was not opposed to the *Code des Chasses;* [53] and Colbert too, who by establishing a surplus of manufactures, caused those of the Cévennes to be destroyed, and neglected agriculture, that mother of all arts and provider for all men. Of all the moderns, Roland seems the one who most closely resembles Cato; but it must here be said that he owed his courage and his talents to his wife.

The twentieth of June "was conceived and prepared" said one of its organizers "in Mme Roland's *salon.*" It's aim was to compel the King to recall "the good ministry." But it was soon for another "day" that plans were being made. "Try to read what Carra's *Annales* say today concerning *the projects.* It develops them rather well," wrote Mme Roland on the seventh of July to Bancal who was then in Paris. On that day Louis XVI sat in the Assembly for the last time. He wore the red cap [54] just as he had worn the tri-colour cockade, in order to mislead public feeling and to gain time. The "projects" in question referred to a plan, conceived by Carra, of an organized insurrection "under cover of the Law." This idea must have appealed to Mme Roland, who was irritated with Vergniaud who had again on the third of July made conciliatory advances from the tribune to Louis XVI. A letter written the same day to Bancal, shows how she felt at the time:

Will Vergniaud be at Mme Dodun's ? If he is, do not fear to tell him that he must accomplish marvels if he wishes to reinstate himself in the good graces of the public; that is if, like an honest man, he still cares about it, which I doubt.

She did not forgive Vergniaud his final attempt to reconcile the
Gironde and the King. At that time more than one Girondist
tried to negotiate with the Court, notably Gensonné, whose
monarchic speech astonished Étienne Dumont. Mme Roland
utterly despised that weakness which she knew full well was to
seal her party's doom. How very different were these men whom
history persists in labelling Girondists !

Mme Roland was a stranger to such uncertainties, as a note
penned by her at this period makes evident:

Anent young Pochet, who is presenting a work already presented by
his father as a claim to the great assistance he solicits. This work, the
National Compass, although containing excellent moral principles, was
not in keeping with the order of the day as to political principles. *He
talks too much of kings and tends to maintain a sort of superstition
in favour of royalty.* Wherefore, the Minister has refused the author's
requests but felt himself obliged to pay one of the children of this
unfortunate family the small sum of fifty francs to soften an unavoid-
able refusal.

This shows clearly how uncompromising were Mme Roland's
views concerning the monarchy, and also bears witness to the kindness of her heart.

One of Mme Roland's letters to Brissot dated the thirty-first of
July 1792, fell into the hands of the great critic Sainte-Beuve, who
spoke of it as "of great historical importance." We acquire some
flavour of it through his analysis:

As the impending crisis of the tenth of August drew near, she no
longer demanded immediate and absolute measures as she had after
Varennes; she now wanted the united sections to ask, not *the deposition*
which it would be difficult to effect without destroying the constitutional act, but the provisional suspension which, as she wrote Brissot,
would be no easy matter but which could be affixed to one of the
articles of the Constitution. . . She complained of the Assembly's silence and of Brissot's uncertain attitude in these threatening circumstances. . . Her letter, which purported to put Brissot on his guard
against that ductility of character and opinion to which he was inclined, gives very precise indications on the principle personages who
composed this fraternal and illustrious group. In a few words each
one is touched on and defined; one after another they pass before us
with all their different characteristics: the worthy Servan (since then a
senator), a genial philosopher accustomed to simple pleasures, but slow

and timid and hence inadequate in a revolution; Gensonné, weak of character and ceremonious in appearance; and Guadet, too hasty, and too ready to be suspicious or contemptuous.

Those who seek to understand the relationship that actually existed between Mme Roland and her friends, will glean some interesting information from another passage of Sainte-Beuve's article:

. . . Vergniaud, whom she decidedly did not like at all (and was later to say so in her own words), was too much of an epicurean, as we know, for this strong-minded Cornelia. Before the final test, she was extremely unjust to him. She did not explain the procrastinations of this carefree and sublime orator as naturally as we do, as the mere caprices and negligences of genius. She went so far as to find fault with his way of dressing, and almost resented that veiled glance which, however, lit up as though by magic when he spoke. . . She sought in vain a great personality who would hearten them in this crisis and rally the good party by his counsels. . . While spurring Brissot to be this very man, it is clear enough that she counted but little on it, that she knew he was *confident to excess, naturally serene, even ingenuous.* . .

By the end of July and the beginning of August, the nervous tension in Paris rose to a pitch hitherto unattained. Robespierre was at the Jacobins; Danton, Camille Desmoulins, and Marat at the Cordeliers. Tempests raged there every day. The Revolutionists were in a state of great anxiety, fearing that the cause of Liberty was about to perish before their eyes. It was at this moment that Grangeneuve, a Girondist, asked Chabot to blow out his brains one evening at a street corner, so that the people would accuse the Court party of the murder and attack the Tuileries.

The manifesto of Brunswick, the leader of the Emigrants, came from Coblenz and brought public feeling to its height. The foreign armies announced that they were on the march to rescue the King and his family, and that everything that resisted them would be destroyed — Paris included — by fire and sword.

At this moment Robespierre made an attempt to win over Barbaroux. "An abbé in rags. . ." came and begged the deputy from Marseilles to go to the Town Hall, where, he said "Panis and Fréron were awaiting him."

PRINCESS DE LAMBALLE

From a lead-pencil drawing by Gabriel
Given by M. Clemenceau to the Musée du Louvre

CAMILLE DESMOULINS

From a contemporary drawing. Original owned by
Mme Georges Claretie

The plan was [said Barbaroux in his memoirs] to persuade the troops from Marseilles to leave their barracks in the upper part of the Chaussée d'Antin and establish themselves in the Cordelier barracks. That position had certain advantages. . . The project was adopted. Their other speeches, however, were cloaked in mystery.

When they told him that "the people required a leader," Barbaroux exclaimed: "Do you mean you want a dictator ?" "No," responded Fréron, "but you know that Brissot wants to be one."

The following day, Robespierre himself "while speaking of the Revolution, made the boast that he had done much to hasten it, insisting, however, that it would come to an end if some extremely popular man did not declare himself its rightful leader and renew its energy."

"I want a dictator no more than I want a king," retorted Rebecquy abruptly, and the conversation ended there.

Barbaroux tells how Étienne Dumont, who had gone to see Duplay, the carpenter, at 366 rue Honoré,

was struck by the ornaments of Robespierre's study. It was a dainty boudoir wherein his own portrait could be seen in every shape and form. He was painted on the right-hand wall, engraved on the left, his bust stood at one end and a bas-relief faced one. Furthermore, there were half a dozen small engravings of Robespierre on the table.

The insurrection of the tenth of August was one of those spontaneous uprisings which should have been well prepared.[55] It was organized by Danton and the Gironde. One can see Mme Roland's hand in Lanthenas' activities in the suburbs, and her influence is no less evident in the enthusiasm of the Marseilles troops of Barbaroux whom she had brought into accord with Pétion. She refused to admit this, however, and said she knew nothing of the preparations for the riot, "having never had any confidence in what one might describe as restricted enterprises." As for Barbaroux, she did say that he came frequently to the rue de la Harpe in the interval between the two administrations, and that, at a certain moment, he led her to believe that an insurrection was under way. "But since he did not confide more deeply in us, we put no questions to him," she said. Barbaroux ceased his visits to them at the end of July, and asked them not to consider him remiss, but that he did not wish to compromise them.

The tocsin sounded at the Cordeliers. Sometimes a mere incident of private life can stamp a great event with universal interest: thus are we greatly moved by the thought of little Lucile Desmoulins who, having watched her husband departing with Danton, knelt by the open window listening to the ominous clanging of the bell.

The Marseilles troops, who were presently to vanquish the Swiss, the last defenders of the monarchy, were at the Cordeliers awaiting the hour to go forth. It was there that the deposition of the King was resolved. Outside, Danton, the Gironde, the Commune, and the Jacobins were each one going their own way and following no coherent plan. The Court was about to send for the Mayor of Paris. As for Robespierre, he invariably ran to cover when there were riots. He let the others do the fighting and compromise themselves as they wished, and then, when all was over, he made his appearance, turning to his own profit what the others had won at the risk of their lives.

With the city in a state of uproar, the Assembly held a meeting before empty benches. The greatest uncertainty prevailed among the Girondists. Hitherto they had sought a compromise between their own irreproachable Republican principles and their weakness in adhering to the person of a king they thought they could not do without. The Court, however, considered them its worst enemies, as dangerous even as the Jacobins. The Girondists recoiled from the idea of a vacant throne. What they feared most was the chaos of a government which would be at the mercy of the warring clubs. The fury of the populace and the triumphant Commune had driven them, in their weakness, further than they had wished, and it was with no conviction that Pétion, who presided at the meeting, rose from his seat and asked what Mme Roland had been demanding for fourteen months — that is, since the arrest at Varennes: the deposition of the King.[56]

Once Louis XVI and his family were imprisoned in the Temple Tower, the Girondists looked in bewilderment upon what they

had done. Robespierre had long awaited this moment. Between
the Jacobins and the Commune, the Incorruptible was now ready
to hold his own in the Assembly and take stern measure of the
Gironde. Till the Convention, that is until September 20, 1792,
forty days of intense opposition were to pass between the Commune
and the Legislative on one hand, and between the Jacobins and
the Gironde on the other.

ON THE tenth of August the Girondist Isnard took the floor in the
Assembly and vehemently demanded the immediate return of
Servan, Clavière, and Roland, the three ministers whom Louis
XVI had had the folly to dismiss. This resolution was passed
unanimously and the three ministers resumed office, but the ballot
also assured Danton of a majority. He had through the insurrection won enormous popularity, and as Minister of Justice he was
to play a rôle of some importance in the Assembly. This latter,
however, retained its own independence of action, as can be seen
by the title of Temporary Executive Council which it gave to the
administration. At that time Danton was almost a daily visitor
at Mme Roland's.

Sometimes [she said] on his way to the Council, he would arrive a
little before time and come into my rooms, or would stop in for
a while afterwards, usually with Fabre d'Églantine; sometimes he would
ask if he might sup, on days other than those on which I entertained.
No-one could have been more zealous, or evidenced a greater love of
Liberty or a keener desire to work in accord with his colleagues in
order to further the good cause. I would look at this repulsive and
atrocious face and although I told myself . . . that I knew of nothing
against him, that the most honest man must necessarily have two
reputations in factious times . . . I found it difficult to reconcile that
face with my conception of an honest man.

At the end of August, Danton and Fabre ceased their visits to
Mme Roland, who concluded that they doubtless did not wish to be
observed by

watchful eyes . . . while they chanted their September matins. From
then on they knew that Roland was too upright a man to take any
part in their intrigues, that neither could his wife be approached, and
that, in short, such a couple could only prove harmful to their
schemes. . . [*Memoirs.*]

And then a terrible blow fell: the Prussians crossed the frontier. France was invaded. The fatherland was in peril.

In moments of desperation, the genius of the race inspires the French with resources that only can be explained as miracles. "When the country is in danger," cried Danton, "everything belongs to the fatherland." And the French of 1793 gave him, indeed, their own persons, their children, and their worldly goods. The Girondists persisted in their opposition to Robespierre, who profited by the general confusion to accuse them of wishing to put Brunswick on the throne of France. Great hopes were placed on the Marseilles troops. An address dated September, the first year of Equality, is entirely in Mme Roland's style and hand:

> The inhabitants of Marseilles are known all over France for their courage and their ardent love of Liberty. When Paris was menaced by despots, they came generously to her defence. The day of the tenth [of August] has demonstrated to the full their ability to lay tyranny low. But public safety now demands that they fly to the attack of the foreign cohorts, that they join with their brothers of the departments to hold them at bay. Anger, however just it be, can, if prolonged, produce the most disastrous disorders; it becomes a frenzy, it leads to culpable excesses by which the children of Liberty should never sully their name. The Law has spoken; it commands the Marseilles troops to leave our walls; there is no doubt but that they will obey, for they would not wish to set the fatal precedent of a remission of duty, of a resistance which would produce the most disastrous chaos, and even dissolution. . .

What a sombre flame burns in this letter which Mme Roland wrote to Bancal:

> Longwy has been betrayed, Thionville invested, Verdun outraged. Presently they will all be at the mercy of the Prussians. They intend to reach Paris, and I know not what can halt them. . . There are no troops. There are no arms. Exhort ardent patriots and send them to us if you would save us; there is not a moment to be lost. . . I say nothing to you of the measures we are taking, but for all our sleepless nights and our working with an activity that is more than human, it is impossible to counteract in a few hours the effects of four years of treason. . . Send us men already armed like those who in olden days sprang from the earth, and send them running to us with gigantic strides. . . It is our mad Commune that clogs the machine; it is at odds with the legislative body, it throws out all the plans of the execu-

tive power; if this goes on we shall soon be undone and perhaps more through the people of Paris than by the Prussians.

When Roland returned to the ministry after the tenth of August, he and his wife were troubled by the presence and even the supremacy in the Council of this Danton who had so bad a reputation.

The Girondists saw clearly that they could not pit a Roland against a Danton. They said in confidence to the couple:

What can be done about it ? He was useful in the Revolution and the people love him. No need to create discontent, we must accept things as they are.

Mme Roland, who could not deny Danton's superiority, probably felt some jealousy and humiliation. She also believed no less sincerely that affairs should be in the hands of the uncorrupt and that the first duty of patriots, once the throne was overturned, was to call men of irreproachable reputation to the government. It was not enough to be able to govern France. One must also be worthy of commanding the respect of all the peoples on earth.

Since her experience in public life, however, her frankness had suffered severe blows. Would she ever have admitted this ? She almost regretted Mirabeau, the man whose unscrupulous passions had so horrified her. But without royalty, Mirabeau alone could never have saved liberty. His dream was to place one in the safe keeping of the other. At the point to which the Revolution had come, it seemed to the out-and-out Girondist that this genius alone would have been able to have got everything in hand again, but "the Mirabeau of the rabble," as Danton was called—him, she detested !

Upon the return of the ministry, Marat—another hideous personage !—had written Roland asking him for 15,000 *livres,* which he required, he said, for the purpose of "publishing some excellent things." Roland, or rather his wife, had responded with an ironical and insufficiently considered refusal.

Mme Roland, who at times wondered if Marat were not an imaginary being, had a whim to see him, "for one must know these monsters." She requested Danton to bring him to her, but he did not seem to believe she was speaking seriously, and Marat avenged himself for the Minister's letter by posting up placards insulting to the Minister's wife, and then, having broken with the Rolands, he appealed to Philippe Égalité whose seat was near his own at the Convention.

Barbaroux had taken Marat's course in optics in 1788, had valued him as a learned man, and wished to renew the acquaintance.

Like Rousseau, Marat was a Swiss. He was short in stature with the head of a batrachian. He called himself a doctor, but there was nothing to prove that he was one. Upon his invitation, Barbaroux went to see him at his home, opposite the Café Richard in the rue Saint-Honoré.

I immediately recognized my professor of optics, but when I heard him speak, I thought he had lost his mind. He told me quite seriously that the French were nothing but petty little Revolutionaries and that he alone had the means of establishing liberty. I wanted to sound out the great man, so I appeared eager for his instructions:

"Give me," said he, "200 Neapolitans armed with daggers and carrying muffs instead of shields on their left arms; with them I could go all over France and I could make the Revolution."

And what he added was of the same stamp; he wanted to prove to me that it was a very feasible reckoning to butcher 260,000 men in one day. Doubtless he had a predilection for that number, for since then he has always asked for 260,000 heads, rarely going as high as 300,000. . .

When the Legislative Assembly impeached him on the third of May 1792, Marat demanded Barbaroux.

An associate of Marat conducted me to a café in the Place de Grève [said Barbaroux] and from there to a woman's house where the conference took place at nine in the evening. It was all the same sort of thing. Above all he urged me to take him to Marseilles. He would disguise himself, he said, as a jockey. . . The evening of the ninth [of August] he again suggested to me that he disguise himself as a jockey. Surely he wasn't giving a thought then to the Revolution: it took place the next day, and ever since Marat has taken upon himself the glory of having been its instigator.

"The National Assembly," Marat added, "can still save France. It should decree that all aristocrats wear a white ribbon on their arms and that they be hanged if three of them be found together. . . No mistake can be made; seize those who have carriages, valets, and silk clothes, or who go to the theatre. You can be sure they are aristocrats.[57]

For his part, Brissot in his memoirs said that Marat was

a mountebank, a buffoon. . . He had neither the courage of an assassin nor that of a philosopher, although he had one day wanted to fight Dr. Charles because he had not evidenced sufficient respect for his experiments, and even though he had one day threatened the Convention that he would blow out his brains at the foot of the tribune with a pistol that was not loaded, although he did, indeed, always speak of bloodshed. . .

Marat always demanded the most atrocious tortures. "Brand them with hot irons. Cut off their thumbs. Slit their tongues," was the daily clamour in the *Ami du Peuple*. In his criminal legislation he suggested that tortures revived from the Middle Ages should punish sacrilege and blasphemy. He wrote that the poor were entitled "to butcher and devour living flesh" so as "to wrest mere necessities from those who had too much."

As a pseudo-scientist, his vanity knew no bounds. After enumerating his scientific works, he would remark placidly: "Twenty volumes of discoveries in physics." And he would add: "I believe I have exhausted all the variations of the human mind on morality, philosophy, and politics."

Mme Roland declared that Marat's attacks worried her very little. Was this quite true ? Indeed she had other things to occupy her mind, for she wrote Bancal:

At the moment I write you the alarm gun is firing, the drums are beating, the tocsin is ringing, and everyone is running to his division. What are the orders ? None have been given. But the Commune has said that tonight everyone must assemble at the Champ de Mars and that 50,000 men must leave Paris tomorrow, without taking into consideration that even 200 cannot be made to go without assuring them of food and lodging. However, the agitated people have sent detachments here asking for arms and believe themselves betrayed because the Minister is not at home at the moment they decide to come.

Here is what actually happened. On the second of September, Roland had just left for the Ministry of the Marine where the Council of Ministers was to meet, when Mme Roland, alone in her room, thought she heard an unusual disturbance rising from the courtyard side. Upon looking from the window, she saw a group of one or two hundred men gesticulating and shouting. From the ante-chamber, she learned that they were determined to see the Minister at all costs and refused to believe he was not at home. With unruffled calm, she gave orders that ten of them enter the house.

They entered; I asked them peacefully what they wanted; they told me they were good citizens ready to leave for Verdun, but as they were in need of arms they had come to ask them of the Minister and they wished to see him.

Confronted with the impossibility of convincing them that the Minister was not there, and, moreover, had no arms at his disposal, she suggested that they go through the house with her. Her cool-headedness finally convinced them.

They withdrew. I stood on the balcony in the courtyard. I saw one coatless furious individual, his shirt-sleeves rolled up above his elbows, sword in hand, declaiming against the treachery of the ministers. My ten deputies circulated through the crowd and finally, to the rolling of drums, persuaded them to leave.

While the valet was carried away as hostage by the rioters, Mme Roland drove off to tell her husband what had taken place:

The Council was not yet under way. . . I found a fair-sized gathering. . . I told the story . . . it was accepted . . . as evidence . . . of the popular ebullition. [*Memoirs.*]

The impotence of the government, the confusion into which the best minds had been thrown, and the general state of disorder, were vividly expressed in the letters Mme Roland continued to write Bancal:

The resolutions of the Assembly are stamped with fear. The mob has stormed the Abbaye; there it has massacred fifteen people and threatens to enter all the prisons. The executive power has summoned all the divisional commissaries to reason with them, to enlighten them if possible, and to point out to them all the ills of anarchy. . . All the horses are being taken away and as this is an operation prevalent everywhere . . . a great many are bound to be lost through lack of care. The gates, which were finally opened yesterday, have been closed again, and the closing of them delays all action, for even the messengers of the executive power are often held up by the Commune in spite of the ministers' safe-conduct. Farewell, I feel my soul cannot be touched by fear, and I am quite capable of pursuing to the last the advance and the measures of disciplined resistance; my worthy friend [Roland] is just as active and even more steadfast than ever. . . Farewell, a few more days will throw great light upon the capital's fate. Wisdom would perhaps dictate the departure of the government, but it is already too late for that. Washington had Congress removed, and it was not through fear.

Three days later, on the fifth of September, horrified by the indescribable massacre of the prisoners, Mme Roland wrote again to Clermont-Ferrand:

We are under the knife of Robespierre and Marat; these men are striving to arouse the people and turn them against the National Assembly and the Council. They have instigated a special tribunal; they have a small army which they pay with what they found or stole from the Château or elsewhere, or with what is given them by Danton who, on the sly, is the leader of this horde. Would you believe that they issued a warrant of arrest against Roland and Brissot, suspecting them of being in league with Brunswick? They insisted upon sealing up their papers, but in their inquisitorial search among Brissot's, they were shamed to find nothing but the contrary of their expectations. They did not dare affix the seals, or even to go on to Roland's and Guadet's; but contented themselves with carrying off letters written in English which they couldn't make head nor tail of. Had they served their warrant, these two excellent citizens would have been taken to the Abbaye and massacred with the others. We are not yet saved, and if the departments do not send a guard to the Assembly and the Council, we shall lose the two of them.

Make haste then to send it to us, on the pretext of alien invasion, for they are sending to the frontiers all the able-bodied men who might defend us. Let all France contribute to the preservation of the two authorities which are hers and which are precious to her. Do not lose a moment if you would save them; farewell.

The capture of Verdun, now occupied like Longwy by the Prussians "in the name of His Majesty the King of France," had served as a pretext for the attack on the prisons. It was perhaps Danton who first received the news, but neither the Mayor of Paris, Pétion, nor the responsible Ministers, Roland, Servan, and Danton, had had them guarded. Certainly the Commune had not taken the Girondists into its confidence concerning these plans which they would have indignantly rejected, and when they wished to take action not only was it too late, but they had no longer any forces at their disposal.

We have the original document in which Roland ordered Santerre, the all-powerful brewer, to march against the assassins and
plunderers:

To M. Santerre, General Commander of the Parisian National
Guard, the fourth of September '92, at three in the afternoon.
In the name of the nation and by order of the National Assembly
and the executive power, I direct you, Monsieur, to make use of all
the forces which the law has placed at your command, to prevent
the safety of life and property from being violated, and I make you
responsible for all attacks made on any citizen whomsoever in the city
of Paris. I am sending you a copy of the law which confirms the
measures I have recommended to you, and I am informing the National Assembly and the Mayor of Paris of the orders I am hereby
transmitting you.

At the same time Roland, greatly distressed, wrote the Assembly
to advise it of the orders given to Santerre and to entreat it to put
a stop to the "outrages." [58]

The following day, Santerre, in a beautiful, even, and ornate
hand, answered Roland with the basest hypocrisy:

September 5, 1792

Sir and Minister,
I know nothing whatsoever of the refusal to go which you apprise me
the federates made under pretext of secret orders. I have just enjoined
the Commanders of the Marseilles and Finistère troops to declare themselves ready to set out against the enemy at the first order I give them.
I shall have the honour of acquainting you with their response.
Every day I give the most precise orders concerning the protection
of the capital; it is only lack of organization that hinders the citizens
from doing regular service. I have strongly urged the General Assemblies of the sections to take up this question without delay.

Up until this time, there had been brawlers and drunkards to
be found among the rioters. From September on there were thieves
and assassins as well. The sinister figures of professional killers
appeared who knew how to make themselves "useful" with such success and impunity that they seemed to have found in this an opportunity for wholesale murder. Several of them were foreigners.
Among them was an Italian, a professor of English; Lazowski, a
Pole, and Rossignol, the cut-throat of the *Force;* Maillard, Judge
at the Abbaye, and this Huguenin who represented the Faubourg

Antoine and the Marquis de Saint-Huruge; last, but decidedly not least, was Fournier l'Americain, the Saint Dominican ex-planter, whose atrocious memory still survives, buckled with three belts of pistols with which he enforced his blood-thirsty curses. Mme Roland's story is curiously interwoven with that of two of these abominable wretches.

At the time when Mme Roland was going from office to office soliciting the patents of Nobility, she had encountered — and she remembered it well — a young Pole named Lazowski who had just come to Paris, and who, under the patronage of the Duke de Lian-court, had been nominated Inspector of Manufactures — just like the austere Roland himself. They created a post especially for him at Soissons "where there was scarcely anything," said Mme Roland, "but the manufacture of priests, and nothing to inspect except nuns." Lazowski

. . . then very elegant, well-coiffed, befrilled, hunching his shoulders and walking on his heels, gave himself that little self-important air which stupid people took at that time as an indication of superiority, while sensible people ridiculed it. But the Revolution ruined his posi-tion. Finding himself penniless, he became a patriot, let his hair go greasy, brayed aloud in his section, and became a *Sans-Culotte* for the simple reason that he was threated with not possessing any [*culottes*]. After the downfall of the monarchy from which, as a "rescuer of the fatherland," he had hoped to benefit, he became a killer on the second of September, particularly of the Saint-Firmin priests, and showed him-self equally "useful" regarding the Orléans prisoners.

As deputy for his division, he presented himself one day at the office of the Minister of the Interior, where Mme Roland perceived

the astonishing transformation. The pretty little gentleman with his slight grimaces had adopted the brutal airs of a rabid patriot, the flushed face of a heavy drinker, and the haggard eye of an assassin.

Among the papers found at Roland's, a letter that was obviously sent on for his attention, holds our interest. It is addressed to Du Bail, vice-president of the Second Division Criminal Court at Paris, 101, rue de Vaugirard. This anonymous letter, which was recog-nized and certified to as authentic by the one to whom it was addressed, declared that "it had been sent to him on the twenty-sixth of October 1792 by Citizen Marcandier, who knew of his love for the fatherland."

Yesterday morning I was at the house of that ferocious person of whom we have spoken several times. A certain individual, also a member of the Cordelier Club, came from the Marseilles section; this miserable soul made a long apology for the second of September and added that that matter was not yet done with, and that another blood-letting was necessary, but an even more copious one than the first. There is, he said, the Roland-Brissot clique to dispose of; we are already seeing to that, and I hope, he went on, that within two weeks at the latest it will be done. Let society profit, I beseech you, by this information I impart.

I did not wish to enquire the individual's name, as I feared they would suspect what use I wished to make of it. However, if you are anxious to know, I can tell you within two days at the latest. It is time, and high time, to arrest the fury of the murderers. I grieve to contemplate the horrors they are preparing for us. Brissot is extremely displeasing to them. Guadet, Vergniaud, La Source, etc. are the ones they accuse of being in Roland's clique. They will hear of no-one but Robespierre.

I do not sign this and you know well enough it is not that I lack confidence but that I fear to compromise you.

Mme Roland was deeply shocked to see Danton "but slightly concerned with his department . . . continuously in the War Offices striving to find situations for his tools, especially as concerned supplies and markets." This was extremely unjust. It was all very well to write speeches to the *Marseillais,* or to ask an Antoine Lemaire to lecture the soldiers, but it was nothing compared to the inspired acts of a Danton. Mme Roland neither saw nor understood the invincible patriotism of the man who had answered Robespierre's sly quibbling with: "All our quarrels won't kill a Prussian !" What would Servan in the War Department have done without the tireless stimulus of Danton ? Was Mme Roland really blinded to the point of wanting the Minister of Justice to be bound by Cabinet procedure rather than occupied with fighting for France by aiding her soldiers ? Nothing was more pressing than to drive back the invading Germans. It was because Danton succeeded in this that Paris erected a statue to him and that his name lives in our hearts.

There was more justice in the terrible implications Mme Roland made concerning the massacres. It is certain that Danton neither thought of nor ordered the slaughter in the prisons. But he was aware of what the Commune was preparing and his policy was to let matters take their course. Mme Roland was revolted, and in spite of herself read on his face "brutal passions," with "the most astounding audacity, half-concealed under the most jovial of manners, an affectation of frankness, and a sort of simple good-naturedness." When her imagination led her, as was its custom, to visualize Danton acting in accordance with his appearance, she always saw the same terrifying vision: Danton, "dagger in hand, inciting by voice and gesture a gang of assassins more timorous or less ferocious than himself." She had learned that Danton in 1789 was "a miserable little lawyer with no practise," unable to support his family had it not been for the *louis* his father-in-law gave him every week.

Having become a partisan of Orléans, he seems to be in easy circumstances. One never sees him working but he brays aloud in the clubs and makes use of every demagogic move which has served to make him the tribune whom the people have forced upon the government. From that time, his advance has been as rapid as it is bold. By bestowing favours, or by protecting them with his own name, he has attached to him those greedy and miserable men who are stimulated by need and vice; he designates terrible people whose ruin must be brought about; he either buys up writers or inspires fanatics to persecute them; he carries the revolutionary devices of blinded patriots or clever rogues to even greater extremes; he invents, decides, and puts into execution plans that strike terror to the heart, annihilate obstacles, bring in money, and mislead public opinion in all these things. By his intrigues, he shapes the electoral body, openly dominates it by his agents, and names the Paris deputation at the Convention in which he takes his part. He goes to Belgium to increase his wealth; he dares confess to a fortune of 1,400,000 *livres,* parading luxury while preaching *Sans-Culottisme,* and sleeps upon heaps of corpses — his victims. . . . As for Fabre d'Églantine, tricked out in a monk's gown, armed with a stiletto, busy hatching a plot for discrediting the innocent or ruining the rich whose fortunes he covets, he is so perfect in his rôle that anyone wishing to depict the most villainous Tartufe need only make his portrait just as he is dressed.

She noticed that Danton was "very much concerned" with the question of secret funds, and did not at all agree with the austere

Roland as to the manner of distributing them. She, a good puritan, was outraged to learn that he had "drawn 100,000 *écus* one day, 60,000 another, still more at another place, without giving any accounting to the Assembly."

On the second of September, Grandpré, Inspector of the Prisons, hastened to Danton, the Minister of Justice, to point out the dangers that threatened the prisoners. Danton was absent at the Council. There Grandpré waited for the ministers to come out. Danton was the first to appear, and Grandpré immediately fell upon him and gave voice to his anxieties. But Danton cut him short with these words: "To h—— with the prisoners! Let happen to them what will" and continued on his way. This occurred in the presence of some twenty persons, says Mme Roland in her *Memoirs*. No doubt she received her information from Grandpré himself.

Danton was an accomplice of those scoundrels who drenched with blood these terrible days of our history.[59] The Orléans prisoners were massacred in spite of Roland's precautionary measures, for Danton had not dared to oppose these new crimes which the Commune had planned.

The murderers then repaired to the Place Vendôme where, shouting beneath his windows, they demanded the minister. Tradition has it that Danton appeared on the balcony and *thanked* them. Meanwhile Marat, who had drawn up an infamous document addressed to the eighty-three departments and which had its bloodthirsty effect, sent it to Minister Danton to be signed. Without a moment's hesitation, Danton affixed his signature, whereupon it became a law.

During this time, a band of rascals was carrying Marat through the streets in triumph; he had already begun — as a philanthropist — to ask for heads — "a few to save many." Danton embraced Marat at the Supervision Committee, then went upstairs to Mayor Pétion.

"Do you know what they want to do now?" he asked. "They have issued a warrant against Roland!"

"Whom do you mean?" asked Pétion.

"That mad committee. . ."

And with these words he tore up the warrant before the eyes of Pétion who was highly amused.

Mme Roland, however, connected this warrant with the invasion of the court of the ministry by 200 fanatics, and thought they had been sent by Marat's group and that Danton had taken this step to ascertain the opinion of Roland's friends.

Furthermore, it is well known that Danton did not deny that he had been involved in the massacre.

"It was my work," he said to the Duke of Chartres. And later, at the Convention:

"What do I care if I am called *drinker of blood !*"

For his part, Robert Lindet came to admit that all he saw in this accumulation of crimes was "the impartial application of the principles of natural law." This same Lindet said that there was no question of a popular movement "but that *all was prearranged. I agree that if one of the three ruling bodies, the Assembly, the Executive Council, or the Mayor of Paris had refused its consent to what was proposed, these events would have never degraded France."*

It is indeed regrettable that Roland did not then hand in his resignation. It would have been an admirable exit.

On the ninth of September, Mme Roland wrote a third letter to Bancal. The riot had not abated. How was it possible to foresee a lull after such elections had just taken place in the capital ?

Robespierre, Danton, Collot d'Herbois, Billault de Varennes and Marat, these are the Paris deputies who have actually been appointed ! . . . Dreadful denunciations against the Assembly and the Council: you will see that the two of them will be sacrificed. You would not believe this possible, but after it has been accomplished you will lament in vain.

My friend Danton directs everything; Robespierre is his puppet, Marat holds his torch and dagger; this savage tribune rules, and, pending the moment when we fall victim to him, we are nothing but poor, oppressed people.

If you knew the horrible details of these expeditions ! The women brutally violated before being torn to pieces by these tigers, their guts slashed into ribbons, gory human flesh devoured ! . . . You know my enthusiasm for the Revolution, well, it has now turned to shame ! It has been disfigured by scoundrels, it has become hideous ! In eight days' time . . . what is there to say ? It is degrading to remain where one is, and it is forbidden to leave Paris; they keep us here so as to cut our throats at the most propitious moment. Farewell, do as did Louvet at the Convention, follow my husband's lead, if there still be an honourable salvation that way. If it be too late for us, at least save the rest of the Empire [60] from the crimes of these mad men.

Brissot was no less desperate. In his memoirs he wrote:

. . . Three words have destroyed the most glorious Revolution which the universe had ever known ! Fire, blood, and plunder. These are the three rallying words of a Revolution where one should have heard only these three consoling and paternal ones: philosophy, tolerance, humanity.

As for Roland, though he was ill with indignation, his famous rigour had begun to yield. His friends had extorted concessions from it. The massacres over, Roland wrote: "One should perhaps draw a veil over yesterday's events. The revenge of the people is terrible, still it contains a certain element of justice. . ."

This was in Mme Roland's style. Because we know that the couple was always in agreement, we know that she too had given way. She believed it her duty to keep silent and she did keep silent. But this was foreign to her nature and her uprightness and constancy must have greatly suffered.

What did the Ministry after this horrible carnage ? Feeling its hands tied, it considered leaving Paris. The question was whether, instigated by the Commune, the popular movement would not abolish the Assembly. Who then would assist the Ministry in its fight against anarchy ? Every part of the country was in confusion. The foreign armies were drawing near. Danton emphatically declared that he was determined to save the State.

As for Robespierre, he answered Louvet and showed his ignoble hypocrisy by disowning Marat:

It is said that one innocent man has perished. It is one too many. It is far too many.

Roland and Servan entreated the Assembly to help them restore order, but no-one heeded them. Mme Roland had not, however, entirely lost her vigour. She induced her husband to write to the

deputies. With misplaced audacity, she threatened to remove the
seat of government from Paris. She said: "The south is full of
ardour, of energy, of courage, and it is quite prepared to secede in
order to insure its independence."

The elections in the provinces were, however, more satisfactory
than in Paris. Mme Roland wrote Bancal: "We are encouraged
by the excellent selection the departments have made." This meant
that Buzot was elected in the Eure, Bancal in the Puy-de-Dôme,
Brissot in the Eure-et-Loir, and that Roland was about to be elected
in the Somme.[61]

It was probably because he felt himself hopelessly constrained
as a minister that Roland presented himself to the people as a candidate. Besides, Mme Roland was more eager than ever for action.
They both agreed that this was an irreproachable way of leaving
office whilst still remaining in the thick of the political battle.

Roland had been so delighted with Pache's simple manners and
excellent office work that he could think of no-one better to take
his place in the Ministry, and with this view in mind he wrote the
Assembly. As usual his wife penned the letter.

I was in Roland's study [said Champagneux] when Mme Roland
came to read the draft of her letter; when she reached the part wherein
were enumerated the virtues and abilities Pache would bring to the
ministry, Roland, greatly moved, embraced his wife and, his eyes damp
with tears, spoke these words which have always remained in my
memory: "Ah, how well you have expressed all that I feel for our
estimable friend !" Who would ever have thought that within a few
months, though neither Roland nor his wife altered in their behaviour
towards him, Pache would become the most implacable and the cruelest
of their enemies.[62]

Brissot and Buzot, however, greatly disapproved of the arrangement. Mme Roland said that Brissot severely upbraided her, and
declared that Roland's resignation would be a "public calamity."
She replied that "his [Roland's] health would cause her too great
anxiety if he persisted in his arduous work, granted he were fortunate enough to escape the tempest that was raging about them."

She, as usual, knew no respite from her activities. Nearby, under
her hand, was a pamphlet she had written. It was warm from the

National Printing Press, and she herself had signed it with Roland's name. Dated September 23, 1792, it was a summing up of the situation which the Convention had ordered to be printed for distribution in the provinces and in the army.

At the very instant that the conspiracy against the capital is breaking out, the fanatics and the nobles are instigating insurrections in several parts of France, especially in the department of the Deux-Sèvres, in the Ardèche, and in the Drôme, where these disturbances have manifested themselves in the most formidable manner, etc.

The Convention began its seances on the twenty-first of September 1792. It was a *bourgeois* Assembly of lawyers, trades-people, doctors, men of letters. Five hundred of its seven hundred and forty-five members belonged neither to the Gironde nor to the Montagne. Owing to a certain veering in public opinion, the Girondists were now seated on the right side of the Assembly. A great number of deputies sought to place themselves between the Gironde and the Montagne. They hated the Gironde, but countenanced it because it was at the head of the administration. This too explains why Abbé Sièyes went sometimes in the evening to the Ministry of the Interior, where the Rolands, ever ingenuous, listened to him with consideration while he insinuated his opinions into their credulous ears.

Danton had no difficulty in believing in his own superiority to Roland, but would have asked nothing better than to make common cause with the couple, and through Roland approach the group who, as it were, took their cue from the ministry in the study of the Minister's wife.

Elected to the Convention as a deputy, Danton did not resign his portfolio, and Roland, always punctilious, was almost as scandalized by this illegality as by the September crimes. Roland protested in two ways: silently, by refusing to attend the Council of Ministers; secondly, by having the Minister of Justice violently attacked by Louvet in the *Sentinelle*.

Like the Lion stung by the fly, Danton began to show signs of annoyance the day when, before the entire Convention, Roland, elected deputy from the Somme, took it into his head to give the

Minister of Justice a lesson by sensationally tendering his own resignation. The Convention protested, but Danton, with rather ponderous sarcasm, suggested that if the Assembly wished to retain Roland it should also declare its opinion of Mme Roland, because "everyone knows that Roland is not alone in the Ministry . . . and since we are speaking our minds, I shall recall to the Assembly that there was a moment when confidence was at so low an ebb that there was no longer any Minister, and that Roland himself considered leaving Paris."

This was a telling blow. So this was what it amounted to, the influence of the celebrated Queen of the Gironde! What, indeed, was the party in the hands of a woman who gave it cowardly advice? Danton's intervention was all the more pernicious to the Girondists in that the rumour of their federalist beliefs, current now for several months, was beginning to take shape and become a menace. It was said that they wished to make of France a confederacy like Switzerland or the United States, and divide it into the republics of Marseilles, Lyons, Rouen, etc. What Danton had done, was to make with dangerous precision an accusation which was much more than an excuse to the extremists, and, unintelligible as it may seem, was to react violently on the people. It was true that Mme Roland had thought that the government should leave Paris under the threat of invasion. She, and those about her, continually cursed the city which they considered the haunt of all vice, and hence unworthy of sheltering the pure. Danton, on the contrary, relied on the capital (where his enormous popularity had brought him to the Council), as the very expression of France. How then could Paris do aught else but follow with increasing enthusiasm wherever he chose to lead?

The Rolands, deeply wounded by Danton's attack, immediately changed their tactics. Roland would remain in the Ministry. He would renounce the repose to which his old age entitled him. Till death came, he would serve his country. He emphatically declared that he had never thought of running away, but that it was the duty of the government in the time of enemy invasion to think first of its own safety. This, he believed, should be apparent to everyone.

Danton's insinuations were perfidious. The Rolands were honourable and courageous, but they were no novices as far as the "Cyclops" was concerned. Their resentment, which sprang from an unseasonable puritanism, advised them ill. Because they paraded their own honesty, they thought they were entitled to insist that others be equally simple. Roland liked to preach; Mme Roland considered that the cause of morality should be avenged. Unwisely but with satisfaction, they had denounced Marat. Now it was Danton's turn. The Commune was already in the hands of atrocious youths such as Tallien, Hébert, Chaumette, who kept on postponing a rendering of their accounts. They were ordered by the Convention to produce them within three days. This was a very tempting opportunity for the Rolands to assail Danton's weakest point. Both of them, like Justice in the pursuit of Crime, rushed headlong to the attack.

Before the Assembly, the Minister of the Interior arrogantly asked the Keeper of the Seals to produce his accounts. But he, who had never kept any, answered disagreeably that for diplomatic and police reasons he had required what are today known as *secret funds*.

While the characteristic short-sightedness and litigious mentality of the Girondists, as well as Mme Roland's Jansenist intelligence, might have brought France to an honourable defeat, who knows whether Danton, experienced in dealing with people, did not simply buy the victory of Valmy, as people are now beginning to say ? On the other hand, had he sufficient funds for this purpose ? And would it not have been natural for him to have confessed to such a success to his colleagues in the privacy of the Cabinet ? One thing is certain, however, and that is that the Gironde never appreciated the force that Danton represented, nor did it understand that to discredit Danton meant granting full power to Robespierre and the Commune. These sincere, verbose, vacillating men had but one chance of success, and that lay in putting themselves under the protection of this vigorous man. It remains to be known, not if this would have been honourable — after all, who cares ? — but whether any good would have come of it.

Mme Roland was less severe with Dumouriez. Barbaroux highly commended her for this, and has told us what took place between Roland and the General:

I witnessed Roland's behaviour toward Dumouriez . . . surely the author of the intrigue which expelled Roland, as well as Clavière and Servan, from the Ministry; but since that time Dumouriez has been of great service to the fatherland; he acted against the orders of the Court and his military talents promised success. Roland forgot his injuries and moved at the Council that Dumouriez be named Commander-in-Chief of the armies, and thus Dumouriez saved France at the Argonne passes.

With greater simplicity, Mme Roland expressed the same thing in her *Memoirs:*

Roland, recalled to the Ministry, considered that the interest of the people and circumstances demanded that he should make an end of the opposition which existed between himself and Dumouriez, because it was their duty to serve the Republic, each in his own way.

Roland (or rather, his wife), wrote the General a witty letter which said in part:

You were enticed into an intrigue which compelled you to damage your colleagues, and in turn you became the toy of that Court with which you were so careful to keep on good terms. Still you bear some resemblance to those doughty knights who at times were guilty of little villainies at which they were themselves the first to laugh, and who, nevertheless, could fight like demons when honour was at stake. It must be admitted that if this character is not entirely in accordance with republican austerity, it is the fault of habits of which we have not yet been able to rid ourselves, and that you must indeed be pardoned if you bring us victories.

And, in truth, the French army under Dumouriez and Kellermann won the victory of Valmy on September twentieth.

The following day, the Convention proclaimed the Republic.

On the evening of that happy day, the Girondists supped at Mme Roland's. At the end of the meal, Vergniaud proposed a toast to "the eternity of the Republic." Mme Roland, her beautiful face aglow, gravely requested him to take one of the roses she wore on her white kerchief and, following the custom of the ancients, scatter the petals of it in his wine. In silence Vergniaud contemplated the fragile petals floating in his glass, and then he drank. Leaning towards Barbaroux who sat beside him, he said in a low voice:

"Barbaroux, not rose petals but cypress leaves should be in our wine tonight."

PILLAGES had taken place in the prisons where a great deal of money and jewels had been taken by the prisoners who were afraid to leave them behind. After the tenth of August, members of the Commune had penetrated into the Château and into the houses of the rich which they had previously put under seal, and there plundered all they could lay their hands upon. Roland had requested, but to no avail, that a guard be set about the furniture repository in the Place de la Révolution.

The plundering took place on the night of the sixteenth of September. All the Crown diamonds were removed, and the *Regent*, pending a bidder, was hidden under a beam in the Ile de la Cité. This caused a great commotion among the people, who accused the Queen. The Royalists retorted by incriminating Danton and even Roland. The following day, Fabre d'Églantine persisted in presenting himself at Mme Roland's where he had long since ceased coming. In her *Memoirs* she accused him of being, with Danton, one of the authors of the theft.[63]

Defections were no rare thing among the Girondists. More than one moderate had abandoned the party to join the Montagne. The current seemed to be moving in that direction, and the fear of being left behind — pending the fear of the guillotine — took the place of real convictions in the minds of many people. Thus it was that, close to the betrayal of her oldest friend Lanthenas, Mme Roland saw with dismay how Couthon, whom she had known through Bancal, was turning more and more towards Robespierre.

Since Buzot's proposal of a departmental guard, Couthon had said that the names of those who proposed it had opened his eyes and that from then on he saw "in this plan the scheme of forming a nucleus of forces . . ." In vain did Mme Roland ask Bancal to enlighten him. From that moment, Couthon belonged to Robespierre. More than ever did Mme Roland suffer from discord, from

jealousies, and from intrigues: "What a curious mania is this perpetual accusation of plotting and ambition against men who have
never used their minds or their abilities except with the greatest
devotion to the common weal and solely to serve it."

No sooner had the victory of Valmy halted the invasion, than
another war, which had been long brooding, broke out between the
capital of France and the departments.

It is quite clear that Mme Roland was the soul of it. Brissot had
been judged a federalist, particularly because he had quoted with
high praise the American *Federalist,* which was a paper, not a man.
But the people of Paris had more definite accusations to make
against the Girondists. For example, Buzot had proposed that a
militia should be selected from the eighty-three departments and
put at the disposal of the Assembly, and the Girondist Lasource
had declared that "Paris should be reduced to its eighty-third fraction of influence." But was it not obvious, in view of the Commune,
Robespierre, and Marat, that the Convention was doomed to lose its
liberty one day ? The proof of this was to be found in d'Hanriot's
canon on the first of the following June. To our mind there are
other reproaches to be made against the Girondists. Before all else
we blame them for having been so un-revolutionary, and for having
so mistrusted all that went beyond the letter of the law. They had
stormed against the monarchy, but when the King took flight, they
put him back by force upon the throne, and there let him work
against them for almost eleven months. After the tenth of August,
they prolonged his sojourn in the Temple, which was not a solution,
and his trial, which should have logically taken place after the
proclaiming of the Republic, was neither rejected nor resolved but
left in the air from September until January. This kept the people
in a state of extreme excitement quite contrary to the fine words
Danton spoke: "When Justice begins to act, public vengeance
should come to an end." The hesitation, or rather the incoherence
of the Gironde was flagrant. It was a Girondist, Valazé, who
demanded the indictment of the King, but it was the Montagne
which spiritedly followed up the question when the orator's party
withdrew and left him in the breach. At bottom the Girondists

wished to save the King. They spoke of a trial, but they were thinking of deposition — at the most.

While they were discussing this subject as they had all the others, it was Danton who took action. No-one paid taxes any longer. The Girondists could not even effect the sale of the property of the Emigrants for the benefit of the country. Roland gave orders which were automatically annulled by the general inertia, and assignats became valueless. The visionary Girondists were satisfied with words, but one of them, in a moment of lucidity, said to another : "You make plans which would perhaps be practicable in the moon."

Nor were the Girondists very much concerned with the poverty of the people. They made no social laws. They had no suggestions to make concerning what we call "the high cost of living." It is almost possible to believe that Robespierre had disgusted them with "the people" for whom they had taken up arms. They confused them, and very wrongly, with the more or less paid agitators, with the street brawlers, with the cheats, and with the fanatical assassins. But Mme Roland was not wrong in reproaching the people of Paris for having allowed the September massacres to take place. We are even justified in reproaching it for supporting the Terror. From time to time, it is true, certain squeamish individuals were heard to say that they could not endure the neighbourhood of the guillotine or the stench of the cemeteries. But to remedy this, all Robespierre had to do was to transport the bodies and heads from the Madeleine Cemetery to the cemetery of the Errancis at Monsseaux. Thus it was that the government cleaver was removed from the Place de la Révolution to the Bastille, where it met with a bad reception. But when it was installed at the Barrière du Trône — in a deserted quarter — everyone was satisfied. Passersby became quite accustomed to the sight of daily victims, those about to die who eyed them with contempt and those who howled with terror. When, after the massacres, Mme Roland said: "All Paris is accursed for me," it is not difficult to understand her exclamation of horror.

To be sure, Mme Roland had not always spoken thus. And what was more natural than that she, a Parisian from the Cité, should have loved the city of her youth ? We need but recall her consternation when, almost below Phlipon's windows, she saw a poor wretch subjected to the torture of the rack. Truly, it cannot be said that "the Rolands took September for granted." A certain great historian of our time insists that it was "through policy that they had pretended to perceive blood upon Danton's outstretched hand." No, she had a fiery heart and resolute ideas. She was too pure to be indulgent, this was the truth. It was Lemontey who saw her as she was.

After having accused her of a hardness of which we can find no trace, this historian said that Mme Roland had infected her political friends with all the "squeamishness of over-refinement, etc."

Indeed she did have a strong distaste for disorder, for uncleanliness, for ugly words. She would not have dreamed of pandering to the people by living in a workingman's home, as did Robespierre, nor would she have been "honoured" as was Pache who, when he became Minister of War, ate dinner at his porter's. Nor would she have sent her pretty daughter Eudora to the Jacobins "to exchange the kiss of peace" with drunkards, as Pache instructed his daughter Silvie to do. Neither did Robespierre fraternize with this "people" of whom he was always speaking. His popularity did not seem to suffer from it. It was Danton who loved the people, who mingled with them, who had the same reactions, the same pleasures; and the plebeian coarseness of Danton repelled Robespierre as much as it did Mme Roland. Robespierre sought that conventional "people" whom Rousseau had sung and Greuze had painted. Finding something entirely different, he kept his distance. Mme Roland, on the other hand, was well acquainted with the people, the true people. Have we not seen her nursing her father's apprentice through a contagious illness, watching over the maid Mignonne until her death, after having put her in her own bed and taken all the housework upon herself ? And at *Le Clos,* and in the village of Theizé, had she not loved and succoured the peasants among whom she lived ?

"The Girondists were ruined by the aristocracy of their tastes, attitudes, one might almost say, the aristocracy of their epidermis," said M. Taine who, among others, wrote that Mme Roland was too isolated from the world. The great historian we have already mentioned has remarked that her "manners were too exquisite." According to the information we possess, we would be more justified in believing that her character, in reality, did not go to extremes. She was not pretentious, neither was she a lady of studied elegance. Our historian thinks the Montagnards could easily have "represented such dandies (the Girondists) as enemies of the people," but did Brissot, for instance, have such fine manners, and who ever reproached Lavoisier for his good-breeding ? Did one need to be either a *"Sans-Culotte"* or *"*a fanatic of the guillotine*"* to be a true Republican ?

It is just as we have said: historians do not always approach Mme Roland with the serenity which befits them nor the neutrality which is her due. She imagined that "future generations" for whom she suffered and died would be at least impartial in their judgment. A hundred and thirty years have elapsed and her hopes have not yet been fulfilled.

FOLLOWING the example of the Convention, Roland wished to give an equal prominence to everything concerned with the glory of France. Although completely lacking in artistic perception, he did not wish to be outdone by those who, setting an example of universal fitness, were at the same time bestowing a lavish interest upon the Beaux Arts and Public Education, upon the Postal Service and Foreign Relations. On the seventeenth of October 1792, he wrote in his own hand to M. David, painter, upon the creating of a Museum at the Galleries (The Louvre). As Minister of the Interior he was "the disposer and curator" of this Gallery.

This Museum must be for the development of the great wealth the nation possesses in painting, sculpture, drawing, etc. . . Also, as I conceive it, it should be open to everyone and each one is at liberty to place his easel before such a painting or such a statue. . . This will be a national monument and there will not be a single individual who has not the right to enjoy it. I believe that the Museum could be one of the most powerful means of rendering the French Republic illustrious.

You, a painter, ask, Monsieur, for the lodging of a goldsmith. . .

Roland granted him the lodging and David thanked him extremely coolly and recommended to him, with the idea that they too might be lodged at the Louvre:

two virtuous artists. . . One has the simple and respectful habits of our first ancestors. The other, a pupil of M. Vien, paints masterpieces, particularly his last one, *Cléopâtre et Rodogune,* especially in the way he has rendered it. . . I would not be so outspoken were you not so kind and if the time of our acqaintance did not date from the seventeenth of July 1791 on the Champs de Mars at the altar of the fatherland.

This twenty-fourth of October 1792, the first year of the Republic.

An autograph letter of Roland shows how he wasted his time answering with emphatic care certain letters which gave him an opportunity of displaying his pedantry.

One instance is his letter of the fifth of October 1792 to M. Gouget-Deslandes, Assistant Judge at the Tribunal of Cassation:

I have read, Monsieur, the address of the citizens of the Quatre Nations section to their fellow-citizens of the forty-seven other sections. I naturally approved of the principles expressed therein, for I myself have often manifested them, and the idea of this throne on which the tables of the law alone would rest has always been my fondest wish. And the rest is fantastical and monstrous and can only be applied to stupid beings. The philosopher, the true Republican can have no regulations other than nature and law, but that all these useful truths may become general, one cannot repeat them too often, propagate them, etc. . .

Had it been in this style that Roland wrote all that bore his signature, his friends would not have long had illusions concerning his ability. But fortunately Mme Roland was always there to make up for his deficiency. At this time, letters show that she was in correspondence with Bernardin de Saint-Pierre, Superintendent of the former Jardin du Roi, which had now become the national Jardin des Plantes, where as a little girl she had been taken walking by her parents; and where as a learned and vivacious young wife, she had with Roland and Lanthenas followed Jussieu's course and made the acquaintance of Louis Bosc who had just attained his twentieth year.

At times Mme Roland's thoughts turned as well to the respectable

pastor, Lavater, who had left her memories so virtuous and touching
that they often restored her faith in humanity. On the fourth of
November he wrote Roland from Zurich to protest against the law
(voted on Buzot's motion on the twenty-third of October 1792),
which ordained the permanent banishment of the Emigrants and a
sentence of death on those who re-entered France.

> One word, my dear Roland de la Platière ! For the first time in my
> life I fall upon my knees in the name of humanity ! I implore you,
> do everything possible and impossible to abolish the unheard of, the
> barbarous and blood-thirsty law which banishes so many of the Emi-
> grants and slaughters all those who return. How many innocent ones
> among them ! How many faithful to their duty ! To this I can but
> add my own name.
>
> JEAN-GASPARD LAVATER

> My good wife asks me in the name of God not to send this to
> M. de Roland. But I answer her: "If you fear that any harm will
> come from this simple word of humanity, you have forgotten the wise
> and just countenance of this man, and the good, loyal face of his wife."
>
> LAVATER

Naturally it was Mme Roland who answered. One feels how
grieved she was to write him that this was a necessary law.[64] It
was Buzot who proposed it, and she was certainly in sympathy with
it. Doubtless they discussed it at length together. She resigned
herself to it because she was subjugated by that resolution she found
in him and which was so lacking in the others. But where, alas,
were the high hopes of '89, when the face of Liberty was radiant
with clemency, with nobleness, and with purity ? It was not yet
known that she would demand blood, nor that so many "crimes
would be committed in her name !"

"In the midst of the political world and the disturbances which
surround us, a memory of friendship brings repose to the spirit and
consolation to the heart," wrote Mme Roland to the worthy Lavater.
She was happy to talk with "an honest man" whom she could trust.
Such a rare thing had it become ! But to come to the point of her
letter:

> Only after mature reflection was the law in question brought before
> the Assembly; it is a harsh measure, but it is perhaps necessary to
> have known all the plans of the Emigrants in general, all their enter-

prises, and above all, the frightening excesses of those who took up arms and as enemies invaded our own soil, before one can appreciate the necessity and the justice of it.

At about this time Mme Roland had a very different letter to write, a letter to the "Prince and Bishop of Rome" — in other words, the Pope.

Two young French artists, Rater, an architect, and a young sculptor, Chinard, had been imprisoned by the pontifical government, under suspicion of being sympathizers with the infamous Revolution which had just proclaimed a Republic in their country. As events were to show, a mere word from the French ambassador would have secured their freedom.[65] But we cannot be far wrong in believing that Mme Roland, still quivering from the insult to France and to Liberty, could not control herself once the idea entered her mind to speak without the slightest reticence — she, Jeanne-Marie Phlipon — to the supreme and sovereign Pontiff of Christianity.

Here is her letter, countersigned by all the ministers:

THE PROVISIONAL EXECUTIVE COUNCIL OF
THE FRENCH REPUBLIC TO THE PRINCE AND BISHOP OF ROME

November 23, 1792

Free Frenchmen, protégés of the arts who have gone to Rome to develop the tastes and talents which are Rome's pride, are now being unjustly persecuted by your order. Torn from their work in the most arbitrary manner, closed away in a severe prison, held up as public examples and treated like guilty men although no court has proved their crime, for there was nothing with which to reproach them save that they let it be known that they respected the rights of humanity and loved a fatherland who exemplified these rights, they may be looked upon as victims of despotism and superstition.

Were it ever allowable to purchase the triumph of a good cause at the cost of innocence, doubtless this abuse might go unchallenged. The tottering reign of the Inquisition ends the very day it again dares show its fury, and the successor to Saint Peter will no longer be prince from the day he countenances that rage. The powerful voice of reason has been heard far and wide; in the heart of oppressed man it has revived a consciousness of his duties and his force; this same voice has broken the sceptre of tyranny and the talisman of royalty; Liberty has become the universal rallying-sign and sovereigns tottering on their thrones must befriend her if they wish to avoid a violent fall. But for the French Republic, it is not enough to foresee the period when tyranny will be annihilated all over Europe, she must as well stay its action on all those who belong to her.

The Minister of Foreign Affairs has already asked the liberation of the Frenchmen arbitrarily imprisoned at Rome. Today it is the Executive Council which asks it, in the name of the Justice they did not offend, in the name of the arts it is your interest to encourage and protect, in the name of reason outraged by this singular persecution, in the name of a free nation, proud and generous, who disdains conquests but who wishes her rights respected, who is ready to avenge herself upon whomsoever may have the audacity to disregard them, and who did not wrest them from the priests and kings to have them outraged by any earthly being.

Pontiff of the Roman Church, still Prince of a State ready to slip through your fingers, you can no longer preserve the State and the Church save by the impartial possession of those evangelical principles which breathe the purest democracy, the tenderest humanity, the most complete equality, and which Christ's successors have assumed only to augment a domination which today is falling into decay. The dark ages are past. Men are now submissive to conviction alone; truth alone can guide them; only their own happiness can bind them, and the art of politics and the secret of government are reduced to a recognition of man's rights and of facilitating for him the practice of the greatest good for all with the least possible injury to any individual; such are today the principles of the French Republic, too just to keep silent even for the sake of diplomacy; too powerful to resort to threats; but also too proud to feign not to notice an outrage, and ready to strike if its demands remain unheeded.

Done in the Executive Council on the twenty-third of November one thousand seven hundred and ninety-two, in the first year of the French Republic.

(signed): Roland, Monge, Clavière, Lebrun, Pache, Garat
The Council.
(signed): Grouvelle, secretary.

Here we see Lemontey's "too perfect woman." Who has ever governed with such uncompromising ingenuousness?

But this letter, although slightly tinged with the flavour of the time,[66] flamed with a civic pride and a freedom of expression which lose none of their thrilling quality. The victory of Jemmapes was but fifteen days old. Would Mme Roland, somewhat earlier, have spoken with so much arrogance in the name of a "free nation"?

In her *Memoirs,* she has written:

A letter to the Pope in the name of the Executive Council, secretly inscribed by a woman in the austere study Marat was pleased to call

a *boudoir,* seemed to me so amusing a thing that I laughed outright
after having done it.

On the twenty second of the preceding May, a Versailles locksmith
called Gamain, had been summoned by Louis XVI to the Tuileries,
to place an iron door over a secret cupboard.[67] On the nineteenth
of the following November, Gamain went to Roland and told him
of the hiding place, offering to accompany him to the Château and
open it in his presence. Heurtier, the architect, went with them.
Roland made a packet of the papers he removed from the cupboard
and entrusted it to a servant. He then proceeded to the Convention where, according to certain testimony, he deposited the packet.
Others have maintained that Roland brought the papers to his wife
and that they examined them together seeking in vain some evidence against Danton.[68]

When we began this work, there was one point which seemed
enigmatic to us: what was the secret reason of Mme Roland's hatred
for Danton ? But as we progressed in the story, this mystery van-
ished into thin air. It dwindled down to the most commonplace
fact: that he was morally and physically antipathetic to her. This
great hulk of a lad (she was five years his elder), with his pock-
marked face and his mouth gashed by the horn of a raging bull,
repelled her more by the grossness of his speech than by the hideous-
ness of his countenance. He never ceased swearing in his "bellow-
ing voice," and no-one could have been more slovenly in his dress.
This was sufficient to keep at a distance a lady who appreciated
good-breeding in those with whom she came in contact.

This natural aversion would not have been important, however,
had she not been convinced that he had been involved in the September massacres — as much, at least, as Pontius Pilate had been
party to the Crucifixion. Further, she resented the man who had
wished to ridicule before the entire Convention the worthy wife of
the Minister of the Interior and then persecuted her ignobly in a
press campaign. Finally, she suspected him of various extortions,
particularly shocking to a couple devoted to the love and practice
of virtue.

A note to Lanthenas, which dates in all probability from the last months of 1792, informs us that Romme, a Montagnard deputy, had solicited an interview with Mme Roland "to save the public weal." He wished to converse with her "without any of the gentlemen of the Gironde or Brissot being present." This was one of the many abortive attempts at a reconciliation between the Gironde and the Montagne. Was Danton involved in this?

The tribune of the Cordeliers felt more and more the need of checking Robespierre and Marat. An understanding with the Gironde seemed the safest and simplest way of attaining this. Mme Roland, however, had, so to speak, irrevocably excommunicated Danton. She was greatly scandalized to learn that Vergniaud had consented to meet him at Julie Talma's, who had given a party to her friends for this purpose, where the great orator of the Gironde had appeared with the brilliant and beautiful Mlle Candeille.

That Danton made an attempt at reconciliation is evident from Mme Roland's own singular story which she told without interpreting and probably without understanding it.

After Jemmapes, Dumouriez had come to Paris glorious and proud of his victory over the Prussians.[69] Mme Roland invited him to dinner among "a great number of other people." He arrived very gallantly, carrying a bouquet of red roses. He was on his way to the Opera, there to permit the crowd to gaze upon the saviour of France. Mme Roland was asked aloud whether she also was not going, and in a puritanical mood she did not respond. It hardly became one of her character and habits to be seen in public at the side of a Court varlet!

After the General's departure she invited Vergniaud to accompany her and her daughter to the Opera. Once there, they were informed by the woman in attendance that the Minister's box was occupied. Mme Roland, knowing very well that she had issued no invitations, had the door opened "despite the protests of three or four Sans-Culottes who looked like cut-throats" and who seemed to be standing guard in the corridor. The performance had begun. From the back, Mme Roland recognized "Danton's inflated figure, as well as Fabre and three or four women of questionable appearance." Danton, leaning towards the adjoining box, was conversing

with Dumouriez. Having taken in the scene at a glance, Mme
Roland withdrew and no-one was the wiser for her presence. No
doubt, Danton, who with his hearty good humour must have found
Mme Roland very ceremonious, had thought of this meeting in
public as a means of proclaiming before the eyes of the victorious
General as well as of the enraptured audience, the reconciliation of
the Gironde and the Montagne. But such an enterprise demanded
a little more care and preparation.

A final interview took place in the greatest secrecy at night in the
Sceaux woods at the end of November. Many notable Girondists,
Brissot in particular, were ready to come to some understanding
with Danton. It was the Roland clique that ruined the plan. The
burly voice of Danton rang out in despair: "Guadet, Guadet, you
know not how to forgive, you know not how to sacrifice your resentment for the sake of your country . . . You are obstinate . . .
you will perish . . ."

Indeed historians unanimously agree that Mme Roland, who
definitely prevented the alliance of the Gironde with Danton, condemned the party of honest people by refusing them the powerful
support which was offered them. This would make Mme Roland
responsible for the Terror. Danton would have been strong enough
to have checked the Montagne, made the Commune act lawfully,
and stopped Robespierre's career. This may seem astonishing, and
to write it is an easy matter. But if Mme Roland considered it
impossible to found upon Danton the politics of her party, she also
had her reasons, and they were good ones. First there was the
alliance with Orléans, then there were the complicities, the extortions. . . There was but one way that she could overcome her disgust, and that was through believing, as we do, in the great patriotic
instinct of this man who had saved France. This she seemed to
ignore. Was it on purpose that she closed her eyes? Did she un-
consciously fear this natural genius? Perhaps one of the deepest
reasons for her aloofness was that she feared to see her own principles attacked. Like all those who have themselves well in hand,
she required immovable foundations for her courage and resistance.
But, even in politics, have fine things ever been achieved by people

who lowered their ideals ? And could not this retort be made to
the historians: "Had the Girondists allied themselves with Danton,
they would have been simple minded indeed to put their confidence
in a man who would have thrown them and their principles over-
board the moment it was to his interest to do so." ?

Towards the end of 1792, Mme Roland went through a bitter
crisis, caused by the conduct of Lanthenas, her oldest friend.

For twelve years she had called him "her brother," and they had
been so intimate that they had resided almost constantly under the
same roof, first at the Hotel de Lyon, then at Amiens, at *Le Clos,*
and finally at the Ministry of the Interior where he held the important post of superintendent of the third section.[70]

The roots of the disagreement were deep in the past. Ten un-
dated notes [71] addressed by Mme Roland to the friend she had
showered with affection and sisterly devotion, prepare us for the
final break. These letters have remained enigmas, and we hasten
to give our interpretation of them. Right or wrong, it is however
worthy of note, that the deductions of all those who have worked
over the originals more or less concur.

This much, however, we can believe:

The change which had taken place in Mme Roland's heart towards the autumn of 1792, must first be considered. She was then
thirty-eight and there was no reason to believe that she had not
been entirely faithful to a husband she tenderly loved and who had
been the object of her constant solicitude. Roland's attachment in
itself proved this before all else.

We know neither when nor how, but someone appeared who
aroused new emotions in this pure heart. No doubt she employed
the best of her strength to resist them, no doubt she used all her
skill to save appearances, and no doubt, too, being in the public
eye, she did not always succeed in concealing her feelings from those
about her. We know that Roland had no suspicions, for it was
she herself who finally made him the romantic confession that
overwhelmed him. Even Mlle Mignot, Eudora's governess, who
lived in the same house and who was odiously to betray before the

Revolutionary Tribunal the trust which the mother of her pupil had placed in her, did not hint that Mme Roland might have been in love. Nor did the Girondists know anything, despite the rumour that ran from the Jacobins to the Cordeliers that the famous "Lucretia," "Cato's wife," had allowed herself to be moved by the attentions of one of the young men over whom she held sway. Several names were mentioned, particularly those of Barbaroux, and Servan, but Buzot was never suspected.

Lanthenas, however, who lived under the same roof as Mme Roland, had been able to see things more clearly. He lived at her side like a "brother" — yes — but his feelings were not those of a brother. As long as she showed no preference, he had accepted Bosc and all the others without a protest. But why, since a certain time, was he meeting Buzot so often in the ante-chamber?

Upon her return to Paris in December 1791, we know that Buzot, a former constituent, had already returned to Evreux as President of the Criminal Court. Mme Roland had not seen him for a year, but she had kept up a regular correspondence with the young deputy until, elected to the Convention, he had returned to Paris in September 1792.

It is probable that Lanthenas imparted his first suspicions without delay to this friend in whom he had confided for so many years. He must have shown himself very much grieved, for in the notes she wrote at that time, Mme Roland evidenced a great distress.

At that time she spent a few days at Monsseaux, in the country, at the house of Gibert, an old friend, who had a little house in that district through which the Avenue de Villiers and the rue de Courcelles pass today. She took with her some work which required calm, at least this was her excuse for leaving the city, a thing she rarely did. Perhaps she wanted some solitude in which to reflect upon her troubles. At any rate, she wrote to Lanthenas [72] inviting him to lunch and said that Roland would probably be there too. The following words arouse our curiosity:

You will find *your sister* who would fain contribute to your happiness, and, though she may possess a thousand blemishes, will never seek *to delude you as to the condition of her heart. Perhaps it is wrong*

*of me to say this to you, but I am hurt at the thought of your grief
and I fear both to speak and to hold my peace.*[73]

What did this mean? It seems evident that Lanthenas had
gently complained to her, and that she was sorry for him but made
no attempt to deceive him. This was consistent with her character.
There was a great deal of anxiety expressed in that last sentence.
This retreat to the country, this voluntary retirement can be explained only as the recoil of a woman determined not to yield, a
woman who strove to defend herself by opposing force to force, but
who, far from possessing her customary assurance, was afraid of
herself and feared another even more.

Lanthenas did not show self-constraint for long, but her tenderness for him remained unaltered.

The thought of your situation troubles me and I find you most
insincere when you say I take pleasure in the pain I cause. . . Come
and see me, either this evening or between noon and two. You know
I will know no peace as long as my brother is unhappy.

And in a following note:

Your expressions, your conjectures of contempt distress me. This is
false. It is not as you say and you know it well.

And here is an even more explicit letter than the one in which
she invited him to Monsseaux. A certain amount of time must
have elapsed:

You distress me, because I hate to cause suffering, because I esteem
you and am attached to you, and I dread hurting you or, in other
words, I am all the more unhappy in that it is you I hurt. But were
you right a thousand times, *the ascendency I recognize is established,
and I can no longer withdraw.* It is false that you wish either my
hatred or my despair; the former is impossible, the latter would make
you perish of remorse, and besides, one feels despair only for the *ruling
being* who alone has the right to bring one to it. *You who invoke
reason and who protest against the caprices of the heart, be generous
enough to be my friend.* This effort can forestall many evils; but no
evil can alter my destiny save by cutting it short.

All these words seem to verify our hypothesis.

This time Mme Roland had come to a decision: love was stronger
than she.

"The ascendency I recognize is established, and I can no longer withdraw." Only the man she loved had the power to reduce her to "despair." She said this to the man she did not love, with a cruelty that is only human, so that there might be no doubt about the situation of things. Lanthenas must have told her that he would prefer to his own happiness the "hatred" she might feel for him or the "despair" to which the one she had chosen might reduce her. But she knew Lanthenas, the dear tried friend, too well to believe he had such sentiments. He knew the affection she bore him would never permit her "hating" him. Moreover, she did not doubt that he would "perish of regret" — no less — if the man she loved treated her ill.

But Lanthenas, far from being moved by her prayers, became more and more bitter every day. Through him we learn that a certain money matter had previously set his great friend against him. She had said nothing of it at the time, however, and one wonders why he brought up this story now. But something more serious was to happen, and this time Mme Roland was cut to the quick. Lanthenas spoke "to third parties" of all that was taking place between them. Lanthenas had been unworthy of her "confidence"; he had been "indelicate" and "dishonourable." In her eyes he was no more than a vulgar person, the victim of emotions she had no wish to qualify and which she "despised." This note, replete with a new harshness, terminated by reproaching Lanthenas for the political ideas he had recently espoused.

I might say a great deal concerning your own alienation, the manifestations of your political opinions and this continual censure of ours.

Here the paper is torn, which makes the letter even more enigmatic:

I know not how or why one can   make accusations of desertion
    when one shows that one is so oneself; but one thing fits into another and I am no longer astonished by anything.

Very harshly did she put him in his place:

. . . Make no more ado as to the care I can take of my own virtue; it depends neither on you nor on anyone, any more than my esteem depends on your opinion or my affection on your will.

And if she invited him to dinner, she made it clear that it was only for the sake of appearances.

However, she was incapable of steeling her heart against friendship, and she presently resumed:

Your excesses outrage pride and justice, still friendship forgives them, attributing them to a regrettable aberration which you should be spared.

If you feel capable of coming to see me and behaving as you should, I shall receive you with the affection you deserve. I warn you, however, that I will not bear with a third scene. I know all that I owe to friendship, but I am incapable of making the least concession to any sort of fear, even if death were involved, for I know what is my due, and I do not permit this to be forgotten.

All this was to end very badly. In the final analysis, Lanthenas behaved like a traitor and, in great contrast with the heroism of the Girondists, he was to be submerged in the oblivion of cowardice." [74]

What lessons she gave him, however! This note, which we have called the eleventh and which does not seem to refer to the same conflict as the others, probably dates from the end of 1792. It is here that we find the admirable words we have already quoted: "I have too much courage to feel the necessity of showing it." Four lines below we find these noble words: "I know men well enough to expect nothing of their justice; moreover, I have no need of it, my conscience stands me in its stead!" Finally, there is this stirring view of the future:

Assuredly it is not clear how the Revolution will end, and its parties will be judged by posterity, but I am convinced that my husband will there find his glory, and I have the presentiment that we shall pay for it with our lives. Perhaps the reign of justice cannot begin until unsullied victims have been sacrificed.

The Commune displayed the fiercest animosity towards the Gironde. Marat, that "man hideous with calumny, malignity, and blood," as Vergniaud had declaimed at the tribune, nursed a virulent resentment against the Rolands ever since they had suppressed the secret funds. In the *Ami du Peuple,* he heaped insults upon them.

One day a contemptible spy called Viard, brought Marat and Chabot [75] "proofs" of a great Girondist conspiracy of which Mme Roland was the moving spirit. Marat seized on this, and that same day made a great din of it in his paper. The Convention then summoned Mme Roland, but she appeared so easy and natural at the bar that the deputies, won by such striking evidence of her loyalty, sought to atone for their action by voting her the honours of the meeting. But Mme Roland, as we have already said, was not always so perfectly controlled. Her powers of resistance were exhausted, and she could scarcely bear up under the unceasing press of labour.

At ten o'clock at night on the fourth of December 1792, Roland received a summons couched in these hardly reassuring terms:

"Citizen and minister, it is imperative that you furnish information concerning a disturbing report upon which immediate action must be taken. Therefore come without delay to the Agricultural Committee where are gathered the Members of the Convention who have been summoned by decree to take a decision upon the Law of Provisions.
The President of the Meeting,
DUGUÉ D'ASSÉ

The next day, Roland wrote the following letter (penned by his wife):

Yesterday, after eleven at night, I attended the United Committees of Trade and Agriculture where the same denunciations [?] were made, and I replied by giving a statement of the amount of grain which had arrived yesterday, and the day before yesterday. All this morning I replied to numerous sectional deputations. Finally, I have just written the Convention, informing it of the actual condition of the manufactures of Paris as furnished by the stock of the Commune. To be sure, I shall neglect no duty that is imposed on me, though I cannot imagine what fresh responsibility could be entrusted to me. That of my office bears entirely on the functions and tasks which I fulfil. If wicked people unknown to me excite a spirit of anxiety and cause uprisings, I am the more to be pitied, but certainly not to be blamed. This is all I have to answer for, and my conduct proves in every instance that I feel the force of this [illegible].

This is the letter of a woman, of a nervous woman, and not the letter of a statesman. Mme Roland had lost her control upon those nerves which most closely touch intellect and action. Her courage was unshaken, but she despaired for the country. Harassed by the invader, a great part of its territory lacerated by civil war, abandoned to the most destructive, incoherent, and irremediable powers of chance, it is almost impossible for us — mere spectators — to understand how France surmounted her difficulties and, furthermore, survived the two Napoleonic adventures.

THE terrible year of 1792 was drawing to a close. An even more terrible year was about to begin.

That Christmas day it was in every mind that on the morrow young de Sèze would speak before the Convention in defence of the King.

Towards evening, Mme Roland in her study wrote to General Servan. She saw clearly how things were going and was not going to let events take her unawares. For several days an uprising of the people of Paris had been feared and on the previous day, Midnight Mass had been dispensed with to avoid any great gathering of the people. Some days before, Mme Roland had already written General Servan a letter of which but a fragment remains: [76]

Paris, 20 X Year I

I finally have news of you from B.; I wrote you three times, once to Coudrieux, the other two occasions to Lyons.

. . . Affairs are going badly. P. [?] is nothing but a stubborn old woman, he fancies he has done a great and wise thing by sequestering himself, and he has only estranged himself from his friends and from able men; he is in the hands of a little clique of rogues who make him perpetrate a thousand stupidities and prepare the way for the ruin of us all.

The Convention is in the grip of thirty or so madmen. . . B. [rissot ?] and the Gironde, with a great deal of characterless ability, act as in the Legislative Assembly, they let things take their course, and this time they will not have an insurrection to save them but surely an outbreak wherein they will perish. Two or three courageous men are risking their lives and are treated as was Maury for not agreeing to a handful of Parisians making the law for eighty-three departments. The Minister of the Interior is detested as the Grand Inquisitor who prevents new massacres. Philippe [Égalité] has his party which torments us all. The corrupted capital merits a king and will probably get one. My friend, a superhuman courage is needed to bear up in this hell ! A ghastly system of calumny goes on, and achieves its end with an art impossible to imagine; one is submerged by floods of lies before one can perceive or prevent their assault. How fortunate you are to be in the south ! *I raise my eyes unto the mountains,* like the prophet king and . . . [the remainder is missing.]

And then, on the twenty-fifth of December, the First Year [1792], in Paris, at eight o'clock in the evening, she wrote:[77]

The date is not without significance for I know not what the morrow may bring; it is possible that many honest people will not be alive at the close of it. Disastrous plots against Louis are on foot, so as to afford an opportunity of going as far as to include the deputies and implicate the Minister of the Interior in this massacre. Warnings are on the increase and various informations attest to the existence of the plot. Can it be foiled by precautionary measures? That is the question. I have sent my daughter off to the country and put my small affairs in order as if for the great journey and, steadfastly, I await what may come. Our social institutions render life so wearisome for honest hearts that it is not a great loss to lose it, and I am so accustomed to the idea of death that I would go out to meet the assassins, were they to come, convinced besides that if there be one thing in existence which could dissuade them, 'twould be the coolness of courage and a contempt for their blows. M. R. [Roland] who has been confined by erysipelas of the leg to his bed or to his room for ten days past, has dragged himself off this morning to the Council which sits at the Tuileries and which will be permanent as long as Louis be out of prison. Warnings of assassination rain upon my table, for people do me the honour of hating me, and I know from whence that comes. When in the first days of the ministry the villain Danton and the hypocrite Fabre were continually hovering about us aping a love for virtue and probity, they saw through me and without my ever saying or doing a thing to confirm their opinion, they judged that I at times made use of the pen. The writings of M. R. [Roland], however, have produced some effect. Therefore, etc. . .

The barker Marat let loose upon me from then on, and has not given me a moment's respite;[78] the number of pamphlets has increased and I doubt if more horrors were printed about Antoinette, to whom they compare me and whose names they call me, than are attributed to me every day. I kept silent, as befitted me, without making any answer save to persevere in my character and duties; this increased their rage; I am Galigaï, Brinvilliers, Voisin, everything monstrous you can think of, and the ladies of the market-place wish to treat me like Mme Lamballe.

In consequence I send you my portrait, for one must leave something of oneself to friends. I am happy to tell you that, save for my husband, my daughter, and one other person, you are the only one to whom I make it known; it is not for the world nor even for the ordinary run of friends.

I know not whither all this is leading; but if Paris be lost, the south must save the rest.

Pache puts the machine out of order; he would make an excellent aid to a man of position and character; he is the most *Jean-fesse* minister it would be possible to find. The term is somewhat *revolutionary,* but how can one avoid becoming so oneself in the midst of continuous revolutions which follow whoever may be the most violent leader !

I know not where to find a wise writer. Would you believe that since Louvet can no longer do the *Sentinelle,* we have vainly tried three men and it has finally failed ? Have a little care for our memory when that is all that is left: they are capable of sullying it and have perhaps already prepared forgeries to insert among our papers.

Almost all our deputies go armed to the teeth; a thousand people implore us to sleep elsewhere than at the house. Delightful indeed is the liberty of Paris !

Ah, well, had you remained we would not be where we are. The moment the federates were under your orders, you would have been able to organize them and to have made of them a respectable support; it was the one way of making up the guard which we did not dare call into being. Pache did naught but disgust them, dismiss them, repeal them. If it be they who save you tomorrow, 't will be of their own doing and in defiance of discipline.

In truth I am weary of this world; it was never made for honest people and there is some logic in ousting them from it. Farewell, good citizen, I honour and love you with all my heart. I shall write you within a few days, if the tempest has not submerged us. If it be so, keep in mind my daughter and our sweet plans; I have placed an excellent woman [79] by her side who serves in my stead. She will go to her uncle at Villefranche, there to pursue her destiny, having good examples in her parents, some glory, an excellent guide, and an honest fortune. I embrace you most affectionately.

ROLAND née PHLIPON

How much this letter contained ! What depths of disgust she expressed ! But she, herself so victimized by slander, might at least, or so it seems to us, have had a grain of pity for the Queen, and even more for the unfortunate Mme de Lamballe. Mme Roland seemed almost to infer that they, after all, had been treated as they deserved. But who in the midst of conflict can boast of ever having been just to the adversary ? To relate without prejudice even the most insignificant incident of revolutionary history, one must keep continually in mind the over-excited state of those who made this history in which the magnificence and the villainy of human kind probably reached their utmost extremes.

One feels how Mme Roland turned to this new friend with an impulsiveness justified by the high moral virtues she recognized in him. Lanthenas' conduct made her mistrust confidence itself. She felt a bitterness insinuating itself into all her emotions, a bitterness equalled by the criminal anarchy of this people who were poisoned by Robespierre's doctrines. In other days she had believed she understood them, and, again in error, she now thought she had fathomed them. What inexplicable ingratitude had been awarded her efforts for the triumph of Liberty! It was to Servan that she sent a portrait which Bosc and Bancal, discarded in the "ordinary run of friends," had never seen. This is rather strange, for Bosc, who had for a period of several months held himself aloof from the ministry and turned a deaf ear to Mme Roland's repeated appeals, had hurried to her side as soon as he had learned of Lanthenas' behaviour. The indignation he gave vent to, as well as the former affection revived in all its pristine freshness, had been a delicious balm to the wounded heart of the perfect friend. Nevertheless, it was to Servan whom she wrote: "Keep in mind my daughter and our sweet plans" [?]. But possibly Servan, a general and a former minister, seemed to her a better protector for her child than older but obscurer friends.

On the same day, this same twenty-fifth of December 1792, which was to be her last Christmas, she wrote to Canon Dominique as well. She wanted to know that she could count on him for Eudora who was only twelve.

In the uncertainty of events, my dear brother, and the impossibility in the midst of their course to make all the arrangements we would wish, I at least do not intend to overlook the opportunity of sending you my embraces and my adieux, of repeating to you the expression of my confidence in your affection for Eudora, and of testifying to my esteem for her governess, Mlle Mignot, who can take my place beside her, who should never leave her, and for whom we pray you to make arrangements so that she shall want for nothing in her old age.

Mme Roland had, moreover, wished that an act be drawn up assuring her husband and herself that their last wishes would be recognized and respected:

We, the undersigned, united in feelings which have never ceased to animate us both, considering that the normal uncertainty of events is increased by the political situation of the Empire and that of the capital in particular; considering that the first duty of a public man

is to remain at his post as long as he can be of service there; and resolved to remain where the fatherland has placed us, but judging that
nothing obliges us to make our cherished child risk the same perils,
we have decided to entrust her to Mlle Mignot, who has already taken
charge of her education, and to send her to the family's country place,
far from the scenes of warfare, there in her peaceful retreat to await
happier days while cultivating her moral faculties, preparing herself
for reverses without dread as for posterity without ambition, with the
examples before her of her parents who lived above reproach and who
will know how to die fearlessly. We rely with confidence upon Mlle
Mignot's affection, care, and her enlightened kindness. We wish her
to exercise upon our dear Eudora all the authority which will assure
her a respectable character which is an essential of her education. Mlle
Mignot will share the existence and the means of her pupil; and when
eight years have elapsed,[80] she will be paid annually from her estate,
an income of a thousand francs for life which she may enjoy with the
completest independence.

Paris, the twenty-fifth of December 1792
J.-M. ROLAND, ROLAND née PHLIPON

This woman considered herself blameless and fearless. It is
understandable that, at the height of the tragedy, it was a satisfaction to her to feel that she had left no duty unperformed.

Affairs, however, were going very badly. The rift dividing the
public authorities was widening. The fury of the clubs, the attacks
of the press, systematically organized delations, illegal requisitions,
arrests without warrants, private revenges — all these contributed to
undermine the firmness of the strongest minds.

In the middle of the month of January, Mme Roland, in a letter
to Lavater, seemed still to be holding her own:

Do not attribute my silence, my dear Lavater, to any cause unworthy
of my friendship. The violent circumstances in which we live permit
me not an instant's liberty. Placed as we are in the centre of the
storm with the public hatchet ready to fall, our way is illumined by
strokes of lightning; and had we not that peace of conscience which
survives all, then we might well indeed be weary of life. But a little
strength of mind accustoms one to facing the most arduous thoughts,
and courage is only a matter of habit. . . My good husband embraces
you, and pursues his career like the honest man he is; proscription
menaces us, but we must stand by our ship, reach port if possible, and
prove worthy of what may come, even ostracism, if that should be
the recompense of virtue.

ROLAND née PHLIPON

The public was greatly astonished when, on January nineteenth, Roland posted on the walls of Paris a placard in which the Minister of the Interior said to the people that he "had continuously protested against the attacks made upon his loyalty and his integrity which he could prove." He gave an accounting of the 100,000 *livres* received as "expenses for correspondence and the printing of writings fitted to enlighten the government upon the criminal plots of the enemies of the State." Of this he had spent [according to the detailed account for which he could supply all vouchers], 32,913 francs and 6 *deniers*. There remained in the National Treasury a sum of 67,088,19, 6. Several remarks followed: "It is false and atrocious to spread abroad that I wish to take flight. I have nothing to conceal, and I know how to die, etc. . ." The entire text is in this worn and nervous tone which makes evident the fact that he who spoke had no longer any authority either upon himself or upon others.

We who are step by step following the husband and wife, we who have at our fingers' ends intimate letters, memoirs, records, we are no more prepared than was the public for a resignation which came with a theatrical suddenness and which was, no doubt, a rash and unpremeditated act.

The hesitations of the Girondists are well known. The people demanded that the King be put on trial. The Girondists were by character averse to violence. In this instance their irresolution became a lack of honesty and courage. Secretly supported by Danton who wished to humour his Royalist and Catholic wife, they made every attempt to avoid the King's trial, and thus they gave every evidence of upholding the "tyrant."

At the Cordeliers, where he was accused of evading the main issue, Danton spoke these noble words: "A nation seeks salvation, not revenge."

Mme Grandchamp wrote:

The Minister and his wife wanted only dethronement. Roland has even announced that he would not retain in his offices those who signed the registers opened in several places [asking the death of the King]. Lanthenas, nominated at the Convention, voted for death because he thought the safety of the State depended on it; he was immediately ordered to leave the house; this sensational break was a blow to politics as well as to a friendship that had lasted fifteen years.

Brissot as well considered that the death of the King would be impolitic and only consented to vote for death on condition that the people ratify the sentence. His intervention at the tribune gave Louis XVI cause to hope, and after his condemnation he repeated pathetically: "I thought that M. Brissot would have saved me. . ." [81]

Buzot, without doubt voicing Mme Roland's thought, voted for the sentence of death with ratification by the people. There were 387 votes for the death sentence and 334 for imprisonment or conditional death.[82]

Vergniaud, who was presiding, announced in a pained voice: "I proclaim in the name of the Convention that the sentence pronounced upon Louis Capet is death."

The following day, January twenty-second, Roland tendered his resignation to the Assembly in the form of a long letter bearing the same date, which Vergniaud, still in the Chair, read on the twenty-third.

The Convention was stupefied. We no less.

We are at liberty to suppose that Roland, having disapproved the condemnation of Louis XVI, resolved to withdraw as soon as possible, but is it not even more likely that Mme Roland chose this moment to make to her husband the bitter confession of her love for Buzot ?

Sainte-Beuve has severely censured her for this confession which he considered unreasonable and barbarous. He would have preferred that she deceive him. "A less unyielding virtue would have shown a greater skill. . . Mme de Sévigné and Mme de Staël were never guilty of such errors ! . . ."

But it is precisely such skill that she would have considered a debasement. The rectitude of her heart and principles imposed an austerity upon her which she considered she was safeguarding by proudly confessing that she had an affection to which she would not succumb. This was in keeping with her stoical ideals, and with her strength of mind, as well as with that secret aspiration to be always superior to events.

Among all those who surrounded her Buzot was perhaps the only one who seemed to her an equal.[83] Let us keep in mind that fine outburst of arrogance in her *Memoirs* in which she swears always "to forego every affection which does not measure up to the height of her destiny." And would not this blow to his personal happiness have deprived Roland of the moral force he required to keep him at his post ? It is highly possible. At any rate, he attempted to mislead historians and to halt investigations by himself furnishing a solution written in his own hand [a precaution so unusual for him that it arouses our suspicions]:

The cause of my leaving the Ministry has been perceived by no-one. . . I am ashamed to say it . . . but there is no man I can mention. . . Yes, could I but find one man who had retained some energy . . . who was not afraid to stand up in the tribune . . . endlessly filled with infamous men, etc. . .

Did he leave because he could not find such a man ? The fact that he did not name Buzot is significant. Moreover, were there not Brissot, Louvet, and Barbaroux ? One or the other of them was always spokesman for the Rolands. When this group asked in one accord that the Bourbons be exiled, and particularly the Orléans branch, the Montagne answered that "it was Roland who should be exiled, for it was to be feared that he himself would become King !" Doubtless we are not far from the truth in discerning a trace of feminine influence in Roland's resignation. The passional crisis which had just been reached had rendered impossible any deliberation or any understanding between the Minister and Buzot. In any case we are certain that the husband and wife were as usual in complete accord upon the principle of so grave a step. The letter Vergniaud read at the tribune was written entirely in Mme Roland's hand. Weariness and disgust, irritation and pain, there was doubtless all this in a dejection which nothing seemed to suggest but a week before, as can be judged from the letter to Lavater.

As they had done in June of the preceding year, so the Rolands retired to the small lodgings in the rue de la Harpe, with their daughter and Mlle Mignot, who for some reason had not left for Beaujolais.

A day or two after his retirement, Roland wrote Lanthenas: [84]

                                                    January 24, 1793
He who leaves his place, loses it, says an old proverb, and if I remember right, I once read in Pibrac that sooth is to be found in proverbs. That is as one may wish. I have talked enough. I am weary. But I do not wish that we should part without, for my part, testifying to that fraternity which I like to think cannot be altered at least between us two. I send you my last will and testament of life or death, and I embrace you very cordially.
                    January twenty-third, the second year of the Republic.

The vulgar press and particularly "the barker Marat" continued to decry the Rolands who, however, no longer saw anyone except Bosc, Barbaroux, Brissot, Bancal, and spent the last four months of their life together retired and even forgotten.[85] They were in danger, nevertheless, and each night threatened to be the last.

About ten o'clock of an evening that Champagneux was calling upon them, they were warned that people very suspicious in appearance were prowling about the house. So strongly was Mme Roland urged to escape in disguise that she began dressing herself as a peasant:

Her head-dress was considered not sufficiently coarse [Champagneux wrote] and this criticism made her burst into a fit of anger which resulted in her discarding the bonnet as well as the rest of the clothing. "I am ashamed," she cried out, "of the rôle I am made to play. I will neither disguise myself nor go hence. If they wish to kill me, they can do it here. I owe this example of strength, and I shall give it."

There is as well a note which Roland wrote to Bosc:

We have been outside the walls for eight or ten days; I am however going to return shortly; the fear of death might become worse than death itself.

In the beginning of February when Danton returned from one of his constant trips to Belgium, he found his Gabrielle [86] had died. She had wished to breathe her last in the little lodging in the Cour du Commerce, far from that accursed building where she had suf-

fered so much from the politics of the regicide and from the
"drinker of blood." On the ninth of March, the Constitution of
the Revolutionary Tribunal was passed in spite of the opposition
of the pure to every exceptional law. Presided over by Fouquier
de Tinville, it was to function until the Thermidor *Coup d'État.*

Did Danton return from Belgium with 1,400,000 confiscated
francs as Mme Roland asserted, or did he, as Robespierre explained
the matter, appropriate the ecclesiastical silver which had been
requisitioned to pay the troops ? Whatever the case, he found that
the people were aroused against him. The Convention likewise
received him badly, not knowing whether or not to believe him an
accomplice of Dumouriez as the Girondist Lasource declared.

THE pension of the former Inspector of Manufactures had never
been paid.[87] Aged and in ill health as he was, it was certainly with
enormous courage that Roland again resumed the steps he had
begun in 1791. But all he wanted was to return to *Le Clos.* In
the first place life was dear in revolutionary Paris and he was
pressed for funds. Fresh air, silence, solitude, these alone could
lave the bitter stains of public life and give him strength to face,
and perhaps one day to master, the situation in which he was
floundering.

Ah, now he knew how wise he had been in Amiens, and during
his trip to Italy; in all those four years how wise he had been to
fight against the charms of that too young and too beautiful girl.
What folly the Prior of Longpont had made him commit ? How
tranquil was his life before his visit to the engraver's home. Ah,
those Cannets ! Certain memories persistently haunted him: the
beginning of a letter he had written to the Convent when the marriage was decided. . . "It is so important to me that you be happy,"
she had said to him at the gate. These words had won him and
upon returning to his hotel, he had repeated them in a letter which
he sent to the Congregation: "It is so important to me that you be
happy ! There is your text, and therein my consolation. Woe to
you if you forget it, or if ever you contradict it !" Now he could
understand Lanthenas ! Truly, he was glad that he had written

him ! A curse upon those twelve years of happiness she had given him ! Had she but taken less care of him during his illnesses, had she kept his house less clean and pleasant, had she exercised less economy in the managing of their fortune, less wisdom in their family relations, and above all, had she not shown so much intelligence in the aid she gave him in the *Dictionnaire des Manufactures,* and later in so many joint tasks, alas, he would not now be losing all ! How could he live without her now, poor man, how tear himself away from his entire well-being ? The one thing that remained to be done was to take her away from Paris, to remove her as quickly as possible from that abode of infamy and corruption, far from that accursed Buzot who merited all the tortures of hell.

Before he had the right to leave this terrible scene of vice, however, he must first render his accounts as the resigning but conscientious minister. The first concern of the strict observer of the Law was to offer these accounts to the Convention at the same time as "his person." This he did — in all eight times ! — and this was due to a ridiculous conception of honesty for which hostile historians have very wrongly reproached him.

On March twenty-third, Roland wrote to the Convention:

> I implore the Convention, through the medium of its President, for the fifth time in two months, to be good enough to grant me my liberty by an auditing of my accounts, which are so obviously clear that but slight examination is required to acquaint oneself with them and shew their accuracy.

In spite of the Convention's hostility, as well as that of the people of Paris, Roland received numerous expressions of regret, of gratitude, and of confidence. In contrast to this, it is of interest to quote a letter from Reverchon, a Member of the Convention, written "to his colleagues of the liberated Commune, the fifteenth of Ventose, the second Year of the Republic one and inseparable," in which he eulogized the civic worth of one of his constituents:

> I cannot repeat too often that [name illegible] has been since the Revolution one of the warmest friends of Liberty and of the people. I may add that it is fourteen years since he was in the body-guard, that he is no longer a noble, that he came to Paris in 1792 solely in

the interest of the affairs he was in engaged in for the Treasury, that he was the first to have Roland burned in effigy at the society of the people, and that, if he be his relative, he is so distantly connected that the instant he learned that the Jacobins had declared Roland unworthy of public confidence, he was the first to enlighten his fellow-citizens upon the perfidy of this man. . .

The letters Roland then wrote, and particularly to Garat, his successor as Minister of the Interior, were bitter indeed. There was nothing in present circumstances to sweeten that acid tone we knew in him of old when he was a younger man and had no excuse for his tartness. One thing is certain — he evidenced not the slightest desire to return to the heart of that furnace wherein his party had remained. He wrote Champagneux:

I can with justice be reproached for the severity of an inflexible character . . . which goes undeviatingly towards good with none of the calculation of self-interest. . .
I have despised despotism of any kind and I protested against it even when it was in power. But those who know me best have had to excuse me only for the harshness of my virtue.

From his pen, as well as from that of his wife, came like a *leit-motif* the ever-recurring hope that they would be rendered justice by posterity. To see Mme Roland in her true character, we must keep in mind the perfect understanding that existed between her and her husband. It might be thought that upon him, as upon others, she was able to impose her point of view. At this time, however, he must have sought to escape her influence.

Life was gloomy in the rue de la Harpe. Mme Roland was thoughtful and anxious, no longer the brilliant rallying centre for the young lovers of Liberty. No longer did they gather in her *salon* waiting the word of command. Moreover, she had no *salon*. The heroic Muse, bereaved of those poets whom she might inspire, was nothing but a little *bourgeoise* whose greatest concern was to calculate to the last sou the expenses of her household. After so much work and so much intensity, it was now the time for repose. She must get away from Paris. Thus seen from afar, the country soothed her weary soul, yes, but she knew that once there tedium and regret would possess her, would be dead ashes thrown upon her burning impulses, would fill the dismal hours with grief, and that every day would be a day lost to her forever. She would no longer experience, perhaps, the nostalgia for action as she had in 1791. For the time being she was broken with fatigue, but what deadly idleness there would be in the midst of her rustic tasks! She remembered the last vintages and how endless they were. Then she had lived only for her return to Paris, which she had left thirsty to quaff a purer air, and with a heart still free.

But that time she had scarcely tasted rest than her destiny had again drawn her to the scene of combat. Her husband resisted? She swept his protests aside. But this time it would be terrible indeed. Her passion for the public weal would give her not a moment's peace — and there was love besides. Would she be strong enough to undertake so arduous a task? And even were she equal to it, what an outlook for this woman whose rich youth had been sacrificed for the benefit of a Roland!

It now happened that "the misfortunes of the fatherland" were somewhat overshadowed by her "own interests." If her husband was greatly changed, she at least at thirty-nine was still fresh and youthful. But her spirits were at a low ebb, and if ever she complained to Bancal of this state of mind, so painful to people of character, he had but to remind himself that she had once said to him at *Le Clos:* "I know that in combat I would recover all my strength and health." This time she would require prison and the scaffold to restore her fire and vigour.

If she had unwittingly lost her heart, she was resolved to keep intact her fidelity, her devotion, and her tenderness towards a "venerable spouse" whom she respected and had never ceased to cherish. Not long before, during the development of the crisis which had resulted in their quarrel, she had written Lanthenas: *"Never will I estrange myself from my husband whose destiny I share. I shall die as I have lived, finding happiness in my duties, whatever it may cost me to perform them."*

Unlike Taine and other historians, we cannot indulge ourselves to the extent of fancying that Roland bored his wife, simply because we ourselves would have found him dull. Mme Roland was serious minded, which meant that she was never bored as long as her extraordinarily avid mind was given nourishment. She herself called it "voracious," Roland's dissertations were to her like grain to the mill. Let us not forget that at the age of seven or eight, the little Manon took pleasure in a *Treatise on Heraldry*. We can readily believe that she enjoyed being what we call *bored,* just as Sganarelle's wife enjoyed being beaten. Moreover, she was too simple and too intense to have much inclination for irony or banter. It is not difficult to imagine that when Sophie Cannet wrote her [rather jestingly], that the "philosopher" she was sending made the mistake of preferring the ancients to the moderns, she was entirely in sympathy with the man who inspired such a criticism. In our opinion she was never for a moment bored with Roland, nor did she ever observe any exaggerated pedantry or austerity in him — at least until that moment when Buzot's youth, his delicate face, and his persuasive speech intervened and forced her to draw comparisons. For this reason certain criticisms of Roland are sensed rather than expressed in the *Memoirs,* because they were written in the last days of her life when all her being was turning to Buzot.

AT THE beginning of March, foreign invasion had again reached serious proportions and even Paris was menaced. The monarchies, outraged by our disrespect for law, dismissed our ambassadors, and the disillusioned Republicans were forced to admit that the oppressed people, whom they had believed ripe for liberty, were not yet ready to throw off their chains. England, "the champion of the liberties of the world" to quote Mme de Staël, bitterly disappointed Mme Roland like all the rest by joining the coalition against France. "France has annihilated morality and abolished law." In virtue of which, the Prussians installed themselves in Dantzig and the English in Toulon. It is true that the latter did not enter Vendée as the Royalist leaders had implored them to do. In vain did M. d'Elbée ask them to send "large troops" to aid the *Vendéens.* In vain did Chevalier de la Roche Saint-André set out for Spain, charged by the Committees to secure military assistance. However, Pitt cheerfully predicted that thenceforth France's place on the map of Europe would be marked by a blank.

With indescribable alarm Paris received the news of Dumouriez'
treason. The Revolutionary Tribunal had been instituted for the
punishment of rebels and traitors, but Robespierre had in mind that
this new court might serve as a weapon against the Gironde.[88]
The Convention immediately arrested a great number of people
who had been part of the following of the fugitive General. It
was scarcely possible to include the former Minister of the Interior
and his virtuous spouse. Everyone knew of their antipathy to the
former *factotum* of Louis XV. However, there were threatening
rumours in the air.

At the end of March 1793 Danton declared before the Convention that Dumouriez had shown him a letter of Roland's in which
he had said: "You must unite with us to crush this Paris party,
and Danton in particular." Roland immediately and indignantly
protested that he had never written such a letter. On March thirty-
first a search warrant was issued against the former minister and
this was followed by the affixing of the seals. Danton's declaration
was but a trick, and the first one that had come into his head. The
truth was both more picturesque and even less permissible.

We have long been puzzled by a singular note of Roland's referring to the sealing of his papers. What did it signify ?

No observations made by the husband, the wife, the Justice of the
Peace, the district commissary as to the absurdity, the impropriety and
the indecency of exceeding the authority of the decree by examining
other papers than Roland's, by pretending to turn a family secret into
a state crime, by destroying all confidence through abusing thus all
that is most sacred, nothing could restrain or halt the youngest of the
Commissaries of the Convention, who, boasting that he was an enthusiastic and ardent Jacobin, thought he could make no more bitter
reproach to Roland than to accuse him of no longer being one.

Upon investigation, it is permissible to conclude that the Committee of National Defence, which ordered this singular police raid
that took place on the night of the thirty-first of March, acted upon
the suggestion of Robespierre, instigated by Camille Desmoulins,
for the purpose of seizing, not the papers of the former minister,
but those of his wife.

Let us retrace our steps to find some explanation of this act.

At the time that Lanthenas was making Mme Roland "unnecessary scenes," some severe words of hers inform us that he had had the indelicacy to "express his displeasure to third parties." We do not know to whom, but it is certain that Mme Roland was becoming the centre of considerable curiosity. The degradation of this Lucretia would have been a triumph for those who stressed her fraility rather than her virtue. However, if they felt that something were on foot, they knew not what it might be, and if Mme Roland had shown some preference, they did not know for whom. This is proved by the ignoble jeers in the *Père Duchesne* concerning Mme Roland's "boudoir," wherein a number of the names of her circle were suggested. Buzot, indeed, was mentioned once, but among many others. Servan, Gorsas, and Barbaroux were the names that most frequently occurred. Here is an instance of the sort of thing Hébert and Marat put in Mme Roland's mouth:

What will happen . . . if friend Gorsas, if my little Louvet, if my heart's favourite, the divine Barbaroux, do not start a civil war in the departments ?

This hardly agreed, by the way, with what they said elsewhere of that "B . . . of a Roland woman . . . that toothless old hag," etc.

There was one, however, more curious than the others, and that was Camille Desmoulins. A street urchin by temperament, a journalist by profession, he was then, at the suggestion of Robespierre, preparing a pamphlet against the Girondists, which he wanted to enliven by some licentious tale that would add a flavour of scandal to the publication. Camille Desmoulins was later heedless to the point of criminality and was to shed sincere tears upon the deaths of those for whose ruin he was largely responsible. In October he was to cry: "It is I who am killing them !" In the meanwhile he had his little jokes, and said laughingly to Brissot: "Brissot, you are a Brissottin."

In the famous *Histoire des Brissottins* we read:

Who knows how many more strange things might have been discovered when the seals were removed [at Roland's] if, when the decree was passed at the Committee of Twenty-five that they should be affixed, a mob of deputies had not immediately left to give the alarm at the rue de la Harpe, so that M. and Mme Roland had six hours in which to empty their desk !

And further:

Jérôme Pétion said to Danton in confidence, referring to the affixing of the seals: "What worries poor Roland is that his domestic troubles will come to light," and how bitterly he took his c . . . dom and how it impaired the serenity of that great mind. We did not find these records of his grief.

"We did not find . . ." Had Camille then slipped in with the police, as has been often asserted, disguised so as not to be recognized by Roland ? [The search was made at night, by candle-light]. We have no proof of this, although he appeared to confess to it without embarassment or evasion. However, as an answer to this "we did not find" we have Roland's complaint which shows there had been a search, and even though nothing was found they had the audacity to ask him the crudest questions. The Jacobin Commissary — "the youngest" of them all, whom nothing could "restrain or halt," was surely not acting upon his own initiative when he made those investigations which exasperated the unfortunate Roland to such a point that he wrote — to whom ? — the singular grievance we have already quoted. Most likely this worthy commissary had been schooled by Desmouslins himself; no doubt he had been promised a reward, which explained his zeal. Instructions had been given him as to what he should look for, and as to what it would be his interest to find and bring back.

It is possible that Roland made confidences to Pétion who passed them on to Danton, who then communicated them to Camille. But this is hardly likely, for if Roland, in the first impact of grief, had felt the need of opening his heart, which was not in keeping with the vanity of his character, he had older and surer friends, Bosc the foremost of them all. If such were indeed the case, Roland at least mentioned no name, for Camille, greatly vexed, was obliged to do without the spicy morsel.

A few months later, Mme Roland, then a prisoner, in a letter to the Ministry of the Interior addressed to the clerk in charge of the care of prisons, with reference to the search made at her home, wrote these words which would no longer seem obscure: "I ask myself whether I have not been the object of cruel curiosity. . ."

It is worthy of note that Roland had implored the Convention "that the commissaries who should be sent to break the seals that had been affixed at his home, be impartial men, suspected neither of being of his party [that of the Law], nor of the opposite party" [anarchists, Jacobins, and Montagnards]. Instead, it was Brival — "that madman of a Brival" — who was entrusted with the mission. This same Deputy Brival had been charged with making a report upon the seizure. To this Roland made answer by a twelve-page pamphlet of observations. Disregarding the main issues, he concentrated upon an explanation of his retirement, stating that he had not wished "to prolong the separation of the Council and Assembly." With force he acknowledged full responsibility for the actions of his ministry. Above all else, he asked the right to live in obscurity, at peace, and requested the permission be finally granted him to return to his property in the Beaujolais. The singular fragment we have quoted may be a part of the rough draft of this reply. It is in Roland's style. Upon reflection — advised or not by his wife — he had had the good sense to leave it out of his text.

Mme Roland was decided to leave Paris without waiting any longer for her husband. In her *Memoirs* she said:

The Roland family had everything to fear, but *this was not my chief reason,* for, weary of all that was happening, I feared nothing for myself. . . But another reason which some day I may write, and an entirely personal one, made me decide upon departure.

In his edition of the *Memoirs,* Champagneux explained this passage, and must have puzzled his readers:

I know the motive to which Citizen Roland referred. She had taken me into her confidence, but the time to make it public has not yet arrived. Malevolent people would seize upon it: this century is too corrupt to believe in the virtuous efforts Citizen Roland made at that time; they are all the more admirable because they were not a public matter and were enclosed within the four walls of her home.

A very stirring paper, dated May 30, 1793, and written in Mme

Roland's hand — with corrections by Roland — was addressed by the ex-Minister of the Interior to the President of the Convention. This was the last entire day the couple were to spend together. On the morrow, he would have taken flight, and she would be arrested.

The letter began in this way: "I have been the minister of a free nation. Is this a reason that liberty should be henceforth denied me ?"

This still referred to the fact that his departure waited on the auditing of his accounts. "The Convention does not propose to refuse me justice." Roland barred the words "does not propose" and wrote above them "does not wish." She wrote: "My claims are sufficient proof that I have nothing to fear." He corrected this and wrote "that I am above all fear," etc.

In the middle of the month of May, Mme Roland had already applied for passports for her daughter and herself. The "zealous *Maratistes*," however, considering her a suspicious character, had made use of every pretext as an excuse for delay. Her request had finally been granted when an acute indisposition forced her to bed for six days, and on the thirty-first of May, when she was feeling somewhat better, the tocsin and the alarm gun kept her from leaving the house.

She had hesitated too long. Her life was over. Thenceforth she was at the mercy of "a government a hundred times more atrocious than the despotism it had abolished."

That day at sunrise, having deliberated all night, the Commune posted the following placard:

RESOLUTION OF THE COMMUNE OF PARIS, MAY 31, 1793
MUNICIPALITY OF PARIS

The Assembly Meeting at the Bishopric has maintained its deliberation.

Several sections have sounded the alarm bell. Some sections are taking up arms, and one of them is disarming suspicious individuals and making arrests, according to the reports which have reached us.

The general captain of the Commune has been in meeting all night. He has ordered the chiefs of the Legion to keep the gates open and has addressed a proclamation to the citizens of the forty-eight sections

requesting them to make no disturbances and to await peaceably the
returns from the Assembly that has been summoned by the departments.

(signed) Pache, Mayor of Paris

May 31st at five o'clock in the morning

Vadier, who was rabidly opposed to the Girondists, was in all
probability one of the most violent instigators of the riot of the
thirty-first of May. Arousing the people's wrath against the
Gironde, he weakly denied that he was a "disciple of Marat, whose
prognostics were at times useful, whose principles were at times
pure and austere, but who did little harm by his advice. . ."

During the evening of the thirty-first of May, the Commissioners
of the Revolutionary Committee of the Commune in insurrection went to the rue de la Harpe to arrest Roland. Roland, who
managed to get rid of them, succeeded in concealing himself in
another part of the house, where his landlord lived, and there he
remained until night fell. A friend, probably Bosc,[89] came to fetch
him after dark, took him home with him, and, crossing Paris, they
left the city by the Porte Saint-Denis. He then conducted him to
the Priory of Sainte-Radegonde, where Roland remained three
weeks in concealment in this remote part of the Montmorency
forest. But here we must refer to one of the most living passages
of the *Memoirs*:

It was five o'clock in the evening when six armed men presented
themselves at my house. One of them read Roland an order from
the Revolutionary Committee, by virtue of which they had come to
place him under arrest.

"I know of no law," said Roland, "which possesses the authority
you speak of, and I will not submit to its orders; if you employ
violence, I can do no more than offer the resistance of a man of my
advanced years, but I will protest against it until the very end." "I have
no orders to employ violence," replied this person, "and I am going
to report your reply to the Council of the Commune; I shall leave
my colleagues here." The idea immediately occurred to me that it
would be well to make before the Convention a sensational denunciation of what was taking place, so as to prevent Roland's arrest, or
to have him promptly released if he were arrested; it took me but a
few minutes to inform my husband of the plan, write a letter to the
President and leave the house. My servant was absent; I left a friend
who was at the house by Roland's side, went off in a cab by myself,
bidding the coachman drive as fast as possible, and I reached the

Carrousel. The court of the Tuileries was filled with armed men;
I crossed it, passed through them swift as a bird; I was clad in a
house-dress and had taken a black shawl and veiled my face. Having
found the doors of the first halls all closed, I came upon sentinels
who would not let me enter, or else who passed me on from door to
door. In vain did I insist, and finally it occurred to me to speak like
a Robespierre devotee: "Well, citizens ! These days when the fatherland is in peril, surrounded by traitors from whom we have everything
to fear, how do you know of what importance may be the notes I
must deliver to the President ? Send me a clerk so that I may entrust them to him." The door opened and I passed into the petitioners'
hall. I asked for a clerk. "Wait till one comes out," responded the
sentinels of the inner hall. A quarter of an hour elapsed; I perceived
Rôze, the one who had brought me the decree from the Convention
summoning me to its bar at the time of the ridiculous denunciation
of Viard, whom I covered with confusion. I asked to be conducted
there now, informing him of the dangers which threatened Roland
and which were so intrinsically a part of the public weal. But though
my rights were the same, opinion had altered; then my presence had
been requested, now I was a suppliant, how could I hope to meet with
the same success ? Rôze took my letter, for he understood my impatience; he went away to give it to the desk and hasten the reading
of it. An hour elapsed. I was pacing up and down; I glanced into
the hall each time the door was opened, but it was immediately closed
again by a guard. Now and then I heard a terrible din. Rôze reap-
peared. "Well, nothing yet; impossible to describe the tumult in the
Assembly; petitioners are now at the bar demanding the arrest of the
Twenty-two. I have just assisted Rabaud to escape without being seen
— they do not wish him to make the report of the Commission of
Twelve. He has been threatened, several others are escaping; we don't
know what to expect." "But who is presiding now ?" "Heraut-
Séchelles." "Ah, my letter will not be read; send me a deputy that
I can talk with." "Whom ?" "Oh, the only ones I know well or
respect are those who have been proscribed; tell Vergniaud that I am
asking for him." Rôze went to fetch him; he finally appeared after
a long delay; we conversed for seven or eight minutes, he then returned to his seat, came back to me and said: "Considering the present
state of the Assembly, I can give you no encouragement; if you are
admitted to the bar, you may, being a woman, obtain a little more
consideration; but the Convention has no longer any power to do
good." "It should have every power !" I cried, "for all that the Paris
majority asks is to know what it should do; if I am admitted I shall
have the courage to say what you yourself could not express without
being accused; I fear nothing on earth, and if I cannot save Roland,
I shall express with vehemence truths which will not be useless to
the Republic. Inform your worthy colleagues, a movement of courage may have a great effect and will at any rate be a great example."

I was indeed in that state of mind which makes one eloquent; filled with indignation, superior to every fear, fired for love of my country the ruin of which was before my very eyes, all I loved in the world exposed to the most deadly perils, feeling with intensity, expressing myself with ease, too proud not to do so nobly; the problems I had to deal with were of the utmost importance, I had some means of defending them, and my situation was such that I could do it to advantage. "But in any case your letter cannot be read before an hour and a half. A resolution in six articles is up for discussion; petitioners and section deputies are waiting at the bar — you see how long you will have to wait." "Well, I shall go home to find out what has happened, and I shall return afterwards; apprize our friends." "Most of them are absent; they have the courage to show themselves when they are here, but they lack assiduity." Unfortunately this was all too true ! I left Vergniaud, I fled to Louvet; I wrote a note telling him what had occurred and what I thought would take place, I flung myself into a cab, giving the address of my house; those accursed horses, however, would hardly stir. Presently some troops on the march impeded our progress; I leapt from the cab, paid the coachman, broke through the files of soldiers, escaped towards the Louvre, rushed to my house in the rue de la Harpe opposite Saint-Côme. The porter whispered to me that Roland had gone to the apartment of the landlord, at the end of the court. I ran there, drenched with perspiration; they brought me a glass of wine and told me that, unable to procure an audience with the Council, the bearer of the warrant had returned. Roland had continued to protest, and these good people had asked him to write out his protest, whereupon they retired. After this, Roland had gone through the landlord's apartment and left the house by the back door. I did the same in order to find him, apprize him of what I had attempted to do and the line of conduct I proposed to follow. I betook myself to a house, but he was not there, I went to another and found him; though the streets were lighted, there were so few people about that I presumed it was late; none the less I intended to return to the Convention. I planned to ignore Roland's retirement and speak as I had in the first instance. I was about to set forth on foot without perceiving that it was after ten o'clock, or reflecting that this was the first day that I had gone out since my illness which required rest and baths. A cab was summoned for me. As I drew near the Carrousel, I saw no more armed men; two cannon and a few men were still before the door of the national palace. I advanced. The meeting was over.

Mme Roland was too enlightened not to fear the worst from the spectacle she saw before her eyes. She crossed the court and met:

an old *Sans-culottes,* evidently well paid to talk propaganda to dupes.

A pretty dog ran against my legs. "Is this poor animal yours?" said the coachman with an accent of tenderness most rare in people of his kind and which struck me with peculiar force. "No, I do not know him," I answered gravely, as though it were the matter of a human being, and already thinking of other things. "You will take me to the Galleries of the Louvre." I wished to see a friend there with whom it was my intention to discuss ways of getting Roland out of Paris. We had not gone twenty paces when the carriage stopped. "What is it?" I said to the coachman. "Oh, he left me like a fool and I wanted to keep him for my little boy who would have a good time with him. Come here, little dog, come here!" I remembered the dog and thought it sweet and pleasant to have this coachman with me at this hour — he was such a good tender-hearted father. "Try to catch him," I cried. "You can put him inside the cab and I will watch him for you." The good man, beaming with happiness, picked up the dog, opened the door and gave me a companion.

. . . Pasquier had just gone to bed. He arose. I told him of my plans. We decided that he should come to my house the next day after seven and I should tell him where to find his friend. I returned to the cab. The sentry post at the Samaritaine halted us. "A little patience," said the coachman in a low voice, turning on his box. "This always happens at this hour." The sergeant arrived, opened the door: "Who is there?" "A citizen." "Where do you come from?" "From the Convention." "That's quite true," put in the coachman, as if he were afraid I should not be believed. "Where are you going?" "Home." "Have you no parcels?" "None, you can see." "But the meeting is over." "Yes, and I am very much vexed, for I had a petition to make." "A woman out at this hour! It is inconceivable and most imprudent." "Doubtless it is not usual, and is certainly not agreeable for me. It only shows that I had important reasons." "But, Madame, all alone?" "Alone, Monsieur? Don't you see that innocence and truth are with me? What more is required?"

At the rue de la Harpe, a man who was lurking in the shadows beneath the carriage entrance, gave Mme Roland a most suspicious warning: Roland was to be arrested that very night. She went upstairs "without quite knowing what to think."

Why, one might ask, circumstances being as they were, did she return to the house? This is how she explained it:

This question is not out of place, for I had been maligned by slanderous tongues, and malevolence could well make sport of me. However, to give a satisfactory reply, I should have to dwell at length on my state of mind and go into details which I am reserving for another time; therefore, I shall confine myself to results. I have a natural distaste for everything which deviates from the clear, free, bold course suitable to innocence. The difficulty of escaping injustice costs me more than submitting to it. . . During the two last months of Roland's ministry our friends often urged us to leave the house and two or three times they succeeded in persuading us to sleep elsewhere, but this was always against my will. It was then assassination that was feared. . . I did not wish to leave the house in January; Roland's bed was placed in my room, so that we should both share the same fate, and I had a revolver under my pillow, not to kill those who might come to murder us, but to save myself from their outrages if they wished to lay a hand on me.

Once returned to private life, obligations were no longer the same and she considered it "an excellent thing that Roland had escaped both the rage of the people and the clutches of his enemies." As for her, she had never believed until now that she was in any real danger, and if another second of September were to be staged, well, she would prefer "to die rather than witness the ruin of her country."

On that day in particular she had no desire for flight. Panckouke had sent his associate Agache to warn her that it was dangerous for her to remain at home and offered her a refuge at Marly-le-Roi:

Since leaving the ministry I had lived in such complete retirement that I saw almost no-one. The owners of one of the houses where I might have concealed myself were in the country; in another they were nursing an invalid which would have made it difficult for them to accept another guest; the one where Roland was in hiding could not receive me without extreme inconvenience and it would have been too marked, impolitic even, to have been concealed in the same place. And I would have suffered as well at abandoning my servants. I therefore decided to return home, calm their anxieties, kiss my child, and I took up my pen to write a note to be delivered early in the morning to my husband.

It was midnight. Hardly was she seated than "a large deputation from the Commune" knocked at the door and demanded Roland. She got rid of them, but sentinels were stationed at both the door of the apartment and the door of the house. Tired out, she had a bite of supper, wrote her note, entrusted it to the maid Fleury, went to bed, and fell asleep. Not an hour had passed when Lecoq, her servant, came to awaken her. Some "gentlemen from the section" were there asking for her. She understood at once that they had come to put her under arrest, and when Fleury expressed surprise at seeing her donning "something other than a dressing-gown" she answered: "One must be decently attired to go out."

The warrant had been issued by a Revolutionary Committee which had no legal authority, and the cause for arrest was left blank. She considered for a moment whether to resist as Roland had done, but reflected that force was on their side and that "resistance was useless and might expose her to danger." The Justice of the Peace arrived. Seals were affixed everywhere.[90] But before this, she had removed her daughter's clothes from the wardrobes and had made her "a little parcel." The officer refused to allow her to write to a friend to whom she wished to send her Eudora, and during this time "fifty, a hundred persons came and went continuously, filling the two rooms, surrounding everything, well able to screen any malicious persons there might be filching or depositing evidence. . . The atmosphere was foul; I was obliged to get to the window of the ante-chamber for a breath of air. . ." The formalities which began to half-past three in the morning lasted until seven. When everything was finally put under stamp and string, Mme Roland was requested to sign the official report of the seals.

For the first time do we see her signature betraying her distress. The first letter of the name *Roland* is irregular, but the *o* was begun twice, the *a* wavers, and the *n* is badly formed. However, the brave woman quickly recovered herself, for the *née Phlipon* is written in her customary hand.

. . . At seven in the morning, I left my daughter and my domestics, after having exhorted them to be calm and patient; I felt their tears honoured me more than oppression could dismay me. "There you have people who love you," said one of the commissaries. "I have never had any near me who do not," I replied, and I descended the stairs.

There Mme Roland passed between two rows of armed men. A cab, surrounded by a crowd, was waiting across the street. Some women shouted: "To the guillotine!"

This unfortunate people, whom those who called themselves its true friends deceived and slaughtered, was drawn by the spectacle and gaped as I drove by. . . "Do you wish the curtains drawn ?" the commissaries obligingly asked me. "No, gentlemen, innocence, however oppressed it may be, never assumes the attitude of guilt; I fear the eye of no-one whosoever he may be." "You have more character than many men; you await justice quietly." "Justice ! if justice were done I should not be at this moment in your power; but an iniquitous procedure will take me to the scaffold, and I shall ascend it as firmly and calmly as I now go to prison. I grieve for my country, I regret those errors which made me fondly believe she was ready for liberty and happiness; but I value life: I fear nothing but crime, I scorn injustice and death.

The poor commissaries understood little or nothing of this fine talk, and probably considered it extremely aristocratic. Faithful to the theories of revolutionary principle, Mme Roland resented more this outrageous breach of law than she did the unjust treatment she herself had suffered.

The carriage, surrounded by its armed escort, halted at the Abbaye, one of the prisons in which the most blood had been shed in the September massacres. One surmises that Mme Roland entered it with that "laughing manner" which was to astound all those who saw it throughout the sombre period of life that still remained to her. During the stormy times of 1792 she had once written Lanthenas: "I have too much courage to have any need of showing it." She was to be convinced of the truth of her words, but a reliable witness was shortly to inform us that she shed tears when she thought herself alone, and it is this that touches our hearts.

The porteress exclaimed that others arriving there "had not this placid air." And then she locked the door and left her prisoner.

Here I am then in prison, say I to myself. Here I sit and commune deeply with myself. I would not exchange these passing moments for those which others might term the sweetest of my life, never shall they leave my memory. In a critical situation with a stormy and uncertain future before me, they have given me a full taste of the strength and virtue that lie in the sincerity of a clear conscience and great courage. . . I recalled the past, speculated upon future events, and if, in heeding this sensitive heart, I found some too-strong affection, I found not one that caused me to blush nor one that did not serve to augment my courage and over which my courage could not still rise supreme. I consecrated myself, as it were, voluntarily to my destiny whatever it was to be; I scorned the hardships of it and put myself in that frame of mind in which one considers only how best to employ the moment, without ulterior anxiety. [*Memoirs.*]

She settled down to await the evening paper, and in deep thought listened to the sounds from the street. Would she be allowed to write, to have visitors ? What would her expenses be ?

In any case, she wrote to Bosc:

Today on the throne, tomorrow in chains. Thus is honesty rewarded by the revolution, my poor friend !

You would not believe how much I have thought of you since this morning. I am convinced you are one of those most concerned with my vicissitudes.

Here am I under a good roof for as long as it may please God. Here, as elsewhere, I shall be on such good terms with myself that I shall suffer little from the change. There is no human power capable of depriving a sane and strong mind of that sort of harmony which sustains it above all circumstances. I embrace you cordially in life and death, esteem and friendship.

ROLAND née PHLIPON

She wrote to Fleury to come and see her.

During her first hours in prison, Grandpré, the good prison inspector, "hastened with touched heart" and urged her to write at once to the Convention.

"I know not how to make my letter read there."
"I shall do all I can."
"Ah, well, I'll write."
"Do, I shall be back in two hours."
He leaves me and I write.

In admirable language she wrote a letter in her husband's and her own name, and her most devoted friends, Bosc and Champagneux,[91] who had hurried to her side, persuaded her to mitigate its most daring passages. She wrote to Garat, Roland's successor as Minister of the Interior, entrusting her letter to him. "I believe that your justice will deem it an honour to present to the Convention the claims that I must have heard against the oppression of which I am a victim," she wrote.

And then she looked around her.

The French of the eighteenth century bestowed upon even their most ordinary objects an exquisite refinement which, from the point of view of taste if not of perfect workmanship, made their art comparable to that of the Far East; but they had not yet felt the need, an elementary one to our minds, of cleanliness. On that question, Mme Roland, like the Queen, was more advanced than her contemporaries. Anything not scrupulously clean filled her with horror. She usually wore washable materials, plain kerchiefs the charm of which lay in their impeccable whiteness, and she was happy only in rooms which servants had waxed until they shone.

She was horribly repulsed in prison by the layer of slime which coated the walls, and by the odour of unaired wretchedness which assailed the nostrils. But if she had no longer her servants at her command, well, she would do without them. She set in to wash the walls and the floor that were bespattered by the blood that had flowed in September. She put a "white cloth over an ugly little table"; this was to be her desk. She preferred to eat on the corner of the mantel so as "to keep the table clean and neat for work. Two great pins fixed in the wall serve as clothes' hooks." She had brought with her "Thomson's poem," equally dear to the heart of Mme de Staël. She made a list of the books she wished brought to her; first of all the Plutarch she had, as a little girl, taken to church instead of the *Semaine Sainte,* then David Hume's *History of England,* and Sheridan's Dictionary.

I smiled at my own preparations . . . for [outside] there was a great commotion; the call to arms was sounding at every instant and I knew not what it meant. They can't keep me from living to the last breath, I said to myself, rejoicing more in my clear conscience than they were ever animated by their fury; if they come, I shall go out to meet them and depart this life as one who goes to rest.

Fleury, the maid, "bathed in tears and choked with sobs," came to see her. Mme Roland reproached herself for her own coldness, reflecting upon the anxiety of those who loved her. With real anguish, her thoughts turned to her husband.

Who then is the one to be pitied in all this? Roland alone, Roland persecuted, outlawed; Roland whose accounts they refuse to examine; Roland, in order to escape the blind rage of men deluded by enemies, obliged to hide himself like a criminal; to tremble for the safety even of those who give him shelter; to eat out his heart in silence over his wife's imprisonment, over the fixing of seals upon all his wordly possessions, and to await in uncertainty the reign of justice which can never indemnify him for all that perversity will have made him suffer.

But before evening, the prisoner was forced to move, for the number of people brought to prison was increasing hourly and her cell could accommodate more than one bed. In order that she be alone, the porter put her in smaller quarters with her small barred window right above the sentry's head.

All night I could hear a thundering voice shouting: "Who goes there? — Corporal! — Patrol!" The houses were lighted and by the number and frequency of the patrols it was easy to see that they feared riots or that there had been some already. I arose early in the morning, I busied myself with housework, that is to say, with making my bed, cleaning my nook and establishing cleanliness upon my own person.

She wrote to the Beaurepaire section (her own quarter), where Roland was "in favour" and which had protested against the incarceration of citizen Roland by issuing an "order" against arbitrary warrants. Mme Roland knew that her letter to the Convention had never been read, and sent her section a copy, asking them to "send deputies to the Convention bar to make heard (her) just complaints." She added that, although imprisoned four days, she had not yet been questioned.[92] Every one of her letters was written in a spirit of perfect dignity. She asked for nothing. In order to make manifest her innocence, the only point she mentioned was that the law had been violated.

Mme Roland wrote to Lauze de Perret,[93] asking him to publish the letter she had officially written to the Convention, addressed to the Minister of the Interior. He answered her with temerity:

Count upon me, virtuous citizen, if but good-will and the most fearless courage are required to help our friends, all honest men, and to deliver you from the dreadful oppression to which your cowardly persecutors have subjected you. Have no doubt but that I will do everything your own generous soul would do for me if I found myself in your plight and appealed to you for aid.

Criminals would in their audacity sacrifice you to their fury, but when one has, as you have, the shield of virtue to hold up before it, one need fear nothing. The scales will soon fall from the eyes of the good people who have been misled, and they will soon make amends to you for the ills that scoundrels have made you suffer. I am more than ever completely your admirer, O respectable citizen.

Your friend,
L. D.

Mme Roland wrote to Gohier, the Minister of Justice. In her opening words she put the case with striking force:

I am oppressed, I therefore have grounds for recalling to you my rights and your duties.

She continued: "The decrees are known to you." But this did not prevent her from enumerating them to him — nor from adding: "I demand that the law be executed, both for my sake and for your own. . ."

In the same lofty tone did she address the Minister of the Interior, Garat, who did not dare to side openly with the prisoner:

As for you, placed between law and dishonour, there can be no question as to your choice, and you are to be pitied if you have not the courage to act in accordance with it.

Champagneux, at times accompanied by his daughter Adèle, came to see Mme Roland almost every day, and often remained with her from five until ten at night.

As soon as Bosc learned of Mme Roland's arrest, he took Eudora under his care and conducted her to the home of the excellent Creuzé-Latouche who "placed her among his own children." He too was a constant visitor to the Abbaye. He carried news to her, and through his friend, André Thouin, the head gardener of the Jardin des Plantes, had beautiful flowers sent to her cell. Roland was in safe hiding at Sainte-Radegonde. Mme Roland was at rest as far as the lot of her family was concerned.

But the deputies!

ORDER OF HANRIOT TO BEAT THE GENERAL
THE FIRST OF JUNE, 1793
General Staff

IN PURSUANCE OF THE ORDERS OF THE COMMITTEE OF PUBLIC SAFETY OF
ALL THE PARIS SECTIONS, THE CITIZENS OF THE LOMBARDS' SECTION WILL
BEAT THE GENERAL; ABOVE ALL LET THE EVENTS TAKE PLACE [*sic*] PRU-
DENTLY AND WITHOUT BLOODSHED.

HANRIOT,
General Commander

[In another handwriting]:

ORDER TO BEAT THE GENERAL WITHIN THE LIMITS OF THE
LOMBARDS' SECTION

We already know that Robespierre's devotees had aroused public
opinion.   Crudest methods were considered the best.   The people
despised the Girondists because they were said to be led by a
woman.   On the twenty-fourth of May, Hébert, in the pay of Pitt,
announced in his paper that the Girondists had seized all grains,
all food supplies, even to the bread in the bakers' shops, with the
intention of throwing it all into the Seine and thus "organizing
a famine."   The confusion of the authorities was aggravated.   More
and more ominous became the popular ebullition.   An outbreak was
brewing.   "Throw the Christians to the lions" was the cry in Rome
when a calamity threatened the *plebs* and the Empire !   Mobs of
wretched women now beat upon the walls of the Convention, yell-
ing: "To the death !   To the death !"   Robespierre, who for some-
time had with difficulty maintained silence, opened the flood-gates
by exclaiming at the Jacobins: "When the people are oppressed,
when naught but themselves remains to them, that man would be
a coward who would not tell them to revolt. . ."   Danton sent
secret warning to the Girondists.

The night of the first of June, several of them who had dined
together, were collected in a house in the rue des Moulins where
Deputy Meilhan lived.   They were not asleep.   They were talking,
talking as they always had.   As usual they were discussing what
plan they should adopt.   The Commune on one hand, the Emigration on the other, they considered themselves lost.   The main
issue was whether or not to go to the meeting.   But long before

this day they had reached the point where they could no longer
make up their minds.[94]

> We had definite information concerning the plot which broke out
> on the thirty-first of May and second of June [wrote Brissot in his
> memoirs]. How was this final catastrophe to be forestalled? Those
> good patriots whom they wished to slay deliberated with the sole end
> of finding an expedient. But what way? Meet force with force?
> And on what force could we draw? We had none and *civil war
> horrified us all*. To await our salvation from the departments meant
> to wait in vain! Their action would necessarily be so uncertain, so
> slow; and even were they roused, would it not be civil war again?
> We discussed at length, and determined nothing.

Since dawn they had heard the tocsin sounding and heard the
General beaten. Presently, as a crowning blow, came the news of
Mme Roland's arrest. In spite of Meilhan, who believed them
as good as massacred if they set foot outside, a holy rage flung them
into the streets. At last, as a final blow, they learned that eight
hundred men had just been betrayed and assassinated at Lyons by
men who called themselves Girondists. Buzot, as can readily be
imagined, was the most furious of them all, and rushed into the
street crying that he would perish at the tribune. Barbaroux was
already there before him. They found the Convention in meeting,
with the benches of the Gironde empty. Ill news from the Vendée
had just come to demoralize even further those who were present.
They were debating what should be done with "the Twenty-two."
This was the number of Girondists deputies the public demanded.
Danton offered himself as hostage. Gnawing his nails, Robespierre
spoke of the trap which had been laid for the people, and coldly
uttered his insensate calumnies: it was the Girondists who had
robbed the furniture repository, Brissot had sent his share out of the
country "and the hypocrite now laughs, lodged in the palace of the
kings." [95]

The Committee of Public Safety sent Barère [96] to address the
meeting in these terms:

"The Committee, out of respect for the situation of the Convention, does not consider it its duty to move the arrest of the accused
members; but, appealing to their patriotism and generosity, it de-

mands that they voluntarily give up their posts." Isnard, Lanthenas, Fauchet, tendered their resignations.

Face to face with Robert Lindet, spokesman for the project of arrest, Buzot and Barbaroux manifested their sublime courage and their republican faith. Barbaroux refused to resign. He had sworn to die at his post and a Marseillais keeps his word. Lanjuinais refused either to resign or to be suspended. The tumult was indescribable, but as yet nothing definite occurred. In spite of the Convention's orders, who feared that a panic might result, the cannon sounded the alarm. Danton cried that "moderatism" must perish to save the Republic. A fabricated plot was denounced at the bar. Somewhat intimidated by Guadet's impetuous fury, Mayor Pache hastily disowned the men of the Commune, at the same time declaring that the Commune and the Convention were in agreement. All over Paris he had placards posted to the effect that full power was in the hands of the Revolutionary Committee and the General Council then in meeting at the Town Hall. In the midst of these indecisions, Louvet proposed that the Girondists should take refuge in their own departments and return to Paris at the head of the provincial militia and liberate the Convention. But the noble hearts of these men were revolted by such a thought. They preferred death to crime. Vergniaud and many others later carved on their prison walls: *Potius mori quam fœdari.*

Outside the doors of the Convention, armed men were on guard, and Deputy Grégoire, wishing to leave, was insulted and struck by them. Hanriot [97] had deployed numerous forces in the Tuileries, and the populace surged back and forth between the National Guard and the Convention. Danton cried that "signal amends" should be made for this outrage. Barère asked for "Hanriot's head," for "laws cannot be made by slaves."

The deputies, led by Hérault de Seychelles, their president, went forth in a body and commanded the chief of the insurgents to disperse his men. But he impudently replied that the Twenty-two must first be delivered over. And he issued this command:

"Gunners, to your guns !"

Subdued by this anarchy, the Convention meekly returned, resumed its sitting, and, upon Couthon's motion, agreed to surrender the Girondists. Several were able to escape. Others obtained the permission to "remain in their homes in a state of arrest, under the protection of the National Convention, the French people, and the loyalty of the citizens of Paris."

In her prison, far from the insurrection, Mme Roland sensed the danger that threatened her party and anxiously awaited news. Finally the *Moniteur* arrived. In it she read the decree arresting the Twenty-two. "My country is lost!" was her first cry. The degradation of the Republic made her forget the peril of her friends.

> . . . The legislative body is in the hands of the Commune . . . the enemy will profit by our dissension . . . the entire Republic is at the mercy of the deadliest havoc. . . [*Memoirs.*]

She wrote to Deputy Dulaure, editor of the *Thermomètre du Jour,* one of the few friends who remained faithful to her. She asked him "to publish in his paper the letter the Convention refused to read," and Dulaure had the courage to comply. "Tomorrow I shall publish Citizen Roland's letter to the National Convention and the one she addressed to the Minister of the Interior."

Indeed, on the eighth of June, Lauze de Perret had said at the Convention:

> Several days ago the Minister of the Interior sent to the Convention the protests of a citizen who was forcibly removed from her home and imprisoned in the Abbaye. The letter, however, has not yet been read. The person in question is Citizen Roland. (Murmurs.) It is pointed out that this matter is not within the province of the Convention. The Assembly proceeded to the order of the day. [*Moniteur.*]

Mme Roland was told that, as minister, Roland had reduced the prisoners' daily expenses from five to two *livres*. The nation supplied them with straw, but they must feed themselves and pay the porter twenty *sous* for bed and furniture. They must also pay for candles and fire.

> I wanted to make an experiment [she wrote in her *Memoirs*] and discover to what extent a human being can, by exerting his will-power, reduce his needs: but to go far in this, one must proceed by degrees. After four days I began by reducing my breakfasts, and substituting

bread and water for coffee and chocolate. I asked that at lunch I be served but one dish of coarse meat and some greens, and at night nothing but a few vegetables and no dessert. In order to break myself of the habit of drinking wine, I drank beer, and then I gave that up too. Since this diet, however, had a moral aim, and since I have naught but contempt for futile economies, my first step was to donate a sum of money to those unfortunate ones who slept on straw, so that while I ate my dry bread in the morning I had the pleasure of knowing that those poor wretches would have something added to their dinner and that they owed it to me. If I remain here six months, I wish to leave fresh and plump, requiring naught but soup and bread and, incognito, having merited a few blessings.

At this time Mme Roland was visited by "shabby flat-faced administrators, some saying they were of the police, others from God knows where; big *Sans-Culottes* with stinking hair."

Finally, on the twelfth of June, after she had been twelve days in prison, a police agent called Louvet came to question the prisoner. This was the result of the publication in Dulaure's paper. He asked her, among other foolish questions, if she "knew anything of a plan to detach the departments from Paris and form a federative republic"; if she "had knowledge of certain pamphlets sent to the departments to rouse them against Paris," and if "her friends, when they spoke of justice and liberty, were not opposed to equality?"

She responded with great self-control, superbly parrying the questions of the agent who would have liked to make her confess to participation in these affairs and, above all, make her divulge the names of the men of her group, who would have been thereby seriously compromised.

After he had gone, she calmly resumed her work. Her first concern was to write a report of the examination she had just undergone and send it to Dulaure who published it in his paper on the twenty-first of June with the following notice:

Whatever the prejudices of the public may be, I deem it my duty to afford accused people a means of justifying themselves. This is why I have decided to publish the examination of *citoyenne* Roland. Only cowards or men with no sense of justice could censure my conduct.

DULAURE

It was probably at this period that Mme Roland began to write certain *Notes*. Was it to find for them a safe depository that she wrote Mme Sophie Grandchamp, with whom she had quarrelled several months before?

> If I esteemed you less, it would be extremely painful for me to see you at this moment. Therefore I feel I give you an unequivocal proof of my affection in accepting your offer and in entrusting you with a matter which demands the utmost confidence.

They were both too noble-minded not to disregard at this time and in a place like the Abbaye, the disagreement which had estranged them, and which was no doubt due to Bosc's exaggerated touchiness. Their friendship and mutual trust were immediately revived. We know that Mme Grandchamp made several visits to the prison, and we also know that Mme Roland later entrusted her with a portion of the *Memoirs*.

On the twentieth of June, Mme Roland was awakened by coarse taunts just beneath her window from a crowd that had been roused by "the *Père Duchesne's* [98] poisonous articles against that infamous Roland woman who was at the Abbaye."

For once the prisoner lost her self-control and vented her anger upon Garat, the most colourless and timorous of the ministers, who, by his silence, had authorized this unjust and unpardonable detention. Her terrifying letter to Garat must be quoted in its entirety. Champagneux (it is true he was Garat's subordinate), found it exaggerated and did his utmost to mitigate its consequences.[99]

> June 20, 1793 (at eight in the morning)
>
> What cries are these I hear? . . . It is the voice of a town crier announcing . . . the discovery of a great conspiracy between the Rolandists, the Buzotins, the Pétionists, the Girondists, and *the Vendée rebels, those tools of England*. One must get hold of old Roland and make him pay the penalty for his crimes, one must open his wife's eyes to her c . . . of a husband. Then a deluge of filthy language, pointed reiterations *that I am at the Abbaye,* and incitements to maltreat me. Right under my window the crier renews his exhortations to the market populace.
>
> Thus is oppressed innocence insulted and thus the people aroused to persecution. And the author of such infamous writings was sup-

ported, protected, defended by Garat at a moment when similar insults to the Convention had caused him to be arrested by order of a Commission of representatives of the people.[100]

Garat ! I hold you responsible for this insult; it is to your cowardice that I owe it, and should worse follow, it is upon your head that I call down the vengeance of heaven.

The brigand who persecutes, the exalted man who reviles, the abused people who assassinate, do but follow their instinct and perform their task; but the man in authority who tolerates them, whatever his pretext may be, is dishonoured for all time.

Turn to your pretty writings; explain events like a philosopher, as well as the passions and errors that accompany them, but posterity will say: *he fortified the party which degraded national representation; he asked the Convention to surrender to a gang of anarchists; he aided and abetted a usurping Commune which refused to recognize legislative authority and which outlawed virtue.*

Indeed, I know what follows such outrageous incitements. What care I ? I have long been ready. In any case, accept this farewell, which I send like a vulture to prey upon your heart.

After the satisfaction of composing and sending this letter, Mme Roland was to experience a great joy, a joy for which she had almost ceased to hope — two letters from Buzot (dated the fifteenth and the seventeenth of June), arrived from Caen [101] where the prisoner had taken refuge. Hitherto she had not dared write him for fear of compromising him, and, to obtain news of him, she had addressed herself in vain to Jerôme Le Tellier at Evreux, a friend and confidant of the fugitive. Nor had she succeeded in getting any information from "young Mme Chollet" (Louvet's Lodoïska), nor from Louvet himself, who both shared her secret.

Buzot, Pétion, Louvet, Barbaroux, Salles, Guadet, Gorsas, and all the others who had managed to escape, had mistrusted the Convention's promise to protect them and had not remained at home to await the Commissioners of the Commune. Some of the Girondists had left their hiding-places in Paris and the suburbs and again encountered each other on the roads of Normandy and Brittany, whereas Vergniaud, Valazé, Ducos, Boyer-Fonfrède, and others had been seized and thrown into gaol. Several of the fugitives had refused to be parted from the women they loved. In striking contrast to the persecution they suffered, unknown sympathizers risked all to assist these unfortunate couples. The deputies who fled from

CHARLES BARBAROUX

From a miniature given by Mme la Comtesse de Jonquières to the Musée du Louvre

MARIE-SOPHIE HARLOW

HIS WIFE

From a miniature belonging to Mme la Comtesse de Jonquières

MADAME ROLAND

From a miniature carried by Buzot during his proscription. Archives Nationales

FRANCOIS-NICHOLAS-LEONARD BUZOT

From a painting which Mme Roland had with her in prison. Bibliothèque municipale de Versailles

Paris after the first of June, could never have made good their escape without the connivance of these partisans whose names have never been revealed to history.

Buzot, probably unable to accomplish anything for Mme Roland, left on the second of June and went to Evreux, which seems to us to have been of the utmost imprudence, as this was his native city. These Girondists, however, were so ingenuous that it never occurred to them to take even the most elementary precautions. Bosc's friends took refuge in the Priory of Sainte-Radegonde, a place he visited frequently, as everyone knew; and, later, he himself was to use it as a hiding-place. Seeking a safe shelter, Roland went to Rouen, to the home of the Malortie sisters, friends of thirty years' standing. As to Guadet, he was to conduct six of his colleagues to Saint-Émilion to the home of his parents, a disastrous step for all concerned.

Buzot and Pétion[102] reached Caen, one in the early part, the other at the end of June. A certain Langeux, secretary of a Society of the people, having recognized "these traitors and madmen" at Rouen, hastened to denounce them to Danton, "in order that he might inform the Committee of Public Safety of Pétion's disguise and of the name Buzot had assumed on his journey." Louvet and his Lodoïska also passed through Evreux on their way to Caen.

And yet Robespierre's victims inspired great devotion. They found many prepared not only to protect their lives and liberty, but eager to console them in their sorrow and isolation. At least eleven — and no doubt more — knew of the secret ties that bound Buzot, the outlaw, to the prisoner in the Abbaye. All these risked their freedom, and their lives as well, to give solace to this persecuted love: Mme Goussard, and her sister, a seamstress[103] Champagneux, Pétion, Barbaroux, Lauze de Perret, Vallée, Louvet, Marguerite Denuelle,[104] Jerôme Letellier, Jany,[105] Bosc, Mme Grandchamp, and in all probability, Sainte-Agathe.

In his memoirs Louvet wrote: "Poor Buzot! Buried deep in his heart he carried bitter sorrows that were known to me alone and which I shall never reveal."

No-one has left one written word divulging this secret. The truth was only known seventy years later, and through Mme Roland herself. In June 1794, five letters she wrote Buzot from prison were returned, after the latter's tragic death, to the Committee of Public Safety, or rather to Robespierre. They were then lost sight of, and came to light again only in 1863 where they were discovered in the possession of Thibaut, Anatole France's father, who had purchased them from an unknown young man.[106]

These letters, far from impairing Mme Roland's memory, reveal her in a new light that shows her worthy of the tenderness of posterity which had until then regarded her with admiration and respect. This splendid human being had in her something of the sublime; virtue seemed her birthright, and frailities were alien to her soul. Hitherto she had seemed above our human imperfections, too great a stranger to the conflicts which are the heritage of human kind. Now no longer was she the "too-perfect" being. No longer did she appear stern and inexorable; a stroke of fortune brought us her justification at the same moment that it revealed her vulnerability, but if she were wounded she was in no way disarmed. Her splendour was never dimmed, but, on the contrary, was purified as it passed through the flame.

These letters [107] reveal to us that, although a Stoic, she was as well a true woman, and that if she had shunned passion for so long a time, she was, in the last analysis, too human a being not to be stirred by it in the end. The beautiful and pathetic part of her story is that passion was ennobled in the purity of her heart.

On the twenty-second of June Mme Roland, still in prison, was seated before her "ugly little table." She was transfigured. The worthy Mme Goussard had come, bringing her two letters from Buzot !

How often have I read them over ! I press them to my heart, I cover them with kisses, for I had lost all hope of hearing from you ! . . . In vain did I appeal to Mme Chollet for news; I wrote once to M. Le Tellier at Evreux so that you should know that I still lived; but the mail is no longer sacred; I did not wish to address a letter to you, for I was sure that your name would cause it to be intercepted and that you would be compromised. I was proud and tranquil when first I came here, filled with good wishes for the defenders of Liberty and still retaining some hope. When I learned that a decree of arrest had been made against the Twenty-two, I cried out: "My country is lost !" Until I received the reassuring news of your escape, I was torn by the cruellest anguish; and again, when I heard of the decree of accusation that concerns you; this was the final affront to your courage ! But the moment I heard you were in Calvados, I recovered my peace of mind. Persist, my friend, in your generous efforts; too readily on the field of Philippi did Brutus despair of the salvation of Rome. As long as a Republican draws breath, as long as he is at liberty and retains his energy, he should and can be of use. In any case, the south offers you a safe abode; there lies the refuge of honest people. If your peril increase, it is there that you must turn and there direct your steps; it is there that you must live, for there you may serve your like and practise your high virtues.

As for myself, I know how to await in peace the return of the reign of justice, or endure the excesses of tyranny in such a way that my example shall not be in vain. If I had any fears, it was that you might risk yourself imprudently on my behalf. My friend, it is by saving your country that you can bring about my salvation ! . . . I shall die in peace if I know that you are efficaciously serving the fatherland. Death, torments, sorrows, are all as naught to me; I defy them all. Go; till my last hour I shall live without wasting an instant of anxiety upon unworthy agitations . . .[108]

And further on:

. . . I dare not say it, and you alone can understand it, but I was not greatly vexed at being arrested.

They will now be less furious, less rabid against R. [Roland] I said to myself. If they attempt some sort of trial, I shall be able to defend him in a way that will serve to glorify him. It seemed to me that I thus acquitted myself of a debt I owed his sorrow. But can you as well believe that, being alone, it is really with you that I remain ? By being thus in prison, I sacrifice myself to my husband and keep myself for my friend. My tormentors have enabled me to reconcile duty and love; so do not pity me.

Others admire my courage, but they do not know my joys; you, who must share them with me, can preserve their beauty by the constancy of your courage. . .

And she finished with these words:

May all this bring some solace to your heart ! Go to, we cannot but both be worthy of the emotion each has inspired in the other's heart; and misery has no place therein. Farewell, my friend ! My beloved, farewell ![109]

On June twenty-fourth — a sensational and unexpected move.

It was mid-day.

Mme Roland, not in the best of health, had that morning remained in bed. The porter's wife came to inform her that an official wished to speak with her. In the waiting-room she found two men. One of them said abruptly:

"I have come to set you free."

She replied that this was all very well, but that she could not go home until the seals were broken. She was told that the order for their removal was about to be given.

Mme Roland returned to her cell to prepare for her departure. The porter was in an even greater hurry, for so many people had been sent to the prison that he was pressed for space. The unfortunate Brissot,[110] whose arrest had been decreed and who, attempting to seek refuge in Switzerland, had managed to get out of Paris, had just been arrested at Moulins and brought to the Abbaye. All unknowing, Mme Roland made way for Brissot, and a fortnight later he was ousted by Charlotte Corday, whose place in turn was taken by Abbé Fauchet. The porter had never believed that a prisoner could be as good humoured as Mme Roland. He marvelled to see her living peacefully among her books and flowers, and he declared that in the future his lugubrious retreat should be known by no other name but Flora's Pavilion.

At this precise moment the good Fleury arrived to pay a visit to her mistress, and she wept for joy as she made up the parcels. Mme Roland asked for a cab, which she entered under the very eyes of the director, having given the address of the rue de la Harpe where she wished to deposit her baggage before flying to embrace her daughter at the home of Creuzé-Latouche.

With nimble step I alight from the cab [she wrote]. In fact I have never been able to descend from a vehicle without jumping. I fly like a bird through the door, crying merrily "Good day, Lamarre!" to the porter. I had not mounted four steps of the stairs when two men at my heels — I know not how they came there — cried out: "*Citoyenne* Roland!" "What do you want?" I asked as I turned about. "We arrest you in the name of the law."

Her release was but a mockery, a stratagem of the Commune to make its position legally sound. It had been somewhat embarrassed by the illegal arrest of the first of June. But such scruples were not long to worry it. It was still a novice in crime, and it felt the need of putting its books in order. Thenceforth, everything would be legal, and the most meticulous jurist could not but agree that although the young woman may have been innocent as she climbed into the cab at the Abbaye, she was certainly guilty as she stopped before the door of her house.

This was indeed a shock, but she immediately made up her mind what to do. Having asked to be shown the warrant, she hastened across the court. "Where are you going ?" shouted the policemen. And she replied: "To my landlord's where I have some business to transact. Follow me."

Mme Cauchois opened the door, her face aglow with pleasure.

Let me sit down and get my breath [wrote Mme Roland] but do not rejoice. . . I have just left the Abbaye. Now they are arresting me to take me to Sainte-Pélagie. I am aware of the resolutions recently taken by my section, and I wish to place myself under its protection. I beg you to take the necessary steps.

The son of the house "with the ardour and indignation of a good young man," hurried to the section. A note added by Bosc to Mme Roland's manuscript, takes our breath away: *"Since then he has been dragged to the scaffold for this deed, and his father died of grief."*

The commissioners of the section arrived. While awaiting them, Mme Roland wrote a few notes to keep her friends informed of what was taking place.

To Lauze de Perret she wrote:

June 24th

They pretend to release me from the Abbaye; I believe I am coming home, they arrest me to take me to Sainte-Pélagie. Who knows whether they will not conduct me elsewhere from there ? Do not forget me.

One must have the originals before one's eyes to know to what extent she was mistress of herself. She had once said: "I am able to control myself." This was true — incredibly true. In writing the above letter, she held her pen as steadily as if she had been in her office at the ministry.

She complied with the request of the section commissioners and followed them to the Town Hall. There lengthy debates were held between the commissioners and the representatives of the Commune. Among the latter she recognized that Louvet who had come to interrogate her at the Abbaye. In spite of everything, she had to give in, and it was at Sainte-Pélagie that they now imprisoned her among prostitutes and assassins.

Once there she found that the State furnished nothing to the prisoners, neither food nor the most elementary and indispensable articles of furniture. The following dialogue took place between her and the warden:

"But how do they live ?" she asked.
"They are allowed a portion of beans only and a pound and a half of bread a day; but you won't be able to eat either of them."
"I admit it is scarcely what I am accustomed to; but I like to know the peculiarities of every situation, and adapt myself to the conditions which surround me: I should like to try some."

And indeed she did, but was unable to persist long in her intentons. She then appealed to the porteress, the worthy Mme Bouchaud, who brought her bread and water in the morning, a chop and some vegetables at noon, and a few greens at night. It was the same diet as at the Abbaye. If Mme Roland stressed these facts, it was because her expenses at Sainte-Pélagie and the "feasts" over which she presided in the porter's lodge, were soon denounced by the strict *Sans-Culottes* of the Observatoire section. In an admirable passage of the *Memoirs,* she wrote:

My courage did not fail me before this new misfortune, but the subtle cruelty of giving me a taste of liberty only to shackle me with new chains, and the barbarous care they took to avail themselves of a decree, aroused my indignation. I was in that frame of mind which intensifies every impression so greatly that they react upon one's health; when I went to bed, I could not sleep, so naturally I dreamed. But these violent crises never lasted long with me; I must needs be always in possession of my faculties for I am accustomed to governing myself. I decided I was a fool to flatter my persecutors by a display of my annoyance with their injustice; they had but committed another outrage and altered very little conditions which I had already been well able to support. Did I not have, as at the Abbaye, books and leisure ? Was I not still myself ? In truth, I was almost indignant

at my own weakness in having succumbed to anxiety, and my sole
thought was now to live my life to the full, and to employ my faculties with that independence which a strong mind retains even behind
prison bars, and which worsts its deadliest foes.

Who could not help but feel a deep respect, and who would not
be dominated by that firmness of character which had now risen
to sublime heights ? It is easy to understand how Champagneux
de Rosières could write of her:

I had truly admired Mme Roland at other periods of her life, but
only when she was in prison did I appreciate her to the full. In gaol
she attained a supreme dignity, and there she lived as if upon a throne.

Mme Roland soon felt that her strength and vitality would suffer
from the diet she had imposed upon herself. In order to retain
the amazing soundness of her splendid organism, she made up her
mind to give up mystic austerities and prepared to indulge in "pleas-
urable amusements." Even in prison would she "live life to the
full" ! She purchased some pencils and took up drawing which
she had given up so long ago. In the mornings she read the poets
and at times the English philosophers. During the day she amused
herself at the *piano-forte* she had had brought to the quarters of
the worthy porteress, and where she was allowed to spend those
hours which the intense heat made unendurable in her cell.[111]

Moreover, the prisoner had convinced herself that she was happy.
Her husband was in a "quiet and secure retreat" where he was
"made much of"; her daughter was well cared for in the home
of "venerable patriarchs"; her friends "received at Caen" had "gathered together considerable forces." Further, "he among them who
is dearest to me, has found a way of giving me news of himself;
I can write to him, and I have confidence that my letters reach
him."

She received visits from "the honest Grandpré who came accompanied by "an interesting woman." [112] As at the Abbaye, "faithful
Bosc" brought lovely freshly cut flowers to her from the Jardin des
Plantes. The tender-hearted Champagneux encouraged her to pursue her writings. Further, Mme Bouchaud, who was pained to

see a lady in such wretched surroundings, which the thinness of the partitions made even more unbearable, had her removed from her cell to "a pretty room with a fire-place" on the ground floor. Replacing the sinister turnkey, she tendered her every care that her kindly heart could imagine, and even put a jasmine plant at the grating, the tiny stems of which twisted about the bars; until the day the inspector angrily discovered the unusual treatment that was being accorded her, and gave orders that "equal conditions be maintained," and sent Mme Roland upstairs "in a hallway," in the quarters reserved for "lost women."

But her work put her beyond the reach of all. It was then that she undertook to write the story of her life. The *Memoirs,* composed in two months' time, and in which scarcely a word has been changed or crossed out, were the outcome of her instinct for resistance, her zest for life, and her taste for work. "I do not control my pen," she wrote, "it takes me whither it will, and I let it fly. Father, mother, friends, husband, I shall describe them all as they were or as they appeared to me." To be sure, the picture she drew of herself was somewhat idealized. But by dint of forcing her nature to model itself upon her ideal, she had reached a point where she fused her personality with it. Where did her real self finish, where did her will-power begin? Mme Roland did but depict the moral character she wished to be.

She wrote with a sort of joy and with an amazing facility, for she was well aware that her work had an original character which would be precious to posterity. At times she was laconic and unhesitatingly admitted the reason for it: "In my last copy book I left off at Vincennes. . . To narrate every event step by step, I should have to write an extensive work and I have not much time to live, so I must limit myself to an outline." When Champagneux, to whom she had entrusted "sufficient manuscript to compose a volume in duodecimo" was compelled, for his own safety, to throw it into the fire, she wrote that she would have preferred to be thrown "herself into the flames." This could be easily understood, she said, for she might be "murdered any day," and "her writings were a comfort to her, for they assured her that her own memory, as well as that of a great number of interesting people, would be justified."

The manuscript of her *Memoirs* profoundly moves the reader who studies it in the quiet hall of manuscripts in the *Bibliothèque Nationale*.[112a] The woman whose hand had touched this paper, and who had penned these words, was in a desperate situation. Still young and still aware of all the rich diversity of life, her whole being had recoiled from the thought of death — DEATH, as she wrote it in heavy capital letters, bordered with wide margins. We know that when she thought she was alone, she sometimes spent three hours weeping at the window. But if she concealed one thing from us, it was her pity for herself, and in no part of the *Memoirs* do we surprise a tear of self-compassion.

The writing is closer than of old, for doubtless she was afraid that her paper might not suffice. One can perceive faded spots of ink between the unwavering lines, and, as time went on, her ink grew paler day by day. The corrections are few. Now and again a sentence was added on the margin, or some passage was barred out with a heavy perpendicular stroke. These *Mémoires Particuliers* were composed with an even greater calm than the *Notes Historiques*. The pages have almost the same appearance as the letters she wrote. It was with an incredibly steady pen, with bold commas, that she wrote — or rather drew — that stirring end: "Nature, open thy bosom. God of Justice, take me," and, beneath the words "at thirty-nine," she signed her work in her habitual way, with her initials and a flourish launched with a superb zest. In the pages entitled *Mes Dernières Pensées,* the inferior paper is soiled, but her letters resemble, in firmness and size, her correspondence of happier days.

On the fifth of September when, in the prisons, they were expecting that the massacres of the previous year would be commemorated by fresh assassinations, she wrote again, in the centre of a blank space: "No-one knows if he still have twenty-four hours to live." M. Auguste Breuil, barrister to the Royal Tribunal of Amiens, and a friend of the Cannet sisters, said that the *Memoirs* formed a hasty and imperfect book, "reminiscent of that iambic that André

Chenier was writing on the seventh of Thermidor, and which he was compelled to leave unfinished so as not to keep the executioner waiting."

In these months of June and July there was terrible news from the frontiers. Alsace was invested, Mayence had fallen, and Cambrai was about to share the same fate; the Austrian light infantry was camping outside Péronne, and, in addition, the Chouans had defeated the Republican army on the Loire.

Saint-Just, "that young monster with the calm and beautiful face . . ." to quote Taine, "emerged from the ranks, and by dint of atrocities established his authority." He requested his master, Robespierre, to place him in charge of the Girondists' indictment (they had been proclaimed "traitors" before any trial had taken place), and made such a terrifying report before the Convention that even Robespierre trembled. "Saint-Just's enthusiasm," said one of his friends, "was based on a mathematical certainty."

Superior to Robespierre in character and ability, Saint-Just would ultimately have condemned Robespierre to whom he had one day remarked, at a time when he knew him but slightly: "You whom I know as one knows God, through his miracles. . ." But once closely associated with him, he was inclined to consider him inferior in ideology. Everyone had believed that Saint-Just was Robespierre's disciple; rather, he was Robespierre's pace-maker and leader.

Had Thermidor not, in one stroke, saved us from these two terrifying mechanisms, the day would have come when Saint-Just would have established a dictatorship in France, and this thought consoles us for the reign of Bonaparte.

The impeachment of the Queen had been decreed, as well as the profanation of the tombs of the kings at Saint-Denis, in celebration of the tenth of August. In retaliation, England and Austria formed an alliance and decided to march on Paris. From one end to the other, France was disorganized; civil war prevailed; anonymous denunciations were followed by arbitrary arrests.

In consequence of an infamous betrayal, the soft-hearted Grandpré was presently arrested and all his papers examined and placed under seal. He fortunately had time to remove a letter which Mme Roland had given him for Brissot. Mme Pétion and her eleven-year-old boy, Étienne, were arrested at Lisieux, and became Mme Roland's neighbours in the gruesome dungeon of Sainte-Pélagie. She went to them, saying: "Never did the thought cross my mind when I was at the Town Hall partaking of your anxieties on the tenth of last August, that we would celebrate the anniversary of that day at Sainte-Pélagie, nor that it would be to the fall of the throne that we would owe our disgrace." Mme Brissot, accused of having held secret political meetings in the Queen's apartments at Saint-Cloud, was also arrested:

Nothing could have been more ridiculous to anyone acquainted with Brissot's wife, addicted as she was to domestic virtues, absorbed in the cares of her household, ironing with her own hands her husband's shirts, and peeping through the keyhole to determine whether or not she should open to those who were knocking at the door.

Champagneux, head clerk of the Ministry of the Interior, underwent a burlesque scene with Collot d'Herbois who had come, quite intoxicated, demanding imaginary carriages. The former actor "swore, stormed, broke the legs of the chairs and tables, and then had Champagneux and the minister both arrested."

Champagneux had been four weeks in prison. It was a great sorrow to him that he was no longer free to visit his friend and sustain her with his warm affection.

She cast a spell of sweetness all about her [he said]. Porters and their wives . . . treated her with the greatest regard. Mme Bouchaud, the porter's wife at Sainte-Pélagie, had the most devoted consideration for her; she and others were kind enough to permit the little afternoon repasts I now and again offered the prisoner and which consisted of fruit and pastry; *citoyenne* Bouchaud supplied the knives and forks and partook of the meal with us.

A plan for escape did not meet with Mme Roland's approval,[113] for she feared that it might result in more painstaking attempts being made to find her husband. "As long as they have me under lock and key, they will leave him alone," she said.

As for Bosc, he was soon to be under suspicion too, and compelled in his turn to conceal himself at Sainte-Radegonde.

On the third of July Mme Roland wrote Buzot,[114] who was still at Caen. Three days later Buzot, whose every thought was for the prisoner, found through generous friends a way of sending her other letters, and she immediately replied in a letter dated the sixth of July. The following day, she even went so far as to extoll "the charms of prison" to her companion of her soul.

July 7 [1793] Sainte-Pélagie
You cannot imagine, my friend, the charms of prison, for here the heart alone takes one to account for the manner in which the moments have been employed. No diversions that pall, no arduous sacrifices, no dull anxieties; none of those duties that are the more exacting because deemed worthy of respect by an upright heart; none of those contradictions between society's laws and prejudices, and nature's sweetest instincts; no jealous glances to spy on one's emotions or on one's chosen occupation; your melancholy or inactivity causes pain to no-one; no-one expects efforts or exacts sentiments which lie not within one's powers. Restored to oneself, restored to truth, with no obstacles to overcome, no conflicts to sustain, one's soul is at liberty to assert its own integrity, and, though apparently a captive, one can retrieve one's moral independence and employ it with an entirety that social relations usually impair. I was not free even to seek this independence and through it deliver myself of the burden of rendering another happy — another whose happiness was not easy to achieve. Events have given me what I could not have otherwise obtained and yet kept my conscience clear. How I prize these shackles which grant me the freedom to love you unreservedly and to think continually of you. Here, all other obligations are suspended; my only duty is to him who loves me and who so greatly merits to be cherished. Pursue your career whole-heartedly, serve your country, save the cause of Liberty; every deed fills me with joy and I triumph in your conduct. . .

THE days passed. Nothing occurred to make any change in Mme Roland's perilous situation. She learned that the Convention had opened the Louvre Museum on the anniversary of the tenth of August 1793, and that David's pupils had played ball, at his suggestion, against the pictures of Boucher and Fragonard. The "restorer of the art of painting" had organized the decorating of Paris, in celebration of the day of triumph of a year ago. Three great plaster statues were erected in the Place de la Révolution.

The central figure represented Liberty and at her feet three thousand living birds were released from captivity. A fountain played
over the ruins of the Bastille, and there eighty-six old men, bearing
the banners of the departments, solemnly drank from its basin.

The prisoner must have considered these gestures futile indeed.
Although she had no faith in the justice of the anarchistic powers
which kept her imprisoned, she refused to consider any plans for
her escape. Her letter to Buzot, dated July third, was purposely
reassuring. In it she wrote:

Poor X [Roland] sent me a person from thirty leagues' distance, instructed to make every attempt.

And three days later:

I rejected plans he had made for me. A person he had sent to carry
them out is still in Paris.

These words are confirmed in the *Memoirs*:

Henriette, free, lively, and affectionate as ever, came to visit me in
my captivity, and wanted to take my place in order to save me.

The reader will here recognize charming Henriette Cannet, the
elder of the two sisters. It was Sophie, however, who had been the
little Phlipon girl's best friend. We have, indeed, heard of a certain
disagreement caused by the "bad behaviour" of their respective husbands, which had occurred at the time the two friends had come
together at Amiens as young married women, ten years before.
But both Henriette and Sophie were Royalists. Moreover, Sophie,
a widow since 1788, was ill. Was this sufficient to explain her
absence at such a moment ? As to Henriette, in 1784 she had
married at the age of thirty-six, a certain M. de Vouglans, a magistrate of seventy-seven, who had at one time considered marrying
the young d'Hangard girl whom he had met at the home of Mesdemoiselles Lamotte and whom Mlle Phlipon was to portray so
cruelly in her letters and *Memoirs*. Widowed since 1791, Henriette had returned to Amiens. Did Roland, then fleeing from
Sainte-Radegonde to Rouen, have a secret meeting with her ? Did
they then consider ways and means to effect the prisoner's escape ?

M. Auguste Breuil has described how Henriette wished to sacrifice herself to save her friend:

The *Memoirs* contain but one sentence concerning this admirable proof of devotion, but Henriette, whom we knew well at Amiens, particularly during the last years of her long life, spoke to me several times of this visit.

"I was a widow," she used to say, "and had no children. Mme Roland, on the contrary, had a husband who was already advanced in years and a charming little girl, and both needed the cares of a wife and mother. What was more natural than that I should risk my useless life to save hers that was so precious to her family? I wished to change clothes with her and stay as a prisoner while she in disguise made an attempt to escape. Well, all my entreaties and tears failed to obtain her consent.

" 'But they will kill you, my good Henriette,' she kept repeating, 'and your blood will be on my head. I prefer to suffer a thousand deaths rather than reproach myself for yours. . .' Realizing that I could not sway her from her resolution, I bade her farewell, and never saw her again."

Mme Roland had at least the consolation of believing that Buzot and the Girondists, then in Normandy, were safe from any immediate danger. And yet, alas, how torn she was by anxieties and uncertainties! When the army of the Convention, advancing under the command of a former beadle, came in sight of the federate army of the Girondists, both retreated in opposite directions. After Marat had been stabbed to death by a young girl from Caen, the Normands took fright and the refugee deputies were ordered to depart immediately with their army. The Brittany batallions were then returning home and offered to take them with them. They were enlisted and left Caen in military service. The Gironde deputies had originally numbered twenty-two. This was the count of destiny: the Convention had in the first place promised the twenty-two Girondists as Hanriot demanded, but on the thirty-first of the following October, after the "trial of the Twenty-two," only one and twenty Girondists went to the scaffold. Eight days later, Mme Roland made up the fatal total.

Brittany had become more and more antagonistic to the Girondists. Hostile to the outlaws, the Jacobin municipalities from Dol to Lamballe advised Loudéac, Pontivy and Saint-Malo that the

Girondists would pass through. A certain Jacobin, François-Allain Launay, who had learned the names of the fugitives, denounced them to the municipalities, and did all he could to effect their arrest, but his efforts met with no success. The entire country was up in arms against them. They went from house to house, hiding here and there, protected by unknown people who risked their lives to save them. It was in these circumstances that Barbaroux caught small-pox and was cured of it. Misery and treachery pursued them everywhere. Gorsas was compelled to abandon his daughter on the road, and Salles his wife and three children, entrusting them to the care of the village priest and giving them what little money they possessed. Mme Buzot expelled from her home, escaped and joined her husband in Quimper. At the same time, Evreux, where Buzot had formerly known but friends, celebrated the enactment of the Convention's resolution, decreeing that Buzot's house should be razed to the ground and his property thenceforth considered as accursed land. Lodoïska and Barbaroux' young wife [115] were the only women who still followed the fugitives.

Undoubtedly, Mme Roland was far from realizing the moral torments of these unfortunate men who, having attempted to find shelter in hostile Brittany, left it for the Gironde which was to prove so fatal to them. On the thirty-first of August 1793, she wrote Buzot the last of the five letters which have come down to us, and perhaps also the last letter ever received by the outlawed man.

This time — acting no doubt upon advice — she concealed her identity and veiled her own emotions. She knew not where he was. She no longer had the small solace of visualizing in a definite place the man she loved.

This letter [116] was addressed to "Brittany," for this was all she knew of his whereabouts. Harassed and desperate, she urged Buzot to embark for America. Instinctively it appeared to her as the only place where he would be safe, and she was not mistaken.

August thirty-first, Sainte-Pélagie
You know, my friend, how your *Sophie's* heart is attached to you. You cannot imagine her emotion and delight when she received your

news. And yet, what uncertainties still fill her mind! To what
anxieties is she still a prey! Why do you not tell her more about your
commercial enterprises, so perilous under present circumstances. The
security of your small holdings and the success you hope to achieve
are the only blessings that could touch her in her present exhausted
state. She lives but to learn of them and would perish should you
suffer. I have undertaken [sic] to answer in her behalf, and you cannot help but feel how great her need to write you if she be willing
to employ a stranger's hand. I can tell you more of her condition than
she herself would have the courage to write. Since you have gone
away, her illness has assumed a most fatal character; it is impossible
to tell how long it will last or how it will end. There are times when
violent attacks seem likely to produce great changes or make one fear
the direst consequences; at times a painful prolongation blackens the
future with sombre worries, relieved only by the faintest glimmers of
hope. When she first fell ill, she considered every possibility and faced
them all with fortitude. The situation of her family and the thought
of your success sustained her at that time. I have seen her, happy
although suffering, retain her equanimity and her mind's free play,
rejoicing in the thought of the good things which she believed fate
held in store for you. Herself she regarded as a propitiatory victim
whose lot it was to accept sacrifice for the sakes of those she held dear.
But now all is changed. Far from her, you are fettered by affairs
which, though they impose rude tasks on you, no longer promise you
a bright perspective; her *old uncle* has fallen into a distressing decline;
it is terrifying how fast he is sinking. His life, although in great danger, may yet be prolonged some time; but feeble, difficult, and suspicious as he is, he finds life a torture and renders it the same for
those about him. She forced him to consent to burn the *testament* [117]
which troubled her so much because of you: this was not an easy
task . . . but she insisted with that authority which the approach of
the last moments lends to the ill, at least when they can profit by
them.

In the early part of her illness, she drew up certain *instructions* she
wished to leave behind; through a most extraordinary misunderstanding
on the part of the executor or rather the depository, they were destroyed. She was greatly affected by this loss, but as she never loses
heart, she summoned all her forces to repair this evil. Her most lucid
moments have been devoted to this pious office, wherein you have not
suffered from neglect.

What, indeed, cannot be borne if one has the knowledge that one
leaves behind memories both serviceable and precious to the beloved
who remains?

If a strange destiny brought you so close to each other only to tear
you apart, at least, my friend, rejoice in the knowledge that you are
cherished by the tenderest heart that ever beat!

What tears I have seen poor Sophie shed as she pressed kisses on your letter and your portait ! Live on for her; it is possible that her youth will survive the injuries she has borne with so much courage, and you are beholden to her love as long as she remains alive.

She has charged me to ask you whether you have considered taking your affairs to America ? She is convinced that, despite the embargo against export but which cannot long endure, it is with the United States that you should deal. She would like you to make every effort in this direction; she is so convinced of the sagacity of this plan that she is troubled by every evasion she sees or imagines in the letter you have written on this subject.

She made every attempt to persuade her old uncle thus to employ a portion of his funds; but you know his obsession, and the idea that you were in some measure a competitor caused him to refuse. Moreover, he has become incapable of attending to any serious affairs, and as she is not in a position to take action, it would not be surprising if he lost his entire property, for he is abandoned to the most melancholy inertia. Show more wisdom, my friend; henceforth, never consider dealing with any save with good Republicans; men of that stamp are the only ones whom you can safely trust. Sophie awaits the news of your resolution concerning this; she considers it the sole means of restoring your fortunes and making it possible for you to unite again one day.

Farewell ! Never was man more loved by heart of woman ! Nothing is lost to you while you retain such a love; whatever may be in store for you, it is forever yours.

The wife of your partner [Mme Pétion ?] came to see Sophie; they are often together and your friend speaks most affectionately of you. She believes her husband is with you at this moment and begs you to give him the enclosed letter.

Josephine [?] is making a change, but surely you have not forgotten little Boufflers [118] and you may write to her on the behalf of your Sophie, for she is well acquainted with our old uncle, and I have nothing on which I can rely except my friendship with her. Farewell ! Oh, how you are loved !

We are approaching September, the anniversary of the massacres of the preceding year. Ninety-three was drawing to a close. The Terror was becoming fiercer and more powerful. In the gaols the prisoners trembled lest the bloodthirsty Septembrists celebrate the last year's butcheries by new crimes. Mme Roland no longer dared to write freely. Two or three times a week, ever since he had been hiding at Sainte-Radegonde, Bosc came regularly to Paris disguised as a market gardener, to bring the prisoner a sentimental nosegay of wild flowers picked for her in the Montmorency woods. But the day came when he could no longer pass, for a "spy had been stationed at the prison wicket."

Mme Roland, separated from everything she loved on earth, deprived of the sweets of friendship, delivered over to the barbarous whims of an anarchistic rabble, had still something precious to keep her company in her solitude. This was Buzot's portrait, that charming little picture which she carried next her heart. At times she reproached herself for the imprudence of this last indulgence and, as her situation grew more perilous each day, she put off till the morrow the bitterness of bidding it farewell. Fearing the risks to which it might be exposed after she was gone, she wrote a notice on a scrap of paper which she inserted into the case.

François Nicolas Léonard Buzot, born in Evreux in 1760, Deputy to the Constituent Assembly in 1789, President of the Communal Tribunal of the department of Eure, Deputy to the Convention, 1792.

Buzot will survive in the memory of honest people. His vigorous thoughts and wise sayings will be quoted, his two letters and commentaries on the sixth and twenty-second of January '93, will be read often. Posterity will honour his memory. His contemporaries will soon regret him, and a day will come when his portrait will be an object of value, and will take its place among those of the generous friends of Liberty who believed in virtue, who were [illegible] as the sole basis of their Republic and who [illegible] the strength to put it into practice.

Nature endowed him with a loving heart, a fine intelligence, and an upright character. His sensibility made him cherish peace and the sweet pleasures of a life of obscurity and private virtues. He was unhappy in love and this added to the melancholy to which he was already inclined. Circumstances forced him into a political career, and he brought to it all the fire of his impetuous courage and the austerity of his inflexible probity. Born to be a Roman at Rome's noblest hour, he hoped in vain to lay the foundations of such an age for a nation that seemed to be awakening to Liberty. Alas, the French are corrupted and unworthy of freedom, they have disowned Liberty's champions, and those they should have cherished and honoured have been outlawed by an assembly of cowards who are ruled by brigands. Declared traitor to the fatherland for which he had made every sacrifice, Buzot's house was razed to the ground and his property was confiscated, but the shame falls on the perpetrators of this crime and on those who passively witnessed it.

We must here take note of an unimportant incident which has already been touched on in a preliminary sketch of the heroine, because it shows singularly well the power of the race and the genius of the species.

The revolutionary prisoners — and each cell contained a tragedy — were not crushed by a uniform or permanent despair. Mme Roland told Buzot that when the worthy Fleury came to the Abbaye bathed in tears, she soon succeeded in making her laugh, and she was to do the same on the way to the guillotine with her companion in the cart, a youth so completely crushed that those who saw him took him to be an old man.

She had but two months to live — two months less six days. Too true a Frenchwoman not to resort at times to gaiety to help her endure her torments, she was asked by those fellow-prisoners whom she saw now and then to write, for the sake of amusement, to a certain M. Montané. He was the husband of a young and lively woman from Toulouse "who sobs and laughs as she awaits the time she will laugh again." This husband, president of the *Tribunal extraordinaire,* had played the Robespierristes false by inopportunely acquitting those he had been told to condemn, whereupon they had put him away in the Force, and, as a precautionary measure, his wife had been imprisoned at Sainte-Pélagie.

But to his other misfortunes this poor man added the pangs of jealousy. He had just learned that the noble Duke of Lauzun,[119] then General Biron, was at Sainte-Pélagie, and that he often wandered about the women's quarters. Lauzun's reputation as a lady-killer greatly disturbed this worthy magistrate. He was perpetually sending instructions to his sprightly wife, and these seemed so comic to the prisoners, that their gaiety still echoes in the jeering letter Mme Roland was asked to write him.

In contrast to this a new note was presently sounded.

Mme Roland was commissioned to tell Mme Pétion that her mother had, without the slightest pretext, been executed.

After the taking of the Bastille, Barras had said: "I was present at that great drama and I saw the victims of arbitrary rule come out of their cells, rescued at last from the cruel vengeance of the rack, the oubliettes, and the torture chamber." Mme Roland wrote a pendant to these words, replete with a bitterness for which she had dearly paid.

I never believed that a more terrible regime or corruption more hideous could exist; and, indeed, who could have imagined it? All the philosophers fell into the same error.

Mme Roland gave up her work to spend her time with Mme Pétion.

We had our meals together and she liked to spend the greater part of her days close to me. I do much less work but I am useful, and this affords me a satisfaction which tyrants do not understand.

She also wrote: "I know that B.[rissot] is to be sacrificed, but I think that the regulation prohibiting the accused to speak a single word in their defence is even more horrible than this."

Not only as an accused, but particularly as a sound theorician of revolutionary principle, did Mme Roland despise this measure. One perceives that she had considered the day when she might find herself before the revolutionary tribunal, and that she had taken pleasure in composing a speech which would put the judges out of countenance. But now she said: "As long as we were allowed to speak, I felt a certain inclination for the guillotine; now there is no choice, and to be tried there or murdered here is all the same." [120]

Toward the latter part of September, a new-comer entered the prisoner's life; this was *Jany*, who proved to be an admirable friend and who sustained her in her last days. His true name long remained unknown, and it is very probable that the intelligent and painstaking inductions of M. Perroud have finally brought it to light.

It was in order not to compromise him — as we can well believe — that Mme Roland called him "Jany." Former historians had taken it for granted that he was Champagneux or Bosc; it is most unlikely that he was Bosc; it could not have been Champagneux, for he was then imprisoned at the Force. M. Perroud thinks that the man in question was the geographer Mentelle,[121] a friend of Brissot. We know that Mentelle had asked Fouquier-Tinville permission to visit Mme Roland, but, though it had been refused, the

LUC-ANTOINE-DONIN DE ROSIERE-CHAMPAGNEUX

*From a contemporary portrait owned by Gen. Marillier, a
direct descendant of Mme Roland*

EDME MENTELLE

From a contemporary engraving

"estimable geographer" had nevertheless managed to see her several times. Was it to him she entrusted, together with her last papers, her farewell letters and her most cherished souvenirs? Indeed, there is good reason to believe so.

Whatever the case may be, we can but pay homage to the truly sublime friend who sustained Mme Roland during the severest of her trials. That he aroused her deepest gratitude is proved in six letters she wrote Jany in which she said that because of his friendship "life still held some sweetness for her."

She asked Jany to pay a daily visit to Mme Grandchamp, no doubt to get news of the unfortunate Girondists, at that time wandering and hunted men. Times were so perilous that she enjoined him to prevent "Pk" [Panckouke] from asking the authorization to visit her. "The only service one can render me," she said, "is not to mention my name to the authorities."

On the eighth of October, she wrote a farewell letter to her daughter, and on that same sordid paper which seems imbued with the wretchedness of prison, she penned a few heart-felt words of consolation to her servant, that humble friend who felt the suffering of her mistress even more keenly than her own. No doubt, before writing, she summoned all her fortitude, convinced that it was the first of a mother's duties to show no weakness before her child.

I know not, my little daughter, whether it will be possible for me to see you or write to you again. *Remember your mother*. The best I can say to you is contained in these few words. You have seen me happy in the fulfillment of my duty and in assisting those who suffer. This is the only way. You have seen me at peace in my misfortune and captivity because I had no remorse and because I possessed the joyous memories that good deeds leave behind them. There is no way but this to endure the misfortunes of life and the vicissitudes of fate.

Perhaps, and I hope so, you will not have to undergo trials similar to mine, but there will be others with which you will have none the less to contend. A severe and busy life is the greatest safeguard against every danger; necessity, as well as wisdom, makes it your duty to labour earnestly.

Be worthy of your parents: they leave you great examples to follow; if you can profit by them, your life will not be lived in vain.

Farewell, dearest child, you whom I have nourished at my breast and whose soul I would like to penetrate with all my sentiments. A day will come when you will understand the effort I am making at this moment to refrain from being moved to tears in contemplation of your sweet image.

I press you to my heart.

Farewell, my Eudora.

To my good Fleury

October eighth

My dear maid, you whose fidelity, whose good services and attachment have been precious to me for thirteen years, receive my embraces and my farewells.

Retain the memory of what I was. This will console you for what I now suffer; honest people go on to glory when they sink into the grave. My sorrows will soon be ended; let yours be assuaged and think of the peace that will be mine and that henceforth no-one will have the power to trouble it. Tell my Agathe that I bear away with me the sweetness of having been cherished since my childhood by her, and the regret of not being able to tell her of my love. I would have liked to help you, at least let me not make you miserable.

Adieu, my poor maid, adieu.

She wished that "the harp she plays" hired at Koliker, instrument maker, rue Fossés-Saint-Germain-des-Prés, should be bought for a hundred écus for Eudora. She wanted the child to go on with her music lessons and claim the piano her mother had paid for out of her own economies. Nor should Eudora neglect her drawing. She did not forget about the income settled on the old Besnards, and wished that their great niece be taken to them. The only jewels she ever owned, two small rings without value which came to her from her father, she left, one to Eudora's adoptive parents, the other to her dear Bosc. She said, in conclusion:

Farewell my child, my husband, my maid, my friends; farewell, sun whose brilliance brought serenity to my soul as it illumined the heavens; farewell, solitary countrysides which have so often moved me, and you, rustic denizens of Theizé who blessed my presence, whose sweating brows I dried, whose miseries I assuaged and whose illnesses I nursed, farewell; farewell, peaceful studies wherein I nourished my mind with truth, where my imagination was charmed by books and where, in the silence of meditation, I learned to govern my senses and hold vanity in contempt.

She invoked her friends:

All of you whom heaven in its kindness gave me as friends, watch and care for my orphan child. . . The hour which has been announced has come, when the people, asking for bread are fed with corpses.

On this same day, October eighth, Mme Roland wrote to the mysterious Jany to bid him farewell. "When you read this, dear Jany, I shall be no more." It was not that she had more reason for disquietude on this particular day, but on the third of October, following Amar's report, forty-two deputies, among whom were the *Twenty-two,* had been indicted, and Madame Roland, believing she would be implicated with the Girondists, felt she was lost.

After mature deliberation, she determined to perish of hunger.[122] Under the same cover she sent Jany those *Dernières Pensées,* that move us so deeply, together with her farewell letters to her daughter [123] and the good Fleury. Perhaps the last pages of the *Mémoires Particuliers* were also enclosed.

Here is the letter which expresses such sublime dignity, and, at the same time, contains such human regrets:

When you read this, dear Jany, I shall be no more. You will see the reasons that have determined me to cheat my gaolers and die of hunger. However, as no violence has inspired this resolve which I wish to consider from every angle, lest I fail in any of my obligations or merit the censure of our friends, I am willing to await the trial of the deputies and then weigh the consequences of my act as well as the moment of putting it into execution.

Should a few days pass before this happen, I shall continue my *Memoirs;* if I am unable to proceed far with them, I shall console myself. If all I have written — now deposited in three different places — is collected, it would be sufficient to throw light on many facts and would help in the justification of many people. This is the trust I bequeath you: it should be sufficient proof of my esteem. Do whatever you wish with these things, do nothing in haste so as to lose nothing, and do not part with anything without a double copy.

My *Dernières Pensées* are indispensable to the adoptive father and mother of my daughter; if the copy I have for them fails to reach them, you will send one to them.

Farewell, Jany, I love and honour you. I die in peace, knowing that you will make all I have made known of myself live again; there are but a few details lacking, and I would give them all had I more time, but none of them would contradict what I have written.

It was the fourteenth of October. The prisoner was ill. Perhaps she had already begun to execute her plan, and her gaolers were frightened by her weak condition. They had brought her a doctor. The following conversation took place:

When he learned my name, he said he was the friend of a man I do not like.

"How do you know? And who is he?"

"Robespierre."

"Robespierre! I knew him well and had a great esteem for him. I thought he was a sincere and ardent champion of Liberty."

"Is he this no longer?"

"I fear he likes power as well. . . I fear he is over fond of vengeance, and above all that he likes to wreak it upon those he thinks do not admire him. I believe that he is very susceptible to prejudice, and this makes him easily give way to passion, and that he thinks everyone guilty who does not share all his views."

"You have not seen him twice."

"I have seen him much more often! Ask him to hearken to his conscience, and you will see if he can then speak ill of me."

If Mme Roland was ill, her character was not affected and, the doctor gone, her thoughts kept returning to this man who "holds her in his clutches." For nearly five months now, all her activity had gone into her writing. Full of spirit, she wrote to Robespierre:

I do not write to entreat you, as you can well imagine. I have never entreated anyone, and it is not in prison that I would begin to do so to anyone who held me in his power.

With a moderation which was not due to cowardice, nor even to caution, so exaltedly did she write that one would imagine there was no longer any reason to be prudent.

I know, moreover, that at the birth of republics, revolutions that are well-nigh inevitable can easily be accounted for by human passion, often making those who have best served their country the victims of their own zeal and of the misinterpretations of their contemporaries. Their own conscience will console them and history will be their avenger.

She set forth her case without grandiloquence, admitting it was insignificant in itself.

What does it matter if the elephant crush beneath his foot one ant more or less, of what import is it to the world? But these [the problems she states] are extremely important in their relation to the present state of liberty and the future happiness of my country. . . Though I am in want of many things, I ask for nothing; I have borne with misfortune, proud of contending with it and trampling it beneath my feet. . .

And she concluded with these words:

Robespierre, it is not to move you to a pity that is beneath me, and which would perhaps offend me, that I paint this mitigated picture; it is for your instruction. . . If you wish to be just and if you reflect on my words, my letter will not be useless to you; and from that moment it will serve my country. Robespierre, there is one thing I know, and you cannot but be aware of it: no-one who has known me could persecute me without remorse.

But how can one argue with an automaton who relentlessly applies a system ? This she understood, and she wrote at the bottom of the page;

The moment my letter serves no purpose, it is out of place. I shall not send it.

Meanwhile France, once more in desperate straits, was working out her own salvation, and great Carnot was organizing the victory. In the writings we know, Mme Roland makes no mention of the great victory of Wattignies nor of the Queen's execution which took place on the same day: October 16, 1793.

But she was ill and she had been sent to the prison infirmary. Can we ascribe to her physical condition her depressed letter to Jany, "her only comforter." From it we learn that she had confided in him and that he knew her secret.

Your sweet letter, dear Jany, did me as much good as your pleasant conversation. Tender compassion is the only balm for an ailing heart. I know the delicacy which makes you detest the idea of ever publishing my secret; this delicate consideration would have prevented me from ever confessing it on paper, had it not already been divined and travestied. As to myself I care for naught but truth; I have never had the slightest temptation to be esteemed above my worth. . . I am not trying to excuse myself, but I am sure that poor R[oland]'s jealousy alone is responsible for my secret being known for he must have confided in many people.[124]

And yet nothing has come down to us to lead us to believe that the secret of "this heart-rending passion," to quote Sainte-Beuve, was ever divulged by her contemporaries.

Jany was acquainted with Buzot.

Yes, you have seen him, and you describe him well. You will find his portrait *painted* and also *written* in a certain box that will be given to you. This is my most cherished possession, and had I not feared it might be defiled, I could not have parted from it. Take good care of it so that you can give it back to him some day.

She clung to this idea.

And concerning this box which contains even more pages of manuscript than you have already, let me know when it can be brought you, that is when your hiding-place will be ready for it. Take every care to preserve it in every possible emergency, so that it will have someone to protect it, if some accident occur.

As for her, all is over.

My liberty will never be restored to me; if it were, I call heaven to witness that I would consecrate it to my unfortunate husband.

She thought Buzot was lost.

Should he ever reach the happy world where your son is farmer,[125] find out all you can, so that you may send him news of me. I know how great is that inclination to remain alive for the sake of him who loves one, *but I belong to others before him,* and I shall never have the opportunity of performing my duties, for all is at an end for me.

It is evident that were she in a position to make plans for the future she would have been the same, and that her loyalty to her child and husband would have taken the first place in her life.

Thus, the prison diet, anxiety, bodily ailments, despair — or rather all that made hope impossible — had not been able to impair the fortitude of her resolution. Her vitality was intact, it was the same woman who three months earlier had written Buzot of the delights of prison, for there alone could she be with him.

On the twenty-fourth of October Mme Roland was taken to the Conciergerie. She was to serve as witness in the trial of the Girondists. Twenty-one deputies had been brought before the Revolutionary Tribunal. They had heard Amar's report. Mme Roland was present. She was then taken to the room set aside for witnesses, where for hours she awaited her turn. Mentelle came there and talked to her. He slipped a note into her hand. Time passed. She was not called.

While she waited she addressed those present, freely, in her clear

voice, and with a vigour and eloquence that seem still to echo in
our ears.

Did the Commune wish the death of those Girondists who were
penned in at the Carmes in four or five attic rooms ? Apparently,
Mme Roland absolved Bazire. It was the Jacobins who were relentless and who had insisted upon the Revolutionary Tribunal. As
to the Hébertistes, they commented on the suffering of the fatherland in these sombre words: "The Girondists are still alive." And
Danton, sullen and wasted, took his ingénue with him and left
for Arcis-sur-Aube. It was the same as in September. When people were being murdered, he turned his back.

Garat had gone to him at the time when the Girondists were
about to be brought to judgment. The Titan had said he was ill.

> I went to Danton [said Garat] and I had not been two minutes
> with him when I saw that his illness consisted of a profound grief. . .
> "I shall not be able to save them," were the first words that left
> his lips and, as he spoke, all the vigour of that man who has been
> compared to an athlete seemed crushed; great tears rolled down that
> face which has been likened to a Tartar's.
> "Twenty times have I offered them peace," he cried. "They re-
> fused to believe me, so as to conserve the right of bringing me to
> ruin." [Garat's *Memoirs*.]

Robespierre, impelled by Saint-Just, considered himself master of
the situation. His principal assistants, Collot d'Herbois, Billaut-
Varennes, Couthon, kept their eyes fixed on the Twenty-two. The
Twenty-two, albeit, were not all there. Some had escaped, others
were dead. The fanatics insisted that this total be made up. But
despite all their efforts they had but twenty-one. There was practically nothing on their police records, and the men were so different that their enemies did not dare charge them all with the
same criminal offence. Fouquier-Tinville abandoned the idea of a
plot, while retaining in the accusation that they had entered into
a compact with La Fayette, Dumouriez, and Orléans. Hébert and
Chaumette were the names of the public prosecutors. No document
was shown to the accused. There were no counsels for the defence.
"It was immediately apparent that it was merely a question of mur-
dering them," Michelet has written. Those who tried to defend

themselves were interrupted. At the end of eight days the worried Jacobins lost their patience and sent deputies to the Convention with this proposition: "That the jury must declare itself resolved on the third day." Robespierre wrote the resolution himself.

Mme Roland wished to make manifest her solidarity with her friends. She said:

I wish to prove worthy of death by giving testimony in their behalf while they are still alive, and I am afraid of losing this opportunity. I await the call to speak as a spirit in torment awaits its liberator.

Adam Lux,[126] also cited as witness, was brought from the Force where he, as well as Champagneux, was imprisoned. The latter commissioned him to give a letter to Mme Roland if it were possible. She took it, read it, and surrounded by spies, two paces from the Revolutionary Tribunal, she had the audacity to reply to it.

Your letter, my dear Champagneux, was given me by Adam Lux, and this excellent man will hand you my reply; I write to you from one of the caves of death, and the pen I am holding will soon, perhaps, write the order for my murder.

I rejoiced that I had been called as witness in the trial of the deputies, but apparently I shall not be heard. The brutes dread the truths I have to tell as well as the energy I would put into my statements. They will find it easier to slaughter me without hearing what I have to say. You will never see Vergniaud nor Valazé again; you may in your heart have nursed some hope; yet how is it that your eyes have not been opened by all that has been happening? We shall all perish, my friend; if we did not, our oppressors would not feel themselves in safety. One of my greatest regrets is that I have exposed you to the risk of having to share our fate. We have torn you away from your retreat; you might still be there were it not for us, and your family would not be scattered and miserable. . . This distresses me more than my own misfortunes; but in the fine days of the revolution, it was not possible to foresee this cruel future. We have all been deceived, my dear Champagneux, or rather we perish as victims to the weakness of honest people [how well she understood her party !]; they thought it sufficient, in order to make virtue triumph, to draw a parallel between it and crime; the latter should have been relentlessly wiped out. . . Farewell. I am sending you what you ask.[127] I write to you almost under the eyes of my tormentors. I somewhat glory in defying them.

That day she would have liked to have had the poison she had asked of Bosc two or three days before.

I had firmly resolved to take advantage of this opportunity [of being before the tribunal] to attain my end more quickly. I wished to lash them to my heart's content, and then die; I considered myself entitled to say everything that was on my mind and thought I should have it [the poison] in my pocket when I went to court; I did not, however, wait for it to get myself in hand. During the hours I waited in the clerk's office, surrounded by officers, judges of the other section, etc. . . in the hearing of Hébert and Chabot who came into the adjoining room, I spoke with as much vigour as freedom. My turn to be heard did not come; then they were to come and fetch me on the second day; the third day is drawing to a close and no-one has appeared. I fear those clowns have suspected that I might create a scandal, and that it is better, after all, to do without me.

On the twenty-fifth of October, she turned again to Jany, her last friend. At the Palais de Justice, the day before, she had been "intensely annoyed" because she could not "converse with him as freely as she pleased." She had been afraid to compromise him. She was "alarmed" for those who were seen talking to her. A few minutes before she had hardly dared acknowledge the bow of someone she recognized. Two days later she addressed to Jany a note-book of rapid observations on Amar's indictment of the deputies: *the deputies who had plotted against the unity and indivisibility of the Republic, and against the Liberty and safety of the French people.* She had listened to it and heard it "very clearly with both ears." Her conscience was revolted to its very depths. Her adherence to the principles for which she was ready to die was on a plane above mere individuals.

Twice had Jany spoken to her of Lanthenas who, as far as we can tell, watched from his obscure corner the impressive agony of the woman who for twelve years had been his friend. What indignation the prisoner must have felt when this memory, which no doubt she did her best to set aside, penetrated into her thoughts like a subtle poison. With that good taste that never failed her, Mme Roland did not wish to humiliate Lanthenas too cruelly by her testimony. Nevertheless we read, in a letter to Jany:

I have refrained from writing about him [Lanthenas]; there is much I might have said, but Lanthenas has loved me so well that I cannot speak ill of him, and I have too much contempt for him to praise him. Well, Jany, I knew that man before the Revolution when he was immersed in earnest and interesting studies, gentle in his manners, human in his affections; he was with me two or three months on end in the country, helping me tend the sick of the neighbouring villages, nursing the poor, and enjoying simple pleasures with a heart that doubtless must have been so too.

Indeed these beginnings hardly presaged a disciple of Marat. It was fright — the "terror" — that influenced the members of the Convention.

In his *"Fragments to illustrate the History of the National Convention"* Dussault has drawn an unforgetable portrait of them:

Their visages were wasted by their arduous, nocturnal labours. The habit and the necessity of secrecy had set their mark upon their sombre faces. There was something sinister about their hollow blood-shot eyes. They had been so long in power that their demeanour and manners had a certain indefinable haughty and contemptuous air.

Besides, they were men wanting in genius and personality to whom had fallen a task which far exceeded their capabilities. Manuel, the Girondist, was not far wrong in exclaiming when the Republic was proclaimed: "Representatives of the people, to fulfil the mission entrusted to you, you need the might and wisdom of the gods." It was by each attempting to outdo his fellow, that they drove one another to the guillotine. They had to make every cowardly concession in order to save their lives, and presently Robespierre was to lose his own through a baseness to which even the courtiers of the ancient kings had never stooped. Only the most abject survived, fit for the domesticity of the Empire.

During this terrifying October, Mme Roland was shocked by the false news that the fugitive deputies had been arrested. Did she, in answer to the letter addressed "to Brittany," receive news from Buzot, or from one of his unfortunate companions ? We do not know. Did she know that they had not heeded her entreaties to embark for America, and that Guadet, whose father lived at Saint-Émilion, had persuaded them on the twentieth of September to set sail for Bec d'Ambez ? What we know for a fact is that, on the sixteenth of October, she read in the *Moniteur* a letter from representative Ysabeau [who had been sent to the Gironde country] in which he stated that the deputies who had been hiding in Calvados had gone to Bordeaux or its vicinity. At the same time she learned of Canon Dominique's arrest.[128] The seals had been affixed at *Le Clos* and at the Villefranche house,[129] and deputy Reverchon had been commissioned to go to Villefranche, where his first steps had been to reform the municipality in accordance with the Robespierrist methods.

About the twentieth of October, we know not why, Mme Roland's suicidal intentions had taken a new form. Perhaps her vigorous organism was revolted at the thought of a lingering death and she lost patience at the thought of the process of gradual decline she would have to endure. Appealing to Bosc, her oldest friend, she had asked for opium, "in order to make her departure immediately before the ceremony." To what test she had put this gentle friend who loved her, and so loyally! Heroically had he made every endeavour to prove himself worthy of her, and he believed in all sincerity that he had succeeded when he pronounced that it was her duty both to her cause and to herself to endure to the bitter end that martyrdom which would bring honour and glory to her party. We understand that he hoped against hope itself, and that Mme Roland was dearer to him than the judgment of posterity, dearer than the very cause itself or anything else on earth. After all, but a short time hence, on the ninth of Thermidor, were not many to be saved, at the very foot of the guillotine?

Here is Bosc's testimony:

During the whole of her imprisonment, until the middle of October 1793, I had, owing to the kind offices of the worthy Mme Bouchaud, wife of the porter, been able to visit Mme Roland two or three times a week; about that time, however, they stationed a spy in the prison wicket, and henceforth it became impossible for me to reach her. It was a few days after this complete confinement, that in a long letter that I concealed so well that I was quite unable to find it at the time her *Memoirs* were first printed, she asked me to send her opium in sufficient quantity to enable her to poison herself. I refused her request, and attempted to persuade her that the cause of Liberty and her own glory would both be served if she resolved to mount the scaffold. This letter caused me greater suffering than any I have ever written in my entire life. Hers of the twenty-sixth of November 1793, was in answer to it.

Mme Roland wrote:

Your letter, my good friend, has done me a great deal of good; it reveals all your soul and your affection which are both rare and precious to me.

She was then drawing the head of the virgin. Having finished it two days later, she wrote at the bottom of the sketch:

I know my friend Bosc will be very pleased to have this sorry picture drawn by the hand of courage and persecuted innocence. I give it to him for the sake of friendship.[130]

And then she again took up with the unfortunate Bosc the question of her suicide. She "takes her oath that it is not prompted by weakness." Bosc had misunderstood her. She did not wish to die then but at the opportune moment.

I flattered myself that I would thus cheat the tyrants of their prey. . . It is possible that profound grief and exaltation due to frightful emotions have, in the secret places of my heart, undermined a resolution which my mind has endowed with excellent motives.

And, a line further on, still bent on showing she was not at the mercy of nervous exhaustion or driven by despair, she wrote these words which have a certain buoyant quality and breathe forth joy:

I am in perfect health; my head is as sound and my spirits as fresh as ever.

Humanity in its iniquity did not give this splendid human being the time to lose her bloom. Twelve days after this letter her head was to fall beneath the knife.

Meanwhile Mme Roland besought Bosc to understand her. She would abide by his decision, but he must make it coldly and not let himself be swayed by his heart.

Keep in mind that your friendship will find the demands I make of it extremely painful, and might even deceive you as to your duty in this respect. Try and think about this affair as if neither you nor I were concerned in it, but as though we were two individuals in like situations awaiting your impartial verdict. Consider how decided I am, weigh my reasons, coldly reflect, and do not forget the small worth of the rabble who will gloat at the spectacle.

Because she was to abide by the decision of her faithful friend, he must scrupulously weigh every word he should write her.

Suddenly, in the middle of the letter, sounded a cry of grief: "My poor little girl — where is she ?"

And indeed Eudora was no longer with the Creuzé-Latouches. It had become too dangerous for them to shelter this unfortunate child. Bosc was of the same opinion, and had chosen for her a suitable boarding-school. The directress, Mme Godefroi, consented to admit the daughter of the former minister only if she came under an assumed name.

M. Barrière, in his edition of the *Memoirs,* wrote:

"Mme Roland was told this a few days before her death. Straightway this steadfast heart was troubled."

And then came the thirtieth of October.

When they heard their death sentence pronounced, the Girondists gave way to their despair; they cried and moaned aloud, with the exception of Vergniaud who uttered not a sound. Valazé [131] pierced his chest with a wretched table knife.

Honoré Riouffe,[132] "under suspicion," and imprisoned at the Conciergerie, saw the Girondists two days before their execution, and for a long time was crushed by this drama which has no parallel. The sight of Ducos leaving his cell pierced him to the heart.

The charming and interesting young man.

Vergniaud, Gensonné, Brissot, Ducos, Fonfrède, Valazé, Duchâtel and their colleagues were the guests I found installed in my new dwelling. . . Their trial was a violation of the most sacred law, for they were deprived of even the right of defending themselves. . . After his condemnation, Lasource quoted a saying of one of the ancients: "I am dying at a time when the people have lost their reason; your turn will come when the people have recovered it again. . ." These stalwart heroes, who represented practically all the talent of French oratory, were dragged into the arena. They were not allowed to make use of their gifts. Only once, with that mellifluous speech that stirred every soul, did Vergniaud release a spark of his genius. Every eye was wet with tears. . .

When they were condemned, we received the promised signal. Patriotic songs burst from every throat. . . They parodied the Marseillaise. All that terrible night their songs were heard. . . This was the first time that such a number of remarkable men were massacred in a body. . . Youth, beauty, genius, valour, talent — every noteworthy quality that men possess was destroyed at one fell swoop. . . Their courage had moved us to such exaltation that we felt this calamity only long after it had happened.

Tradition has it that an unknown friend sent them a final meal. Abbé Fauchet and Marquis de Sillery were the only ones to be confessed. There have been recorded many instances of the sublime friendship which united them. Liberty whom they had honoured and cherished seemed to have turned against her very defenders. However, they had not lost all hope in her. They were piled into five carts, all standing, except Valazé, whose corpse was beheaded like the bodies of the living. Before the scaffold, they sang the Marseillaise in a way that will never be forgotten. Each time the blade fell, one voice stopped singing, but the others continued. Vergniaud was the last to sing.

At the same time, Mme Roland left Sainte-Pélagie and was conducted to the Conciergerie, into a loathsome hole, close to the cell of the Queen, whence Vergniaud and Brissot had been just removed.

She knew her doom was sealed. Injunctions became so strict that she could no longer receive anyone. Mme Grandchamp relates how the excellent Mme Bouchaud contrived a last meeting between the two women, but only on condition that the friend of the great Girondist should make herself unrecognizable. She spent the entire night disguising herself, and arrived just when the gates were being opened. She said: "Mme Bouchaud made me slip into the linen-room, where she had had my unfortunate friend brought before daybreak. . . Her good health and the freshness of her complexion showed that her mind was at rest."

Mme Roland requested Mme Grandchamp to be present at her last moments, "in order to bear true witness of what happened." She had hardly finished her words when she covered her face with her hands and cried:

"Oh, this is terrible. My own request fills me with horror. Merely promise to see me pass. Your presence will take away some of the terror I feel when I think of that odious journey. . . You shall be proud of me. I shall not make you suffer." "So be it. Where do you want me to be ?" "At the end of the Pont-Neuf, near the first step, leaning against the parapet, dressed as you are today."
We conversed for three hours, but I have never been able to recol-

lect a single word we spoke. At last Mme Roland called the porteress and asked her to take me away.

For his part, Champagneux said:

She spent five months in her several prisons and, with the exception of two or three true friends whom these places did not terrify and who came to grieve with her, not upon her fate, but upon the misfortunes of France, there is not a single man who showed the slightest interest or compassion for her. Either in the papers or books of the time one does not read a single objection, a single word in her favour, all applauded her imprisonment and murder. . .

The *Moniteur* (No. 59, November 19, 1793) says:
In a short space of time the Revolutionary Tribunal has given women a great example which shall not be in vain. . . Marie-Antoinette, Olympe de Gouges. The Roland woman, a sort of note-paper philosopher, who was queen for an hour, and was surrounded by mercenary writers to whom she gave suppers and distributed favours, posts, and money, was a *Monster* from every standpoint.
That the *Père Duchesne* should vomit such loathsome slander would neither have surprised nor humiliated me, but should one have expected to read them in the *Moniteur*?

The following note [was it written to Bosc or Jany?] still bears the stamp of that dauntless character.

I think, my friend, that one must hide one's head, for verily, it is such a sorry spectacle that it is no hardship to quit this stage; I have been very poor in health, but the last catastrophes have restored my vigour, for they presage that there will be others to endure. Farewell, I continue living, only to detach myself from life.

On the eve of her death, ordered to appear next day before the Revolutionary Tribunal, she wrote to Mme Godefroi, a letter that may have been her last — in any case the last we know — to ask her to care for the "child from whom she had been wrenched." As in her other farewell letters, she wrote with moderation. Till the very last moment she wished to control the anguish which she never expressed, but which can be sensed in every word.

As soon as the Girondists had been executed, the Revolutionary Tribunal seized on Mme Roland.

In one of the cells of the Conciergerie, lying upon the sheetless bed that a prisoner had kindly lent her, she was questioned on the first of November and again on the third. She was continually interrupted, and told she "talked too much" if she answered. Her judges required her to confine her replies to yes or no.

On the night of her examination she drew up her defence, a proud address, which she wished to read before the tribunal. It terminated with these words:

. . . and it is for you to judge whether it is to your interest to condemn me on mere opinions, without evidence and without the jurisdiction of any law.

Immediately after the heart-rendering execution of the Girondists, Riouff saw Mme Roland. The sight of "this comely Frenchwoman whose scaffold was then in preparation" moved him to grief and admiration, and he has left us a valuable account of his impressions.

In that part of the Conciergerie where I had been placed, was the women's prison, separated from the men's by a grating. The men communicated with the women through this grating, and through the windows of two rooms which opened onto the court. There it was that I saw enter an innumerable crowd of victims of every age and description. The blood of the Twenty-two was still warm when citizen Roland arrived. Though well aware of the fate that awaited her, her peace of mind seemed in no way shaken. Though not in the prime of life, she was full of charm; she was tall and well shaped. Her countenance was extremely intellectual, but her sorrows and her long imprisonment had left traces of melancholy upon her face which detracted from its natural vivacity. This woman possessed the mind of a Republican, although her exterior bespoke a certain court refinement. In her large black eyes, so filled with sweetness and expression, there was something more than is usually seen in the eyes of a woman; she went often to the grating and spoke with the freedom and courage of a man. This Republican speech, issuing from the lips of a comely Frenchwoman whose scaffold was then in preparation, was one of those marvels of the Revolution to which we were not yet accustomed. We listened attentively to her, in a sort of stupour and admiration. Her conversation was grave without being cold; she expressed herself with such purity, such cadence and rhythm that her speech was like a sort of music which never palled on our ears. When she spoke of the deputies who had just perished, it was with respect but without effeminate pity and she reproached them even for not having taken stronger measures. When she mentioned them, she usually called them *our friends;* she often sent for Clavière to converse with him. Sometimes the woman in her came to the fore, and one saw that she had wept at the memory of her daughter and her husband. This blend of natural softness and of strength made her all the more interesting. The woman who served her said to me one day: "She musters all her strength before you all, but when she is in her room she sometimes remains three hours on end, leaning against the window, shedding tears."

Count Beugnot, who also saw her at the Conciergerie, wrote:

She lacked the beauty of regularity, but her face was pleasing. . . Her eyes were expressive, and even when in repose her face had something winning and noble.

On the eighth of November, Mme Roland was summoned.

It was the eighteenth of Brumaire, a Friday.

She untied the little packet I had seen her prepare [said Mme Grandchamp]. It contained what she called her death apparel. She carefully placed a linen scarf over her black hair, donned a white dress, and went into the Tribunal.

The Tribunal, which consisted of five judges, sat in a bare hall at a square table which had been draped as though for a banquet. Fouquier-Tinville sat on the left. The President and the Public Prosecutor were high and mighty people. Just as the Redskins, in order to fascinate their foes, wore bristling feathers and painted their faces, so these men wore hats extravagantly adorned with plumes.

Mme Roland rose from her seat. Behind her stood a tall soldier holding a naked sword. To the beplumed President who questioned her, and who was also standing, she made reply. The clerks were bending over their papers. Before the public stood a large detachment of pike-bearers. As to her counsel, the accused besought Chauveau-Lagarde, who was to plead for her, not to be present. It was said that she feared to compromise him. But he was already compromised. Was it not more probable that it did not befit the wife of Cato to have the Queen's counsel at her side? A certain Guillot, or Guyot, who had four months previously pleaded for Charlotte Corday, was officially designated to defend the victim of the day. Verily, she would not have needed him nor any other had she been allowed to speak. This was the one thing, however, that they did not wish to have occur.

This was to be expected. However, upon reading the records of this *trial,* it is almost impossible to believe that such scanty evidence could have sufficed to pronounce *legally* the suppression of a human life. The hypocrisy of Robespierre's government revolts us as much as does its brutality.

The judge had the floor. He accused Mme Roland of "having corresponded with conspirators despite the fact that she was in a house of arrest," and of "having held secret meetings of which she was the ruling spirit." Her letters to Lauze de Perret and several letters from Barbaroux were the counts of the indictment.

The Tribunal was aware of certain rumours reflecting on the honour of the prisoner, and would not have objected to receiving some information on this point.

Questioned as to whether among those denominated and formerly questioned by us, there were not some with whom she had had special and more intimate relations
[she], answered that Roland and she were since the Constituent Assembly closely connected with Brissot, Pétion, and Buzot.
The respondent being repeatedly asked whether particularly and apart from Roland, her husband, she had not had particular relations with any of the afore-denominated,
[she] replied that she had known them with Roland and through Roland, and, having known them, had for them the degree of esteem and attachment which each appeared to her to deserve.

The venemous testimony of Mlle Mignot must have bitterly wounded the noble-hearted woman who had let herself be so deceived.

The old spinster named a great number of deputies who came habitually "to the house." Brissot, Buzot, Gorsas, Gensonné, Louvet, more frequently than the others, had direct relations with Roland's wife whom they often visited in her study. She declared that they lived at rue de la Harpe in such incessant fright and terror, that they often had to sleep out, that this appeared "suspicious" to her, and that the day had come when "no longer able to endure this sort of life, she had decided to go away, about the twentieth of May."

On the other hand it seemed quite natural to Lecoq and Fleury to speak the truth.

A senseless denunciation had induced Fouquier-Tinville to call

MADAME ROLAND

*From an engraving by Lips from a sketch made by Bréa while she was
before the Revolutionary Tribunal*

the maid Fleury as witness against her mistress. It was his intention to compel the poor girl to say "that she was well aware that
Roland and his friends wished to rule over France and share the
provinces between them." Moreover, had she not been enjoined to
consider Roland's daughter as if she were the daughter of a
king ? [133]

Fouquier-Tinville's indictment had cited the letters in which Barbaroux besought Lauze de Perret to make every effort to see "that
estimable citizen" [Mme Roland] and bring her in her prison every
possible consolation, giving her the good news and best wishes of
the twenty-two proscripts . . . and to tell her that the twenty-two
proscripts . . . that all honest men shared her misfortunes. . .

According to the contents of the aforementioned letters [concluded
Fouquier-Tinville], it is impossible to doubt that the Roland woman,
aforementioned, was one of the principal agents and accomplices of
the conspiracy. The Public Prosecutor has drawn up the present indictment against Marie-Jeanne Phlipon . . . for having wickedly and
intentionally taken part in the conspiracy against the unity and indivisibility of the Republic, and against the security of the French
people; by, in private meetings, assembling the principal leaders of this
conspiracy, and maintaining with them correspondences intended to
encourage their liberticide projects.
    Signed: RENÉ FRANÇOIS DUMAS, ÉTIENNE FOUCAULT, ANTOINE
MARIE MAIRE, CLAUDE EMMANUEL DOBSEN, Judges.

At the foot of each page, Mme Roland was bidden to sign her
name. We notice that her hand trembled on the first two signa-
tures, but that she soon controlled herself and recovered her habitual
steadiness.

The order of execution [134] bore a special injunction. The words
very urgent, underlined, can be clearly read, as well as the particular instructions to "the General commanding the Army of Paris, at
the Town Hall":

Written this day and instant, calling his attention to the fact that
it is the wife of the ex-Minister and that it is to the interest of the
people that the execution take place today.
                                      Paris, eighteenth of Brumaire

Riouffe saw her leave the Tribunal. Here is further invaluable
testimony:

The day she went to the interrogatory, she passed me with her customary assurance: when she came back, her eyes were wet with tears. With such harshness had she been treated, even her honour questioned, that as she gave vent to her indignation she had been unable to hold back her tears. A mercenary pedant had coldly insulted this woman who was renowned for her intelligence and who, at the bar of the Convention, had silenced her enemies by the charm of her eloquence and had compelled their admiration. She remained eight days at the Conciergerie, and her sweetness endeared her to all the prisoners who sincerely mourned her.

On the day of her condemnation she was clad in white, her black dishevelled hair falling to her girdle. She would have softened the most ferocious hearts. This, however, was not her intention. She had chosen this dress as a symbol of the purity of her soul. There seemed to be some joy in the quickness of her step as she passed through the wicket after her condemnation. She indicated by a movement of her hand that she had been condemned to death. . . My heart that was to be torn by so many tortures in this horrible place, has never known more bitter pain than that caused by the death of this woman whose name will never perish. The memory of her assassination will in my soul unite with that of my unfortunate friends and shall be shrouded with inconsolable mourning till I breathe my last.

This execution marked *very urgent* was to be so indeed, for in justice to Robespierre it must be admitted that sentences were put into effect the same day. If the condemned woman was hurrying, as Riouffe said, it was no doubt because she was eager to regain her cell. She needed to muster all her strength to combat the protest of every natural instinct. She had settled everything that concerned her family and everything that was to safeguard her memory. Jany had taken her last manuscripts, as well as the little portrait from which she had derived such joy. She had also given him her own portrait, her husband's, and her watch.

How many hours then elapsed?

Which is one to credit — the order of execution which says half-past three, or general testimony which repeatedly puts the hour at five or half past? In November it is almost dark at four o'clock. No-one has spoken of torch-light executions. Was she alone, or was another prisoner keeping her company while she waited? Did a gaoler give her a moment of compassion, offer her the solace of company or of a human voice? Poor woman, how cold she must have been in her muslin dress. According to Mme Grandchamp

18 Brumaire

TRIBUNAL CRIMINEL

Révolutionnaire établi par la Loi du **10** mars 1793, l'an 2e. de la République.

———————

L'exécuteur des Jugemens criminels ne fera faute de se rendre *ce jourd'hui* ~~1793~~, à la Maison de Justice pour y mettre à exécution le jugement qui condamne *la ve Noë P^e Rolland & Lamarche*

à la peine de *mort*

———————

l'exécution aura lieu à *trois* heures ½ du *soir* sur la place de *la Révolution*

l'Accusateur public.

A. Q. Fouquier

Au Tribunal ce *18 Brumaire l'an 2e. de la Répub.*

THE ORDER FOR MADAME ROLAND'S EXECUTION

From the collection of Dr. Clerc

she took her last meal with the condemned man who was to die
with her, and she besought him to take nourishment while she
talked gaily with him "She suffered the approach of the executioner with great calm," says Champagneux. "Without a murmur
she let him cut her hair and tie her hands."

And now, the fatal moment so close upon her, she felt how futile
it had been to strive to picture the final scene. Now, she had to
die. She discovered that although she had long thought herself
prepared, she had not yet grasped the meaning of that word *death,*
a word she had so deeply pondered over since she had been in
prison in order that she would be ready to face it when the time
came. And now, how could she really comprehend, that before
night fell she would be dead, torn from every sensibility, hurled
into eternity, and presently lost forever in the infinite ?

A deist, she must certainly have refused the priest who doubtless
came to her. In the last lines of her *Memoirs* she wrote "take
me" to that "God of Justice." She needed no intermediary between
herself and him. She came to Him with her clear conscience and
feared neither the encounter nor the judgment.

"Her courage was as fresh as ever" when she heard the steps of
the gross men who were coming to take her to cut off her head.
She left the dark Conciergerie. The cart was already waiting in
the court. It contained a man so trembling and broken that everyone thought him an old man. And yet this other "enemy of the
people" was but thirty-four. His name was Lamarche, formerly
director of the assignat factory, "accused of having tried to defraud
and betray the interests of the Republic, and of having been guilty
of appropriating the *denier* of the Republic."

At the sight of this lamentable creature, Mme Roland regained
all her self-possession. She entered the cart and steadied herself
against the side and, standing very straight, she hastened to speak
to him and brought a smile to the face of this companion whom
chance had given her for the last half hour of her life. Amid
vociferations, the cart moved slowly behind the pike-bearers of the
Commune. Mme Grandchamp had already been waiting some
time at the corner of the Pont-Neuf — the appointed place. Sud-

denly cries broke forth from the populace: "It is she." "To the guillotine." "There she is." "There she is." On the other side of the river, the house of the Quai de l'Horloge was also faithful to the rendezvous. From the window of her study, the shade of the little Phlipon girl watched the passing of the victim of the day.

She was fresh, calm, and gay [says Sophie Grandchamp]; one could see she was attempting to infuse some energy into the poor wretch whose pallor and dejection formed a striking contrast to the high colour and confident bearing of his companion. She looked for me as she drew near the bridge, and I read in her eyes the pleasure she felt at seeing me at this final and unforgettable appointment. When she passed before me, a movement of her eyes accompanied by a smile told me that she was glad to have obtained what she desired; I controlled myself a few moments longer, but as soon as she was so far away that I could no longer see her nor be seen by her . . . my head spun . . . I know not how I reached my house.

Did not this glance and smile arouse in her a forlorn emotion and come perilously near to shaking the courage of this condemned woman? Fortunately the miserable Lamarche was there, claiming his share of his companion's strength. He served his purpose by diverting her from the cowardly insults, the cries for death, the spiteful grimaces and threatening fists around them. And even while she spoke to him she forced herself to stand erect, in spite of the jolts that shook the cart from side to side.

They passed before Robespierre's house. A little further the long rue Saint-Honoré terminated at the rue Royale, then called the Rue de la Révolution. She saw the pikes of the soldiers ahead of her bear to the left, turn, and almost immediately they were in the Place de la Révolution. Just at the entrance, Louis XVI's scaffold had been erected, and on this day the entire square was filled with armed troops.

The Place de la Concorde did not then offer the classical appearance it does today. On the side of the Orangerie was a sort of yard where the stones from the Bastille had been brought and piled up for the construction of the Pont de la Concorde. The balustrades which Gabriel had designed to break the monotony of this wide expanse protected the passersby from deep trenches. On the beau-

THE PONT NEUF

From a painting by Raguenet m 1760 [Musée Carnavalet]

tiful pedestals on which Louis-Philippe later caused his dull statues
to be erected, the great designer had placed superb ornamentations,
the style of which was in keeping with that of the other two
palaces.

In 1793 the statue of Louis XV [135] had been temporarily replaced
by David's decorative figures. Between these and the walls of the
Tuileries, which communicated with the square by a revolving
bridge, stood, guarded by soldiers, the guillotine. It had attracted
an entire populace of itinerants who well knew how to turn this
popular passion to account. These clever creatures had been quick
to meet the requirements of the rabid vociferating crowd, which,
more or less dense, more or less brutal, seethed on this square from
morn till night. Hand carts, wooden stools, straw chairs were hired
by the most eager for as much as six to twelve sous and occupied
the best places. On days when "great batches" were executed, they
were retained for the entire night. Sellers of lemonade, cake ven-
dors, peasants with their fruit stalls, peddlars with their trumpery,
offered their various wares and vied in their efforts to refresh the
"abused people" during the course of that torrid summer. There
was drinking, singing, jeering; loud yells greeted the appearance
of the cart when, surrounded by the soldiers of the Commune, it
emerged from the Rue de la Révolution.

The scaffold stood high, so that the people might see how its
enemies were dealt with by its vigilant rulers who, in the ardour
of their devotion, discovered new foes every day. Facing the scaffold was David's statute of *Liberty,* that murderous *Liberty* that
should have been smeared with gore to show her as she really was
and as he understood her — the goddess who demanded blood to
slake her thirst.

The day was dark and there was rain in the air. Night was
falling. The trees of the two gardens were but black slippery
skeletons of their summer selves. Dead leaves were blowing in
the bleak wind. Mme Roland raised her intrepid eyes to that
pitiless blade that waited in the November fog.

That day there was no great crowd about the guillotine. Champagneux' second son, Pierre-Léon, a fifteen-year-old boy who was to

marry Eudora Roland three years later, had run away from home
to look upon "that amazing woman" of whom his father and his
sister Adèle spoke with such enthusiasm. Later he was to tell Mme
Marillier, his granddaughter, his memories of that day:

As I saw her standing in the cart [he said], she appeared to me a
true aristocrat.[136]

When she alighted, the servants of the horrible machine laid
hands upon her. It was then that the young man heard her voice.
Its calm was unbelievable.

"Go first, Monsieur," she said to Lamarche. "The sight of my
blood would make you feel death twice. I wish to spare you the
grief of seeing my head fall." But the executioner protested, saying
that this was not the custom. He ventured, however, to say no
more when she said with an assurance that young Champagneux
was never to forget:

"I shall not find it difficult to wait."

Perhaps, in these last moments that remained to her, her thoughts
returned to those happy days of her youth when, on a fine summer
morning, the Odes of J.-B. Rousseau in her hand, she would go
down the Seine to Meudon, her father and mother by her side.
How radiantly the sun shone in those bygone days! Heavens
above! The vintages at *Le Clos* were not so far distant. Alas,
even the winter days had contained a certain charm. Had she not
written from *Le Clos,* in this selfsame month of November, but a
few years past:

Thus, before the fire, at eleven in the morning, after a peaceful
night and the various duties of the morning done, my husband at his
desk, my little girl knitting, and I, talking with one and directing
another, enjoying the warmth and happiness of being in the bosom
of my dear little family while the snow falls on so many unfortunate
beings who are crushed with grief and harassed by troubles, I pity
their lot and meditate quietly on my own.

As for her lot — this was its term, this its terrific climax. Injustice
lent it a philosophical beauty. That fatal stimulus which had
urged her on throughout her life was but to lead to this! Passionately had she consecrated herself to her vocation, but she was

compelled to admit — and with her this almost amounts to a denial: "we [women] are more useful to society by our virtues than by our intelligence." How cold it was! She shivered in that "garment of death" which was symbolic of "the purity of her soul." Why did they not cover her with the crimson mantle of the parricides in which, last July, Mlle de Corday d'Armont had appeared so beautiful to Danton and Camille who too had gone to the corner of the Pont-Neuf to see her pass.

Of a sudden her courage faltered. Anything but death. Only yesterday had she thought that she preferred the scaffold to a life wasted in the provinces. But now she was afraid. She was afraid for herself and her poor little girl. She was afraid for Buzot. She was already regretting the light of day, even the wan light of this desolate November. *A wretched life is far better than a noble death.*

Her mind turned to her beloved. She remembered that she had one day said to Buzot, that could she give her last breath to him alone, she would willingly sacrifice her life to Roland. It was with her love that she was about to perish. Death would be her liberator. This time it was Buzot who was coming to "abide with her," never to leave her again. The hour had come at last. Death would bring him the woman that life denied him. This is no doubt why it has been said that she mounted the scaffold triumphantly.

Once on the platform, it must have been with pity rather than with contempt that she looked upon the people, for she still had a thought for Liberty, for whose sake she had lived so passionately and for whom she was about to die. Turning toward the impassive statue which had already witnessed so many human sacrifices, she gazed on it without reproach, for she had lost none of her love for it; her only grief was that she left so noble a friend in such infamous hands. Like the very personification of Justice she addressed herself this time to "impartial posterity," as she had promised herself to do in prison, and she said with gravity:

"Liberty, what crimes are committed in thy name."

Then the executioners cast down that superb body. Her hands were tied, so that she could not modestly draw about her the folds of her white gown. A last thought winged toward the West, seeking a proscribed man — a thought arrested, cut short, by the descent of the suspended blade.

The official report of Mme Roland's execution, entered without fee on the register, says that it took place at five o'clock. Further one reads: Resolution of the tenth of March 1793, without appeal to the Court of Cassation. Re: Marie-Jeanne Phlipon Roland.

The bodies of the executed were taken from the Place de la Révolution to the cemetery of the Madeleine of the Ville-l'Evêque, a piece of ground Louis XVIII purchased in 1815 in order to erect the expiatory chapel.

We shall draw a veil over the nameless outrages to which the grave diggers submitted the bodies of the executed.

In the terraced garden of Percier and Fontaine's memorial, a central alley passes between two grassy banks fragrant with roses and bordered with ivy. Here, among other victims, lie Mme Roland and the Twenty-one. On the other side, beneath the arcades, are great stone sarcophagi consecrated to the Swiss who defended the Tuileries on the tenth of August 1792. At one end, to the right, lies Charlotte Corday. Facing her, is Philippe Égalité. Danton is also there — one knows not where.

In the middle of 1794, there being no more space in this cemetery, another burial ground had to be found. The guillotined were then interred at Monsseaux or Montceaux, in the Errancis cemetery, which extended beyond the park of the Comte d'Artois, in the place that today lies between the boulevard Malesherbes and the rue du Rocher, [formerly des Rochers]. It was there that Robespierre was buried when his turn came. It was said that on his grave a white rose bush was planted by an unknown hand and there bloomed for many a year.

Today, Robespierre and his accomplices lie in the catacombs.

EPILOGUE

A GREAT idealist, and one so richly endowed with vital qualities, does not suddenly cease to exist, even if decapitated.

An entire book could well be written upon the posthumous history of Mme Roland. We cannot conclude by abandoning to their fate — in more than one instance a tragic one — those who sentimentally depended upon her.

Referring to her condemnation, which she knew was inevitable, she had said:

"Roland will kill himself."

When the former minister reached Rouen, coming from Sainte-Radegonde, he had immediately gone to his old friends, the Malortie sisters. Always devoted to him, they did not hesitate to conceal him in their house, rue de l'Ours, where he remained almost five months. From this place he soon found a way of communicating with his wife who, from the twenty-second of June, knew that he was in safety. Till the very end, she continued to receive news from him — how, we know not — and from afar she exercized so great an influence upon the unfortunate outlaw, that she persuaded him to burn those "venomous writings" in which he had sought relief for his hatred by delivering Buzot over to the "execration of the public."

M. Auguste Breuil, the friend of the Cannets, was also well acquainted with the Malorties. He has bequeathed us a priceless document upon the silent drama of Roland's death. Mme Grandchamp has done the same.

"I know not how I reached my house," said Mme Grandchamp on her return from the Pont-Neuf . . . "Mentelle arrived. . ." They were grieving together when Bosc joined them. "I thought the violence of his sobs would prove fatal to him," said Mme Grand-champ. "He was the man who most sincerely regretted Mme Roland."

When he was somewhat calmed, Bosc wrote Roland that his wife had been *condemned* that morning. Roland received the letter on November tenth, the following day. M. Breuil wrote:

The Malorties had made every attempt to calm Roland's despair. When they were convinced that it was impossible to dissuade him from his resolution, they had the courage to deliberate with him upon the manner of taking his life.

Two methods of suicide were discussed. One, that he betake himself incognito to Paris, force his way into the Convention, and shock it into listening to truths that he considered of import to his country. He was then to demand to die on the scaffold, "where his wife had just been murdered." Upon reflection he came to the conclusion that this act would entail the confiscation of his property, and that his daughter would be left destitute.

Despite the bitterness of his rage, the wretched man decided to disappear in silence. His long, pointed nose protruding from beneath his wide-brimmed hat, he turned up the collar of his great-coat, and leaning on the sword-stick Bosc had given him with which to defend himself in case of need, he left the house in the rue de l'Ours at six in the evening and disappeared into the winter night. He crossed the town, took the Fleury-sur-Andelle road, and with no other companion than his thoughts, walked four leagues through the countryside. He stopped at Bourg-Baudouin. He then passed into the Avenue of Coquetot Chateau. It was there, having seated himself on the bank, and no doubt giving his last thoughts to his wife, that he pierced himself three times with the point of his sword, which broke and remained in the wound. It probably took him a long time to die.

His body was discovered on the morning of the eleventh of November. In his pocket was a paper he could well have left unsigned, so typically was it his in style. It bore witness to his patriotism and courage, as well as to the confusion of his ideas.

Whosoever you are who find me here, respect my remains; they are those of a man who died as he lived, in honesty and virtue. A day will come, and it is not far distant, when you will have a terrible judgment to give; await this day; you will then be able to act with a thorough knowledge of the matter and you will understand the reason for this injunction.

May my country come to abhor so many crimes and return to human and sociable sentiments.

J.-M. ROLAND

He turned the page over and, underlying them, he wrote the following words:

Not fear, but indignation.
I left my refuge at the moment I learned my wife was to be murdered and I no longer wish to remain in a land which is the prey of crimes.

Another paper was found in his pocket; it bore the address of citizen Aimée Malortie, an inexplicable imprudence, which led to the arrest of this devoted friend.

Two representatives from the Convention, Delacroix and Legendre,[1] the butcher, discovered Roland's body and, according to Champagneux, who heard this from a former priest present at the time, these two men addressed "infamous insults to the inanimate remains." By order of the two members of the Convention, Roland was finally interred, but without a coffin, at the corner of the Avenue and the high road to Paris.

THROUGH Mme Clarisse Bader, we learn that Eudora, then in Mme Godefroi's boarding-school under another name, overheard a visitor, on the evening of her mother's execution, relate the story of her death. Knowing that her grief would have betrayed Mme Godefroi, she had the courage to contain "her despair till the moment . . . she could break into heart-rending sobs." That day, indeed, might Mme Roland well have been proud of her daughter.

As soon as he had somewhat recovered from his grief, Bosc had no thought save for the sweet and charming child he had known since her infancy. He made himself her guardian, and as soon as public events permitted it, he took her to live with him. But he was without resources, not wishing to return to the Post Office lest he find there one of those people who had betrayed him and had him discharged in 1793. It was then he thought of publishing Mme Roland's *Memoirs,* under the title she had herself chosen: *Appel à l'impartiale postérité.* Louvet, who had become a bookseller, published the book, and Bosc conscientiously and ardently made numerous corrections. Twelve thousand copies were sold, bringing in more than ninety-eight thousand francs, but these were only assignats.

Bosc worked without respite to secure the little girl's heritage for her.

Citizen Marie-Thérèze Eudora Roland, daughter of the ex-Minister of the Interior, had reason to believe that the notoriety the Convention gave the death of her unfortunate father, 21st of Brumaire 1793, would prevent any consequences arising from the possible accusation of emigration. In spite of her claims, the furniture of the apartment Roland occupied in Paris has just been sold as the property of an emigrant, and steps are being taken to dispose of the remainder of the estate.

[signed] Bosc

He was mistaken. The furniture was not sold. In the presence of Bosc, January 7, 1795, Eudora was given the authorization to remove the effects intended for her, notably her mother's *fortepiano,* so that she might "pursue her studies."

The following July, the young girl, having regained possession of her parents' property, arrived at Villefranche with her guardian.

He kept Eudora's accounts with extreme care, and among notes of so much spent on veal broth and fine gloves, we learn of a *hat remodelled* for the sum of twenty-five francs. Concerned with her education in every respect, he objected to her taking her first communion.

In August 1795 things came to an unexpected pass: Bosc perceived that he had, little by little, fallen in love with this fourteen-year-old girl he had taken under his protection. He was then thirty-seven years of age. He immediately wrote to Mlle Aimée Malortie who came from Rouen to fetch the child and brought her to her home in the rue de l'Ours where she remained seven months. Ward and guardian were in constant correspondence. There came a day when poor Bosc thought he was loved in return, but he soon

MARIE-THERESE-EUDORA ROLAND

From a painting by Eléonore Godefroid, belonging to Mme Marion, now in the
Château de Rosière

discovered his mistake and asked La Révellière-Lepeaux[2] to send him to the United States as consul.

In the beginning of July 1796, he left for Bordeaux on foot, lacking the means to travel otherwise, after having entrusted Eudora to Creuzé-Latouche and Champagneux. No boat was sailing when he reached Bordeaux, so there he waited a month, and arrived in Charlestown in the middle of October. Once there he was bitterly disappointed that the Americans did not accord him the welcome he thought due a friend of Liberty and one of the founders of the Republic. Appointed vice-consul in Wilmington in July 1797, and, a year later, consul in New York, he decided to return to France. He had learned that Eudora had married Champagneux' second son, Pierre Léon, a lad of no more than eighteen. He arrived in Paris towards the end of 1798, but did not go to Paris before making a pilgrimage to Saint-Émilion, where his friends, the Girondists, had perished.

Next year, having been appointed Horticultural Inspector, he married his cousin Suzanne Bosc, who bore him six children. In 1801, when he had the misfortune to lose his first child, he bought from Bancal two *arpents* of the little property of Sainte-Radegonde, where one can see the tombs of his family today. He was buried there himself, July 20, 1828, after a long and painful illness.

Eudora survived him by thirty years. Married at fifteen years of age, the little girl with yellow curls had become a charming young woman who lived a quiet life undisturbed by intellectual interests. After the death of her daughter Malvina in 1832, she became so devout that she adopted a sort of religious uniform and lived in her family almost as though in a convent.

MME ROLAND knew that the fugitive deputies had set sail from Brittany. She hoped they would go to America, which was what she had advised Buzot to do. In leaving France, however, Buzot would have thought he was deserting her, and, to his misfortune, he heeded Guadet's advice.

The Committee of Public Safety had finally discovered that the Girondists were in the Finistère. In his memoirs Buzot wrote that he had seen a letter from Gohier, "commanding that the prisoners be delivered bound hand and foot." The Revolutionary Tribunal sent Héron, one of its most implacable representatives, to arrest them. They were forced to embark very suddenly, and there was no room for the women.

Guadet was under the illusion that he and his friends — Buzot, Barbaroux, Pétion, Louvet, Salles, Valady — would be in safety in his country. This he did not long believe. The outlaws had hardly landed at Bec d'Ambez when they learned that the guillotine was functioning under Tallien at Bordeaux. Even more dangerously menaced than in Brittany, they spent many long days concealed in the woods.

It was then that Mme Bouquey, Guadet's young sister-in-law, was told that the unfortunate proscripts were hiding in the vicinity of Saint-Émilion. She posted to this little town where she owned a house built over a number of vast caves, and having collected these tracked men, she managed to shelter and nourish them by incredible and valorous feats that bear witness to her ingenuity, devotion, and good humour.

But in Paris Tallien had been severely censured for allowing the Girondists to wander with impunity in the Bordelais. A day came when the odious Marc-Antoine Jullien, Robespierre's agent, more than suspected the presence of the deputies in the house of Mme Bouquey. He was like a hound on their trail. It was the thirteenth of November. After having held a final council, and unwilling to expose their protector to greater risks, they decided to separate into two groups, so as to attract less notice. Louvet, who could no longer live without his Lodoïska, declared he would return to Paris to find her, and, impossible as it seemed, he actually succeeded, and was the only one to be saved. Valady went off alone and was guillotined at Périgueux. Salles and Guadet managed to remain concealed several months in the house of Guadet's father at Saint-Émilion. Buzot, Barbaroux, and Pétion went at random through the countryside. They spent six months of wretched misery wandering about the Castillon country, hunted from thickets to quarries, from hovels to barns. When Buzot learned of Mme Roland's execution, his despair terrified his friends. He wrote a heart-rending letter to Jérôme Le Tellier: "She is no more, she is no more, my friend. The ruffians have murdered her. Tell me if there is anything left to live for ! When you hear of my death, burn her letters. I know not why I want you to keep a *portrait for you alone*. You were equally dear to both of us." But Le Tellier had been in prison since September. He killed himself there in January 1794. He must have had time, however, to destroy the compromising letters with which he had been entrusted. At any rate they have never been found.

An unknown person sheltered the fugitives for a short time at Saint-Émilion. The three unfortunate men again saw Mme Bouquey, to whom they confided their papers and most precious souvenirs, which she placed in a tin box. Then a barber called Troquart, who lived by himself, consented to hide them in his loft. He kept them till the day four hundred armed men made a sudden irruption into the little town. Jullien brought his blood hounds, famous for their ferocity, which in the presence of the terrified population he let loose in the vaults of Mme Bouquey's house.

Through the cracks in the walls, Buzot, Pétion, and Barbaroux saw their friends, as well as Mme Bouquey and hers, leave for Bordeaux in the cart of the commissaries. Salles and Guadet were immediately executed [June 18, 1794]. The following day it was the turn of Guadet's father, his aunt, Marie Guadet, and his brother, Saint-Brice Guadet; and then Mme Bouquey, wild with rage, and also old Dupeyrat, her father.

Troquart, the barber, refused to run any further risks and forced his boarders to leave. They departed at night, not knowing whither they were going. Before their departure, however, they scrawled their farewells to those who remained to them.

Buzot and Pétion wrote to their wives, Barbaroux to his mother. It is with great difficulty that we decipher a few words of these tragic letters.[3] Barbaroux' note, however, can be made out:

O my dear, good mother; I have no time to say more to you. I am trusting in God's Providence to find a refuge; despair not for my lot and, if you can, reward the good man who will give you this note or have it sent to you. Adieu, good mother. Your son kisses you.

A short time previously he had written some very beautiful words to his son:

O my son, if you escape from the calamities that are lacerating your country, hearken to me: do not avenge your father, avenge Liberty.

Buzot, Barbaroux, and Pétion left the town. In the Castillon plain they thought themselves surrounded. Barbaroux, who was hiding under a great oak, shot himself in the head. Pétion and Buzot, who lay concealed in the wheat, killed themselves at the same time. Barbaroux [4] was still breathing when he was discovered. The Bordeaux municipality had him removed "with great care." He was almost dead when he was guillotined. Dogs had devoured the faces of the other two corpses when they were found at harvest time.

At the moment of Mme Bouquey's arrest, she had told her little maid, Anne Bérard, to throw the tin box left by the Girondists into the "privies." It contained Pétion's, Buzot's and Barbaroux' memoirs; "a tragedy of Salles entitled *Satan cédant le fauteuil à Marat,* a poem of Barbaroux, and finally "Buzot's correspondence with a very intelligent woman and a diamond-studded picture of a woman." This was, it is believed, the miniature of Mme Roland which is conserved at the Archives, and the five letters we have already cited.

Young Anne Bérard was terrified into revealing the existence of the tin box which Jullien, anxious to display his zeal, found and sent to the Committee of Public Safety, to be given to Robespierre. History does not tell us whether the diamonds arrived. At any rate, there are none on the frame of the miniature, nor is there any visible sign of where they were.

If the contents were faithfully delivered to the dictator, we know not why the letters were not immediately identified by the portrait of a woman whom all the people of the Commune had seen and whose face and handwriting were equally well known to Robespierre.

NOTES

PART I

[1] In accordance with the custom of the times, the little girl had been boarded out with a nurse. She lived for two years in the house of a peasant woman at Arpajon.

[2] She was born in the rue de la Lanterne, in the Cité, the seventeenth of March 1754. The following day, she was christened at Sainte-Croix.

[3] The Cannets were a wealthy Amiens *bourgeois* family.

[4] The inventory of the apartment, a document discovered by M. Calemard, tells us that Mignonne, the nurse, was called Marie Renard, and that she was the widow of Pierre Montignon, a soldier. Her wages were 100 *livres* a year.

[5] The ancestors of the future Mme Roland came from the common people. About 1500, we find a wool comber from Château-Renault, in Touraine, then a series of wine merchants. Nothing but small artisans and shopkeepers.

[6] The Revolution was to call it the Jardin des Plantes.

[7] This correspondence lasted nearly fifteen years.

[8] Mercier, *Tableaux de Paris*.

[9] When, after an absence of seven years, M. de Sainte-Lette came back to France, he found that the daughter of his friend Phlipon had been married two weeks.

[10] This property never left the family and now belongs to General Marillier, a direct descendant of Mme Roland.

[11] Cousin-Despréaux, 1743–1818, a merchant and a man of letters. He had written a history of Greece in sixteen volumes to which Roland had contributed. He belonged to the Academies of Villefranche and Rouen. He was known as *Plato* in the literary society of "The Greeks."

[12] When he passed through Geneva, Roland went to see Voltaire at Ferney, bearing letters of introduction from M. de Cideville, a name well known to the readers of the *Correspondence*. Roland was received very cordially and was amazed by the fresh and vivacious mind this man still retained.

[13] They often corresponded in Italian. Roland had studied the language and urged his young friend to do the same.

[14] Phlipon, born in 1724, was one year younger than his wife, who was one and fifty when she died.

[15] These names were taken from Italian pastorals they had read together. In several of the letters addressed to Italy she signed herself "Amanda."

[16] Sévelinges, who was about sixty, had scarcely any means. At the time Mlle Phlipon considered marrying him, she had thought of learning the engraver's craft in order to supplement their funds.

[17] After the debts had been settled, there remained to be shared between father and daughter 17,034 *livres*, 15 *sols*, and 6 *deniers*. Included in this amount was the silver, priced at 1041 *livres*, and the furniture at 4011 *livres*.

[18] M. Perroud had the happy idea of collecting in a single volume the letters exchanged between Roland and Mlle Phlipon during this long and arduous engagement.

[19] It is probable that Phlipon did not believe in Roland's affection for his daughter

333

and asked her to show him Roland's letters so that he might be convinced. This she refused to do.

[20] The request to see Roland's letters.

[21] This church was transformed into a theatre by the Revolution. It has since then been destroyed.

[22] These were the notes Roland had compiled during his journey to Italy, augmented by others he had added on his return. Cousin-Despréaux had undertaken to correct and publish them, but took his time about it. The volume was finally published in Amsterdam in 1782. The sale was exceedingly small.

PART II

[1] In 1782 Sophie married the Chevalier de Gomiécourt, captain in the Grenadiers. Mme Roland acted as witness.
The following year, Henriette married M. de Vouglans, an elderly magistrate.

[2] Marie was Mme Roland's name, and Roland's mother was called Thérèse. The parents probably found the name Eudora in some romance they read together.

[3] Anent these circumstances, Mme Roland left her daughter a document which contained many precise instructions. It was entitled: "Advice to my daughter when she comes of age and if about to become a mother." She strongly urged Eudora to perform her maternal duties and nurse her child herself.

[4] This correspondence attained enormous proportions, and though many letters still remain, they form but a small fraction of the whole. MM. Pilastre, Bosc's descendants, have but a single letter from Mme Roland to Bosc which they bought at Charavay. It seems that Bosc's untidiness was proverbial.

[5] This, indeed, was the first public performance.

[6] Thérèse Lavasseur was quite illiterate. *La fâme de gangaque* was her spelling for *la femme de Jean-Jacques*. [Translator's Note.]

[7] Delolme, who came from Geneva, was the author of *Constitution d'Angleterre,* one of Mlle Phlipon's favorite books.

[8] At that time Lanthenas, who lacked the courage to leave his friends, considered establishing himself as a doctor at Villefranche.

[9] The inhabitants of Villefranche were called "Caladois."

[10] At that time the Rolands entertained André Michaux, the naturalist, who had been introduced to them by Bosc. He had just come from Persia, and was about to sail for the United States where he was to remain eleven years and found a garden of natural history at Charleston, South Carolina. It was with the idea of finding him again that Bosc went to America in 1796.

[11] Phlipon was over sixty when he died. According to his death certificate, he died in Paris, rue Fossé Saint-Jacques, on the twentieth of January 1789. His furniture was sold for 380 francs, while the old-clothes dealer gave 288 francs for his wardrobe. He was still doing a little work when he died, for Odiot, the celebrated engraver, presented a bill for 315 *livres.* After everything had been settled on May 15, 1791, there remained 14,349 *livres* and 17 *sous* for his heirs.

[12] Lanthenas had been working since 1785 on a treatise entitled: *Sur les Inconvénients du droit d'ainesse.* It was published only in 1789.

PART III

[1] He had finally received his doctor's degree at Reims, where the examiners were notoriously slack. The subject of his thesis was: "The remote causes of every illness, and frequently their direct causes as well, can be attributed to education." Instead of establishing himself, however, he continued to lead an idle life. He spent most of his time with the Rolands who for some reason pitied and loved "good sensitive Lanthenas." He resided with them at *Le Clos,* at their Lyons apartment, returning at times to Paris where he lived with Bosc.

² Rabaut Saint-Etienne, 1743–1793, future Aube deputy to the Convention.

³ This was Roland's great work.

⁴ Roland thought that English would some day become the universal language.

⁵ He died on the twenty-third of November 1789.

⁶ "A great number of pamphlets," said Brissot, "have appeared since the Revolution. But while they shed much light upon the questions which were to be discussed, they could be read only by a limited number of individuals. . . I thought of a less expensive and more expedient way of instructing all my fellow citizens, and with this end in view I started a paper called the *Patriote Français*. This was the one means of educating a populous nation which wished to rid itself of slavery and ignorance." The first number appeared July 28, 1789, with the following notice: "A liberal gazette is an outpost sentinel perpetually on guard for the people."

The principal papers of the time were:

Mirabeau's *Le Courrier de Provence;* Gorsas' *Le Courrier de Versailles;* Barère's *Le Point du Jour;* Marat's *L'Ami du Peuple;* Les *Annales Patriotiques* edited by Carra and Mercier; Camille Desmoulins' *Le Courrier de Brabant;* Fréron's *l'Orateur du Peuple,* and lastly, a Royalist sheet entitled *l'Ami du Roi.*

⁷ From Roland's letter to the King, composed by his wife when he was Minister of the Interior, June 10, 1792.

⁸ It was Bancal who first had the idea of secularizing education. His project for a law to that effect dates from the twenty-fourth of December 1792, and was couched in accordance with Mme Roland's ideas.

⁹ Bancal paid 8150 *livres* for Sainte-Radegonde but never lived there, although Bosc made long sojourns and there concealed many Girondists (notably Roland) in 1793.

¹⁰ At that time," said Brissot in his memoirs, "women of quality were enthusiastic about Saint-John de Crèvecœur's *Letters of an American Farmer.* I shared their enthusiasm and was eager to meet the author. . . He was lodged very simply in the home of the Countess d'Houtetot, the mistress of Saint-Lambert, whom Rousseau's *Confessions* was to make so famous. It will be recalled that he fell violently in love with her when he was fifty years of age, and that she was the inspiration of Julie. I saw this lady in 1787. She was old, ugly, witty, but full of pretentions. . . She had all the prejudices of her cast and, proud of possessing an American savage, she wished to tame him and bring him out in society. He had the intelligence to refuse, and confined himself to several groups of men of letters who gathered at her house. When Crèvecœur saw these men of worldwide reputation, he could scarcely be restrained from falling on his knees before them. But how his admiration faded into thin air when he heard how viciously they reviled and disparaged one another."

¹¹ Mme Roland's letter was addressed to M. Henri Bancal, but she signed herself Phlipon Delaplatière. He had called himself M. des Issarts when he had come to see her, and she could not quite reconcile herself to being simply Mme Roland. She knew, however, that to sign de la Platière in three words would compromise her republican principles. Thus she solved the difficulty by writing it Delaplatière.

¹² The first number appeared on the first of September 1789. Champagneux continued to edit it after the Rolands' departure, and it soon acquired considerable importance. The Rolands were frequent contributors.

Donin de Rosière-Champagneux (1744–1807), lawyer, landowner, settled in Bourgoin, where he entertained Rousseau in 1768, and acted as witness to his marriage to Thérèse Levasseur. Having himself married a young woman from Lyons, he came to that city in 1785, where he met the Rolands and became one of their most devoted friends.

¹³ Brissot's biographer and editor.

¹⁴ Pétion de Villeneuve, deputed to the States-General by the Eure et Loir, and a Member of the Convention. He appeared for the first time in Mme Roland's correspondence at the end of 1790.

[15] Mme Roland's friends blamed Bancal for remaining in England. She herself wrote: "I know not what good you are doing in England, but had you been here and willing to help me, I think you would have been more useful."

[16] Viscount Louis de Noailles (1756–1804), son of the Marshal, had fought in the American War of Independence. He had given his adherence to the Revolution, and on the night of the fourth of August he proposed the abolition of feudal rights.

[17] It was a certain Sieur Bouquey—a name to keep in mind—whom Roland had appointed steward at Saint-Cloud, who lodged Brissot in an attic. He was the brother-in-law of Guadet.

[18] Part of this letter to Brissot was published in the *Patriote Français*.

[19] On returning from London, Bancal went to Auvergne. Thanks to his singular persistency in refusing to live in Paris where his ideas and principles should have drawn him, we have his important and beautiful correspondence with Mme Roland.

[20] Malouet (1740–1814), elected to the States-General by the bailiwick of Riom. Like Mirabeau, he wanted to combine monarchy and liberty.

[21] Duport (1759–1798), member of the Constituent Assembly. A liberal monarchist, he was sought for after the uprising of the tenth of August, but managed to escape to Switzerland where he died.

[22] Tallien was to say at the Jacobins on the eighth of October 1792, that Buzot had been a Republican at a time when it was dangerous to mention the word Republic. And Buzot himself said at the Convention a few days later: "I was not present to take my oath when you declared the Republic, but when the very thought made everyone tremble in 1791, I was on the spot and voted for it."

On the third of July 1791, at the Jacobin Club, of Clermont-Ferrand, Bancal moved that the monarchy should be overthrown and the Republic established. His motion was received with great enthusiasm.

[23] This was the first mention Mme Roland made of Danton. She still spelled his name D'Anton.

[24] Anent the Revolutionists' mania for the heroes and ideas of antiquity: Léonard Bourdon had founded a school based on the Institutions of Lycurgus, and when the Constitution of '93 was being drawn up, Hérault de Seychelles had thought it amusing to send the legislators a collection of the Laws of King Minos.

[25] The story of the return from Varennes should be read in Pétion's memoirs. He had been sent by the Assembly with Barnave to bring back the fugitives. It is known that the Queen made the conquest of Barnave during the journey. And it would not have surprised Pétion had he been favoured by a royal princess. As he represented the National Assembly he sat inside the carriage, Marie-Antoinette on his left, and Mme Elizabeth facing him. "I may have been in error," he said, "for it is very easy to mistake the sensibility of grief for the sensibility of pleasure, still I do believe that had we been by ourselves, and if, as though by enchantment, everyone else had disappeared, she [Mme Elizabeth] would have fallen into my arms and abandoned herself to the impulses of nature, etc."

[26] Mme Roland reveals the fact that a great many of the speeches to be made in the provinces demanding a republican form of government, had been composed at her house. She had inspired the address Bancal wrote on the behalf of the Puy-de-Dome. The gist of his declaration to the Assembly was that France was quite prepared to dispense with it and manage her affairs herself.

[27] At this time there was nothing more than a friendly feeling between Mme Roland and Buzot. In her own words: "I had singled him out because of the excellent advice he gave as well as for that decisiveness which is invariably the stamp of a just man. He lived fairly close to us; his wife, although not his equal, was an honest woman, and we saw each other frequently." Buzot was then thirty-five, married to a cousin who was lacking in looks, intelligence, and who was, moreover, thirteen years his elder. It was Pétion, most likely, who brought Buzot to the Rolands.

[28] He never forgave Mme Roland for refusing him the post of Ambassador to Constantinople.

[29] Among the papers bequeathed to the *Bibliothèque Nationale* by M. Faugère's widow, are a few pages of memoirs that relate to Mme Roland. M. Faugère acquired these from Baron Girardot. They bear no signature, but the quality of the paper, the handwriting, and a number of other details, have caused M. Perroud to attribute them to Mme Sophie Grandchamp. With every reservation as to the authenticity of this document, we shall in quoting it refer to it as *Les Souvenirs de Mme Grandchamp*. M. Perroud published extensive fragments of these memoirs in M. Aulard's *Revue de la Révolution Française,* and inserted it *in toto* in his edition of Mme Roland's *Memoirs*. The *Morisson* collection in England possesses one of Mme Grandchamp's letters. It would be interesting to compare the handwriting of it with the pages in the *Bibliothèque Nationale*.

[30] Bancal was not elected.

[31] *Souvenirs de Mme Grandchamp.*

[32] All these details are supplied by Mme Sophie Grandchamp.

[33] The landlord, a *bourgeois* named Cauchois, belonged to the Jacobin Club and was to prove faithful to the Rolands to the very end.

[34] The Legislative Assembly lasted until the twentieth of September 1792.

[35] Condorcet never spoke from the tribune and very seldom indulged in conversation. He was called "the mad sheep." There was no love lost between him and the Rolands: they had had some difficulty with him regarding one of Roland's publications in 1781; and later in '93, he wrote a very malicious letter about Mme Roland which was published in the *Chronique de Paris.*

[36] Camille Desmoulins' pamphlet, which caused the ruin of the Girondists, was entitled: *Histoire des Brissotins.* (May 1793.)

[37] On the ninth of March the King replaced Narbonne, Minister of War, by the Marquis de Grave, and the following day the Assembly retaliated by impeaching the Minister for Foreign Affairs. Cahier handed in his resignation at the same time, and his example was followed the next day by Bertrand de Molleville, Minister of the Navy. On the fifteenth, the King called Dumouriez to the Foreign Office.

[38] Dumouriez was a native of Provence. A Huzzar at twenty, he had taken part in numerous wars. He was a typical courtier. In 1792, he was fifty-six years of age.

[39] Since December 1791, Brissot had exercised great authority at the Jacobin Club. At the time he proposed Roland for the Ministry of the Interior, he suggested Clavière for Finance. After Roland had brought about Servan's appointment as Minister of War, Brissot had three friends in the Cabinet. He supported them with all the strength of his position. After the tenth of August, his power seemed supreme.

[40] Clavière, a Genevan banker, had been exiled from his country because of his advanced ideas. When he came to France, he offered his services to the revolutionary party. Upon proposing to the Constituent Assembly his scheme for printing assignats, he found his chief enemy was the American Minister, Morris, who was on excellent terms with the Court. This was the same Morris who had deplored that there had been *so little firing* at the Champ-de-Mars. Clavière stressed the hard conditions France had suffered when she borrowed in order to lend money to the United States. In '92, when France, in her last extremities, requested a partial repayment of this loan, Morris refused his signature.

[41] Roland had charge as well of the Department of Justice, until April thirteenth when the Girondist Duronthon was appointed.

[42] Étienne Dumont, a Genevan, had come to France from England at the time of Necker's return. He had sought to have annulled the guarantee treaty between France and Switzerland. Having worked with Mirabeau, he had known the most important members of the Constituent Assembly. During the Revolution, he looked on as a mere spectator.

43 Bosc, touchy as usual, was convinced that the Rolands had little use for him since they had been called to their high position. During Roland's first ministry, he continued to resist Mme Roland's appeals and refused her invitations. [Translator's Note.]

44 Née Marquise de Grouchy. She was twenty-one when she married Condorcet who was twenty-two years her senior.

45 In like manner he had, at the Constituent Assembly, always been in opposition to violent measures. He stood out for peace in '92, as he had opposed the death penalty and martial law in '91.

46 This letter, which M. Perroud has not included in the correspondence, and of which we found a copy in the archives, does not begin with these words and, as we shall see, makes no mention of secrecy. It has been impossible to discover the origin of É. Dumont's assertion, but it is quite true that Mme Roland urged her husband to send the famous letter to the Assembly.

47 One of the leaders of the Revolution at Marseilles, elected as deputy to the Convention.

48 Joseph Servan de Gerbey (1741–1808). He handed in his resignation as minister on the third of October 1792, and was appointed Divisional-General in the Pyrenées-Orientales. Disgraced after the arrest of the Girondists, he was discharged May '93, arrested, and imprisoned in the Abbaye. He was released in 1795 and given a subaltern appointment by Bonaparte.

49 Year IV meant the fourth year of Liberty, and dated from the taking of the Bastille. After the proclamation of the Republic, the years started on the twenty-first of September 1792.

50 Marquis de Grave.

51 Referring to Louis XVI's diary, Arthur Young has called it a huntsman's diary. If we look to it for the true thoughts of the King on the fifth of October 1789, we find: "October 5. Went shooting at the Porte de Chatillon. Killed eighty-one head. Interrupted by public events."

52 The metaphor was Buzot's.

53 The King was entitled to hunt over any part of the territory.

54 This cap was the head-dress of the French peasant, dyed red by the Revolutionists who wore it as the symbol of equality.

55 Bonaparte, who was walking with Bourienne along the quays that morning, saw the rioters from the Faubourg pass by. Tradition has it that he said disdainfully that a few hundred soldiers could have managed them with the utmost ease.

56 Brissot in his memoirs, wishing to indicate how monarchy was then discredited, quoted a list of the "scale of beings" as drawn up by an English Republican: "God, angel, tyranicide, philanthropist, honest man, labourer, citizen, idler, devotee, priest, monk, saint, martyr, soldier, hero, noble, king, pope, devil."

57 Barbaroux' memoirs.

58 David, who has been called "the restorer of the art of painting," was at the Force, drawing from nature scenes of the September massacres. When Reboul, a deputy, reproached him, he answered: "I am recording the last manifestations of nature in these scoundrels." In April 1794, he posted himself at the Café de la Régence, to await the cart that was taking his friends Danton and Camille Desmoulins to the scaffold. "It was there," according to Courtois, "that he indecently caricatured those pain-distorted faces." No-one has ever known what became of these drawings.

59 This massacre assumed such terrible proportions that it was long believed that the prisons had been attacked by a great mob of furious people. Danton said nothing could have stopped them. Today we have reason to believe that the assassins were fewer than a hundred.

60 We are astonished by this term—the Empire. It appears frequently in the writings of the time.

61 The positions of deputy and minister could not be filled by the same person at the same time.

NOTES

339

62 On the third of the following October, Servan, who had resigned, was succeeded by Pache at the War Ministry. It was immediately invaded by the Jacobins. Pache managed to get out of the Terror prisons. His troubles, however, were not over. A new Gironde, come back into power, saw in him one of the men of May thirty-first.

63 *Memoirs*. Pages 271–272. Dauban edition.

64 Mme Roland never wrote her views on the death penalty. It was probably most repugnant to her, but as her friends judged it necessary, she must have decided that her personal feelings were due to lack of courage and that it behooved her as a citizen to have more virile views.

65 Mme Chinard had appealed to Mme Roland on the twenty-fifth of October. Roland wrote to Lebrun, minister of Foreign Affairs, demanding that he take immediate action. Lebrun must have acted quickly, for Chinard and Rater had already recovered their freedom when Mme Roland's letter reached Rome.

66 At that time it was considered fine writing to say: "inertia has arms" and "intestine quarrels give forth a glow which serves as a beacon to the enemies of the fatherland."

67 All of this was to be denied by Louis XVI.

68 Mme Roland said nothing of the sort. She agreed that her husband had acted imprudently, but "like an honorable man."

69 Dumouriez had placed the young Duke of Chartres (later on Louis-Philippe) in the first lines. In the armies he acquired a lasting popularity.

70 Lanthenas had been elected deputy to the Convention by the department of Rhône-et-Loire.

71 There is an eleventh letter, referring, apparently, to another period.

72 As we have already said, these letters bear no date. We have attempted to classify them in accordance with the development of the sentiments therein expressed.

73 In this and the letters that follow, the italics are the author's.

74 Lanthenas, who was inclining more and more to the left, was saved by Marat who justified himself for this compassionate act by declaring that Lanthenas was nothing but a "weak-minded man."

75 The famous Capuchin monk, beheaded in 1794.

76 General Servan was no longer Minister of War. Attacked by Dumouriez, he had resigned on the third of October. He was replaced by Pache, who was discharged on January 2, 1793, and was a short time later indemnified by the people of Paris who made him Mayor.

77 This letter was published for the first time by Mme Louise Colet in her book entitled: *Charlotte Corday and Madame Roland*.

78 Treachery had penetrated even into her *salon*. A conversation in which Buzot praised Switzerland, the United States, and ancient Greece, was denounced by Anacharsis Cloots as a conspiracy to detach the departments from Paris and federalize France. Cloots, a wealthy Prussian baron, became a Jacobin and a Cordelier, and was guillotined by the Hébertists on the twenty-fourth of March, 1794.

79 The perfidious Mlle Mignot.

80 Eudora would then be twenty.

81 After the ninth of Thermidor, Brissot's wife and children, whom he had entrusted to the nation, were voted pensions. One of his sons refused his oath of allegiance to the Emperor. The third son, who had been made penniless through disastrous enterprises, was saved by some old friends of Brissot who opened a subscription in his behalf, and by a noble Royalist out of gratitude to Brissot's speech in defence of the King. [*Introduction to the Memoirs of Brissot by M. de Lescure.*]

82 Vadier said on the day of the trial: "In casting my vote for death, I am but a passive applier of the law." Many of those who voted for the death of the King, took great satisfaction in evidencing their delight. Tradition has it that a certain deputy from Gascony pasted likenesses of the King and Queen to

one of his doors in such a way that they were beheaded in effigy each time anyone entered the room. [Albert Tournier, *The President of the Committee of
Public Safety during the Terror*.]

83 She reproached him with idleness, however.

84 Bosc never consented to see Lanthenas again. When Bosc published Mme
Roland's *Memoirs* in '95, Lanthenas seemed greatly surprised and wounded,
although Bosc had deleted several passages which concerned him. After the arrest
of the Girondists, Lanthenas drifted with events. He went to the country in
1794 and was not seen in Paris again before the ninth of Thermidor. He was
appointed a member of the Council of the Five Hundred where he again found
Bancal.

On the thirtieth of March 1793, Bancal had been sent with three other commissioners to the armies of Beurnonville, Minister of War, to demand Dumouriez'
submission. The latter, however, delivered them over to the Austrians. They
remained twenty months in the dungeon of Olmütz, and were then exchanged
for Louis XVI's daughter and were able to return to France in 1795.

While in prison, Bancal turned again to religion, at the same time remaining
a disciple of Rousseau and a good Republican. At the age of fifty-three he married a notary's daughter who bore him six children. He died in Paris in 1826.

As for Lanthenas, poor, alone and ill, he died in Paris on the second of January
1799, at the age of forty-five.

85 We have no indication of Buzot's attitude towards the Rolands at this period.

86 His great friend Robespierre mourned with him and wrote him the following
letter:

February 15, Year II

My dear Danton,

If in the throes of a grief which alone could agitate a mind such as yours,
the assurance that you have a tender and devoted friend can afford you any consolation, know that it be true. I feel for you in this moment, as though it were
myself who was bereaved. Do not close your heart to the voice of a friend who
suffers all your pain. Let us mourn our friends together and make those tyrants
who are the authors of public misfortune and of private woe, soon feel the effects
of our profound grief. My friend, I had already addressed the sentiments of my
heart to Belgium. I would have been ere now at your side, had I not respected
the first moments of your justifiable sorrow.

Embrace your friend

ROBESPIERRE

There is no document apprizing us of Robespierre's private attitude to the
Rolands. At any rate, there was never any pretense of affection between them.

87 Brissot obtained from the provisional Executive Council a pension for Roland
of 3000 *livres*.

88 On the eighth of May Robespierre moved at the Jacobins that those *under
suspicion* should be arrested.

89 Bosc had been arrested at his home in the rue des Prouvaires on the morning
of the thirty-first of May. Released a short time later, he concerned himself with
the fate of his friends, disregarding his own safety.

90 The apartment remained uninhabited and under seal from the day of the
arrest, the first of June 1793, until the twenty-first of January 1795, the day when
Bosc went with Eudora to Commissary Richebraque and obtained the authorization
for Eudora to resume possession of her rightful property.

91 Champagneux was arrested and imprisoned in August '93. During his second
ministry, Roland made him the director of his most important department. He
performed his duties so efficiently that Garat, Roland's successor, was loath to let
him go. Champagneux wrote seven hundred letters a month, according to Garat.

It was his relations with the Girondists and in particular with Mme Roland,
whom he visited in prison, which caused the Committee of Public Safety to suspect Champagneux. He was arrested when a letter from Barbaroux, then in flight,

was discovered at Lauze de Perret's. This letter contained news of the fugitives for Mme Roland's benefit and indicated Champagneux as a person able to assist her. Before being taken to the Force, Champagneux had time to destroy certain manuscripts Mme Roland had confided to him. He was saved by the ninth of Thermidor. He died at his own home in 1807, after having rejected the advances of Portalis, who had been charged by the imperial regime to sound out his views.

[92] "Every accused person must be questioned within twenty-four hours following his arrest." (Constitution of 1791, Chapter V, Article II, Law of the 16–29 September 1791.)

[93] Lauze de Perret (1747–1793) deputed by the Bouches-du-Rhône to the Legislative Assembly and the Convention. In July, Barbaroux sent Charlotte Corday to him from Caen. While Lauze de Perret was conducting her to the Ministry of the Interior, the seals were affixed at his house and the correspondence with Barbaroux seized. It contained some letters from Mme Roland which were produced at her trial and served as further pretext for her condemnation. Arrested after Marat's death, Lauze de Perret perished on the scaffold amid the twenty-one Girondists.

[94] The Girondists were too individualistic to constitute a group. Meilhan said: "We were so little disposed to form a party that the mere thought of taking concerted action was repugnant to us."

[95] Nothing could have been more false than this accusation. Brissot was lodged with his family in a garret in the Château de Saint-Cloud. The Girondists were poor men. It was said that most of the time Vergniaud had not sufficient to pay his laundress.

[96] Barère de Vieuxzac, surnamed the Anacreon of the guillotine.

[97] "Hanriot, Commander of the National Guard, first a lackey, a clerk at the city gates, and then assassin at Saint-Firmin, breaks the seals, empties the cellars, removes the furniture, etc. . ." [Mme Roland's *Memoirs*.]

[98] An article of Hébert. (No. 248 of the *Père Duchesne*.)

[99] In his *Discours Préliminaire* of his edition of Mme Roland's writings, Champagneux recounted how he prevented Garat from sending an extremely harsh answer to this letter and even persuaded him to write to the Committee of General Safety stating Mme Roland's recriminations. Garat's letter received the following response, dated the first of July 1793, and signed by Chabot and Ingrand, two members of the Committee:

"The Committee of General Safety arrested Mme Roland for assisting in the escape of her husband who at the present moment is inciting civil war in the department of Rhône-et-Loire . . ."

[100] Indeed, in May, Garat had been cowardly enough to protest against Hébert's arrest.

[101] The Caen municipality had voted the formation of a federal force that would go to Paris to safeguard the freedom of the Convention. The neighbouring departments of Mayenne and Brittany joined this movement. General Wimpfen was put at the head of these groups. The first deputies who reached Caen were hailed with great enthusiasm. The Parisian anarchists had horrified the surrounding country and the Girondists were at first considered Royalists. Duval, Meillan, Henry-Larivière, Lesage, and others, joined Mme Roland's friends. They were feasted and presented with a guard of honour, and lodged in the superb *Hotel de l'Intendance*.

[102] During July Mme Pétion, her friend Mme Goussard, Barbaroux' young wife, and Louvet's Lodoïska made frequent trips from Caen to Paris with letters from the fugitives.

[103] Mme Goussard and her sister concealed Pétion at their house until he was able to make his escape. Buzot's letters from Caen had been given Mme Roland by Pétion who had received them from Lauze de Perret.

[104] Marguerite Denuelle was the daughter of a Paris *bourgeois* who refused to allow her to marry Louvet, a mere clerk in a book shop, whom she had loved

since her childhood. At the age of fifteen she was married to a Lyonese goldsmith called Chollet. In order to win her, Louvet became a writer and published *Faublas,* a book which met with great success. Later he became a journalist
and was appointed deputy for the Loiret. A sort of legendary love bound him to
this little *bourgeoise* whom he called Lodoïska after one of the heroines in his novel.

105 As we shall later see, he was to be her great friend at the end.

106 Thibaut sold them to Plon, publisher, who gave them to the *Bibliothèque
Nationale.*

107 Four of these five letters to Buzot were written between June twenty-second
and July seventh, the fifth one on August thirty-first. The author has given them
in full. Owing to lack of space—the letters are very long—we must, unfortunately, confine ourselves to fragments of them. In spite of the high interest and
beauty of these letters which bear testimony to Mme Roland's dauntless fortitude
and courage, as well as to the strength, purity, and delicacy of her love for
Buzot, and the uncompromising enthusiasm of her political ideas, their abridge-
ment does not leave a gap, for the same ground is covered in the author's text
as well as in the selections quoted from the *Memoirs.* [Translator's Note.]

108 She dwells upon her occupations in prison; the kindness of the porter; the
books she reads; her letter to Garat; the situation of Eudora; Roland's plight, and
other things already well known to the reader. [Translator's Note.]

109 In her comments upon this letter, the author says:

"This letter, as we have seen, is not a love letter in the strict sense of the
word. It was inspired by love, but love is not its theme. The fatherland is its
theme. It deals with Liberty. . . It tells us how suffering should be borne.
Her constant concern was to be equal to events, 'superior to destiny,' and, if she
loved Buzot it was because he had shown himself 'a proud free spirit,' 'superior
to destiny,' 'engaged in noble plans.'" [Translator's Note.]

110 Lescure says: "The provinces were extremely hostile to the Girondists who
were then in flight. When Brissot was arrested at Moulins, the people of that
town rose up against this sincere and convinced precursor of Republican principle,
crying: 'To the guillotine!'"

Among other vile calumnies, he was accused of being a Royalist spy and a
letter was found to prove the "truth" of this accusation. True, there was such a
document written by a certain Watteville. It was an easy matter for Brissot's
enemies to change Watteville to Warville. The document was published by Marat
in *L'Ami du Peuple.*

When Brissot wished to escape from Paris on the thirty-first of May, he had
not one *sou,* and he had to wait until the fourth of June. It was upon Mme
Roland's suggestion that he wrote his *Memoirs.* Though she was at Sainte-
Pélagie and he at the Abbaye, they managed to correspond. He was thirty-nine
at the time.

111 The summer of 1793 was torrid.

112 Probably Mme Grandchamp, who lived with Grandpré and brought up
his son.

112ᵃ Bosc had hidden at Sainte-Radegonde the first manuscripts he had received,
and another part must have been confided to Mme Grandchamp. Miss Helena
Williams, whom Mme Roland had known through Bancal, said in her *Letters
Upon the Events of May 31st to the 9th of Thermidor* that she had received
a note-book from Mme Roland but that she had destroyed it in a moment of
anxiety. Mentelle, the geographer, said in his letter to Champagneux, dated
1800: "*It is to me that Mme Roland entrusted her Memoirs.*" It is probable
that she made several copies.

113 In her letter of July sixth to Buzot, Mme Roland referred to these plans
for her escape: "I shall not dwell upon the dangers and difficulties incumbent
upon any attempt to escape from this place, due to the disposition of the building
and the number of guards. Nothing would keep me from joining you were I
the only one to defy them, but to expose our friends and throw off the shackles

with which the wicked persecute and honour me only to take on others which no-one sees but which I could not avoid, these are things I am in no hurry to do."

And further on: "From the point of view of politics, it would be detestable, just as it would be insane for those deputies who remain here to escape now. My person is not as important as theirs, because I represent only myself; but my oppression is even more odious because it is the more gratuitous. The duration of my captivity is a daily proof of the most revolting tyranny; it shows an extreme stupidity on their part to nourish thus the hatred of the people, and it would be very rash of us to remove its cause." [Translator's Note.]

114 In this letter Mme Roland again told Buzot that her imprisonment was not difficult to bear. On the contrary, she found herself now in a position to love him as she wished.

"Proud of being persecuted in these times when honesty and character are outlawed, I would even without you have been able to bear my lot with dignity, but you render it dear and sweet to me besides. The wicked think to subdue me with their chains. . . Insensate ones! What care I if I live here or there? Have I not my heart with me everywhere I go, and do they not, in putting me in prison, surrender me unreservedly to it? He whom I love—this is my company; to think of my love, this is my care."

And further on: "I delighted in combining service to Roland with a life that permitted me to give my thoughts to you. I would sacrifice my life to him if I, by so doing, but earned the right to bestow my last breath on you alone."

In this final sentence, the author finds proof that the relations between Buzot and Mme Roland were beyond reproach. "Would a woman who possessed such scruples and who recognized that her husband had such absolute rights on her most intimate feelings, have considered herself free to bestow on another what was less avowable and more forbidden?"

Other sentences in this letter induce her to form the same conclusions: "Tell me, do you know any sweeter moments than those spent in the charm of an affection which nature sanctions and which is governed by delicacy, which duty honours by the privations it imposes, and which is nourished by the very strength that gives us the power to endure them." " 'Sweeter moments.' Does this not imply that Buzot had known no others?" writes the author. She further supports her thesis from a quotation from the *Dernières Pensées,* from the invocation to Buzot: "You, whom I dare not name. . . You, whom even the most fiery passion does not cause to overstep the barriers of virtue . . ." [Translator's Note.]

115 Barbaroux' wife was a young Englishwoman, Mary Sophy Harlowe or Arlove, the daughter of an English manufacturer, and not a shop girl he had met in Marseilles as was long believed.

116 Thibaut did not believe that this letter was addressed to Buzot, but to a tradesman, Sophie Cannet's husband. It was M. Faugère who purchased it, identified it, and bequeathed it to the *Bibliothèque Nationale.*

117 Roland had also employed his leisure hours writing memoirs, in which he spoke violently of Buzot. Mme Roland persuaded him to burn them, a proof of the influence she still had over her husband.

118 Sister Sainte-Agathe who lived nearby the prison so as to be close to Mme Roland whom she called her daughter.

119 Mirabeau, Lafayette, and many others who had belonged to the Court party joined the Revolution. The handsome Lauzun became General Biron and was appointed Commander in Chief of the armies of the Rhine. Having signalled certain embezzlements in the Ministry of War, he was summoned to Paris to furnish explanations. This proved a trap, for the General was arrested upon his arrival, imprisoned, and guillotined on the thirty-first of December 1793.

120 Faure, Deputy of the Haute-Loire, in order to augment the "produce" of the Revolutionary Tribunal, moved "that after the pleading there should be no defence speech on the part of the defender."

[121] Edme Mentelle, born in Paris in 1730, "the most estimable geographer of the century." He was a great friend of Brissot for whom he stood bail in 1784 when Brissot was imprisoned in the Bastille. He lived during the Terror in one of the twenty-six lodgings installed in the great Louvre Gallery.

[122] "I shall never forget," said Brissot in his memoirs, "an opinion Buzot very forcibly expressed on the night of the thirty-first of May. The question was whether, in the event that we were impeached, voluntary death was not preferable to the shame of going to the scaffold. Buzot was in favor of the latter alternative and demonstrated that death on the scaffold was more courageous, more befitting a patriot, and that it would better serve the cause of Liberty. It is noteworthy that these ideas made Mme Roland reject the idea of suicide, while Buzot, on the contrary, killed himself rather than be dragged to the guillotine."

[123] There are two copies of this letter, both authentic: one at the *Bibliothèque Nationale*, the other at the Château de Rosière. Probably Mme Roland feared her farewell to her daughter might be lost and entrusted a copy to Mentelle, and another to some other person, perhaps Mme Grandchamp.

[124] She seemed to have forgotten Lanthenas' indiscretion.

[125] M. Perroud considered this passage further proof that Jany and Mentelle were one and the same person. Mentelle's son was then in America and had been there some time.

[126] Adam Lux, deputy from Mayence, had made no secret of his admiration for Charlotte Corday. For this he was arrested in July and executed on November fourth.

[127] A lock of her hair.

[128] Roland's brother was executed at Lyons, December 22, 1793.

[129] Everything at the Villefranche house and *Le Clos* was sold at auction. A part of Mme Roland's furniture was bought back from the purchasers and is now at the Château de Rosière. The property of Rosière was bought by Joseph Chaley, Eudora's son-in-law. It belongs today to Mme Marion, a direct descendant of the Rolands.

[130] This drawing was given to Eudora and then to Mme Champagneux by Bosc's son, after the death of his father.

[131] Valazé (1751–1793), lawyer, Deputy from the Orne to the Convention.

[132] Honoré Riouffe, born in Bordeaux in 1764, administrator, man of letters, was arrested in Bordeaux as a suspect and saved by the ninth of Thermidor. He published *Mémoires d'un detenu pour servir à l'histoire de la tyranie* [*sic*] *de Robespierre,* a book which had great success. He became a Bonapartist, was made a baron, appointed *prefect,* and died in 1813.

[133] The maid Fleury was arrested the following day for saying in the porter's lodge of the rue de la Harpe that her mistress had been unjustly condemned. She remained six months in prison, and was then acquitted. Such was not the case with Lecoq, who was guillotined. Shortly after regaining her freedom, Fleury joined Eudora, and remained in her service. The rest of her life was spent quietly at *Le Clos.* She was nearly a hundred when she died.

[134] The order for Mme Roland's execution, which belonged to M. Alfred Sensier, is now in the possession of Dr. Clerc. It is dated the eighteenth of Brumaire and bears these words:

"The following named Roland woman and Lamarche shall be executed at half-past three on the Place de la Révolution."

The orders were printed, leaving the name and the hour in blank. When a person was condemned, the blanks were filled in and the order sent to Fouquier-Tinville who affixed his signature.

[135] The statue of Louis XV was torn down on the morrow of the tenth of August, and was sent to the melting-pot.

[136] "She crossed Paris," wrote Champagneux, "amid great hue and cry, and met death with heroic fortitude and serenity. She would have taken poison without a murmur, and she went to the scaffold in the same way. When she died

she had but one regret, that she could not record the new and extraordinary sentiments that she experienced on the way. . . She asked for pen and paper, which were refused her; she would have written at the foot of the scaffold as she had in her study, that is, without anxiety and with a tranquillity and wisdom which those who did not know her intimately would not have believed possible."

Dauban reproached Faugère—doubtless influenced by Champagneux—for having said that Mme Roland requested writing materials at the foot of the guillotine. He found this idea absurd.

Carlyle, on the contrary, credited this story, while Sainte-Beuve considered it most improbable. We might incline to the former opinion were we not aware of the fact that the condemned had their hands tied behind their backs.

"Like a white Grecian statue," wrote Carlyle, "serenely complete, she shines in that black wreck of things—long memorable."

EPILOGUE

[1] He was the Roland's butcher in Paris.

[2] The Director of the Post Office.

[3] These are in the National Archives. Many words have been blotted out by humidity. The barber Troquart was arrested the same day that these letters were confided to him. They remained eight months buried in the ground. When Troquart was released, he sent them to Louvet, who read them to the Convention on July 12, 1795.

[4] Barbaroux suffered a long and horrible agony. Only after six days was he brought to Bordeaux where he was guillotined on the twenty-fifth of June 1794.